The Job

The
Job

WORK AND ITS FUTURE
IN A TIME OF
RADICAL CHANGE

ELLEN RUPPEL SHELL

CURRENCY
NEW YORK

To Avery, whose work has just begun

In the highest sense, work is meant to be the servant of man, not the master.

—EDMOND BORDEAUX SZÉKELY

Contents

Introduction: A Measure of Our Sanity 1

Prologue: The Unbroken 15

PART I: OUR NATIONAL JOBS DISORDER 21

    1: SUFFERING LESS 23

    2: COMING OUT OF THE COFFIN 49

    3: SHOULD ROBOTS PAY TAXES? 68

    4: LET THEM EAT APPS 84

PART II: CHOICES 95

    5: THE PASSION PARADOX 97

    6: HABITS OF THE HEART 116

PART III: LEARNING TO LABOR 135

    7: A CHILD'S WORK 137

    8: MIND THE (SKILLS) GAP 158

    9: THE THOUSAND-MILE STARE 176

    10: WHEN THE SPIRIT CATCHES YOU 194

PART IV: THINKING ANEW 211

    11: THE FINNISH LINE 213

    12: ABOLISH HUMAN RENTALS 237

    13: PUNK MAKERS 266

    14: HOMO FABER 289

    Acknowledgments 323

    Notes 327

    Index 387

Introduction

A Measure of Our Sanity

A man's work does not satisfy his material needs alone. In a very deep sense, it gives him a measure of his sanity.

—ELLIOTT JAQUES

Work holds dominion over us. It's through work that we exercise our talents and build an identity, through work that we fit into this world. And while our most cherished memories don't always revolve around our jobs, our hopes and dreams for our future—and the future of our children—generally do.

Americans are raised to believe in the sanctity of work: whether in school, at home, or from the pulpit, there is no higher praise than "a job well done." Political hopefuls can't seem to say enough about work—in stump speeches the word or its equivalent is more common than *liberty* and *justice* combined. In most matters rhetorical, even *freedom* takes a backseat to *work*.

Little wonder, then, that Donald Trump's campaign was built on a vow to return "real work" to America's shores, to wrench twenty-five million jobs back from the grip of "not fair" trade treaties and "bad deal" immigration policies and lay them at our feet like the spoils of war. "I will be the greatest job producer that God ever created," our future president bellowed. "It will be amazing to watch. You watch, it'll happen."

And watch we did . . . how could we not? Jobs mean so very

much to us, and on so many levels. Americans spend more time on the job than in any other waking activity: roughly six times the amount we spend with our families. Jobs are not only our lifeline but our lifeblood, as individuals and as a society. The ebb and flow of job numbers shape our national mood: they steer financial markets, sway voters, and decide elections. They bring dread and hope. Yet while numbers can tell us a good deal about many things, they can't explain the way so many of us feel today—namely, that work is just not working for us.

What we're feeling is real. America was built on the "grand career narrative," by which almost anyone could, through hard and concerted effort, scale the occupational ladder to a middle-class life and beyond. Not everyone followed that trajectory, but enough did to make it seem like a reasonable expectation. Thanks to this steady progress, the prospects of children were expected to exceed those of their parents. And throughout most of the last century, those expectations were largely met.

But that was then. In the twenty-first century, job growth has not led to a significant decline in poverty or to a rise in the middle class. Instead, the postindustrial "digital" economy has brought a trickle of fancy, high-paying jobs and a torrent of not-so-fancy low-wage jobs, and with them a soaring inequality that threatens the very premise of our free-market democracy: the promise that hard work will take almost any one of us where we need—and want—to go.

Today's glaring uncertainties make navigating a career seem less like scaling a firmly braced ladder than like clawing up a rock face slick with ice, where any misstep can lead to disaster. Even kindergarteners are hip to the drill. Chris Brown, an educational researcher at the University of Texas, told me that five-year-olds quickly "get the message that they're supposed to worry not about now but about what comes next—first grade, middle school, high school, college, all pointed toward what they'll do in the future. And by that I mean *the job*."

Of course, it's not unhealthy for youngsters to gravitate toward an occupation; many of us as children dreamed of becoming fire-fighters or teachers or ballerinas or—speaking for myself—a deep-sea diver. But how many of us recall our five-year-old selves being *worried* about getting a good job? A middle-class kid with dreams of becoming a deep-sea diver is one thing; a middle-class kid growing up fearful of her future is quite another.

This was not supposed to happen. On the contrary, the digital age promised abundance via unfettered access to information, networks, and markets by which each of us would captain our own destiny. Certainly, that promise was fulfilled for some. But technology did not—as predicted—level the playing field. On the contrary, it rutted that field with steeper peaks and deeper pits. We've been taught to believe that the best way to prepare for a life of good work is to hone our skill set through formal education or training or a combination of both. But as we'll see, this advice is incomplete, as it fails to fully acknowledge that progress has its price.

One of the central lessons of artificial intelligence is that a variety of tasks that are easy for humans are difficult for machines, while a variety of tasks that are difficult for humans are easy for machines. For example, the tasks of giving manicures and pedicures or placing water glasses just so on a restaurant table, while rather easy for many humans, can be extremely difficult for a machine, while tasks that involve high-level reasoning—bookkeeping, accounting, many banking functions, and the analysis of legal documents and medical scans—are relatively easy for machines. For this and other reasons, skilled, middle-wage jobs are often more at risk of being reduced or eliminated by technology than are many low-paying jobs. The "middle" is under seige, and this does not bode well for our sweet American dreams.

A twenty-six-year-old entrepreneur I spoke with in Detroit put it this way:

> The Internet hollows out the middle and elevates extremes.
> What's in trouble is the in-between. To understand how

this plays out on a corporate level, think about how we buy books. Customers can go online to track down rare volumes at a tiny bookstore run by some grumpy old guy, so there is still that niche market. And then there's the mass market, which is Amazon. But the people who worked at Borders Books and companies like it, well . . . let's face it, those jobs are gone. And what's true for books is true for so many other industries . . . most industries, actually.

The mantra of our time, "Average is over," comes laced with an implicit threat that the middle no longer exists—that if you're not at the top, you're at or falling toward the bottom. But by definition, not all of us can be better than the rest. Rather, in most things humans tend to fall along a normal curve, a sort of inverted letter U with small numbers of us at each end and the vast bulk of us crowded into the middle. So clearly, if average is over, so are most of us, at least when it comes to a job suited to our needs, capabilities, and dispositions. At least, that's what many pundits argue and many of us have come to believe.

The mounting pressure to excel or to step aside for those who do pits us against one another, and not in a good way. In matters of income, most of us rank so far below the top that the "winners" might as well inhabit another planet: a mere 1,600 Americans possess as much wealth as the bottom 90 percent combined. Such dramatic disparities have ramped up public expectations of what a job should—and can—do to elevate us above the norm. And it has inclined us to adopt and even rationalize winner-take-all behaviors and policies that undermine our ability to be happy with or make meaning from our work.

Matters of national policy, do, of course, play a role in this book. But my motive for taking on this thorny, contentious, and—for me—fascinating topic was as personal as political. As a parent and a teacher, I could hardly avoid the issue. I'd witnessed the confusion and paralyzing anxiety in so many kids and the growing resentment and anger in so many young adults. I'd seen how the shameless shilling behind making ourselves and our children "job ready" diminished our educational system and weakened our convictions. I'd watched as almost any "accomplishment"—no matter how trivial its purpose—was applauded if it boosted a résumé, and also watched as so many heartfelt endeavors with no clear self-promotional payoff were devalued, neglected, even mocked and ridiculed. I'd seen firsthand how the mounting anxiety over jobs was transforming many people—especially the young—into risk-averse strivers, terrified of making the wrong move. (Memorably, one of my own students saw no choice but to drop his "selfish" literature major to pursue a "practical" business degree, for which he confessed he had little aptitude and no stomach.) And I'd seen these personal observations reflected in our national panic that somehow our economy and our workforce were losing ground to shadowy, unknowable "foreigners" in China, India, Mexico, and other nations whose citizens were also struggling to make sense of an ever more fickle and precarious global economy.

No question, work has changed in America and around the globe. The offshoring of jobs—both blue and white collar—and the rise of contingent "gig" work have added to our unease. The contract between worker and boss—the trade-off of loyal service for security—is no longer implicit. And technology seems to have grown a mind of its own. These and other factors have turned work into a problem that as a nation we seem unable to face, let alone deal with openly and with courage. This book is a heartfelt leap into the breach. I won't promise easy solutions or even attempt to convince you that there are easy solutions. Rather, my intention is to roil the waters—to challenge received wisdom and expose hard truths, not a few of them urgent. For after all, in the broadest sense, the way we work represents our most profound engagement with the world, both individually and as a nation.

One caveat: while I think you'll agree that a national conversation on work and its future is both essential and long overdue, you may doubt that the current state of public discourse is up to the task. Your skepticism is justified. In an era when vapid pandering and partisan vitriol can pass for reasoned argument, when empty rhetoric comes disguised as a promise ("We *will* bring back coal mining!"), and promises come cloaked as done deals ("Twenty-five million new jobs!"), it's hard to imagine a fruitful dialogue on almost any topic, let alone one so complex. So before going further I'd like to acknowledge two very real but surmountable obstacles.

The first obstacle is the underlying assumption of scalable efficiency as *the* essential driver of progress. That assumption no longer holds in the way it once did. In the industrial age, the push for efficiency led employers to tightly specify tasks and standardize them under a theory of organization that relied on people fitting into narrow roles—be it shoveling coal to stoke a furnace or trimming cloth to make shirt collars. This was the logic behind the many innovations that de-skilled labor, a strategy that was highly disruptive over the short term but of great economic and social benefit over the long term. Thanks to automation, we could make more for less, thereby increasing productivity and growth while lowering prices. And throughout the industrial age, many workers—especially those in sectors affiliated with a labor union—were rewarded for their increased productivity with a steadily increasing wage, solid benefits, and in some cases greater control over their working lives. Growing efficiencies increased prosperity, reduced poverty, and stablized democracy. Enhanced productivity contributed to the rise of the American middle class.

But in the digital age, this logic is flawed. Our sometimes unquestioning pursuit of efficiency has led us to underrate the importance of quality, of both work and life. It has led us to judge farmers not by the nutritive value or taste of their produce but by its price; doctors not by the lives they save and better but on the number of patients they treat; teachers not by the students they enlighten and inspire but by the test scores those students generate. It has led us to overvalue certain sorts of work and undervalue other sorts, driving many of us—like that aspiring humanist I mentioned earlier—to pursue jobs that hold little meaning for ourselves and only questionable value for society. Our fixation on efficiency has led us to generate more goods and services that we may desire but don't need and not enough goods and services that we both desire and desperately need.

Another troubling trend is that as workers we no longer profit proportionally from our efforts: since 1973 our productivity has grown almost six times faster than has our wages. With so few capturing the value of the work of so many, we can no longer rely on growth—or even jobs per se—as a highway to prosperity. In fact, the fraction of living-wage jobs has declined in the US, as has the fraction of Americans earning middle-class wages: in 1971, 61 percent of Americans qualified as middle class, but in the most recent surveys that number fell to just under 50 percent. One of the goals laid out in this book is that we recalibrate our metrics to balance the endless quest for worker efficiency and productivity with our indelible human need to *be* productive and to be fairly rewarded for our contributions.

The second obstacle to an open and honest dialogue is the assumption that acquiring and sustaining good work is by its very nature a winner-take-most proposition by which the victories of the few condemn the many to defeat. On its face, this assumption might seem justified. For many of us the job "hunt" has become a sort of Hunger Game, a cutthroat competition to survive in a world where jobs have been automated away, or shifted from higher-wage nations like the United States to lower-wage nations like China and India. Donald Trump acknowledged—and exploited—this trend when pledging to bring jobs "back home." The problem with this claim is that in a global economy not all jobs have any particular "home"—many can happily land almost anywhere, and when they land in low-wage nations the benefits sometimes return to

American consumers in the form of lower-priced goods. So, while I do not argue that jobs be farmed out willy-nilly to the lowest bidder, nor do I argue that jobs remain in nations no longer suited to host them. Indeed, another premise of this book is that while many American jobs have succumbed and will succumb to the one-two punch of globalization and automation, good work is, in practical terms, infinite, expansive enough to meet the demands and needs of all who seek it, no matter their nationality.

All of which raises the inevitable question: What do we mean when we talk about *work*? The very word conjures up different things for different people, so before going further, let me set some terms. Work is often judged by its most measurable component: income. So we could easily define work as any paid effort. But maybe we shouldn't. Certainly this one-dimensional view of work is incomplete, as it tends to legitimize work only of a certain sort, while discounting work of every other sort. For example, the value of parents caring for their children is not included in calculations of the Gross Domestic Product (GDP). Nor is the value of countless volunteers—charity fund-raisers, church choir singers, club soccer coaches, Wikipedia contributors, or blood donors, to name a few. And yet this unpaid work is typically of great value, certainly of equal or even more value than many forms of paid work. Volunteer firefighters and pro bono attorneys provide real benefit to our society and communities, yet it's not at all clear that the same can be said of cigarette manufacturers and creators of online pop-up ads, no matter how well they're paid.

So I think we can agree that good work can be and often is precious beyond its market value. Nonetheless, in what follows I default mostly to the sort of work that brings a paycheck. An all-embracing definition—say one that included "any activity that brings value to oneself or others"—would lead us down a rabbit hole of ambiguity and equivocation. Still, whenever possible I try to draw a distinction between *work* and a *job*. Work is a natural human inclination—infants "work" to find their toes, to smile, to make their needs known, but as we'll see, no one is born with a natural inclination to hold a job.

Traced to its sixteenth-century origins, the word *job* is defined as "to rob or cheat," a sordid bit of business meant to extract money from others. While surely many peasants and craftspeople dreamed of owning land or workshops in which to make their mark, it's unlikely many dreamed of earning a wage by helping others to make theirs. It was not until the industrial age that the term *job* broadened to engulf work, as though "work" were a mere subset of "job." But of course, it's the other way around—a job is a mere subset of the far larger universe of work, and not necessarily the most desirable or stable corner of that universe. A job, no matter how good, can turn on us, while good work, I think most of us would agree, never does.

Jobs, then, have their limits, and in the digital age those limits loom large: at this writing the official unemployment rate has reached a seventeen-year low point, but that brings many of us little comfort. It's the quality of jobs, not the quantity, that has come to matter most, and in many cases, the quality is just not there. The most recent government statistics indicate that half of all American workers earn less than $30,000 a year and only about a quarter make more than $50,000. Meanwhile, the cost of almost everything that matters continues to climb. Annual premiums for family health insurance plans average north of $12,000, with a whopping $8,000 deductible. In two-thirds of the country, the rise in housing prices outpaces wage growth. College tuition, which once consumed just a modest chunk of the average worker's yearly income, today eats up roughly 30 percent—for in-state public school tuition, excluding housing, books, fees, and other related costs. And the cost of day care? Just ask any parent of young children.

For a growing number of Americans, then, having "a job" is not enough. So, does this mean that jobs as we know them are fading? Some say yes. The young Detroit entrepreneur I spoke with saw things this way: "In the future, work will be seen more as *outside* the employment context."

Work outside the employment context. That is quite a concept, and one we'll explore in depth later in the book. But first allow me to set a few more guideposts. Work is a sprawling concept and difficult to capture in the abstract. So throughout the book I've tried to ground the narrative in actual working lives: a marketing executive in eastern Massachusetts "reinventing" himself when his job is downsized; a former marketing manager whose job once was to help companies ship jobs overseas; an autoworker in the Midwest retraining for a job in "advanced manufacturing"; a disillusioned twenty-something accountant in Manhattan; a father of three in Charlotte, North Carolina, passionate about his job at a convenience store chain; a Cleveland-based army veteran and onetime cocaine dealer who found salvation through the promise of ownership at a commercial laundry; an art school dropout shaping the look of Hollywood blockbusters from her cottage in southern Maine; young men in rural Kentucky contemplating a future beyond the coal mines. We'll hear their stories, and those of firefighters, zookeepers, hospital cleaners, motorcycle designers, and a China scholar turned real estate agent, among others. And to help make sense of all this, we'll also hear from workers of another sort—economists, philosophers, psychologists, computer scientists, sociologists, and historians. Their insights are likely to surprise you, and perhaps even incline you to see work—including your own—in a stark new light.

The book is divided into four sections that proceed in a roughly linear fashion (with a few detours) from the problem of work to intriguing—even exciting—remedies. I begin with a prologue, the tale of Marienthal, an Austrian hamlet mired in the Great Depression of the late 1920s. We start at this unlikely place because what happened in that small village nearly a century ago forced the world to recognize what today we take for granted: work in all its richness, complexity, joy, and pain is essential for people to flourish.

The story of Marienthal makes all the more urgent the message of the book's first section, "Our National Jobs Disorder," that chronicles the disruption of work in the digital age. I make no argument here for swapping cell phones for landlines—innovation is and always will be key to our future. But I do warn that in recent decades innovation has brought a number of surprises that have thrown work out of whack.

In late 2017, announcing the opening of a new institute for the study of robotics and artificial intelligence, the United Nations sketched out the problem: "Rapid advancements in the field of robotics coupled with the rise of computing power during the latter half of the twentieth century has exponentially increased the range of tasks that can be assigned to robots and systems based on an artificial intelligence (AI), as well as the autonomy with which such technologies operate. While this can be beneficial for global development and societal change . . . it also raises legal, ethical and societal concerns and challenges."

Indeed, in an era of Uber, freelance app designers, and online brokers that outsource tasks to the lowest bidder, it has become hard to pin down what it even means to be "employed." We're reassured that technology that destroys old opportunities will be applied to create new opportunities for more than a favored few, but the question is, how? Faced with this dilemma, economists and computer scientists who just a few years ago scoffed at the specter of technology replacing human intellectual capital in the workplace now warn that it is doing just that. In this section we take a hard look at these and other less visible forces shaping the way we work and the powerful influence these forces have over our democracy, our economy, and our lives.

The book's second section centers on the psychology of work. How do we make meaning from our jobs, and from what aspects of work do we derive our identity? We may assume that meaning is conferred by our employers and that our identities are linked to the institutions that employ us. Fair enough. But what happens when we don't identify with the goals of our employers, when we don't feel valued by our employers, or, as is increasingly common, we are not employed by any particular institution? Under these conditions, with what do we identify, and how do we make meaning of our work? In addressing these and related questions, we're guided by a number of big thinkers, among them Yale management school psychologist Amy Wrzesniewski, whose work is making sense of how we make sense of ours. She has shown that *what* we do for a living does not always determine how we *feel* about what we do for a living, at least not in the ways we have come to expect. For example, a Walmart greeter may rightfully see her work as a calling, while a doctor might rightfully regard curing the sick as "just" a job. And while most employers would prefer that we treat our jobs as callings, giving our all to what we do every day, Wrzesniewski contends that most of us probably shouldn't: the "called" are far more likely to be underpaid, undermined, and generally taken for granted, while those of us with "just a job" are in fact less likely to fall into a similar trap. Indeed, too often employers who lure us with the promise of "meaningful work" are like Greeks bearing gifts—the package they offer is filled with trinkets meant to lure us into the corporate culture rather than to bring us real value. As we'll see, making meaning of work is ultimately very much a DIY proposition.

Global competition generates what seems like an insatiable demand for a skilled and knowledgeable workforce. Americans are expected to rise to the challenge. But how? Is it safer or wiser to train ourselves and our kids for the jobs of today or to prepare them to address and even shape the work of tomorrow? Is formal education in the traditional sense the best way to ready the twenty-first-century workforce, or is there a newer, better way? Is the college experience—already overpriced—also overrated as a job strategy? What about job-training programs and apprenticeships? What of the "skills gap"—is that even a thing, and if so, how do we close it?

In the book's third section, I trace these and related questions into today's schools and training grounds and beyond. It's a fundamental section, and perhaps a contentious one. Most of us have strong beliefs about the purpose and promise of education, and those beliefs are important. But my goal here is to sort out belief from what's actually happening on the ground. Among the places and people I highlight are a large community college deep in the Rust Belt preparing the next generation of drone pilots, and a small liberal arts institution in the heart of Appalachia preparing the next generation of deep thinkers and innovators. What becomes clear is that people everywhere wish for the same thing—an education that will launch them into a life of productive, purposeful, and fairly compensated work. Wishes not being horses, only some will ride—and we'll see why. And we'll also get a hint of what we need (beyond wishes) to boost more of us up into the saddle.

The fourth and final section is where the future of work comes alive: a philosopher turned sausage maker in Helsinki, Finland; a designer of motorcycles in Brooklyn; a twenty-four-year-old broom maker in Kentucky; a basketball shoe magnate in Philadelphia; the founder of a national convenience store chain in Tulsa, Oklahoma. Though wildly different in many ways, they share one common purpose: to get work right. We'll follow their journeys and hear their thoughts, and also those of some of the nation's—and the world's—cutting-edge thinkers on work and its future. If you are anything like me, their insights will convince you that work as it can and should be is well within our reach.

As I noted earlier, my intention in what follows is to challenge received wisdom and provoke new thinking, not swamp you with my own views. But allow me a few thoughts that have, at intervals, occurred to me along the way. Chief among them is that work is far too vital a human need to trust to the vagaries of a fickle global marketplace. Nor can it be dismissed as a mere happy side effect of corporate innovation. There is no "trickle-down" solution to the problem of work. On the contrary, sustaining good work must be made one of the explicit *goals* of innovation, a challenge to be addressed—and met—with openness, transparency, and a sense of urgency. We cannot rely on conventional wisdom based on rusty industrial age strategies. We need a new approach that comports with the new realities.

In what follows, I make the case to squarely place the innovation of sustainable and worthy work on our public agenda. No single stakeholder—business, government, educators, citizens—can go it alone; this must be a collaborative effort agreed upon by all. This strategy is not optional but essential to our survival not only as a nation but as citizens of the free world. And I mean that quite literally.

For work determines to a great degree what comes to pass on this planet. Good work brings stability of the sort that staves off conflict, and a clearness of mind that disinclines us to destroy and inclines us to create. That's the big picture, but not the only one. On an individual level, few things in life bring us a greater sense of purpose as we ourselves define it. In the end, this book is about the centrality of work in our lives—economically, historically, and psychologically. And it is also about the dignity that good work brings, and the unique role work plays in making us fully aware of our humanity.

Prologue

The Unbroken

The industrious races find it extremely difficult to tolerate
idleness; it was a stroke of genius on the part of the English
instinct to spend Sundays in tedium . . . so that English people
would unconsciously lust for their workdays.

—FRIEDRICH NIETZSCHE

Two hundred years or so ago the tiny community of Marienthal,
Austria, emerged shanty by shanty on the muddy banks of the Fis-
cha River, fifteen miles southeast of Vienna. The thin soil made
farming dicey, but the river flowed briskly and almost never froze,
gushing a steady source of hydropower. The Industrial Revolution
roused the hamlet's sleepy economy, and the struggling farmers
abandoned their cabbage and potato fields for a new life in the
factory.

The Imperial and Royally-Privileged Marienthal Cotton-
Spinning Mill and Woolens-Manufacturing Company hummed
day and night. Men, women, and children perched shoulder to
shoulder on long benches, making blue and pink cotton prints for
export to Hungary and the Balkans. The pay was low and the job
demanding, but the work was steady and sure—there were no worries over foul weather or pests as there had been on the farm. By all
accounts the good people of Marienthal were happy, and grateful
for the opportunities that progress had brought them.

Viennese financier and philanthropist Hermann Todesco was
the founding father of Marienthal and the owner of the factory,

among the first of its kind in Europe. Born in 1791 to a family of peddlers in Bratislava, Todesco was a self-made man who rose from the ghetto to become one of the wealthiest men of his time. Well liked and benevolent, he and his sons were by almost any standard model employers. They built worker housing, a kindergarten, and a primary school. They installed a hospital and offered their workers free health care. Their largesse was repaid many times over in employee loyalty and productivity—the business prospered, and under new ownership grew into one of the largest textile mills in the Austro-Hungarian Empire.

Marienthal's fortunes were tied to the factory, so it, too, boomed. It was known for festivals, theater, and dances and was especially festive during Winter Carnival season. The charming Manor Garden Park, with its lovely lake and bathing hut, music pavilion, and tennis courts, was a great attraction: families and friends thronged there on weekends, strolling the dappled lanes and manicured lawns. The town sponsored a workers' library, a soccer league, a radio club, a theater club, a rabbit breeders' association, a women's handball team, and a bicycle dance club for men—in a photo, the cyclists dazzle in white shirts and black trousers.

Marienthal was by all accounts a safe and lively place for ordinary folk to make their mark and raise a family. But this utopia was not to last. The Great Depression smothered the Austrian economy much as it did that of the United States. Currency inflated dramatically, the banks collapsed, and consumer demand shriveled. Almost no one was in the market for pink and blue striped cloth or much of anything else. In the summer of 1929 the factory began its slow and steady decline: the spinning mill, the printing works, and the bleaching plant were all demolished by heavily muscled men wielding sledgehammers. In a final blow, the great looms were dismantled and sold off. More than 1,200 lost their jobs. Come winter, the good people of Marienthal were surrounded by the ruins of their former working lives—dented boilers, broken transmission wheels, crumbling factory walls. Most of them were where they hoped never to be: on the dole. They despaired.

Newlyweds Paul Lazarsfeld and Marie Jahoda were blissfully unaware of the troubles plaguing the hamlet to the south. Both social psychologists, their attention was fixed closer to home, in Vienna. Committed socialists, the young couple was delighted when the mandated hours for factory workers were reduced. They proposed a research project designed to help these workers make good use of their hard-earned leisure. But when they brought this plan to Social Democratic Party boss Otto Bauer, he blanched. Did they not realize that the Austrian economy was in the toilet? The critical question was not how workers spent their spare time. The critical question was how workers survived when their jobs went away. Unemployment was rampant, he fumed, and Marienthal was ground zero.

Chastened, Lazarsfeld and Jahoda dispatched to Marienthal accompanied by legal scholar Hans Zeisel and eight colleagues from the Vienna Psychological Institute. Given that Marienthal was a stronghold of the Social Democratic Labor movement, it was widely assumed that this "breakdown in capitalism" would prompt political action, maybe even revolt. The mission of the researchers was to bear witness to a revolution of the unemployed and to document the process. To that end, they compiled an in-depth record of 478 village families and their daily activities. They checked membership lists of political and civic societies, tallied grocery store and butcher shop receipts, and monitored newspaper subscriptions and library withdrawals. They crouched behind trees, stopwatches in hand, recording the pace of pedestrians as they crossed the street. They dropped in on clubs and social gatherings and conducted lengthy interviews with families in their homes. They assigned schoolchildren to write essays on such themes as "what I want most of all" and "what I want to be." After some months, the researchers gathered to analyze their data. And what they found was chilling.

Deprived of their livelihood, the villagers did not unite in protest or incite political action. Rather, they withdrew. The once bustling library emptied. The park, abandoned, was choked with weeds. Public debate cooled. Social clubs disbanded. And children lost their resolve. In his assigned essay, one twelve-year-old wrote: "I want to be an aviator, a captain of a submarine, an Indian chief, and an engineer. But I am afraid that it will be very difficult to find a good job." (It's interesting to note that the boy linked what he "wanted to be" to a job and the lack thereof.)

In Marienthal, joblessness itself had *become* a job, a thankless, miserable one that set citizens into revolt not against the system but against one another. People were isolated, pessimistic, and bitter. They spied and snitched on one another, especially around issues of money—welfare recipients thought to be "cheating" were quickly reported to the authorities by their neighbors and former friends. And there was mischief: family pets vanished from backyards and porches; the occasional cat, but mostly dogs. The title of a monograph from the period, "When Men Eat Dogs," tells us all we need know about where those pets ended up. One Marienthal resident explained: "When a dog or cat disappears, the owner no longer bothers to report the loss, he knows that someone must have eaten the animal, and he does not want to find out who."

Yet the weirdest thing in Marienthal was not dog on dinner plates. It was that men abandoned their sense of time. They quit wearing watches and were habitually late for meals. Their pace slowed, in some cases to a crawl. Asked where they had been and what they had done with their day, many men admitted they simply could not recall. One man wrote of his empty mornings, "In the meantime, midday comes around."

The researchers were stunned. Poverty was a terrible thing, but poverty alone was not enough to explain this tragedy. The villagers were poor but not starving—most had unemployment insurance and some had pensions. They had their homes, their families, and, of course, one another. Yet rather than unite to do what they could—take their children to the library, form study groups, perhaps even rise up to demand more from the government, the community was atomized, with individuals scrambling to snatch any personal advantage. Life on the dole, the researchers concluded, was neither the galvanizing experience socialist scholars thought it should be nor the excuse to "kick back and enjoy a life of leisure" that critics of the poor thought it would be. Joblessness was an evil unto itself: demoralizing, soul killing, and dangerous. In the preface to the American edition of their study published in 1971, the researchers sum up their findings this way: "Leisure proves to be a tragic gift."

The Marienthal investigation was the first systematic effort to lay out in detail the true cost of unemployment—financial, psychological, and spiritual. The authors described the "latent functions" that work supports, such as structured activity, shared experience, status, and collective purpose, without which society and so many individuals fell apart. And they went even further—linking the idleness and malaise in Marienthal to the Nazi conquest of Austria. When Hitler—with his promise of good jobs—invaded Austria in 1938, and the factory was reopened and "Aryanized," the people of Marienthal breathed a collective sigh of relief. Years later, Jahoda wrote, "Only the provision of any work could counter the resignation that comes with unemployment."

You may well be thinking that Marienthal before World War II was very little like the United States today. And you'd be right. Yet there's a plot twist to this cautionary tale that's entirely relevant to our times, a twist rarely mentioned in its retelling. For while some men in Marienthal stopped wearing watches, ratted out one another, and even stole their neighbors' pets, the same could not be said for everyone, especially not the women. Losing their jobs didn't rob many of the women of Marienthal of their sense of agency or purpose. And it didn't lead them to passive resignation. After the factory closed they slept on average ninety fewer minutes each night than did the men, rising early in the morning, just as they had always done. They kept a tight rein on the family budget, even putting a bit of cash aside for the children's holiday gifts. They opened cottage businesses, planted vegetable gardens, and raised rabbits. In short, other than their paid jobs, they did everything they had done when the factory was open, and a little more. As one young mother put it: "Although I now have much less to do than before, I am actually busy the whole day." Though this may seem a contradiction, the researchers understood what she meant. "The term 'unemployed,'" they concluded, "applies in the strict sense only to the men, for the women are merely unpaid, not really unemployed."

Unpaid, not unemployed . . . so it goes for daughters, mothers, and wives. But gender played a smaller role in Marienthal than it might appear. Buried deep in the study is the fact that some men, too, carried on when the factory closed. They also cultivated vegetable gardens and raised rabbits. They also spent time with their children. Though not technically employed, they clung tenaciously to the purposeful tasks that anchored them in the world and gave structure to their days. Their work did not depend on an employer; it was indelibly part of who they were. As the young Detroit entrepreneur I mentioned in this book's introduction so aptly phrased it, these women and men were able to sustain work "outside of the employment context," to cobble together not only a better living but a more meaningful life. The authors had a name for these stalwart men and women. They called them "the Unbroken." And as we'll see in the following chapters, their story of survival in the throes of tumultuous change has much to inform our own time.

Part I

Our National Jobs Disorder

We are going to fight for every last American job.

—PRESIDENT DONALD TRUMP

1

SUFFERING LESS

How many years of fatigue and punishment it takes to
learn the simple truth that work, that disagreeable thing,
is the only way of not suffering in life, or at all events,
of suffering less.

—CHARLES BAUDELAIRE

If the American dream came packaged in human form, Abe Gorelick
would be a perfect match. Crisp, youthful, and tirelessly upbeat, his
hair has just the right touch of gray, his smile just the right blend
of humility and charm. He lives in a fine house on a cul-de-sac in a
million-dollar neighborhood known for its good schools. He drives
his three kids to soccer practice in a forest-green Jaguar the likes
of which his own father—a retired high school Spanish teacher—
could barely imagine. He sits on two philanthropic boards and
holds a leadership role at his synagogue. He plays league softball
and basketball and can't help feeling proud of his three-point shot.

One glance at Gorelick's résumé makes clear that this seem-
ing prosperity was well earned: titles like "senior vice president,"
"general manager," and "principal consultant" all funnel into an
Ivy League degree capped with an MBA from the University of
Chicago. A veteran strategist, Gorelick had partnered with major
financial institutions, airlines, pharmaceutical companies, global
retailers, and start-ups large and small. Digitally savvy and forward
thinking, he was by all appearances a winner—a member of the top
4 or 5 percent flying high in the knowledge economy.

But that was then, just short of his fifty-seventh birthday. Just shy of his fifty-eighth, Gorelick was still proud of his three-point shot. But the rest of his life had come unhinged from his résumé. When we first met in person, he was driving a cab, manning a cash register at Whole Foods, and peddling neckties at Lord and Taylor. The take-home pay for these part-time gigs paled compared to his previous earnings, most recently as principal for global strategy and innovation at an international marketing firm. Gorelick was unceremoniously "downsized" from that job for reasons that elude him, but he tried not to dwell on that. He was clinging to what he called the "bright side." He enjoyed bantering with customers at Whole Foods. He was pleased when an elderly woman brought him a treat after he helped her get in and out of his cab—it felt great to make a difference in people's lives and to be appreciated. Still, he wanted his *career* back. He knew the obstacles—his age, for one, worked against him. He wasn't naive. But he didn't believe that age was the essential problem. He believed the problem was *him*. And he had plans to fix that. He had enlisted a job counselor, had joined a support group, and, with his wife, was spending long hours rehashing the past in an attempt to make right whatever was holding him back, as well as preserve their marriage in the face of these new headwinds and challenges. The marriage, he said, teetered on the edge of his fragile ego, and his ego depended on his professional success.

"For a long time I wanted to be who I am," he confided over chamomile tea in a café outside Boston. "And I think that hurt me. Most companies, you've got to fit into their culture. And I guess I didn't always do that. I was always, you know, *me*. And I guess that wasn't what they were looking for."

Gorelick's career successes surpass those of most Americans. With all his savvy and privilege, we might believe, he should have known and planned better. He freely acknowledges that, and agrees that there is no shame in driving a cab or bagging groceries.

Still, to many of us the outline of Gorelick's story may strike a familiar chord. We know how he feels because we've felt the same way, or know someone who has. Our job title is a sort of shorthand that in just one or two words captures who we are and where we stand in the minds of others, and in our own. If you doubt it, try this thought experiment. Close your eyes and picture Abe the fifty-eight-year-old supermarket cashier/cabdriver/retail clerk. Now picture Abe the fifty-eight-year-old senior vice president of marketing strategy. In your mind's eye do these men—really two versions of one man—look anything alike?

I've introduced Abe Gorelick so early in the book not to evoke your sympathy but to sound the alarm. By almost any objective measure, he has done everything right. With his advanced degrees, sterling résumé, and upbeat outlook, he is not the sort of guy we associate with bad job karma. He is an eager and well-connected networker, a flexible thinker, a generous volunteer. There are no obvious gaps in his skill set, and no grass growing beneath his feet. But while his case might not be typical, his response to his situation is: like so many of us, he blames himself—not the system—for every setback. And that self-blame takes a heavy toll on far too many of us. Clinging to the canard that we—as individuals—have near-complete control over our vocational trajectories has brought misery, as public policies built on this myth risk being not only counterproductive but in some cases dangerously divisive. And as Gorelick's case makes clear, that divisiveness can hit terribly close to home.

Sociologist Ofer Sharone knows Abe Gorelick well, and he knows quite a few other people like him. Not only has he made a study of them, but not all that long ago he was one of them, at least in some ways. Before entering academia, Sharone practiced international law, circling the globe to negotiate deals in several languages. He felt powerful and important. Like Gorelick, by conventional standards he had done everything right. But on one overnight flight from Israel to Japan, he started to question himself. The money and status were intoxicating, but the power—well, that wasn't quite real. Many of his everyday tasks seemed silly and futile, yet like a nagging toothache these matters demanded his full and near-constant attention. "I found it horrifying that I was expected to give myself to a job over which I had almost no control," he told me. Even more sobering was the realization that he was sacrificing so much of his life for a job. And here is where Sharone and the people he studies part ways. Rather than contort himself to maintain his career identity, he began to plot his escape.

Sharone quit the law and entered graduate school to study sociology and grapple with the question of why he—and so many people he knew—felt trapped by jobs that afforded them so little control. To truly understand the problem, he needed a base of comparison: Did workers in other nations feel the same way? Born in Israel, he figured that was a natural place to have a look. So he gathered his frequent flier points and went off to investigate.

Israel and the United States have many things in common: both are market economies with low labor union participation rates and relatively flexible private sector labor markets. They share important economic structures, including a thriving high-tech sector. And they are business allies. "Since the 1990s, Israelis considered the American economic model synonymous with progress and efficiency," Sharone said. Yet despite these commonalities, Sharone observed that Israelis and American workers related to their jobs quite differently.

Sharone noted that Americans felt less control over their working lives than did their Israeli peers. Even in high-pressure sectors like corporate law or finance, Israelis were better able to negotiate the terms of their employment and to find a balance between their professional and personal lives. A critical factor underlying this difference, Sharone told me, was the very process of securing employment.

In Israel, rejected job applicants tend to blame the system. In the United States, rejected job applicants are far more likely to blame themselves.

Sharone attributes this contrast in attitudes to what he describes as two very different hiring strategies. In Israel, job candidates are screened in a depersonalized and fairly objective process focused on demonstrated skills and credentials. In what Sharone calls the "specs game," applicants are grilled and pretested on their abilities and are sometimes eliminated because of technicalities or attributes—like their age—that don't necessarily relate to the job. This might make them angry, but it tends not to diminish their self-esteem. They consider it not their fault but the fault of an imperfect and sometimes unjust system that is beyond their control.

In the United States, by contrast, job seekers engage in what Sharone calls the "chemistry game." While demonstrated skills and credentials are generally essential to getting an interview, they are typically not sufficient to clinch the deal. For that, job seekers need to conjure up what Sharone calls "interpersonal chemistry"—that is, to show a deep commitment not only to the job but to the institution behind it. It's not enough to merely want and need the job or be qualified for the job. As one online job site advises: "Standing out from the equally-qualified pack and getting that job offer most often boils down to 'fit.'"

Sharone attributes this focus on "fit" in part to what he calls the "career self-help industry," the legion of job coaches, counselors, and consultants who insist that it's not enough to impress employers with one's work ethic, experience, and skills—one must also come across as the right *sort* of person. "In the US, having your identity constantly put to the test generates a lot of the objective experience of work," he told me from his office at the University of Massachusetts, Amherst. "The self-help industry convinces us they have a secret, and they will help us become the sort of person employers are looking for. We're warned that you can't just pretend to have that passion for the job, you have to make yourself feel it. What this means for many American workers is that any urge to distance yourself from your job identity is undermined by what it takes just to *get* the job."

This edict applies not only to the sort of high-paying white-collar jobs sought by people like Gorelick but also to the basic entry-level jobs sought by recent graduates. Where I teach, students are advised to prepare for interviews with an "elevator speech" that at once showers praise on their potential employer and reflects their ability to conform to the company's presiding "corporate culture." Concocting such "interpersonal chemistry" requires a substantial outlay of what Sharone calls "hard emotional labor" to sustain "a whole new persona." This includes meticulously crafting a rhetorical style that projects a passion for career goals that match the objectives of the employer. Job seekers must portray themselves as team players also willing to take initiative while at the same time conveying an undying enthusiasm for whatever service or product the company delivers. In the course of playing this "chemistry game," many applicants experience a decline in feelings of self-worth—blaming not the job or the employer or the system but themselves for any failure. Many workers with whom I spoke—machinists, waiters, chemists—ascribed their difficulties on the job, or, especially, in getting a job, to personal failings rather than to economic forces beyond their control. Sharone told me this was typical: in his surveys, asked whether "something is wrong with me," 84 percent of unemployed American job seekers responded yes.

The idea that we must sell ourselves—not merely our time, effort, and skills—to get and keep a job is so commonplace in the United States that it's become a subject for parody. In an outtake of the hit television series *Girls*, Hannah Horvarth, played by Lena Dunham, enters a bakery where she has previously dropped off a résumé. Equipped with a freshly minted—but apparently useless—college degree from a prestigious liberal arts college, she is clearly desperate for a job. As she approaches the manager, he winces. "I'm sorry, the position is filled," he says, pointing to a newly hired employee spreading frosting on a cupcake in what appears to be a state of ecstasy. Nodding sagely at the cupcake, Hannah is humbled. "Wow, you must totally be a baker, because those look amazing, and it must be very hard to do." The cupcake-froster looks up from her handiwork and smiles dreamily. "No," she says, "I just learned this *right now*." The manager cocks an eyebrow at Hannah and explains, "She just totally fits in with our vibe. Can I give you a friendly rec? If you are looking for a job, you should probably do it with a little more, like, buoyancy." Hannah gratefully accepts his advice, and in turn the manager promises to keep her résumé on file—a promise they both know is empty.

While the cupcake scene is parody, we laugh because we also know it's in the largest sense also real. Most of us have experienced similar humiliations or know someone who has—the message that it's not our skills or knowledge or abilities that are keeping us from a job, but—well—who we are. Probably the most memorable case in my experience is an acquaintance of mine whom I will call Elizabeth to protect her privacy. Elizabeth, a thirty-three-year-old account executive in Washington, D.C., was eagerly recruited by a firm in Atlanta, Georgia. Though she hadn't been actively looking for a job, Elizabeth prepared carefully for the interview and pulled together what she hoped was an impressive PowerPoint presentation. She arrived at corporate headquarters directly from her flight, overnight bag in hand. After a warm welcome and introductions all around, Elizabeth was told to put her PowerPoint aside for now and "suit up" to join the sales team in a group jog. Elizabeth suffers from asthma. Nonetheless, she pulled a pair of shorts and a T-shirt from her overnight bag and plodded through four breathless miles. Returning to the office and to what she thought would be her presentation, she was detoured once again, this time to join a postjog prayer session—the staff had joined hands in a circle and were bowing their heads. She respectfully declined. After the prayer circle dispersed, she went on with her presentation, which all agreed went quite well. Flying home, she decided to take the position—yes, it was a rather unusual office, but the pay and benefits were excellent, the work suited her, and her presentation had prompted applause. Later that week, Elizabeth got a surprising e-mail: she had been judged a "less than perfect fit," and had been passed over for the job.

Certainly, it is well within an employer's rights to pass on a candidate who appears to be a bad fit. It's also common for human resource experts to argue that "fit" with the company culture is the number one thing to look for in a new employee and that "poor fit" all but inevitably predicts "poor performance." But this leads to an essential question—what do we mean by *fit*, and how does one achieve it? The term is sometimes vaguely defined as the likelihood that an employee will reflect and be able to adapt to the core beliefs, attitudes, and behaviors that make up a particular organization. This sounds reasonable; after all, an outspoken vegetarian may not be a great fit for a sales position at a meat-processing plant, or a claustrophobe the best fit for an underground coal-mining operation. But when employers talk about "fit" they are not necessarily talking about individual preferences and proclivities. Rather, wittingly or not, they are more often describing the very behaviors and attitudes that comport with their own.

Like most of us, employers gravitate toward those who most resemble themselves. This tendency is attributed to what psychologists rather grandly call the "mere exposure effect": that is, the inclination to feel most at ease with people of the sort we've been exposed to in the past—relatives, school chums, neighbors—generally those of similar ethnicities, educations, and socioeconomic standing. Under this principle, familiarity breeds not contempt but comfort. Some might even trace this back to "Hamilton's Rule," an adage of evolutionary biology that predicts that social behavior evolves around specific combinations of relatedness: the more closely related individuals are—by blood or by tribe—the more likely they are to trust one another. It's no surprise, then, that as a whole, employers are biased toward job candidates who share or reflect their own background, values, and beliefs—the sort of people they grew up with or, crudely put, people whom they recognize as members of their own tribe. This is true for workers in every sector—both blue and white collar. Whether consciously or not, we tend to assume that in order to be a "good fit" for any given job, an employee must share the values, interests, and goals of fellow employees and certainly those of management.

This reasoning might seem to make good sense—no one enjoys a fractious work environment, and oddballs can gum up the works. But insisting that employees "fit" into a certain "culture" essentially reduces them to stereotypes and risks creating an echo chamber in which too many people within an organization too readily agree with one another and thereby fail to anticipate problems—or see solutions—that those with a greater diversity of perspectives might see. Requiring that employees "fit" a predetermined mold can also result in the exclusion of highly qualified people who for whatever reason don't seem to represent the sort of person we believe should have the job—be it a factor of their age, race, or disposition. The high-tech industry, for example, is notorious for pronouncing applicants over the age of thirty-five to be a "bad fit," and the construction industry has a difficult time imagining most women as a "good fit" for the job. A focus on "fit" also helps explain why so many employers find themselves unable to locate "qualified" employees, by which they sometimes mean "people who resemble me." Gorelick for one was stymied when an employer declined his application, only to reopen the hunt to search for someone with precisely his credentials.

A few years ago, sociologist Lauren Rivera made note of this "hire yourself" phenomenon in a yearlong study of the recruitment and hiring practices of law, banking, and consulting firms. From what she witnessed and recorded, evaluators at these firms sought not merely colleagues but soul mates: people who shared their values, thinking, and pedigrees. She writes, "Interviewers often privileged their personal feelings of comfort, validation, and excitement over identifying candidates with superior cognitive or technical skills. In many respects, they hired in a manner more closely resembling the choice of friends or romantic partners than how sociologists typically portray employers selecting new workers." Rivera was surprised to find shared *leisure* interests to be one of the most important factors in evaluating a new hire. That is, if the job candidate was a Red Sox fan and her evaluator was, too, she was far more likely to be deemed a "good fit" for the company. In another, more recent study, Rivera and her colleague András Tilcsik of the University of Toronto found that male applicants to top law firms who listed circumstances or interests thought to reflect an upper-class background, such as classical music and sailing, were far more likely to score a job interview than were equally qualified candidates who listed circumstances and interests associated with a working-class background, such as getting financial aid via an athletic scholarship or listening to country music. (Upper-class female candidates enjoyed no such advantage, as employers assumed that since they "didn't need the money" they were more likely to quit.) Similarly, sociologist Sharon Koppman of the University of California, Irvine, found that candidates for "creative" jobs in advertising and related industries were judged less by the quality of their work than by their cultural identity. Koppman interviewed employers who freely admitted that they cared relatively little about a candidate's educational credentials, résumé, or past experience but rather were looking for "cultural omnivores" conversant in a certain lingua franca of fashion, food, music, art, and literature. Candidates who had been exposed to these cultural pursuits in childhood—generally more affluent candidates—were judged to be "more creative" by employers, even though by objective measures many were not especially creative. Koppman writes: "Members of creative departments saw themselves as different and interesting and favored candidates who were different and interesting like them."

Complicating matters is that employers tend to shift their hiring criteria to justify their personal beliefs about what does—and does not—make a good "fit." For example, it's widely agreed that to be considered for even a modest leadership role, an applicant must be perceived as confident and ambitious. However, a trio of Rutgers University psychologists discovered that this measure does not apply across the board. In their study, men who came across as confident and ambitious were—as expected—more likely than other men to be hired as a computer laboratory manager, regardless of their perceived social skills. But when women were evaluated, the emphasis was reversed: skilled, confident, and ambitious women were seen as competent but were unlikely to be hired if judged "socially deficient" in such stereotypical feminine traits as being caring and deferential. The authors conclude: "To combat the perceived lack of fit, female leadership candidates must present themselves as unambiguously agentic (e.g., ambitious, competitive, and capable) to ensure they are perceived to be as competent as men. However, women face interpersonal penalties when they exhibit agency.... New to the present research, social skills predicted hiring decisions more than competence for agentic women; for all other applicants, competence received more weight than social skills. Thus, evaluators shifted the job criteria away from agentic women's strong suit (competence) and toward their perceived deficit (social skills) to justify hiring discrimination."

This selective "objectivity" plays out differently in the blue-collar sector, but only a bit differently. In the hiring of construction managers and police officers, for instance, gender sways priorities. When male applicants have more education than experience, education takes precedence. When female applicants have more education than experience, "street smarts" takes precedence. As with white-collar workers, the criteria for "fit" shifts with the person whose fitness is being measured. What this suggests is that "fit" may not be the best measure of an individual's ability to perform well on any particular job.

Personality and attitude play an important role in how we approach and perform our jobs, and no one would suggest that employers ignore this when screening job candidates. But efforts to tease out "cultural fitness" in job interviews are rarely helpful.

Indeed, some question whether an employer's instinctual response to a candidate should play any significant role in the hiring process. "One hundred years of data tell us that typical job interviews don't have much value," organizational psychologist Scott Highhouse told me. "Arguably, the most significant technological advance in my field in decades is the development of decision aids like tests and structured interviews that substantially reduce error in the prediction of employee performance. And perhaps the greatest failure of my field has been our inability to convince employers to use them."

To be fair, a growing number of employers are in fact looking for more objective methods by which to judge job candidates. One relatively common approach is what's known as a "simulation," whereby an applicant is asked to address an actual job-related task, like solving a problem or giving a presentation in real time. In theory this approach seems fair, but in practice it also carries a risk of subjectivity, as employers might look at a solution or presentation differently depending on who is solving or presenting. So in an effort at achieving true objectivity, some employers are turning to a new approach, "recrutainment."

Knack is one of several Silicon Valley ventures that has developed a scheme to essentially replace the job interview with a video game. Former attorney Guy Halfteck, who was once vice commander of the Israeli navy and holds a doctorate in management, founded Knack after he himself was deemed "not creative enough" for a job at a hedge fund. Rather than inducing despair, the rejection led him to look for a better way for job candidates like himself to signal their talent and potential. Looking back to his academic work, he found what he thought was the key to solving the problem: game theory, a branch of mathematics that grapples with competitive situations in which the outcome of a participant's actions depends critically on the actions of the other participants. In creating Knack, Halfteck brought together a team of mathematicians, psychologists, software engineers, educators, and others to develop and bring to market a technology platform that weaves behavioral science and data analytics into games that reveal a job candidate's potential on a number of metrics. For example, in Dashi Dash, Knack's signature game, candidates are asked to play the role of a virtual server in a Japanese restaurant who must predict customers' food preferences on the basis of their facial expressions while greeting and serving other customers. Halfteck said that one's performance in Dashi Dash can within ten minutes sort out such attributes as emotional intelligence, risk tolerance, and adaptability to change. And it seems that not a few hiring managers agree: Knack claimed more than two hundred corporate clients in 2017. Yet while Knack and similar efforts are growing in popularity, there's scant evidence that games offer a genuine improvement over more subjective methods of hiring.

What is more certain is that in many sectors hiring *has* become a game. In recent years the ratio of job applicants to job opportunities has declined radically from the spring of 2009, when unemployment was at its height. But competition for most jobs remains fierce and shows little sign of abating. According to a 2017 survey commissioned by the job site Glassdoor, the average job announcement brought more than 250 résumés, and only 2 percent of applicants were called in for an interview. Indeed, the vast majority of job candidates fail to get any response, let alone land any particular job they apply for, regardless of their ability to master a video game or, for that matter, win over a human recruiter. Yet despite this reality, many resist the idea that a scarcity of good jobs underlies our job search difficulties or our unhappiness with the job we have. When I asked Sharone why this was the case, his response bore a tinge of frustration. "We want to live in a world where every talented person can get a job they enjoy," he told me. The reality—that many very capable people cannot find a job that suits their abilities, education, and talents in a job "market" that increasingly resembles a discount store—is too disturbing for many of us to face. So instead, we hunker down in an effort to make ourselves a "good match."

Making ourselves a good match is not easy, especially for jobs of the sort that once sustained us and the nation. For while America is rich and getting richer, most Americans are not. For the past two decades, median household income has essentially stagnated, a problem made worse by the 2007–11 recession, which resulted in a free fall in household wealth, where one-fourth of American families lost at least 75 percent of their financial holdings and more than half of all families lost at least 25 percent. (This loss of wealth was particularly dire for people of color, who had less wealth to begin with and therefore suffered greater proportional loss. In 2013, the wealth of white households was on average thirteen times greater than that of black households, which, when controlling for various factors, was deemed the greatest disparity in the three decades for which the data was available.) At the same time, the number of stable, living-wage jobs has plummeted. The real compensation for recent high school graduates fell 4.3 percent between 2000 and 2017, and that's for those lucky enough to have jobs: in 2017, 26.6 percent of twenty-five- to fifty-four-year-olds who lacked a college degree had no job of any kind. That figure is 5 percentage points higher than it was in 2000. And college graduates are not immune: in its most recent analysis the New York Federal Reserve Bank reports that between 30 and 40 percent of recent college graduates are underemployed, meaning they have jobs that don't technically require a degree. Indeed, while the official unemployment rate has declined markedly since the December 2007–June 2009 recession, the number of Americans with a *good job* has also declined. Perhaps even more surprisingly, the percentage of people who believe themselves to have very poor or no job prospects has increased. Thirty years ago, only one in sixteen American men of prime working age (twenty-five to fifty-four) were neither working nor looking for work. Today, that ratio is one in eight. For women, it's one in four. This is not the case in the rest of the developed world. In a Federal Reserve comparison of eight nations—the United States, Sweden, Germany, France, the United Kingdom, Canada, Spain, and Japan—the United States had the lowest prime-age labor participation rate. In another study the United States lagged behind Poland, Latvia, Portugal, and even Columbia. And while millions of baby boomers have delayed retirement to remain in the workforce, as of May 2018 only 62.7 percent of working-age adults were either employed or looking for work.

Admittedly, some people in the prime-employment age of twenty-four to fifty-four opt out of a job in order to go to graduate school or attend to young children. However, these factors do not entirely explain the decline in labor participation. Social scientists offer multiple theories for what has been called this "flight from work," not all of them convincing. But most agree that it boils down to the measurable deterioration of economic and social well-being, especially in what was once America's thriving working class. For many working-class Americans, getting a job just doesn't seem worth the trouble and, in fact, may not be when compared with the alternatives.

One-third of prime-working-age men not in the labor force receive Social Security disability payments, compared to 2.6 percent of employed prime-working-age men. Yet, despite public perception, the disabled are not slackers—the average person collecting Social Security disability has worked for twenty-two years. Fully half of people not in the labor force take pain medication every day. As one primary care physician told me, "I get so many requests to fill out disability forms. Many of these people are able to work, but they don't see the purpose in it. They simply don't see themselves part of something bigger than they are." Princeton economists Anne Case and Angus Deaton have shown that addiction, depression, suicide, heart disease, and cancer are on the rise, as is midlife mortality—but only for white, prime-working-age men and women. While the economists do not insist that these "deaths of despair" are *caused* by a dearth of good jobs, they do correlate the rising level of pain, distress, and social dysfunction in the lives of working people with a decline in blue-collar prosperity.

Case and Deaton caution that declining wage incomes and prospects do not entirely explain the rise in the poor health of America's white working class. The income and prospects of African Americans and Hispanics have also declined, yet the health of these groups has if anything improved. Likewise, in Europe mortality trends do not synch with income trends, even when incomes decline sharply, as they did in the world financial meltdown. So what causes these "deaths of despair" in white, working-class America? While they can't prove it, Case and Deaton have a compelling theory: hope—or, rather, the lack of it. While African Americans, Hispanic Americans, and Europeans may hold little or no expectation of economic advancement from generation to generation, white Americans most certainly do. And it is the dashing of this hope, rather than unemployment itself, that seems to correlate most strongly with failing health and early death.

When we fail to measure up to our own expectations, we tend to assume we are doing something "wrong." This worry sows the seeds of anxiety. The World Health Organization reports that the United States is among the most anxious nations on the planet, and much if not most of that stress stems from feeling a lack of agency on the job. According to the American Institute for Stress, excessive work stress costs the US economy over $300 billion annually in health care, missed work, and stress reduction treatments. Perhaps surprisingly, this goes for workers in every sector. While it may seem obvious that hard-charging white-collar workers are under stress, studies show that blue-collar workers—line cooks, factory workers, practical nurses—are even more vulnerable, because of what Ofer Sharone described as the toxic confluence of high demand for their efforts and low control over their working lives. Demanding jobs do not necessarily make us sick, but demanding jobs that give us no agency over what we do or the way we do it are quite likely to. For growing numbers of Americans—no matter how successful—these pressures have transformed work from a source of satisfaction and pride to an anxiety-ridden bout of shadowboxing. "We have our identity constantly put to the test," Sharone told me. "Insecurity, anxiety, that's everywhere."

Much has been written about the importance of our taking "psychological ownership" of our jobs. Generally that seems to mean having a stake in our work, a stake akin to that of an entrepreneur. But not all of us buy into this idea. On the contrary, some of us prefer to "rent" our jobs, and for good reason. When we own a home or a car, we take responsibility for its maintenance and improvement in part because we see it as a wise investment, for ourselves and possibly for our children. A job, by contrast, is not necessarily a wise investment, as most of us serve at the pleasure of our employers. So, it is no small irony that those of us who claim "ownership" over our jobs are among the most likely to be owned by our jobs.

University of Pennsylvania management scholar Alexandra Michel has both studied this job-ownership paradox and experienced it firsthand. Michel, with her penchant for wearing pearls above black décolleté frocks, retains the style and instincts of the successful investment banker she once was. But not the priorities. "When I was recruited to Goldman Sachs right out of college, management told me I'd have very few opportunities to enjoy a private life," she said. "That was okay with me. It was thrilling as a twenty-two-year-old to have the opportunity to be surrounded by such smart, driven people. It felt like I had my finger on the pulse of the world economy." But as her twenties ebbed, Michel started to have doubts, chief among them the question that also haunted Ofer Sharone: Why would bankers sacrifice virtually every waking hour to an enterprise over which they exerted so little control?

Like Sharone, Michel left her high-paying job to enter academia to search for answers.

"Bankers are supposedly 'masters of the universe,'" she told me. "They have no real boss, so it *seems* like their work is autonomous, self-imposed, and self-regulated. But every young banker I knew behaved in a similar manner—they all worked eighty- to one-hundred-hour weeks, and no one had much of a life. And that puzzled me. Why, if they have so much freedom, were they all behaving in precisely the same way?"

The well-worn "work hard/play hard" cliché did not entirely explain what Michel was sensing, namely, that she and her colleagues had somehow become complicit in their own exploitation. While it was never entirely clear precisely why this was happening, history offered some clues. Decades earlier, in 1954, William H. Whyte Jr. had taken a stab at answering a related question. Whyte is best known for his widely influential book *The Organization Man*, published in 1956. At the time, he was editor of *Fortune* magazine, where he and his team set out to document what was thought to be a new management trend. As he wrote,

> There is an interesting fiction these days that goes something like this: Executives are at last getting sensible about work. The worker long ago cut down his workweek to 40 hours or less, and now the executive is doing the same. Why shouldn't he? Taxes, as top executives themselves so frequently say, have taken away the incentive to overwork. Furthermore, the argument goes, the trend to "multiple management" makes the extra hours unnecessary anyway. Indeed, it makes them downright undesirable. The effective executive is the rested man who prizes his leisure and encourages his subordinates to do the same.

Through interviews with 221 managers and executives, Whyte and his team discovered the truth: most men in their sample spent more time on office work than they did on anything else. As Whyte put it, "It is difficult to see how they could possibly work harder." Official work hours were kept from 8 or 9 a.m. to 5 or 6 p.m., but for most this was just a start. Nights and weekends were filled with paperwork, phone calls, and business meetings. Whyte clocked the average workweek of these highfliers at a grueling fifty-seven to sixty hours. Their efforts, while not always rewarded financially, were loudly applauded. "Executives . . . were unanimous that their superiors approved highly of their putting in a fifty-hour week and liked the sixty- and sixty-five-hour week even better," he wrote.

In many ways, this finding was counterintuitive. In earlier eras slavish hours were most closely associated not with elites but with workers in low-paid jobs: clerks, factory workers, and farmhands who had little choice in the matter. The wealthy pitied the "striving classes" and relished and took pride in their leisure. Why break a sweat when you have everything you need and plenty of what you desire? As economist Thorstein Veblen wrote in *The Theory of the Leisure Class*, "Conspicuous abstention from labor . . . becomes the conventional mark of superior pecuniary achievement."

It's hard to know just when the tables turned—that is, when working long hours became a signal of high status and power. It was almost certainly linked to the post–World War II economic boom and a rising consumerism that inclined workers to swap leisure for extra cash. But this does not entirely explain the behavior of high-paid executives. Whyte had his own theory: "We have, in sum, a man who is so completely involved in this work that he cannot distinguish between work and the rest of his life—and he is happy he cannot." By this measure, today's high-paid employees must be very happy indeed. Recent research shows that the best-paid white-collar workers are twice as likely to put in "overtime" as the lowest-paid blue-collar workers, though in the case of white-collar workers this overtime is largely uncompensated. To put it simply, it seems that over the past two decades the nation's wealthiest have seen the greatest decline in their leisure time, or at least that is the image they strive to project. There is perhaps no more apt example than our current president, Donald Trump, who proudly proclaims himself the "workaholic in chief."

While it's not certain why so many wealthy people are so eager to brag of their extraordinary work ethic, some social scientists trace it to a matter of scarcity—the simple economic principle that when there is less of something desirable—be it vintage port, Dutch master paintings, gold, or human effort—we regard it as extra special and desire it more. So, the theory goes, working long hours is a way to seem extra special—that is, to seem indispensable to superiors and peers. As one researcher observed, voluntary overwork is "driven by the perceptions that a busy person possesses desired human capital characteristics (competence, ambition) and is scarce and in demand on the job market." And there's another, perhaps more sinister factor that affects many of us, not just the wealthy: the often mistaken belief that what's good for the job is ipso facto good for the person doing the job.

Wall Street is a rarefied place, and not much like the workplaces where most of us ply our trades. Wall Street bankers are essentially "coin operated"—the harder they work, the larger their pile of coins, at least in theory—and this calculation does not apply to teachers or firefighters or book editors, among many others. Nonetheless, Michel argues persuasively that on a fundamental level the lessons she learned on Wall Street have much to teach all of us.

To glean those lessons, Michel shadowed a gaggle of young bankers for several years, getting close enough to hear their sometimes shocking personal stories. Not surprisingly, the bankers were fiercely competitive and self-driven; they had no need to keep track of their vacation days because they rarely took any. Most measured their self-worth in dollar signs, and their bosses did everything they could to reinforce that inclination, and to keep young bankers at their workstations. Their every need was catered to—meals, car service, dry-cleaning, round-the-clock support. Coffee and sweets were delivered unbidden—the jolt of caffeine and sugar generating what Michel described as "a state of constant nervous stimulation."

Najahyia Chinchilla, a Detroit-based architect who once designed office spaces for New York City investment banks, confirmed Michel's observations. "The banks want people to stay close to their desks, so we made sure that they had everything they needed—for example, we put kitchens adjacent to every workspace. And today, that's pretty much caught on across industry sectors. We no longer design spaces for people who work 8 to 5, that just doesn't happen anymore. Work today is 24/7, and we design spaces with that in mind."

Many employers advocate and publicly promote the *idea* of work-life balance, but it's not always clear what that means on the ground. As one senior director at Goldman Sachs told Michel: "The more you talk about work-life balance, the more you create the problem that you want to solve. Why make a distinction between work and life in the first place? The more you can blend them together, the more you'll get out of your people."

The young bankers Michel followed embraced this philosophy, bragging of their stamina and mocking anyone who showed the slightest weakness. After a few years of this, many broke down in what Michel called a "full-body rebellion": back pain, migraines, insomnia, eating disorders. They self-medicated with alcohol, drugs, pornography, shopping, food, and sex. Michel recalled one banker complaining that no matter how much Red Bull he drank, no matter how much nicotine gum he chewed, he could simply not get enough done. "It's like a war," he complained. "Me against me. My body is my worst enemy." A few weeks later, Michel noticed blood on another banker's shirt. "I asked what was wrong, and he brushed me off," she said. "His assistant told me he'd been at the office for three days and nights and that he keeps vomiting into the trash can. She thought he had pneumonia. But he refused to go home. And this guy believed *he* was in control."

I'll acknowledge again that all this talk of investment bankers and their woes may seem not to apply to the rest of us—after all, these are *investment bankers,* not social workers. But Michel persuaded me that bankers are canaries in a coal mine that many of us inhabit. The prioritizing of "energy" over experience, the normalization of a 24/7 work cycle, the conflation of job and home are all hallmarks of today's high-pressure workplaces—whether in a New York City skyscraper or a warehouse in Memphis. Even the seemingly innocuous open office, evocative of the trading floors of investment banks, has become a weapon in a battle for control. "Open offices make employees feel they are under surveillance," Michel said. "Everyone is watching everyone else, and that creates a web of control that did not exist when people had the privacy of their own offices."

Michel links the way investment banks are run to the rise of so-called flat corporate structures, organizational arrangements with few levels of management between staff and the top brass. This organizational structure is said to encourage employee decision making and what some believe is a true democratization of the workplace. In investment banks, the flat hierarchies minimize power differentials among bankers—all bankers hired in the same year advance together, and rapidly. It's possible to reach the highest level of the organization—managing director—in less than ten years. This means that all perceived power differentials are seen as temporary—a mere obstacle to be quickly hurtled.

Flat structures are increasingly popular today not only in investment banks and other financial institutions but in consulting firms, law firms, and media and IT companies. One commonly cited pioneer of this strategy is Valve Corporation, a video game maker that has garnered enthusiastic praise for its toppling of the corporate hierarchy. Affectionately known as "Flatland," Valve boasts of having no clear chain of command and no central business plan: employees are free to choose their own projects, can organize their own time, and are even included in hiring decisions. Staff members rate one another on technical skills, productivity, and teamwork under a principle known as "360 degree feedback," whereby employees get a stream of anonymous, confidential reviews on their strengths and weaknesses from peers. The scores are aggregated and used to generate a figure representing an employee's "relative value" to the company. All this is meant to make staff members feel empowered to judge one another, rather than be judged by an overseer.

Gabe Newell is Valve's cofounder and managing director. A scruffy, soft-spoken Harvard dropout and former Microsoft executive, Newell makes every effort to stimulate and encourage creativity and collaboration at the firm. The company lavishes employees with unlimited vacation and sick leave and rewards them with all-expenses-paid vacations for themselves and their families. Newell prizes intellectual flexibility and verve in his staff and rejects job titles, which, he once said, "don't map really well to creating the best possible experience for your customers."

As you may have guessed, "Flatland" also has a dark side. With no managers to turn to for adjudication or support, there is enormous pressure on employees to "fit in" with the prevailing corporate culture. Those who fail to do so are sometimes marginalized or ejected in an "off the island"–style banishment. Several years ago, the company "voted out" more than two dozen top engineers, including inventor Jeri Ellsworth, a legend in game design circles. Ellsworth, who went on to cofound a new venture, described the Valve structure as "pseudoflat" with a hidden layer of authority that she compared to "popular kids in a high school clique." Since a large portion of employee compensation at the company is based on individual performance as perceived by one's peers, Ellsworth said most engineers gravitated toward high-profile projects that were both visible and almost certain to succeed. Basically, she told me, her colleagues were incentivized to avoid taking the very risks companies like Valve claim to encourage.

Valve is certainly a pioneering company, but its management structure is hardly novel. Since the 1990s consultants have advised American businesses to flatten their hierarchies to empower workers to think for themselves and to respond to customer needs more quickly. In doing so companies have eliminated many middle-management positions while sometimes increasing the number of top managers. This adjustment clearly correlates with top brass making more money (at this writing, Gabe Newell has a reported net worth of $5.5 billion), but its success at spawning innovation is less clear. "Flat hierarchies are supposed to result in disruptive innovation," Ellsworth said. "But what happened at Valve wasn't innovative. It was just disruptive."

The concept of "disruptive innovation," popularized by Harvard Business School economist Clayton Christensen in his 1997 best seller *The Innovator's Dilemma*, is all but de rigueur in business circles, particularly in the tech industry. Yet while it's common for employers to encourage staff to be "disruptive," what they actually mean by this is uncertain, even, one suspects, to the employers themselves. What it seems to imply is the expectation that employees function like entrepreneurs within their organizations, fearlessly innovating and taking risks to solve company problems. Unfortunately, the assumption that every one of us can and should make galvanizing change from within an organizational structure imposes what poet Gary Snyder once called "a double burden." It implies that existing processes are at best inadequate and then, as Snyder writes, force us to "do something supposedly better and different." MIT cultural historian Rosalind Williams once observed that under this thinking any resistance to change—any honoring of the processes, innovations, and accomplishments of those who precede us—becomes "an accusation rather than an irreplaceable and necessary aspect of human life." That is, rather than studying and learning from our past, we reflexively dismiss it as passé and even irrelevant.

Such hubris comes with consequences, some of which affect each of us on a very personal level. We might imagine our industrial past as a collection of ossified and stiflingly hierarchal institutions managed by a cigar-smoking elite resistant to change. And we might also imagine our "postindustrial" present as a collection of decentralized, participatory workplaces from which control and direction emerge, not from rules and regulations, but from the agreed-upon values and actions of the employees themselves. But while this makes for a promising ideal, in practice the promise is rarely kept.

Some years ago, management theorist James Barker took a close look at one small manufacturer's self-proclaimed transformation from a hierarchical bureaucracy to a "holocracy," a congregation of self-managing teams. Barker observed that when team members were released from management oversight, they tended to exert more control over one another than their former bosses had exerted over them. With no externally imposed structure, the employees formed their own hierarchies and tyrannies, worked longer hours, and sacrificed personal time, family time, and their health in their eagerness to be seen as worthy team members. "The powerful combination of peer pressure and rational rules . . . creates a new iron cage whose bars are almost invisible to the workers it incarcerates," Barker wrote.

Ofer Sharone stepped into that cage nearly a decade ago, at a large Seattle-based software company he called "Megatech" (a transparent pseudonym). There, as today at many other firms, employees were expected to engage in what was called "competitive self-management." To out-compete their coworkers, before leaving for the day some workers draped spare parkas or rain jackets across their desk chairs in an attempt to fool management into thinking they were hard at work late into the night. Such gamesmanship was made all the more demeaning by the fact that most employees actually did work impossibly long hours: on average sixty-seven a week, and some as many as eighty. Many felt they had no choice. For despite the supposed "flat hierarchy," the company ranked employees on a curve, where in any particular ranking period roughly 20 percent of employees were automatically condemned as "below average." Ten percent of staff were dismissed every year, even those whose performance surpassed their official job description. This resulted in a toxic atmosphere in which even top players felt under threat.

Neuroscientists have found that when we suspect we are being compared unfavorably to others, our natural fight-or-flight response kicks in, releasing stress-related hormones that illicit irritability, sleeplessness, and anxiety. This certainly seemed to be the case at Megatech. The prospect of being "ranked and yanked" pushed some employees to the point of sabotaging their peers. As one exhausted engineer told Sharone: "It's this treadmill where you are blowing out your expectations by doing more, then they get reset, and then you have to do even more."

When Abe Gorelick and I spoke a year or so after our first meeting, he was back on that treadmill. He had recently nailed an assignment with a large advertising firm, heading up the digital account for Subway Restaurants in Canada. The new job demanded only a fraction of his experience and capabilities, and the pay wasn't what he had hoped for. Also, it was temporary. Still, he was thrilled to be "back in the saddle." He was no longer driving a cab or selling neckties. But he told me cheerfully that he was holding on to the gig at Whole Foods, at least for the time being. It was tough getting out of bed Saturday mornings to work the early shift, but he said he wanted to keep the job for now "to remember how things have been." What he didn't say but was surely thinking was "and how things might be again." Ten months later, when we spoke again, Abe had completed his assignment at the ad agency and was back on the job market. He was nearly sixty, but that did nothing to diminish his determination. It was a matter, he said, of attitude, and of keeping ahead of the curve. "I'm still working on myself," he told me. "I'm determined to get better, better every day."

COMING OUT OF THE COFFIN

I first met Amy Cotterman at an informal gathering in Dayton, Ohio. I felt lucky to meet her. A few years earlier, *Forbes* magazine had declared Dayton one of the nation's "Ten Fastest Dying Cities." That same year a Dayton boy stumbled upon a neighbor's mummi-fied body swinging in a closet of an abandoned house—facing fore-closure, the man had hanged himself five years earlier. The bank holding the mortgage didn't investigate or try to recoup the loss, as the property—like so many properties in Dayton—was essentially worthless. Cotterman had heard the story, and it troubled her. But she told me it didn't change the way she felt about her birthplace. She'd traveled the world, but she was proud to call Dayton home.

Cotterman had built her remarkable career on a rather humble foundation. A middling student, she dropped out of college in the mid-1980s to grab a job at a company that designed and sold soft-ware to car dealers. She had no particular interest in software or cars, but nonetheless quickly became the firm's rising star, pushing past older and more experienced colleagues. It was a heady time when desktop computers were just catching on, and she mastered them. And then, in 1991, the World Wide Web went public. "The web changed everything," Cotterman told me. "We'd develop software at company headquarters in the US, run it through antiviral software, and ship it off to our partners in India. They'd work on it through our night, check it for viruses, and ship it back the next morning. My boss said, 'You work for me twenty-four hours a day, seven days a week, and you work your life around it.' This was not a suggestion; it was a *directive*."

Cotterman took pride in rising to the challenge. "I was killing it," she recalled. But when the firm was sold, she sensed change coming, and not the sort that would work in her favor. So she quit and opened her own consulting business helping clients ship their manufacturing operations overseas. Somehow she found the time to marry a former colleague who shared her priorities. They tried to see each other twice a month, but sometimes that didn't happen. She was terribly busy. "American companies were getting tax breaks to pack up and leave the country," she said. "And I made it happen."

Coffinize is the word Cotterman coined to describe the process of breaking down a factory piece by piece in preparation for shipping it abroad. "You dismantle all the machinery, equipment, shelves, everything—take photographs, write instructions on how to rebuild it, and pack it up in boxes," she explained. "It's step-by-step, very IKEA. You put lids on the boxes and line them up in trucks in rows, like racks and racks of coffins. And after that, you think, 'Wow, death of the American factory.'"

Cotterman had no time to fret over the death of American factory jobs. Her job was very much alive, and she was at it seven days a week. Nights, though, were different; that's when the free-floating anxiety piled on. She suffered from insomnia and migraines. She wasn't sure why, but her friends thought they knew. "They told me I was living *Up in the Air*," she said. "I had no idea what they meant, not back then. I had no time to go to the movies."

For those of us who did have the time, the film *Up in the Air* hit a nerve. George Clooney stars as Ryan Bingham, an Armani-clad "termination facilitator" who swoops down on companies bearing pink slips hand-delivered to employees on behalf of managers too cowardly to do so themselves. A twenty-first-century J. Alfred Prufrock, Bingham measures his life not in coffee spoons but in frequent-flier miles. Spouseless, childless, rootless, he is in some respects what Cotterman once strove to be—the quintessential "zero-drag employee" unencumbered by family, civic responsibilities, or other distractions that might come between him and his job. *Up in the Air* reminds us that "having it all" can mean giving our all to a job that does not return the favor.

Okay, we get it, overwork is not good, but that doesn't mean we are in a position to cut back. Our reasons are both myriad and mysterious. We need the money, of course, but that doesn't entirely explain it, because many of us prefer to be on the job even when we're paid not to be. According to government surveys, the average private sector employee in the United States receives about ten days of paid vacation and six holidays, fewer than the minimum legal standard set in most other wealthy economies across the globe. Yet most of us fail to take them.

So why do we labor so faithfully for "the man," even when we know the man is not faithful to us? Surveys of workers cite fear of reprisal for "slacking" from bosses and coworkers. But there's another reason, one that resonates with Cotterman. Asked in a survey why they didn't take the vacation days they'd earned, more than 10 percent of respondents checked the box that read: "Because the job *is* my life."

But is there anything wrong with this? After all, Freud declared work a "cornerstone of humanness," on a par with love. (Of course, Freud was a self-confessed neurotic for whom work was a life-sucking obsession. He once confided to a friend, "I cannot imagine life without work as really comfortable," adding, "The chief patient I am preoccupied with is myself.") And even Freud must have understood that, unlike ants, humans are not naturally inclined toward busyness.

Indeed, it's been decades since evolutionary anthropologist Marshall Sahlins made the case that when given the option most of us would choose leisure over labor. Like a handful of other anthropologists of the 1960s and '70s, Sahlins had come to question the once iron-clad assumption that the life of hunter-gatherers was a short and brutish one devoid of almost anything but thankless toil. In his landmark metastudy of a number of modern hunter-gatherer societies, Sahlins observed that in the absence of hunger most people were content to socialize, play games, make art, or simply rest. He wrote: "Their wandering, rather than anxious, takes on all the qualities of a picnic outing on the Thames." Were society not pointing an accusing finger, Sahlins concludes, few humans would feel any compulsion to hold a steady job. "The present human condition of man slaving to bridge the gap between his unlimited wants and his insufficient means," he wrote, "is a tragedy of modern times."

Sahlins and his colleagues may have been the first to document this observation, but they were not the first to make it. German philosopher Georg Wilhelm Friedrich Hegel, who struggled for much of his life to get paid for his own efforts, reasoned that toil in the absence of need is not a natural inclination. "The barbarian is lazy and differs from the educated man in his dull and solitary brooding," he wrote, "for practical education consists precisely in the need and habit of being occupied." Yet while the gentry might have been occupied in Victorian times, it was not generally with what many of us today would call an occupation. Aristocrats harbored no ambition to be "employed," and many looked down on those who did. (Fans of the addictive PBS costume drama *Downton Abbey* saw Richard Clarkson, a physician, patronized by the aristocracy as a sort of high-class servant, as was the teacher Sarah Bunting.) Indeed, leisure historian Benjamin Hunnicutt has shown that through most of human history progress meant "opening up a life beyond pecuniary—to family, community, the life of the mind":

that is, toiling no more than absolutely necessary to sustain a decent life.

The Protestant work ethic rose—in part—in response to this view. The industrial age brought growth and status to middle-class merchants, tradesmen, craftsmen, and artisans who saw no shame in wanting more, or in serving the demands of those who did. This growing bourgeoisie came together in praise of the "dignity" of work, pushing back on the "idle rich" and their ruling-class snobbery. At the same time, Protestant dogma seemed to encourage what nineteenth-century German sociologist Max Weber once called "salvation anxiety," an abiding unease for which the faithful execution of hard labor was the one sure cure. Sloth was a sin, the thinking went, while toil cleared a path to heaven. As Scottish philosopher and essayist Thomas Carlyle wrote in 1843: "Doubt, Desire, Sorrow, Remorse, Indignation, Despair itself, all these like helldogs lie beleaguering the soul of the poor dayworker, as of every man: but he bends himself with free valour against his task, and all these are stilled, all these shrink murmuring far off into their caves. The man is now a man."

Carlyle's admiration for what he called "the chivalry of work" was absolute, at least rhetorically—he once declared "Giant Labour" the "truest emblem of God." But it's worth noting that Carlyle penned those famous lines when his country was in the midst of an economic crisis—a time when work was scarce and when untold thousands of his fellow Scots were fleeing the Highland potato famine. It is also worth mentioning that in matters of employment Carlyle himself did not always "bend himself with free valour" to the task at hand. As a young man he earned his living as a teacher, and confided in a letter to a friend: "It is true! I hate teaching . . . in all its branches; yet what can a solitary person do? The inhabitant of Bridewell hates beating hemp; but he hates flogging still worse." (Bridewell Prison was a London poorhouse where inmates were required to pound hemp with a mallet to break down the fibers in preparation for making rope for use in nooses, among other things.) Carlyle quit teaching as soon as he could and reserved his own "free valour" for a life of reading, writing, and what he once described as his chief occupation: "strolling about the fields, revolving most dreamy thoughts."

The great nineteenth-century essayest, poet, and designer William Morris was an admirer and protégé of Carlyle's, but he had little tolerance for the older man's hypocrisy. He wrote: "It has become an article of the creed of modern morality that all labour is good in itself—a convenient belief to those who live on the labour of others." Morris was horrified by the heavy toll industrialization had begun to take on the working class. Factories, he warned, threatened to rid work itself of any intrinsic human value beyond keeping the bills paid and hands busy. And this was especially true in the United States, where paid work seemed to be privileged over most other human endeavors. As German-born mathematician and journalist Francis Grund observed of his new home in America: "There is, probably, no people on earth with whom business constitutes pleasure, and industry amusement, in an equal degree with the inhabitants of the United States of America. Active occupation is not only the principal source of their happiness, and the foundation of their national greatness, but they are absolutely wretched without it, and instead of the 'dolce far niente,' know but the horrors of idleness."

Thomas Jefferson drew a sharp contrast between what he called "a natural aristocracy of talent and virtue" in the New World and the presumably unnatural aristocracy of the Old World. By this he meant that in America residents earned their privilege, while in Britain they inherited it. Yet, with some exceptions (as fans of the Broadway hit *Hamilton* are especially aware), the Founding Fathers were themselves men of privilege with a snobbish disdain for the laboring class. George Washington argued that only "the lower classes" should risk their lives as foot soldiers, while Jefferson envisioned a public school system that would rake a handful of talented students from the "rubbish" of the working class. James Madison, who worried about a tyranny of the masses, argued that the Senate "ought to come from and represent the wealth of the nation," or, as he went on to explain, the "more capable set of men."

Of course, neither slaves nor Native Americans nor most women had much chance of rising above their station in colonial America. Yet America has throughout its history imagined itself a meritocracy. For some reason, the idea that those of low or moderate birth could readily pull themselves into the ruling class was so tantalizing, it not only took hold but dominated public thinking. And oddly, this belief was particularly potent when class divides were widest—for example, in the period of rapid industrialization following the Civil War known as the Gilded Age.

In 1868, Horatio Alger published *Street Life in New York with the Boot Blacks*, about a poor white boy who through perseverance and effort rises from destitution to prosperity. Alger, a defrocked minister, published nearly one hundred novels built around this theme, a message given credence by wealthy industrialists of the time whose fondest boast was of being "self-made." As French historian Alexis de Tocqueville wryly observed, Americans seemed to "owe nothing to any man, they expect nothing from any man; they acquire the habit of always considering themselves as standing alone, and they are apt to imagine that their whole destiny is in their own hands."

Tocqueville found it endearingly naive that Americans were "apt to imagine" they had full charge over their own destinies. For, after all, he observed, had they such control they would be rich, while the "number of large fortunes (in America) is quite small." And while today many politicians continue to promote the fuzzy hope that hard work and plenty of it is all it takes to make it, many Americans are beginning to see Tocqueville's point. Most of us still believe in the value of hard work, of course, but we have also come to realize that it is not so much how hard we labor but the sort of labor we do that makes the real difference. And the sort of labor we do very much depends on the circumstances to which we were born.

Stanford University sociologist David Grusky is an expert on inequality, its causes, and its consequences. "Equality of opportunity is a fundamental value for Americans, basically—it's written in our DNA," he told me. "But the evidence is very clear that there are gross departures from this ideal." For example, over their lifetimes, those born into the bottom 10 percent of income distribution earn on average about one-third as much as those born into the top 10 percent. There are many obstacles faced by those born into disadvantage, notably a lack of positive role models and access to good schools. But Grusky said there are other, perhaps even more important factors.

"The general thinking is that the digital revolution increased the demand for skilled labor and diminished the demand for unskilled labor," he said. "Okay, that sounds right, but what skills are we talking about here? No one seemed to know—not economists, not other social scientists, no one. It seemed fairly obvious that this is an important question to answer—if we don't know what skills will really pay, what skills should people acquire? So we decided to deconstruct the concept of skill, to find out which skills—specifically—had the biggest payoff."

Grusky and his colleagues took a hard look at the assumptions social scientists had made about the links between skills and good jobs. And what they found surprised them. "Everyone thought that computer skills were key," he said. "But from our findings, they were not. What sticks out are analytic skills—critical thinking, logic, and reasoning." And honing those analytic skills, Grusky said, is far easier for those born into circumstances that have allowed them the opportunity to practice those skills through the course of their daily lives.

Analytic skill is the ability to weigh evidence, recognize patterns, and conceptualize and solve problems on the basis of available information, even when that information is imperfect or incomplete. It differs from quantitative skill in that it involves not only knowing the rules but also how and when to break the rules. So, while it's become customary to argue that all students be armed with "math and computer skills," those skills are not enough. To succeed, they need more than technical skill—they also must know how best to apply that skill to real-world problems, and to which problems to apply it. Analytic thinking typically requires imagining various scenarios and perspectives, conceiving effective strategies to deal with them, and then making judgments based on the persuasiveness of each alternative. Generally, people born into relative wealth have far more experience with and exposure to this challenging way of thinking than do the less advantaged, as the wealthy have a greater opportunity to put their minds to matters that extend beyond the immediate demands of daily life.

"We live in a moment in history when you need flexibility," Grusky said. "Training into a fixed set of skills might be fine in the short run, but it is far less likely than it once was to have a long-term payoff. What matters now is not fixed skills on their own but the capacity to see opportunities, seize them, and make the most of them."

For example, a high school student might decide to train as a welder, a job that according to government statistics is in immediate need of workers. But skilled welders require extensive education and experience, which makes their services rather costly. As a consequence, welding has become a target for automation. And while robot welders do and will undoubtedly continue to require human guidance, only the most highly trained and skilled welders are in a position to offer that guidance. Given that robots are far more efficient than humans, fewer traditional welders will be required. So young people interested in pursuing this trade need to be in a position to think well beyond acquiring immediate skills.

Grusky went on to say that the decline of the middle class has left Americans with less access to what he called the "good" jobs that demand these skills. And while it may seem that what qualifies as a "good" job is a matter of opinion, in 2012 economist John Schmitt at the Center for Economic and Policy Research and his colleague Janelle Jones set some actual guidelines. By their reckoning, the minimum standard for a "good" job was an annual salary of at least $37,000 (roughly equivalent to $38,900 at this writing), with health insurance and a retirement plan. By this standard, fewer than one in four Americans had a good job. Roughly half of these people had the bad-luck trifecta—a low-paying job with no benefits and no retirement plan. Looking at the data, Schmitt and Jones were shocked to note that the American economy had since 1979 lost fully one-third of its power to generate good jobs. And much if not most of that power seemed to have been lost to technological advance.

Historically, this had not been the case, at least not over the long term. Throughout the nineteenth and early twentieth centuries, a cavalcade of astonishing inventions—the steam engine, the assembly line, the railroads, electrification, the internal combustion engine, petroleum processing, airplanes, automobiles—led to a *temporary* loss of some jobs, followed by the creation of new jobs. For example, the internal combustion engine put any number of horse trainers, blacksmiths, and harness makers out to pasture but also laid the groundwork for an automobile industry that directly or indirectly employed tens of millions of Americans in transportation, manufacture, sales, insurance, road construction, and other sectors. From this and similar historical examples, it has long been argued that a temporary decline in what William Morris called "worthy work" is to be expected, collateral damage in a process by which over the long term technology creates more and better jobs.

Yet while innovations of the industrial age often resulted in significant job creation, it's far from certain the same can be said of the digital age. Indeed, some experts argue that automation and digitalization are more likely to be linked to a general *decline* in job creation. Economist Robert Gordon, for one, points out that as electronic data becomes cost-free, its marginal benefit in terms of labor creation approaches zero. Facebook and other information providers rely on customers to create content—all those messages, photos, videos, comments, likes, and pokes generate plenty of revenue for Facebook and its investors without necessarily creating many jobs. Indeed, despite their staggering market caps, no American Internet information provider has come close to providing the 443,000 American jobs (many of them union jobs) directly supported by Kroger, the nation's largest supermarket chain. In 2017 Apple, the nation's most profitable company, had only 77,000 direct US employees.

There's a fancy word for this phenomenon: *ephemeralization*, coined by Buckminster Fuller in the 1930s to describe the concept of "doing more with less." Throughout human history, doing more with less resulted in efficiencies that helped make our world a better place. But arguably, we have reached a limit. By building more human-like capabilities into our machines, we seem to have reduced the need for humans in most positions along the value chain in a growing number of industries. Digital technology has made workers more productive than ever before, but over time this increase in productivity has not always led to a boost in wages or job quality. Nor has it resulted in more people attaining more challenging, higher-skilled jobs. In fact, here's the stunner: overall, digital technology has led to a *decline* in the demand for the high-level skills that command a high-level wage.

A decline in demand for skill? To many if not most of us, this statement sounds preposterous. We've heard so much about the knowledge economy and its nearly insatiable demand for technological and managerial acumen. Skills are the key to the twenty-first-century kingdom, right?

Once again, it's complicated. No one doubts that acquiring skills can help broaden an individual's prospects. But in the aggregate, there are convincing signs that the *demand* for skills has cooled. Economist Paul Beaudry and his colleagues at the University of British Columbia and York University first reported this startling trend in 2013, though to surprisingly little fanfare. "In the late 1980s and especially the 1990s, there was great demand for high-level skills," Beaudry told me. "Organizations were integrating computers into the workplace, and this integration generated demand for all sorts of business and management services. But once the automated systems were up and running, the demand for skill tapered off. In this, the maturity era of the IT revolution, having a college degree is only partly about obtaining access to high-paying managerial and technology jobs. It is also about beating out less-educated workers for barista and clerical jobs."

It appears that digital-age capitalism threatens digital-age democracy by polarizing employment opportunities—adding a few more jobs at the top and many more jobs at the bottom, while squeezing out many solid, middle-level jobs. Data from the US Bureau of Labor Statistics indicates that the fastest-growing jobs are low-paid—nursing assistant, home health care aide, personal care aide, restaurant food preparer (including fast food), maid, and janitor. While well-paid jobs like software designer and computer analyst are also growing, they are growing at a far slower rate.

"The most vigorous job growth is not at the highest tiers," MIT economist David Autor told me. "It's at the bottom third of the wage scale." While we may choose to believe that our economy needs many more engineers and scientists, the far greater demand is for service workers who—at least technically—are far less skilled and require far less education.

In 2016, the country had recovered most of the jobs it had lost in the Great Recession; unemployment shrank to below 5 percent, and politicians cheered. But many Americans had reason to feel less gleeful. Fully 58 percent of the job growth was in occupations with a wage of $7.69 to $13.83 an hour, while 60 percent of jobs in the midrange—$13.84 to $21.13 per hour—had vanished. It was as if a rogue wave had crashed onto our shores, leaving millions of bad jobs in its wake, and retreated to carry millions of good ones out to sea. Often, when employers complain that they cannot find enough "good workers," it's not because there are not enough good workers available, but rather because good workers cannot afford to invest in poorly paying and precarious jobs.

British economist Guy Standing has written extensively on what he describes as a breakdown in the twentieth-century income distribution system, whereby wealth was reflected in one's wages. By contrast today, wealth is channeled away from workers to "rentiers"–that is, owners of financial, physical, or intellectual property, like software. He coined the term *precariat* to describe a new class of workers left to stew in a toxic mix of what he calls the "four A's"—anxiety, anomie, alienation, and anger. In setting the terms of employment, employers fully expect this "precariat" to willingly push aside the demands of their personal lives to accommodate unpredictable schedules and uncertain career prospects. Not a few employers make these demands under the cheerful guise of offering workplace "freedom" and "flexibility"—as though workers should be grateful to not know from one week to the next what their schedules, or paychecks, will be.

"We've idealized the idea of portable work, promoting the notion of people roaming about with a portfolio of skills they can sell at a price they set themselves," Standing told me. "Some are able to do that, of course. But to think that we can build a society on this platform, with no protections, is fanciful. The person who works for himself works for a tyrant—you are only as good as your last job and your last performance. You are constantly being evaluated and graded. Having to worry so much about where the next bit of bread is coming from means people losing control over their lives."

One way to grasp the implications of this trend toward precarity is to look at a specific employment category. Rather than choose an occupation in obvious decline, like travel agent or highway toll collector, let's take a look at an occupation that experts agree is in robust and growing demand: college instructor. College teaching is not immune to innovation—it can and does take place remotely, for example, through "Massive Open Online Courses" (MOOCs) whereby a single instructor can reach hundreds of thousands of people around the globe. Still, most college instruction happens live and in real time—one teacher, one classroom. Given the growing pressure on Americans to seek postsecondary education, experts predict that the demand for college instructors will grow substantially, certainly faster than the average for all occupations. And yet, counter to what classic economic models might predict, robust *demand* for college instructors will not necessarily result in improved terms of employment for college instructors.

To understand why, it may be helpful to compare college instruction with another job category—farmhand. While it might be difficult to imagine that college instructors laboring in College Park, Maryland, have anything in common with artichoke pickers laboring in the fields of Castroville, California, they do. Most farmhands work contingently and are paid by the piece. Most adjunct college instructors work contingently and are paid by the class. Both farmhands and adjunct instructors are vulnerable to last-minute schedule changes that can result in lost income—in the case of field workers for bad weather or weak harvests, in the case of instructors for low enrollments leading to the cancellation of a class. Neither field hands nor college instructors are likely to have employer-subsidized health insurance, a retirement package, or other benefits through their job. Nor are they likely to be on the first rung of a "career ladder" leading to more promising prospects.

Yet there is great demand for both farmhands and college instructors, which suggests that there should be some upward pressure on their wages, and also pressure to improve their terms of employment. So why not? The answer is that despite protests to the contrary, there in fact are sufficient qualified college instructors and farm laborers to meet the growing demand.

You have every reason to doubt this assertion. Given the recent complaints about the dearth of farm labor, one would assume that farmhands—at least—are in short supply. And starting around 2010 farm owners across the nation did indeed report they were unable to find farmhands, thanks in part to Obama administration crackdowns on undocumented workers. By 2015 the shortage was so dire, it was reported, that farm owners had no choice but to cut back production of fruits and vegetables by 9.5 percent, supposedly costing growers $3.1 billion in lost revenues. So does this imply a labor shortage? Not necessarily.

By almost any standard, farmhand is not a good job. The median pay in 2016 was $10.83 per hour, and in California, the nation's largest agricultural state, farmworkers working fewer than ten hours a day were only recently entitled to overtime pay. Many farmworkers are unable to make minimum wage. In general, hands are hired without contracts and are under constant pressure to work quickly or lose their jobs. So, the inevitable question: Was there a true shortage of farmworkers, or simply a shortage of farmworkers willing and able to labor under these draconian terms?

We are fortunate that a "natural experiment" provided an answer. That experiment was conducted by Christopher Ranch, the nation's largest garlic producer, based in Gilroy, California, tucked into the southern tip of Santa Clara County, home of Silicon Valley. As of late 2016, Christopher Ranch was short fifty workers needed to peel, package, and roast garlic at a wage of $11 an hour—high by farmhand standards, but apparently not high enough in prosperous Santa Clara County, where full-time workers earned an average of $121,212 annually. So in January 2017, the ranch upped its wages to $13 an hour. Within the month, Christopher Ranch was fully staffed and had over 150 people on its employee applicant waiting list—some willing to commute up to two hours for the opportunity to peel and package garlic.

Cases like Christopher Ranch suggest that while employers may complain of the "difficulty" of finding farmhands—or adjunct instructors—this difficulty does not necessarily stem from a true labor shortage. On the contrary, basic economic principles suggest that an excess—not a shortfall—of labor is what makes it possible for employers to offer substandard terms. When improving those terms results in a landslide of job applications, the phrase "labor shortage" simply does not seem to apply.

President William McKinley once famously declared, "Cheap merchandise means cheap men and cheap men mean a cheap country, and that is not the kind of Government our fathers founded." Given America's history of slavery, indentured servitude, and sweatshops, McKinley could not have been more wrong on this point. The nation was indeed built on a foundation of cheap labor, and since the steady decline of unions in the 1970s, we've come to rely on that cheap labor to prop up industries whose jobs, we're warned, will fall victim to automation if workers who perform them dare to demand higher wages or better terms and conditions of employment. Indeed, the Bureau of Labor Statistics predicts that despite growing demand for agricultural products over the next decade, an increased demand for agricultural *workers* is unlikely, as their jobs are being steadily automated.

Adjunct college instructors, farm laborers, and others working as contractors may have the flexibility to move between and among gigs, but there's a good chance that many if not most would gladly trade that flexibility for the opportunity to exert more control over their working lives. The same holds for the millions of Americans working in IT firms, warehouses, banks, insurance agencies, and assembly lines under contracts that promise flexibility but no paid holidays, sick days, employee-sponsored health insurance, or other benefits routinely offered permanent employees. While it's not known precisely how many Americans work as contractors, there is no question that the number is growing—and quickly. According to some estimates, by the decade's end nearly half of the US private sector workforce will have spent at least some time in this precarious state. As one contractor wrote in response to a *Wall Street Journal* survey, "The flexibility so beloved of large corporations translates to continuous gnawing anxiety over whether the next day will bring an announcement that you're 'excess to needs.'"

Nearly a decade ago, a global study carried out by professional services company Willis Towers Watson surveyed twenty thousand employees in twenty-two countries. They found that most workers no longer prized "flexibility" on the job. What they craved was stability and job security. Fully one-third of respondents said they would prefer to work for a single company for their entire career, and another third said they would prefer to work for no more than a total of three. Other than compensation, stability and job security took precedence over every other variable, including such vaunted factors as "challenge" and "autonomy." Some experts chalked this up to postrecession shell shock and predicted that worker attitudes would change once the economy gathered steam. But the feelings persisted. In a follow-up survey of 31,000 employees conducted in 2016, job stability remained a top priority.

Linguist and social critic Noam Chomsky once declared the hiring of temporary workers to be integral to a corporate business model aimed at reducing labor costs and increasing "labor servility." Certainly, for a growing number of us his words ring true. Without security, we have little or no leverage to apply whatever hard-won flexibility we might be granted—indeed, not a few of us are shouldering more than one job just to make ends meet. Our increasingly precarious relationship to work provokes stress of the sort that can lead to poor relationships, poor health, and a sense of powerlessness that makes it difficult for people to take charge and make change.

How to reconcile ourselves to an age of increasingly precarious work? That's not an easy question to answer, nor does it lend itself to generalizations. There is no one approach, no one sure solution. But for many if not most of us, the first step is to question the hard-held assumption that we must *make ourselves* a good fit for the job rather than create work that is right for us, work that we control rather than a job that controls us.

You'll recall Amy Cotterman, the successful consultant we met in Dayton at the opening of the chapter. When she and I last spoke, I learned a part of her story that she doesn't always reveal. She told me her husband had died unexpectedly, and relatively young. After his death she came to a startling realization. She felt unmoored and without purpose. Looking forward into the future, she saw more of the same. So rather than stay the course, as she had always done in the past, she took a moment to reconsider. And she concluded that despite what others called her "success," her work simply wasn't working for her.

She had returned to her hometown of Dayton with high expectations, she told me, but not of the sort one might assume. "This is the Rust Belt," she said. "I'm aware that full-time, permanent knowledge jobs are not plentiful here. That time has passed." So rather than polish her résumé and strive to duplicate the career she once had, she carefully crafted a life that made sense for her. And that life, she decided, would center not on a job leading to success but on work as an end in itself.

She returned to college to study culinary science, with a specialty in baking, and after graduation cofounded a baking cooperative. She took a part-time position as catering manager at a local deli and signed on to teach baking at her local community college. She took on volunteer work and became active in the larger Dayton community. And she settled into the sort of life she'd never dreamed she would want, but now knows she always did: a life where her sense of self comes not from a career identity but from work from which *she* can make meaning. For the first time in her life, she said, she felt at peace.

"We're trained from childhood that it's all about success," she told me. "But no one tells you that when you get to success, there's a whole lot of maintenance involved—always knowing the right people, always having the right ideas, always being the smartest one, always hustling, never knowing how long it will last. When I let go of all of that, a whole new world opened up to me. It's not a precarious life, but really, the opposite—there's nothing precarious about doing what needs to get done, in doing what feels right and doing it well on my own terms. It was hard to let go of my old self, but also thrilling. When I let go of my obsession with success, I finally found real meaning in my work. And for the first time in my life, it's me—not the job—that's in control."

SHOULD ROBOTS PAY TAXES?

There is something tragic in the fact that as soon as man
invented a machine to do his work he began to starve.
— OSCAR WILDE

Route 9 skims by Boston and cuts clear across Massachusetts to
Pittsfield, a city of roughly fifty thousand, the largest in Berk-
shire County. Well east of Pittsfield, Route 9 becomes Worcester
Road, named for a city that in earlier times was the nation's largest
manufacturer of wire—barbed wire, electrical wire, telephone wire,
and the wire used in the making of undergarments by the Royal
Worcester Corset Company, once the largest employer of women
in the United States. Older Worcester residents can still recall the
factory bells pealing to signal the start and end of the workday.
Now the bells are silent, and the wire and corset factories have been
replaced with three of the nation's largest employers: Walmart, Target, and Home Depot.

If this sounds familiar, it should. It's been nearly two decades
since retail overtook manufacture as the nation's most important
job creator, employing roughly one of every nine American workers. That's more workers than in health care and construction *combined.* That's a lot of jobs. Unfortunately, by the standards set out
in the last chapter, retail jobs do not often qualify as good jobs.
At this writing the average hourly wage for a nonsupervisory retail

worker is $10.14, less than half of the national average, and less than half of retail workers receive benefits of any kind.

As a nation, we've come to a sort of uneasy peace with this trend. We know that iPads and Macs aren't made in America, and that neither are many televisions, appliances, tools, toys, or clothes. We also know that a great many of us make our living designing, marketing, advertising, transporting, and—especially—hawking those things. Retail has become the world as we know it, a world where the consumer—not the worker—is king and queen. After all, a Walmart outlet all but runs itself, especially with the recent roll-out of those adorable shelf-scanning robots. Thanks to these and other innovations, sales per employee have in recent years doubled across the retail sector.

Still, in matters of productivity, no brick-and-mortar retail store—no matter how efficient—can hold a candle to online commerce, which since 2014 has become by far the fastest-growing retail sector. China's Alibaba Group—Asia's most valuable company—is the world's largest player in this rough-and-tumble sphere. Alibaba holds such sway that in January 2017, company founder Jack Ma became the first Chinese businessman to meet publicly with Donald Trump after the US election. Nonetheless, for various reasons Alibaba has so far failed to gain a foothold in the United States. In America, Amazon reigns supreme.

Analysts predict that by 2020 one-fifth of the US $3.6 trillion retail market will have shifted online and that Amazon alone will reap two-thirds of that bounty. The company already captures one of every two dollars Americans spend online and is by far the nation's biggest seller of books, music, video games, cell phones, electronics, small appliances, toys, magazine subscriptions, and what seems like almost everything else—hence its nickname, "The Everything Store." Amazon captures gobs of market share in nearly every retail category, including its own private-label food line. And with every click, it gathers critical information—our addresses and credit histories, and also the identity of everything we've ever bought or even looked at on the Amazon site—and uses the data to build an even more intimate relationship with each of us, with the goal of cultivating still more of our business. In May 2018, Amazon had 100 million Prime members who paid $99 annually for the service and an average of nearly $1,300 for Amazon merchandise. This is in addition to the untold millions who chose not to subscribe to Prime but nonetheless shop on the site. The company produces television shows and movies, manufactures thousands of products from batteries to baby food, and owns such familiar brands as Zappos, Shopbop, IMDb, Audible, and Twitch. Amazon Handmade is poised to challenge Etsy, and Amazon Business is aiming a death blow at Staples and other independent office suppliers. Analysts generally prefer to hedge their bets, but on one thing they seem to agree: Amazon is on the glide path toward becoming the world's first trillion-dollar company.

Whether or not Amazon CEO Jeff Bezos is, as some claim, a "people person," it's clear that one of his business missions is having as few people as possible on the payroll. To be fair, the company is so efficient that it needs relatively few people, reaping roughly $400,000 in revenue for every employee, nearly twice the revenue per employee of Walmart, the nation's most efficient big-box retailer. Given this enormous success, the company is leading the way for many established retailers—from Walmart to Best Buy to Bloomingdale's—to also sell online, or to die trying. Indeed, other than gas stations, new- and used-vehicle dealers, and grocery and liquor stores, brick-and-mortar retail is slipping, while e-commerce soars.

E-commerce, it seems, represents the future. So it was perhaps unsurprising that President Barack Obama delivered his stirring July 2013 "Morning in America"–style jobs speech at a cavernous Amazon distribution center in Chattanooga, Tennessee. Like Worchester and so many small American cities, Chattanooga was once a booming factory town; its central location, easy access to roads and rails, and willing workforce made it an extremely popular manufacturing base. At its manufacturing peak in 1979, about one of every three Chattanoogans made their living making things—textiles, furniture, iron, steel, and over-the-counter drugs like Rolaids. But as the 1970s bled into the 1980s, most of that work disappeared, leaving Chattanooga to search for a new way to feed, clothe, and house its citizens. Amazon seemed like a part of the solution: a twenty-first-century company for a twenty-first-century Chattanooga.

Chattanooga had by then lured dozens of companies with tax incentives and land grants, including a half-billion-dollar package to Volkswagen that soon swelled to nearly a billion dollars. Amazon's deal was not nearly as rich—but the multimillion-dollar proposition did include a chunk of former army land, and no property tax for a decade. In exchange, the company promised jobs. And unlike the jobs at companies like Volkswagen down the road, most of the Amazon jobs were jobs that almost anyone could do. Warehouse "pickers" would spend their shifts taking orders through a pair of headphones, rolling a cart to a designated shelf, retrieving an object from a designated bin, placing that object in a basket, and rolling that basket to the next object in need of retrieval. That walk was sometimes very long because the warehouse was huge. Before delivering his speech, President Obama marveled at the more than a million square feet of it, the size of twenty-eight football fields! Beaming as he looked around the cavernous space, he christened it the "North Pole of the South" and praised the assembled workforce as "good-looking elves." A handful of naysayers objected to the president's choice of words, but their grumbles were barely audible over the applause of the thrilled assembly.

A few years earlier, Amazon had opened a similar facility in Irving, Texas, not far from Dallas–Fort Worth International Airport. Like Chattanooga, Dallas is well situated as a major distribution hub: In forty-eight hours or less, shipments from Dallas can reach over 35 percent of the US population by truck and over 99 percent by rail. And like Chattanooga, when it comes to luring jobs, Texas thinks and acts big. Irving ponied up $269 million in tax breaks and other incentives at the prospect of what Dave Clark, then Amazon's vice president for global customer fulfillment, described as "great jobs." What the good people of Irving weren't told was whether those jobs would stick around, or what sort of jobs they'd be. But Texas was on a roll, and Amazon got swept into it.

Under then governor Rick Perry, Texas offered up more incentives to lure jobs than did any other state—roughly $19 billion annually. In the 2010s, this generosity helped make Texas home to half of all newly created private sector jobs in the nation. In boasting of this very real accomplishment, the governor failed to acknowledge that Texas also rated quite high in poverty and that an inordinate number of Texans labored for less than the minimum wage. Part of the reason for this was that many Texans weren't exactly "employees" of the companies they seemed to be employed by. And in that sense, Texas was at the head of a fast-growing pack.

Starting with the economic meltdown and continuing through the recovery, the number of Americans working for contract agencies rose to sixteen million—a faster rate of growth than that of overall employment. Such statistics make clear what reported labor numbers do not: that the economic recovery brought a dramatic rise in temporary contracts (at an average duration of about three months) as well as a growth in independent contractors tied to labor platforms like Uber and Lyft. The pay for these "alternative" gigs typically averages about $17 an hour, compared with the US average of $24.57 an hour. Often they are part time, occasional, or seasonal.

In Irving, contract employees working at Amazon received about $8 an hour, minus a portion retained by the employment agency for transportation and check-cashing fees. This meant that their take-home pay sometimes dipped below minimum wage. But all this became moot when Amazon got into a tussle with the Texas comptroller over unpaid back taxes, pulled up roots, and closed its warehouse and installed a new one in a friendlier location: Chattanooga, Tennessee.

Chattanooga worked hard to woo Amazon—the city council voted unanimously for a $30 million incentives package. It also gifted the company the eighty-acre site and spent $4 million on preparing the site. In exchange, Amazon promised 1,476 full-time jobs and 2,400 seasonal positions. Those lucky enough to join the permanent staff earned $11.25 an hour, the temps whatever the employment agencies were willing to share with them. To ward off theft, employees were checked twice daily with a metal detector on their own time, which cut significantly into their hourly earnings.

President Obama seemed to suggest that Amazon had created many solid middle-class jobs in Chattanooga, but not everyone saw things that way. One commentator likened the president's Amazon warehouse speech to "announcing a fitness initiative in a grocery store's snack aisle, and nodding approvingly as unhealthy-looking Americans toss giant bags of potato chips into their carts." Amazon itself may not object to this critic's characterization. After all, Jeff Bezos regularly offers workers throughout the company money to *quit*, and makes no secret of his robot fixation. Worldwide, his company has installed over one hundred thousand robots to labor in "perfect symbiosis" with humans in its warehouses and has plans to install many thousands more. While it's not clear what constitutes a perfect symbiosis, the robots are said to save the company $22 million annually, per warehouse. The company's master plan of an autonomous future also includes goods delivered by drones and self-driving vehicles. While Bezos insists that none of these innovations will eradicate jobs, it's hard to take him seriously on that point. For while Amazon continues to open warehouses around the globe, and to staff them with what it predicts will be an additional one hundred thousand human beings, estimates are that every human on the Amazon payroll—whether full or part time—displaces two humans at traditional brick-and-mortar operations. As Tim Lindner, a veteran IT analyst, confided in a note to industry insiders, eradicating jobs is the explicit goal of any online retailer. Lindner continues, "Labor is the highest-cost factor in warehouse operations. It is no secret that Amazon is moving to highly auto-mated operations within its distribution centers, and ... it has ad-ditional technology that can further reduce the number of humans it needs to process customer orders. . . . You have heard the old pro-grammer's phrase, 'Garbage in, garbage out.' . . . [With] the dimin-ishing reading abilities of humans on the Receiving dock, finding an automated solution to eliminate the 'garbage in' problem is the Holy Grail. Amazon may have just patented it."

By *garbage*, Lindner meant human error, the alternative to which is apparently robotic precision. And yet robots are far from precise. For as we've seen, they seem to have the most difficulty complet-ing tasks that humans find simplest, like picking delicate items off a shelf. Computer scientist Gary Bradski, a Silicon Valley entre-preneur, is cofounder of Industrial Perception, a start-up acquired years ago by Google that developed computer vision systems and robotic arms for loading and unloading trucks. "For Amazon and all Internet retailers, moving things from one place to another is just about their entire cost," he told me. "Basically people in that industry are used as an extension of a forklift. Human forklift ex-tenders are pretty expensive. Robot arms cut that cost drastically."

Sawyer, an industrial robot created by Boston-based Rethink Robotics, offers an impressive illustration of how all-embracing those arms can be. Sawyer is the brainchild of Rodney Brooks, the inventor of both Roomba, the vacuum-cleaning robot, and Pack-Bot, the robot used to clear bunkers in Iraq and Afghanistan and the World Trade Center after 9/11. Unlike Roomba and PackBot, Sawyer looks almost human—it has an animated flat-screen face and wheels where its legs should be. Simply grabbing and adjust-ing its monkey-like arm and guiding it through a series of motions "teaches" Sawyer whatever repeatable procedure one needs it to get done. The robot can sense and manipulate objects almost as quickly and as fluidly as a human and demands very little in re-turn: while traditional industrial robots require costly engineers and programmers to write and debug their code, a high school dropout can learn to program Sawyer in less than five minutes. Brooks once estimated that, all told, Sawyer (and his older brother, the two-armed Baxter robot) would work for a "wage" equivalent to less than $4 an hour.

Robots loom large in discussions of work and its future, a conversation that can get mired in false assumptions. Until recently, many economists were skeptical that automation could permanently displace human workers on a large scale. People have always shifted away from work better done by machines, but the economic principle of "comparative advantage" predicts that humans will maintain an edge in fields where they are the least disadvantaged. Under this logic, technology will not displace us but set us free to do less dangerous, more challenging things, essentially the very things that make humans human.

For example, in 2016, the National Highway Traffic Safety Administration officially recognized "software" as a driver of self-driving cars, thereby putting the nation's 4.1 million paid motor-vehicle operators—drivers of taxis, trucks, buses, and Uber—on notice. But under the rubric of competitive advantage, this will not simply unemploy people but free them to fill new roles—for example, to invent new sorts of engines or design new sorts of fenders or tackle other challenges better suited to uniquely human capabilities. The problem with this argument is that in recent years most experts have come to believe it's built on a false premise—namely, that humans will have a real advantage in undertaking most tasks.

In March 2015, scores of scientists, engineers, and business leaders from around the world gathered in Cambridge, Massachusetts, for a conference aptly titled "Robo Madness." The first speaker, Democratic senator Mark Warner from Virginia, spoke movingly and with passion about the challenge of "inventing work"—work that embraced technological change while giving more people a stronger foothold in the economy. "People in my state made their living in tobacco, textiles, furniture," he told the crowd. "They need a new structure within capitalism, and a future where they are regarded as an asset, not a cost." Senator Warner wasn't sure what that future might look like, but he reminded the audience that predicting the future was not his job. He stepped down from the podium, leaving MIT computer scientist Daniela Rus, a leading roboticist, to take up the challenge.

Rus grew up in Romania and traced her fascination with robots to childhood afternoons spent with *Lost in Space* reruns, watching in awe as B-9, a robot endowed with superhuman strength and futuristic weaponry, displayed emotions and played the guitar. Robots, she said, would soon weave themselves into the fabric of everyday life and become "indistinguishable" from that fabric. As an example, she cited a robot maid "waking up" in the morning, sensing its owner's desire for coffee or orange juice, and—noting that there was none at hand—jumping into a self-driving car to the grocery store, where it would be waited on by other robots. Humans who desired to get their own coffee or juice could of course do so, Rus said, but that seemed unlikely, because robots—not other people—would man the store, allowing little opportunity for human interaction, and therefore little incentive to endure the inconvenience.

In painting this rosy future, Rus did not acknowledge the millions of Americans who made their living driving vehicles, nor those who made theirs serving coffee and orange juice. Nor did she raise the possibility that some—perhaps many—of us might enjoy picking up our own coffee or juice, and chatting with a salesperson. I knew I did, and as the meeting paused for a break, this small point weighed heavily on my mind. And for some reason, I thought it might also be on the mind of Leo Sprecher, a rather puzzled-looking man standing behind me in the coffee line. Sprecher introduced himself and told me he held several degrees in computer science, which, he said, served him well as CEO of Mrs. Budd's pies. Given that we were on break at a robotics meeting at MIT, I suppose I can be forgiven for assuming that Mrs. Budd's pies was meant ironically, perhaps as a code name for an high-tech start-up. But as it turned out, Sprecher told me, Mrs. Budd's pies is precisely what its name implies. Intrigued, I pressed for details, and Sprecher said he'd be happy to elaborate.

When we met for lunch the next week, Sprecher slowly and carefully unfurled the story of his firm's humble beginnings in a small New Hampshire poultry shop owned by Irving Budd. It was the early 1950s, and the economy was flirting with a brief recession. Chicken sales were not bad but could have been better. The question was, how to make them better? Budd had no idea, until a salesman passing through town introduced him to rotisserie chicken, a "value-added" product he promised would multiply Budd's profits several times over. Budd bit, and the rotisserie birds did sell well, but not as well as the salesman had promised. At the end of the day there were usually a few left over. Budd dutifully brought these stragglers home, where his mom—Mrs. Budd—baked them into an old family recipe. The rest is chicken pot pie history.

Mrs. Budd's built its reputation and customer base on claims like "fresh," "never frozen," "local," and "homemade." Its Facebook page and website feature testimonials from grateful eaters and happy workers in hair nets smiling proudly as they heft trays of perfect pies with golden crusts and chunky fillings, every bit as tasty as your grandma's. The avowed company mission is to craft "each pie as if they are serving their families, because they are! You, our customers are an extension of the Mrs. Budd family. You bring us home with you and create memories with your own families."

A sucker for homemade pie, I praised Sprecher for sticking to his guns. But rather than smile humbly, as I expected, he groaned. "We're automating," he said, staring deep into his coffee cup. "We have eighty-five people in manufacturing, and we plan to reduce that to twenty-five, maybe fewer. If you've ever had to deal with people on a production floor, you'd know why. Machines don't have attitudes, they don't have ups and downs, they don't have 'issues.' And automation has never been cheaper; a massive pie-making machine can pay for itself in two years, sometimes even less. With consumers demanding low price (never more than five dollars for a pie that serves four!) and stockholders pressing you for the highest return on investment, there really is no choice but to bring on the machines."

I couldn't help but sympathize. Humans are complicated, and replacing them with machines is not necessarily a bad thing. Unlike the happy folks making pies at Mrs. Budd's, many of us do not like the jobs we do. We get tired, hungry, distracted, angry, confused. We make mistakes, sometimes egregious ones. Machines lack our frailties and our biases and are better equipped to weigh evidence fairly, without prejudice or false assumptions. Perhaps most critically, machines can retain and process data far more accurately than we can, and that data is growing exponentially.

Every minute of every day Google services 3.6 million searches in the United States alone. Spammers send 100 million e-mails. Snapchatters send 527,000 photos, and the Weather Channel broadcasts 18 million forecasts. This and so much more data—properly collected, codified, and analyzed—can be applied to automate almost any high-order task. Data can also serve as a surrogate for human experience and intuition. Online shopping and social media sites "learn" our preferences and use that information to make values-based assessments to influence our decisions and, ultimately, our behavior. What might this portend for the future of work? The answer to that question is as nervous making as it is uncertain.

What we do know is that the allocation of tasks between humans and machines depends on the productivity of each—when humans do a job cheaper or faster than machines, they generally get to keep it. But there is no economic principle to support the idea that humans will frequently come out ahead. As in the case of Mrs. Budd's "homemade" pies, when humans no longer keep pace, it is they who are sent home.

Reports of machines outpacing human performance in tasks from flipping hamburgers to playing chess to performing surgery are so commonplace they have become media clichés, pulled out on a regular basis to set the scene for any number of business narratives. And by all accounts, these cases are just the start of an escalating trend. At a meeting of the American Association for the Advancement of Science focused on this issue, I asked computer scientist Moshe Vardi why so many economists—and politicians—had such difficulty coming to grips with this looming threat.

"It's because until roughly 2009 there was no real threat," he told me. "Since then, there's been a dramatic change. Computers are able to see and hear, and have face recognition capabilities that are significantly better than humans'. Machines understand the human world far better than they did just a few years ago. And we haven't discovered anything in the human brain that can't be modeled. We're at a unique point in human history. We are sitting on the cusp of an enormous change."

One striking hallmark of that change came in March 2016, when the Google artificial intelligence program AlphaGo beat South Korean world master Lee Sedol in Go, an ancient board game known for its baffling complexity. Each game of Go has 10,360 possible moves, an unimaginably large number that makes exhaustive evaluation of individual moves utterly unrealistic. This complexity makes the game far more unpredictable than chess; rather than see possibilities, players *perceive* possibilities either consciously or unconsciously by gazing at the pieces on the board. To do something similar, AlphaGo relies on what scientists call neural networks, essentially mathematical versions of the networks of nerve cells operating in biological systems. Much like the human brain, AlphaGo has an unquenchable ability to learn, and not only from "observing" games played by human experts. The program is designed to play millions of games against itself, continuously improving its performance without any human intervention. In other words, AlphaGo seems to have what in the previous chapter was deemed critical for good work in the digital age—analytic skill. That is, these machines have the ability to visualize, articulate, conceptualize, or solve problems by making decisions that are sensible given the available information. And they are getting better and better at it.

AlphaGo is just a sample of what scientists hope to accomplish with this line of research, and any number of corporations—large and small—are hot on the trail. For example, tech giant IBM boasts that "over the next five years, machine learning applications will lead to new breakthroughs that will amplify human abilities, assist us in making good choices, look out for us and help us navigate our world in powerful new ways." The company targets five arenas ripe for disruption: medicine, education, retail, online security, and what it calls "sentient cities"—apparently, cities that through technology know what residents want and need before the residents themselves do. These are of course extremely broad categories encompassing an inestimable number of jobs. And IBM is but one of hundreds of players in this effort, most of them brand-new, or nearly so. Just a few years ago, only four laboratories around the world were working to develop man-made neural networks. Today it's one of the hottest areas of research in computer science. But it may not employ many actual workers: in the spring of 2018, IBM laid off what was thought to be thousands of American employees, most of them highly educated and many of them experts in machine learning and artificial intelligence.

Bart Selman is a professor of computer science at Cornell University and an expert in knowledge representation—basically, translating the real world into terms computers can understand and act upon. He cautioned that computers do not yet have full human capabilities. For example, they lack "common sense" and an ability to grasp the deep meaning of language. But he predicts that's about to change. "The AI community believes that machines will match human intelligence within the next fifteen to twenty years," he told me. As an example, he cited the field of medicine. "Doctors do very standard things 99 percent of the time, their work is really very routine. And a lot of what's not routine can be done by machines. Machines are already better at diagnosis. Soon machines will know a lot more than doctors. Physicians are resisting this; they don't want to allow machines to take over. But in ten, maybe fifteen years, most doctors' jobs will be obviated."

While this may sound like an extreme view, Selman is certainly not the only one to express it. Though other computer scientists I spoke with generally agreed that human judgment will for some time be essential for critical decision making in medicine, they also agreed that automation will soon offer a higher quality of care, broader access, and lower costs that will likely eliminate the roles of some—perhaps many—physicians. After all, robots need not be perfect, only equal to—or a tad better than—complicated and expensive humans. And given that physician error is after heart disease and cancer the third leading cause of death in America, robots seem a sensible and perhaps preferable alternative. To err, after all, is *human*.

Hod Lipson, a professor of mechanical engineering, directs the Creative Machines Lab at Columbia University, where he and his students train machines to be reflective, curious, and, yes, creative—including in the kitchen. When we spoke, he was putting the final touches on a device that uses software to concoct beautifully composed gourmet delights from a jumble of pastes, gels, powders, and liquid ingredients. From the looks of it, this machine could compete with a three-star Michelin chef. Certainly it could construct a Mrs. Budd's pie, allowing Sprecher to pare his staff down to a couple of technicians, perhaps, or maybe none at all. When I ran this thought by Lipson, he groaned. He said scientists and engineers like himself have a reflexive urge to automate almost every difficult task. The whole point of engineering, he said, is to alleviate drudgery and increase productivity—in the past, that was almost always the right thing to do, the good thing to do. But now he's not so sure.

Nor are most experts I spoke with. For, while we all know that routine jobs are under threat (especially the sorts of jobs that once commanded high wages), as are a number of "knowledge" jobs like bookkeeping and document searching, we're often assured that "creative" jobs—jobs that require decision making and individual initiative—will for the foreseeable future remain in the human domain. But after speaking to scores of computer scientists, engineers, and economists, I realized that it's not always the least complex jobs that are most at risk. In some cases, it's the most complex.

For example, fast-food restaurant chains are not rushing to automate burger flipping even though it's long been possible to do so. The reason for this is that flipping burgers is fairly easy, and without unions to back them the people who do it are not in a position to command high wages. But the same cannot be said for people who perform heart surgery, lawyer divorce proceedings, peddle expert financial advice, or create architectural renderings and automotive designs. Automating these and other complex and costly tasks will result in a big payoff because the expense of the machines doing them will be quickly recouped by the savings in salaries. So while we may have come to believe that only certain jobs are most at risk—generally low-wage, routine jobs—this does not always comport with what scientists and technologists predict, or are seeing on the ground. In fact, when humans organize to improve labor conditions—as is happening today with the "$15 an hour" minimum-wage movement, it's become almost routine for bosses to threaten to replace them with machines. And they can.

"Automation and AI will take all our jobs away," Lipson told me. "Or pretty much all of them. If not within our lifetime, then certainly within our grandchildren's lifetime. How do we keep people engaged in a jobless future? What will we all do to derive meaning from our lives? That's the new grand challenge for any engineer, and we haven't even fully articulated the problem. This is a totally new situation in human history, and we're not in the least prepared for it. Maybe we think we are, but we're not. Yes, of course, we could be better educated, be better prepared. That would be great, but it's not the answer. Not all of us can be technologists or scientists or mathematicians, and even if we could, who would pay us to do it when machines will do it for free? Yes, a few of us will be making those machines, writing the code, and thinking the big thoughts. But let's face it, not all of us can work for Google."

4

LET THEM EAT APPS

I know that starting and growing a business takes
tremendous grit and that facing the unknown requires
determination. I also know that taking on that risk makes
our Nation and our world a better place.
—PRESIDENT DONALD J. TRUMP

Google's "connected campus" in Cambridge, Massachusetts, spreads
across two office towers tucked behind a gourmet vegetarian sandwich shop. It's surprisingly difficult to find, so difficult that visitors typically walk past it once or twice before asking passersby
just where it's located—a tacit reminder, perhaps, that Google has
no need to trumpet a brand that is among the world's most recog-
nizable. This is especially true when it comes to attracting talent.
Google, it seems, is the dream job of bright young people almost
everywhere on the planet. In surveys, one of every five American
college graduates cited Google as his or her employer of choice. A
poll of college students *the world over* drew a similar response. No
other company comes close.

Google is also, after Apple, the world's most valuable brand. The
company invests in such a broad array of endeavors that even its
employees have difficulty keeping track: a browser called Chrome, a
smartphone operating system called Android, a suite of cloud computing platforms called Google Cloud Platform, a video-sharing
platform called YouTube, and online services that include Google
Maps, Gmail, and Google Docs. Alphabet, Google's parent com-

pany, is a force in the self-driving car realm, and its investment arm, GV, has a piece of more than three hundred other companies, including Uber. All this is mind-bogglingly impressive, but incomplete, as it neglects the segment of Google business that generates the vast bulk of its revenue stream.

Roughly 90 percent of Google's revenue comes from advertising, more than three-quarters of it plastered across the company's own websites. This bounty requires the paid efforts of relatively few human beings. Neither the beauty nor the profitability of this arrangement escapes the company's legion of faithful investors.

A Googling of Google brings the expected—fanciful spaces filled with what look like toys and an array of tempting snack options. And it also brings the less expected—for example, images of marketing manager Shawn Aukland in a Google company lunchroom in London, proposing marriage to his boyfriend and fellow Googler, Michael, while being serenaded by a Google a cappella group crooning Bruno Mars's "I Think I Want to Marry You." Not all of us would relish this experience, but apparently enough of us would to make it unremarkable that so many people the world over have set their sights on scoring a Google employee ID badge. What *is* remarkable are the odds against any one of these hopefuls making the cut: with an estimated 3 million applicants in a single year, only 1 in 428 got the offer. As a point of comparison, the odds of an applicant getting into Harvard are quite a bit better: 1 in 14.

Andrew McAfee, coauthor of *The Second Machine Age* and principal research scientist at the Center for Digital Business at MIT's Sloan School of Business, joined me to mull over the implications of all this at Legal Seafoods, a popular restaurant just a few steps from Google's Cambridge campus. At the time, McAfee seemed a tad preoccupied, as though he, too, was dreaming of Google. And in a way, he was. While simultaneously checking his e-mail and ordering a crab cake sandwich, McAfee grabbed a pen and scribbled four words on a napkin—Amazon, Apple, Facebook, and yes, Google (aka Alphabet). In the summer of 2016, these "Four Horsemen" (as he called them) had a market cap of more than $1.8 trillion, roughly equivalent to the gross domestic product of India. India is home to more than 1.25 billion people. In 2016 the Four Horsemen together employed fewer than four hundred thousand Americans, including those working in Apple retail stores and Amazon warehouses. (Amazon had yet to purchase Whole Foods or to hire the one hundred thousand employees—most of them warehouse employees—it claimed it would in 2018.) "That's less than the number of net new jobs we need *every three months* to hold the employment rate steady," McAfee said. Indeed, he continued, while wildly successful at attracting both capital and the public eye, in the matter of sustainable job creation, not one of these tech dynamos stood up to legacy companies like Kroger, Home Depot, Hewlett-Packard, General Electric, IBM, and Walmart.

McAfee is an avid booster of technology, which he habitually calls "a creator of abundance." Certainly it works for him, and for that happy band of Googlers hacking and snacking in Google offices next door. And he points out that it works for all of us— Instagram, Facebook, SnapChat, YouTube, Twitter, and of course Google Search are all part of what McAfee calls "the bounty." But he acknowledges that this bounty is created through the efforts of relatively few paid employees. That's the nature of the digital age beast. "What we're looking at is an economy that is incredibly wealthy without needing work in the way that we came to think about it in the industrial age," he said.

So how has our thinking about work changed? Consider two companies: Instagram, a product of the digital age, and Eastman Kodak, a product of the late industrial age. Instagram, cofounded by Mike Krieger and Kevin Systrom, gathered a small team of young engineers and marketers in a small San Francisco space to create and market a single app through which hundreds of millions of people share billions of photographs. Kodak, founded by George Eastman, gathered as many as 145,000 employees in an expansive industrial park to build an iconic firm that in its heyday furnished 90 percent of the nation's film and 85 percent of its cameras.

Within less than two years of its founding in 2010, Instagram was sold to Facebook for $1 billion—leaving a baker's dozen of instant multimillionaires in its wake. A few months before the sale of Instagram, Kodak—a 132-year-old company that held 110,000 patents—declared bankruptcy, leaving scores of loyal employees in the lurch.

In the age of Kodak, productivity, employment, and median income rose as one. Company founder George Eastman felt an obligation to his employees, and also to the city where he and most of them lived—Rochester, New York. One of the most generous philanthropists of all time, Eastman made unprecedented donations to M.I.T. and the Tuskegee Institute, as well to various institutions in his hometown—the University of Rochester, various hospitals, dental health clinics, an orchestra hall and music school—and to his employees, in the form of many millions of dollars worth of stock. In a letter to a colleague he wrote, "I want to make Rochester for the thousands of people I have gathered here the best place on the face of the earth to live in and bring up their families."

Today, there is far less to motivate such largesse: the Internet knows no geographical boundaries, and while many successful business owners are philanthropic, the global economy demands and expects far less of employers in matters of employee or community loyalty.

In George Eastman's time, the impact of innovation on workers and citizens was fairly clear. Thanks in part to Eastman Kodak innovations, almost anyone could operate a camera, and the making, selling, and distributing of those cameras and film resulted in untold numbers of good jobs that enabled workers to purchase cameras of their own. The digital age, by contrast, brings with it what one observer called the "yawning disparity" between the "subjective experience of innovation and the objective measures of its real economic impact." That is, innovation affects us differently depending on whether we are buyers or makers. As consumers, many millions of users reap the "abundance" that McAfee described. But as workers, not so much. "Our nation is tremendous at creating abundance," he told me. "But we have only one way to tap into it—by offering up our labor. That's not working for everyone. I don't think that's a trivial problem, but it's not my job to solve it."

So, if it's not the job of our national representatives (see Senator Warner in the previous chapter) or economic thinkers to solve the problem of work in the digital age, whose job is it? Politicians and pundits on both sides of the aisle tend to put their faith in entrepreneurs. At the Global Entrepreneurial Summit at Stanford University in 2016, President Obama declared entrepreneurship "the engine of growth . . . that creates good-paying jobs; that puts rising economies on the path to prosperity, and empowers people to come together and tackle our most pressing global problems." Presidential candidate Hillary Clinton pledged to find a way to forgive student loans to graduates who start a new company or join a start-up. President Donald Trump makes no secret of his worship of entrepreneurship, a strategy that holds great appeal for millions of voters.

Indeed, America as a whole has a soft spot for risk takers willing to gamble almost everything in an effort to create new business opportunities. While in Europe schoolchildren are taught to revere poets and philosophers, in the United States schoolchildren are primed to lionize entrepreneurs like Steve Jobs, Bill Gates, and Elon Musk. The very term *business hero* has a distinctly American ring. And by *hero*, we generally mean "innovator," regardless of what that innovation foretells for our futures, both individually and as a nation. For the question remains, innovation of what and for whom?

Harvard economist Joseph Schumpeter coined the phrase *creative destruction* to describe the process by which innovation creates new technologies, businesses, and jobs at the cost of the old. The classic example of this is the aforementioned automobile—the innovation of the car brought untold numbers of new opportunities for factory workers, managers, administrators, engineers, designers, marketers, and salespeople, while killing off old opportunities for blacksmiths, harness makers, and others. The same can be said for many innovations. Schumpeter, who died in 1950, argued that innovation is the driving force of both capitalism and economic growth, as are the entrepreneurs who commercialize those innovations. In *Capitalism, Socialism, and Democracy* (1942) he wrote, "The opening up of new markets, foreign or domestic, and the organizational development from the craft shop to such concerns as U.S. Steel illustrate the same process of industrial mutation—if I may use that biological term—that incessantly revolutionizes the economic structure from within, incessantly destroying the old one, incessantly creating a new one. This process of Creative Destruction is the essential fact about capitalism."

Schumpeter's argument that new, innovative firms drove the bulk of job growth galvanized economic thinking, as did the work of David L. Birch, a business consultant and researcher at the Massachusetts Institute of Technology. In a slim, fifty-two-page report, *The Job Generation Process*, published in 1979, Birch estimated that only 15 percent of new jobs were created by established firms with five hundred or more employees and that six of ten jobs were generated by firms with twenty or fewer employees, most of these newly established firms. Later, he amended those figures to support the astonishing claim that new small businesses created fully eight of every ten new jobs.

Birch's claim that small, new companies created the lion's share of new jobs played into an ongoing David and Goliath narrative that captured the public imagination and the approbation of policy makers. The idea that scrappy, risk-taking entrepreneurs could—free of government intervention and union meddling—sustain and grow the nation through job creation held great appeal at a time when industry deregulation was widely embraced by both liberals and conservatives. Suddenly, small entrepreneurial efforts were no longer mere "Mom and Pop" anachronisms but veritable job generation machines. And such prolific job creators, politicians agreed, should be given substantial regulatory leeway and taxpayer support.

Two decades later, in 2010, the Ewing Marion Kauffman Foundation published findings that seemed to bolster this view. In a widely quoted analysis, then Kauffman economist Tim J. Kane concluded that for most years between 1977 and 2005, established firms were net job *destroyers*, costing Americans about a million jobs a year (that is, these firms fired a million more people than they hired). Start-ups, by his reckoning, created an average of three million jobs annually. Kane's thundering conclusion: "Start-ups aren't everything when it comes to job growth. They're the *only* thing." While many analysts were left rubbing their head in puzzlement—how could it be that only start-ups create jobs?—it's nearly impossible to overstate the influence of Kane's report. The Kauffman Foundation was called upon to help craft the bipartisan Startup Acts 2.0 and 3.0, legislation aimed at (among other things) exempting individual start-up investors from capital gains tax and reducing other regulatory burdens, as well as making it easier for foreign entrepreneurs to acquire US visas. The foundation was also behind the 2012 Jumpstart Our Business Startups (JOBS) Act aimed at reducing regulations on new businesses. And the passage of the tax cuts put into place by the Trump administration relied heavily on the central claim that reducing taxes on corporations and wealthy individuals would spark entrepreneurship that would generate jobs.

The problem with all this is that the link between entrepreneurship and job growth is far more tenuous than policy makers claim. The puzzle to be solved is this: Are start-ups really creating permanent jobs, or do we simply believe they do and cherry-pick our facts to prove it? Before tackling that vital and enormously complicated question, it's helpful to acknowledge that the terms *start-up* and *entrepreneur* mean different things to different people.

Hearing the word *start-up* we may think of companies like

McAfee's Four Horsemen—dazzlingly innovative firms with sky-high market caps. But actually a start-up is defined as any newly registered firm with at least one employee, and that one employee is often the founder. Broadly defined, entrepreneurs are anyone who creates a new business—whether a hot dog vendor or a maker of a groundbreaking medical device. Economists, though, break things down a bit—making a distinction between "replicative" entrepreneurs and "innovative" entrepreneurs. Replicative entrepreneurs (for example, the hot dog vendor) reproduce an existing business model, while innovative entrepreneurs (like the medical device maker) create something new.

For the purposes of his survey Kane counted as a "job creator" *any* new business that created at least one job—including that hot dog vendor who—like most entrepreneurs—"created" a job only for himself. Moreover, in this study a company that went bust and let all its employees go—as do most new businesses within five years—also counted as a "job creator" because it had, after all, created at least one job. The most important measure is *net* job creation—that is, jobs created minus jobs lost. And once that calculation was made, it was fairly clear that entrepreneurs actually created relatively few lasting jobs in the United States or, for that matter, around the world.

Entrepreneurship, then, does not necessarily lead to job creation or economic growth. Indeed, a nation's level of entrepreneurship tends to be *negatively* correlated with its competitiveness. In Uganda, the world's most entrepreneurial nation, more than 28 percent of workers are entrepreneurs. The world's second most entrepreneurial nation is Thailand, followed by Brazil, Cameroon, Vietnam, Angola, Jamaica, and Botswana. Few of us would mistake these nations as powerhouses of innovation or prosperity: in 2016, Uganda had a per capita income of less than $700. Nor would we mistake most American small business owners—of nail salons, barber shops, cafés, cleaning and landscaping services, and the like—as what Schumpeter called "engines of progress." These replicative small businesses may well be entrepreneurial, but they create few jobs and fewer living-wage jobs. Indeed, the vast majority of new small business owners have no intention of building a company in which to employ others, but rather are setting themselves up for self-employment.

Nor are start-ups more innovative or productive than legacy companies. On the contrary, a firm's innovation and productivity tend to increase with age. What this means is that long-established, "stogey" firms are more likely to innovate in a productive manner than are new, agile start-ups, the life span of which generally ends at five years or less.

The truth is that even David Birch came to question the power of small new companies to create jobs. In 1994, he penned an essay in collaboration with one of his most vocal critics, Harvard economist James Medoff, in which they concocted a sort of taxonomy of American companies: elephants, mice, and gazelles. Elephants are large, lumbering companies that employ plenty of people but do not generate many *new* jobs (think Walmart). Mice are small, twitchy businesses that ultimately generate little value and few jobs (think that hot dog stand). Gazelles are nimble, rapidly expanding firms that—though far less stable than elephants—create real value and real jobs. Gazelles can be found in almost every sector, and not necessarily those we associate with innovation: in the 1990s a disproportionate number were technology firms, but in the early 2000s many were in housing-related services. Birch and Medoff concluded that high-impact gazelles made up less than 4 percent of US companies and created 70 percent of the new jobs. On average, gazelles are twenty-five years old—that is, elders by Silicon Valley standards.

Paul Nightingale, a former industrial chemist and professor of strategy at the Science Policy Research Unit at the University of Sussex, told me that entrepreneurship per se has never been a powerful engine of economic growth. Jobs generated by start-ups are typically less productive and lower paying than jobs at established firms, he said, and far less stable. "Entrepreneurial firms actually tend to be less innovative than established firms," he said. "Most entrepreneurial activity just generates churn, workers shifting from one job to another, not the creation of new jobs." Nightingale added that the extraordinary success of a handful of firms, especially new technology and social media companies like Google, Facebook, Amazon, and Twitter, has blinded us to the reality that roughly nine out of ten new companies fail quickly and completely, dragging their workforce (if any) down with them.

As Scott Shane, a professor of entrepreneurial studies at Case Western Reserve, once observed, it takes forty-three entrepreneurs starting new companies to create nine jobs that last even a decade. He added that this woesome record is not exactly "the spectacular yield you might think we'd get if you read the press reports about the job creation of start-ups."

Our constant search for novelty—whether a new app, a new diet aid, or a new video game—sometimes causes us to underrate innovation of the sort that can create real value and lead to lasting, well-paying jobs. But innovation of the sort that leads to real improvement in our lives doesn't come easy or, for that matter, cheap. The private sector once played a much greater role in basic research, especially as co-investors with the public in big, risky, high-payoff ventures such as those once conducted at research divisions of major corporations like Xerox PARC, IBM Research, DuPont Labs, Bell Labs, and Microsoft Research Silicon Valley Lab. But in recent decades, these and similar institutions have been sold off, closed down, or cut back. In many cases, rather than invest in these long-term projects, business efforts have been redirected to meet the immediate demands of investors. And something similar is happening in the public sphere. The American Association for the Advancement of Science reported that as a share of the total federal budget, research and development fell from 11.7 percent in 1965 to a low of roughly 3.4 percent in 2016. But even that was deemed far too high by the Trump administration, whose 2018 budget stipulates further cuts of up to 22 percent in key research agencies.

New companies can and do thrive and grow—Instagram, Facebook, and yes, Google are all-powerful examples. Entrepreneurship and technological innovation do contribute to what economists call the "bounty." But increasingly that bounty is not being shared in the form of good jobs. The truth is that start-ups employ less than 3 percent of US workers—not much of a platform upon which to build a strong economy. And clinging to the idea that the future of work hinges on our incentivizing entrepreneurship risks urging on what economists call "unproductive entrepreneurs" who create little value and few if any new jobs.

Our capacity to create ever more efficient machines that shrink the market demand for human labor seems almost limitless, and yet pales when compared to the capacity of digital technology to diminish the market demand for human *thought*. We're at a turning point, a critical juncture at which past experience is not a reliable guide to the future. We have a pressing obligation to reconsider the prospects and purpose of work and to lay out a plan based not on laissez-faire nostrums but on evidence. The first step is to sort out the elements of work that we need to preserve, elements that expand the narrow confines of what it means to have a "job" to something more fundamental. That is, to sort out and fiercely protect those critical elements of work that are essential not only to our economy and our democracy but to our very humanity.

Part II

Choices

Only if a man works can he live, but only if the work he
does seems productive and meaningful can he bear the life
that his work makes possible.

—LANGDON GILKEY

THE PASSION PARADOX

In every vocation, the meaning of the work is less
in the thing done than in the growth of the
man through the doing.
—EDWARD HOWARD GRIGGS

Michael Pratt has the sturdy look of a varsity athlete who in middle age still makes the time to keep up with his game. Charming and charismatic, he holds an endowed chair at Boston College's Carroll School of Management, and as a consultant he could pad his wallet enlightening executives in ways to more thickly pad theirs. But it's not wallets or what's in them that holds Pratt's interest. Rather, he spends his time pondering matters mostly beyond price—among them, the ways each of us makes meaning of our work.

Pratt doesn't claim to have all the answers, nor, to his knowledge, does anyone else. Glib generalizations are suspect, he said, as the very term *meaning* is relative and individual. Work is not a product, not something you can hold in your hand. It's a "life domain," he told me, and a deeply personal one. Still, he's convinced that the quest for meaning through work is among life's most powerful drivers, and also the most misunderstood.

"When theorists—economists, social scientists, and their popularizers—talk about work, they don't talk about the work that people actually do," he told me. "And most of the time, they don't talk to the people doing the work. They make assumptions about what's important and what's not. And often, they get it wrong."

When trying to tease out the elements of work that matter to people—nurses, Amway distributors, firefighters—Pratt spends time listening to them, a lot of time. He tends to focus on the concrete—what it is precisely that people expect and hope of their work. Often, he's found, what they hope for is not what is generally assumed. For one thing, not everyone seeks to find their passion.

As an example of this he cites his own grandfather, a glazier. The man wasn't especially drawn to installing and repairing windows; it wasn't something he dreamed about or even talked a lot about. It wasn't his passion. And yet Pratt said his grandfather believed that the quality of his work reflected back on himself and on his family, and for this and other reasons he took great pains to do it well. Focusing on the task and seeing it through to a successful completion, it seems, brought him a level of satisfaction that was difficult to duplicate in other arenas of his life—whether intellectual, interpersonal, or spiritual. The job brought him what he needed.

Pratt's grandfather was raised in an age when few Americans had the luxury to consider the meaning of their work, or even knew what that might entail. Back then, as it is today, only a privileged few could earn an adequate living giving free expression to their capabilities; and back then, unlike today, not many expected to—not even craftspeople like Pratt's grandfather. On the contrary, plying a craft often entailed taming one's creative inclinations to suit the demands of the marketplace. Yet many craftsmen found those constraints in some sense freeing. Did Pratt's grandfather make *meaning* of his work? He never said, but Pratt believes he did. "When I asked my grandfather, 'What did you do today?' he could tell me precisely," Pratt told me. "And he took great satisfaction and pride in that." But for many of us, that satisfaction is elusive. "If we're not producing something tangible, and especially if we don't know the standards for good work versus bad work, it becomes quite difficult to derive meaning from it."

Karl Marx once envisioned a utopia in which citizens "carried out production as human beings . . . our [work] products would be so many mirrors in which we saw reflected our essential nature." Marx and other social critics blamed industrialization for obscuring and distorting that reflection, by distancing workers from their labor. He wrote: "Like every other instrument for increasing the productivity of labour, machinery is intended to cheapen commodities and, by shortening the part of the working day in which the worker works for himself, to lengthen the other part, the part he gives to the capitalist for nothing. The machine is a means for producing surplus-value."

Certainly, this was a legitimate and serious concern. As one late-nineteenth-century observer wrote, "We can understand the fierce opposition of the hand loom weavers, for the loom was the breadwinner in the family of the textile trades . . . [just as] in later days, the tailor objected to the sewing machines used in the branch of his trade." Before automation, craft workers were responsible for both the conceptual and the manual labor required to produce a commodity and generally exerted substantial control over the labor process. Machines diminished that control.

Still, as the story of Marienthal implies, machines also brought compensations. Agriculture and craft production were often unreliable enterprises, the success of which rested largely on the effort of individuals. By contrast, millions of people found fulfillment in factories that brought stability, focus, and community to their lives. Like the textile mill of Marienthal, the paper mills of Maine, the furniture factories of North Carolina, and the automotive factories of the Midwest all brought prosperity and unity of purpose. Factories pull together people of various backgrounds and proclivities, affording them the opportunity to form a community that can transcend the one they grew up in. Factories can also bring employees a sense of place, and of contributing to something tangibly larger than anything they could tackle on their own. Unions, of course, amplified these feelings of solidarity—uniting workers in common cause, and sometimes lifting them, almost as one, into the middle class. But unions were not always for the good, or always needed. For many workers, factories can be a kind of second home, and fellow workers a second family.

Centralized workplaces that offer such a home—whether factories or offices—are still with us, of course, but in declining numbers. Increasingly "noncore" work functions—whether IT or transportation, food delivery or janitorial services—are outsourced to contracters and freelancers, or in some cases sent off to be done in places where labor is cheaper. So we find ourselves faced with the challenge of making meaning of work in which the workplace itself plays a far less central role. In a sense, we are circling back to the time of the independent tradesman, farmer, and craftsman, and toward an economy in which our working identity relies less on any particular institution and more on our relationship to the work itself.

To be sure, relying on institutions to make meaning for us has never been a good bet. In the late 1970s, Hungarian-born psychologist Mihaly Csikszentmihalyi noted that while 80 percent of adults claimed they would prefer to work even if they didn't need the money, the vast majority also said they could hardly wait to leave their jobs every night. From this he concluded that while humans very much desired work, many did not desire their jobs. So he set out to uncover what it was about work that held appeal, and what it was about jobs that did not. To that end, he studied people at work, and one thing in particular surprised him: that some of the happiest and most satisfied workers feel no real connection to the end product of their labors.

This may seem to contradict Michael Pratt's story of his grandfather, who found meaning through the creation of things tangible. But looking closely, it was not the window his grandfather made that brought him meaning, it was the process of making that window. Early in his career Csikszentmihalyi found something similar. He observed a group of visual artists, with the goal of figuring out what motivated them. He noted that these artists pursued their work with great intensity, so much so that they sometimes forgot to eat or sleep. That was hardly surprising. But what was surprising was that while the artists clearly relished their work, they seemed to care very little about its fruits. For rather than proudly display their completed paintings, they stacked them in piles like so much cordwood, then went back to work on the next piece. What made this behavior so intriguing was that it seemed to contradict a widely held paradigm of behavioral psychology: that people are motivated to work largely by the expectation of a reward—like food, sex, money, or praise. The artists readily agreed that their paintings were not likely to be purchased or even acknowledged by the general public, so it wasn't money or praise that kept them going. (Certainly, it wasn't sex—they got plenty of that for free.) For them, it was the process of creation—not the resulting objects—that made meaning.

Over the years, Csikszentmihalyi and his colleagues turned their attention to other categories of workers: farmers, surgeons, computer programmers, teachers, and skilled craftsmen who, like the artists, claimed to love their work above most other things and approached it with great intensity and focus. What all these people had in common, Csikszentmihalyi concluded, was the ability to engage in what he called "flow." Csikszentmihalyi characterized flow as a state of mindfulness in which people are absorbed in an activity for its own sake, so much so that self-consciousness vanishes and their sense of time slips away. And it's not only lofty professionals like artists and surgeons who find flow in their work, but also blue-collar workers. As an example, Csikszentmihalyi sometimes cites the case of "Joe the Welder," a barely literate man in his early sixties who worked for a railroad car assembly plant in South Chicago.

————

Joe the Welder spent the bulk of most weekdays holed up in one of three cavernous, hangar-like structures, welding enormous steel plates to the wheel bases of freight cars. The hangars were hot in the summer, frigid in the winter, and cacophonous year-round. Not surprisingly, Joe's fellow welders despaired of the tedium and discomfort. But not Joe, who attacked his job with good humor and mastery. Joe's secret, as Csikszentmihalyi tells it, was finding flow on the job and, through work, in his life. Joe and his wife owned a small bungalow where he carved out terraces and planted gardens watered by a sprinkler system of his own design. He ringed the garden with floodlights tuned to the sun's spectrum, and at night watched as the light bounced off the sprinkler and misted into rainbows.

Csikszentmihalyi described Joe as "autotelic," in that he could create flow experiences in environments other folks would find ghastly. It is a rare gift. While Joe made rainbows in his garden, as Csikszentmihalyi decribed it, his colleagues "squandered" their leisure at "saloons" or at home guzzling beer in front of the TV, ignoring the demands of their wives. "The rest of the welders we interviewed regarded their jobs as burdens to be escaped as promptly as possible," Csikszentmihalyi wrote.

Csikszentmihalyi seems to imply that the parable of Joe the Welder is a tale not only of work but of moral rectitude. By finding ways to enjoy a job others found noisome, Joe is portrayed as a superior being who lived in harmony not only with his colleagues and superiors but with nature and his wife. His story became a favorite of ministers and management consultants, an allegory of a working life well lived. But what does Joe's experience really teach us about the role of work in our own lives? Is flow a prerequisite to happiness on the job, and if so, should we strive to find it?

Csikszentmihalyi seems to think so, as do his many followers. In his books and speeches he urges the cultivation of three key prerequisites of flow: maintaining a clear sense of purpose and progress, focusing psychic energy on the project, and maintaining a balance of challenge and skills—the task should be challenging but not daunting. Joe is lionized for achieving all three of these conditions. But Joe was extraordinary in that he seemed inclined by his very nature to find the silver lining in the darkest clouds, silver linings that by chance aligned with the goals of his employer. While enthusiasts might congratulate Joe for finding flow, and while consultants might advise employers to seek out more employees like Joe, the less charitable among us might discount Joe as a foolish sap willing to deal with whatever indignity management threw his way—be it a freezing hangar or a burning-hot one.

Flow seems to me a fancy word for an everyday concept—the phrases "in the groove" or "in the zone" perhaps work just as well. Many of us have experienced these states through sports, hobbies, and leisure pursuits like dancing, making music, gardening, cooking, or playing chess or video games. But while we might find flow in these and any number of other activities, those activities don't necessarily correlate with the objectives of our employer. Indeed, playing video games is one of the surest ways to get into the flow state, as video games provide every requirement—they provoke focus, a sense of progress, and an increasing, but manageable, level of challenge, something that cannot be said of a good many jobs. And yet it's unlikely that advocates of flow would encourage employers to turn tasks into a video game.

As Csikszentmihalyi later discovered, few of us are able to attain a flow state when we are being monitored, timed, and judged by others. And unlike Joe, who took pride in every carefully executed weld, not all of us are given the opportunity to "focus" very long on any particular task. For example, while a chef at a pricey restaurant might feel a sense of flow in the creation and execution of an exquisite dish, a fast-food employee whose job it is to stock the fryer with frozen potatoes and hot oil, serve customers, man the cash register, and swab the floor might find it difficult, if not unnerving, to suddenly find himself in a state of "flow." While a clerk in a high-end boutique might feel confident in his or her knowledge of fabrics and cut, and might attain a sense of flow in sharing that expertise with customers, a clerk in a discount store might have trouble finding flow in the constant interruptions of answering the phone, ringing up purchases, folding clothing, and stacking shelves. And while an author working in solitude might find flow in the execution of her latest novel, a copywriter juggling multiple projects, deadlines, and meetings while fielding a deluge of texts and e-mails might consider finding flow as elusive as finding a vacant seat on the subway home.

The idea of flow could well have sprung from the writings of Friedrich Nietzsche, the philosopher who stressed the importance of maintaining an upbeat and productive attitude, writing: "Not merely bear what is necessary, but love it." But in this, Nietzsche was not implying that we learn to love our job. On the contrary, he writes:

> In the glorification of "work," in the unwearied talk of the "blessing of work," I see the same covert idea as in the praise of useful impersonal actions: that of fear of everything individual. Fundamentally, one now feels at the sight of work—one always means by work that hard industriousness from early till late—that such work is the best policeman, that it keeps everyone in bounds and can mightily hinder the development of reason, covetousness, desire for independence. For it uses up an extraordinary amount of nervous energy, which is thus denied to reflection, brooding, dreaming, worrying, loving, hating; it sets a small goal always in sight and guarantees easy and regular satisfactions. Thus a society in which there is continual hard work will have more security: and security is now worshipped as the supreme divinity.

As Nietzsche implied and Csikszentmihalyi acknowledged, most of us are dissatisfied with our jobs, a matter made all the more complicated—and guilt provoking—by the modern expectation that we feel *passionate* about them. A search of Google Books' Ngram Viewer finds that the term *follow your passion* appeared nearly 450 times more frequently in 2008 than it did in 1980, when it was barely used at all. Think back to that scene in *Girls* where the heroine—a college graduate—gets turned down for a job frosting cupcakes because, well, she doesn't express enough passion for frosting cupcakes. The skit is so funny because it rings so true. "Do what you love and you'll never work another day in your life" is a sentiment we've all heard countless times. See, for example, Steve Jobs's iconic commencement address at Stanford University:

> You've got to find what you love. And that is as true for your work as it is for your lovers. Your work is going to fill a large part of your life, and the only way to be truly satisfied is to do what you believe is great work. And the only way to do great work is to love what you do. If you haven't found it yet, keep looking. Don't settle. As with all matters of the heart, you'll know when you find it. And, like any great relationship, it just gets better and better as the years roll on. So keep looking until you find it. Don't settle.

"Don't settle." Okay, we know what this meant for Steve Jobs. But what does it really mean for the rest of us? That each and every one of us should throw off convention (and the advice of others) to become a self-made visionary of our own heroic futures? Yes, this is an enduring American fantasy, but a fantasy nonetheless. Most of us cannot begin to achieve this goal, which, if you think about it, is rather arbitrary. After all, what does this advice to "not settle" even mean? What does it portend for those of us whose passions—no matter how well executed—do not command a paycheck? After all, Jobs's first passion was Zen Buddhism, but he didn't make a career of it. Does that mean he "settled" for a life in IT? Is Jobs really advising us to pursue our passions in the face of insolvency? Or should we discipline ourselves to be—or pretend to be—passionate about a paying job that holds no relation to our true passions?

The admonishment to "follow your passion" seems at once comforting and daring, as though we can succeed in the conventional sense while at the same time throwing convention to the winds. While on its face extremely appealing, such advice relies on the slippery assumption that each of us is endowed with a passion that can—with hard work, discipline, and determination—be channeled into a remunerative career. But this happy coincidence is far less common than some of us would like to believe. "There are many things motivating work, and many ways to find meaning in it," Pratt told me. "But it's a dangerous business to advise young people to 'follow their passion.' Most of us never find one, at least not one that pays the bills."

If Pratt himself has a passion, it is directed less at his job than at people like his grandfather: nurses, police officers, librarians, and others whose quiet labors do not seem to align with the modern quest for a passionate workforce. Recently, his attentions have landed most firmly on firefighters. He told me that despite what we might have seen on TV and in the movies, the job of firefighter is not all that perilous: fishermen, loggers, garbage collectors, roofers, coal miners, machine operators, cabdrivers, and farmers are statistically more likely to die in the line of duty. It's not that fires aren't dangerous—of course they are. It's that most firefighters don't spend a lot of time fighting them. Mostly they attend to other things: balky elevators, frozen pipes, gas leaks, fender benders, chirping smoke alarms, and frantic calls from elderly citizens mistaking the ache in their lonely hearts for a heart attack.

So, I wondered, how do firefighters make meaning of any of this? In popular accounts and self-help books, meaningful work is typically linked to three factors: autonomy, complexity, and a clear relationship between the work and a reward. But firefighters spend most of their time on the job performing routine tasks for which the link to reward is—at best—frustratingly obscure. (Some might argue that scrubbing the firehouse floor is a reward in itself, but probably the firefighters themselves would not.) As for complexity? A relative term, of course, but Pratt has found that firefighters prefer simplicity, predictability, and clarity—they'd rather deal with a routine call than tangle with something they've never experienced before. In a sense, they prefer not to be challenged by novelty, which in their line of work can spell danger. Autonomy, too, is subjective, though generally it means freedom from external controls. Like many of us, firefighters resent being micromanaged, and they take pride in making their own decisions on the ground. But at the same time, their profession requires them to work together, to adhere carefully to rules and procedures, and to insist that others adhere to them as well. While there is certainly room for independent judgment on the job, true autonomy in the firehouse would slow down and confuse the process, endangering both the firefighters and those they are pledged to protect.

So if not through autonomy, complexity, or reward, what do firefighters seek to make meaning from their work? Following Pratt's advice, I put that question to an actual firefighter: Patrick Sullivan III, deputy fire chief in his hometown of Somerville, Massachusetts, the most densely populated city in New England. Portly and mustachioed, his mild blue eyes framed in wire-rim glasses, Sullivan exhibits none of the bravado some of us associate with his vocation. For Sullivan, a father of three, fighting fires is simply the family business. "My father served thirty-eight years in the Somerville unit, and my uncles were lifers, too," he told me. "Firefighting was all I wanted to do, nothing else entered my mind."

As a kid, Sullivan hung around the firehouse most afternoons; on lucky days he got hoisted into the fire engine cab, which offered a terrific view. So Sullivan kindly insisted that I, too, take the view, a claustrophobic experience that to me felt nothing like lucky. Sullivan clambered into the cab behind me to explain the purpose of every gadget in the cockpit, then led the way out and up to the firehouse kitchen, where four burly firefighters in crewcuts and rubber gloves were yanking yellow skin off chilled chicken parts to make chicken pot pies—no Mrs. Budd's for them! I was admiring their culinary determination when suddenly a landline blared with an urgent plea—an elderly woman was on the line, frantic that her grandson was choking to death. The firefighters stripped off their gloves and sprang into action—decending to the waiting fire engine by way of an actual pole. In less than two minutes (they were timed) they arrived at the woman's door to find precisely what they had expected to find: Grandma was slightly embarassed, but the boy was fine.

I wondered how chicken skinning and false alarms added up to meaningful work. So I asked Sullivan. He excused himself to make a fresh pot of coffee before leaning into his thoughts. Like most firefighters, he said, he recalls his first deadly fire with painful acuity. He was a new father at the time, exhausted from too many sleepless nights. Still, he couldn't help feeling a thrill when he got the call at 2 a.m. But when he walked into that roaring conflagration, any expectations he had about the job vaporized. Squinting through the smoke he could just make out the vague outline of what looked like a human figure slumped in a chair, engulfed in flames. He froze for a split second, then rushed in to resuscitate. But as he got closer, he realized it was too late, the man was gone. And that, he said, changed him. "Cops, they're always taking things away—booze from teenagers, children from abusers, a license from a DWI," he said. "Mostly, we firefighters give things back—a home, a life. We're supposed to *help* people. And this time, we couldn't. We couldn't do a damn thing for the guy."

Sullivan said that horrifying night set him back, at least for a while. But then came another incident—not a fire, a car crash. Some wise guy had wrapped his Corvette around a telephone pole, and Sullivan and his team worked for hours to pry him out in one piece. Things were looking bad; the man's left leg was stuck in the wreckage and wouldn't budge. The medics insisted they needed to amputate immediately and asked Sullivan and his team to step aside. Sullivan said sure, all right, just give us one more minute. "Five months later, the guy comes in to thank us. He's walking with a cane, but he's got the leg. So that's something, right?" Sullivan takes no personal credit for any of this, no "craftsman's pride" in a job well done. He has never heard the expression "flow," and when I explained it to him he shook his head. It's not the act of work that matters to him so much as the actors doing the work. "We experience things like that *together*," he said. "And that's what keeps us going. Who else could you talk to about something like that? Who else but these guys would understand? In the twenty-eight years I've been at this station, I can count on one hand the number of people who have left this job. We do not come and go. We're family."

Firefighters don't necessarily make meaning from their work the way we're told we do—from autonomy, complexity, and actions linked to clear rewards. Rather, they seem to make meaning through connectedness, the "band of brothers" kinship that also makes meaning for police officers and soldiers, and many of the rest of us. As *New York Times* culture critic Charles McGrath once wrote, the appeal of television "work dramas" is "that for a lot of us work is where we live more of the time; that, like it or not, our job relationships are often as intimate as our family relationships." And for many of us, it is those relationships—not necessarily the job itself—that gets us out of bed in the morning.

People driven by a need to connect to others through their work, Pratt told me, tend to fall into one of two categories: the *called* and the *city workers*. The *called* are motivated by a sense of duty or destiny, or both. They are there for themselves but also for their mates—they need to be needed. *City workers*, by contrast, are attracted to the job for its predictability. They show up every day knowing what to expect—the same old reliable group of colleagues, the same steady paycheck. City workers yearn not for novelty or challenge but for stability. Hearing this, I made the assumption that the called are generally better at their job. But Sullivan set me straight.

"The [firefighters] who are in it for the steady paycheck, they often do fine," he said. "They do their job." But apparently the same cannot always be said of the called, especially of a subgroup of firefighters Pratt dubbed "the sparks." Sparks stay glued to their scanners even when they are off duty and tend to appear unbidden at fires when they're not on call. This exercise in unpaid overtime may seem like a good thing, but sometimes it's not. You probably know one or two of these overeager Type A characters; they can get in the way, screw up the works. Sullivan said he's seen his share of them, and has a particularly bad memory of one on his team a few years back. "He was an arsonist," he told me, flatly. "He did it for the excitement, you know, he wanted to be a hero. When you think about it, passion on the job isn't always such a good thing."

The dictionary defines *passion* as a strong and barely controllable emotion, not something we necessarily want to see played out on the job. A "passionate" social worker may overidentify with a client to that client's detriment, a "passionate" engineer may sabotage a colleague in a misguided effort to pull ahead, a "passionate" cop may mistake a water pistol for a gun. While few would deny that many jobs require commitment, passion is perhaps better reserved for matters of the heart.

So from where stems the idea that passion—that most ineffable of qualities—is necessary for a meaningful working life? That's hard to say, but some trace it to the work of psychologist Abraham Maslow. Maslow was born and raised poor in Brooklyn, the oldest of seven children in a very unhappy family; he loathed his abusive parents and as a young man he loathed himself. But in graduate school, he came to believe that there were indeed good people in the world, and that Freudian theory placed too much emphasis on psychopathologies and not enough on human strengths. Rather than focus on illnesses, he chose to focus his research on happiness and self-fulfillment—essentially, on how people like himself managed not only to survive a rocky start but to thrive.

Maslow is best remembered for popularizing the "hierarchy of needs," a theoretical pyramid on which he believed people built their lives. At the base of the pyramid are the basics—food, shelter, sleep, sex. Maslow argued sensibly that these fundamentals must be met before people can move up the hierarchy toward fulfilling increasingly complex needs: for emotional and financial security; for love, belonging, and friendship; and for self-esteem. Once all these needs are met, people might strive toward the pinnacle—self-actualization—a lofty perch from which they could express their creativity, spontaneity, morality, and problem-solving ability. The self-actualized were upbeat, open-minded, optimistic, independent thinkers, the very qualities many managers today claim to desire in an employee. Unfortunately, Maslow believed, very few human beings—perhaps one out of a hundred—are in a position to self-actualize, and most of us are doomed to live our lives on a far more mundane plane.

Maslow's theories took hold in the post–World War II era, a time when pundits publicly bemoaned the sad fate of the working stiff, who was typically characterized as lumpish and exploited. "Overspecialization, petty rules, humiliation, and fatigue are manifestations of the poor quality of working life for the average rank and file worker," wrote one scholar of the period. A popular textbook noted the "considerable revulsion by young workers to working in mass production, highly rationalized jobs . . . even at premium pay." Certainly, Maslow would agree. He argued that managers have a responsibility to help workers see beyond their basic needs, and to aspire toward self-actualization. This represented a shift away from thinking about the employee-employer relationship as one that was largely transactional, in which workers expected little more than their pay from employers, to one that was "relational," in which employers promised employees opportunities for personal fulfillment.

And yet, while all this made solid intuitive sense, Maslow offered very little empirical evidence to support either his needs hierarchy or the theory that employers were in a position to shape employee aspirations. And the truth is that self-actualization or no, worker satisfaction in his heyday was relatively high, and substantially higher than it is today. Surveys show that in the 1950s and 1960s and into the 1970s—when many Americans labored in factories, and when fewer employers offered "meaningful" jobs—as many as 92 percent of US workers reported being satisfied with their jobs. And not all respondents were satisfied for the same reasons. White-collar workers—a small minority at the time—rated challenging work as the most important factor in job satisfaction. Blue-collar workers—who were most workers at the time—prioritized financial reward. Blue-collar workers also assigned greater importance than did white-collar workers to relationships with coworkers, duration of work hours, fringe benefits, and job security. Basically, blue-collar workers were far less concerned with being challenged than they were with job security, working conditions, and relationships. Of course, this was a time when union membership was at its peak, when real wages and benefits were on the rise, and when federal and state regulations were enacted to support and protect workers. For example, 1962 saw the passage of both the Manpower Development and Training Act, the nation's first major job-training scheme, and the Public Welfare Amendment to the Social Security Act, providing support for job training and placement. Eight years later, in 1970, President Richard Nixon signed into law the Williams-Steiger Occupational Safety and Health Act, giving the federal government the authority to set and enforce safety and health standards for most of the nation's workers. Though not all workers benefited from these policies, and many full-time workers still earned a poverty wage, conditions had improved for millions of American workers. And while many if not most workers might not have felt "self-actualized," or even challenged by their jobs, they did feel a sense of security and belonging that made them claim to be satisfied with their working lives.

In the 1980s, job satisfaction in the United States began the steady decline from which it has yet to recover. Since the turn of the century through this writing, fewer than half of all Americans claim to be satisfied with their jobs—giving low marks to such factors as compensation and benefit levels, opportunity for advancement, treatment by supervisors, training opportunities, and job security, among other things. The vast majority—hovering at 70 percent—also confess that they are not engaged with their jobs, by which they mean that they are not particularly interested in doing them. Naturally, this does not bode well for innovation, for people who are disengaged from their work are unlikely to want to go beyond the minimum that's demanded of them.

Several years ago, in an effort to put a human face on this rather concerning turn of events, I invited readers of the online edition of the *Atlantic* magazine to share their personal experience of work. I was astonished by the scope and depth of the responses, especially from people in their twenties. The comments varied greatly in tone and focus, but almost all of them conveyed a similar sense of stark disappointment. They also made clear that people can be satisfied with the actual terms of their job while at the same time being disengaged from it.

A twenty-four-year-old certified public accountant wrote: "I'm employed by a large public accounting firm and by many accounts, I'm quite successful. I'm thankful. . . . I'm seriously debating, however, giving most of that up because my job contributes zero meaning to my life. Sure, I've learned how to do my job well and I've built up some skill sets that can take me further down this particular career path; but the question I find myself asking—day in and day out—is why I continue to wake up every morning and go to a job that I actually dislike. I'm not who I thought I would be; my job doesn't contribute to my sense of self."

A twenty-six-year-old analyst explained that he "grew up in the age of the big boom, with economic and cultural idealism" stoked by "parents, teachers and mentors telling us we could achieve anything we set our minds to and reasonably find a career that satisfied us personally and paid the bills. I can't think of how many times I was told to find something that me happy, because if I was passionate about it then I would make money, and even if I didn't make money, I'd still be happy at the end of the day." But things hadn't worked out as predicted; his job—though challenging—offered him little more than a decent paycheck. He concluded: "I'm struck by the profound lack of meaning and fulfillment I get from my 8–5."

Such concerns are easy to dismiss: Should it really alarm us that these twenty-somethings feel alienated from their "8–5"? This question was illuminated in depth by another respondent, a newly minted college graduate.

> I strongly believe my generation has been trained to value only time spent in activities that are investments in the future. The pursuit of personal interests is not valued as an investment, and so we seek to make work our personal interest. We try to make work fit the mold of a passion, or our passions fit the mold of work. The result is a feeling of immense failure when we are unable to land the jobs we want. The search for identity is terribly flawed because it forces the individual to surrender a part of himself in order to find himself. A character is defined by desire; that is, his own desire. Landing a job requires the alignment of desires, that of the seeker and that of the employer. If work is to give purpose to an individual, he must depend on another for his purpose. His identity is thus at the mercy of another human being.

Hearing these and similar thoughts, Howard Weiss, professor and chair of psychology at the Georgia Institute of Technology, said that they sounded disturbingly familiar. Weiss has spent much of his career trying to distill and decode the human experience of work, an experience, he said, that remains mostly a mystery. Answers to questions such as whether we should seek passion, purpose, and satisfaction on the job are elusive, he said, because so little is known of the individual experience. Most research has focused not on workers per se, but on how employers might best engage with them, ultimately, to get the most out of them. The result of this, he said, is not that people are happier on the job, but rather that they are more anxious about not feeling happier on the job.

"There are so many questions that we haven't studied because the paradigm we've followed developed out of a demand to understand the human component of *organizations*," he said. "But organization-centric focus can't provide the insights we need. We haven't looked hard enough at work in a way that people actually experience it. Extracting the essential qualities of what makes work meaningful is a critical step because, you know, people are being put in circumstances where the psychological benefits of the work experience will have to accrue outside of the employment context. It's time we step back and see work from the *worker's* point of view."

HABITS OF THE HEART

The real social revolution of the last 30 years, one we are
still living through, is the switch from a life that is largely
organized for us to a world in which we are all forced to be
in charge of our own destiny.
—CHARLES HANDY

The morning we met, Amy Wrzesniewski was windblown and rav-
enous. She'd been up since 3 a.m., stealing a few solitary hours grad-
ing papers before her kids woke up, then stuffing her toddler into
play clothes, feeding her newborn, and pedaling her three-speed to
her office at Yale School of Management. Sipping her third caffeine
of the day, she likened the "current chapter of my life" to the task of
emptying a swimming pool with an ice cream scoop. "Every night
it rains and the pool fills up again," she said. "And in the morning
you wake up and start scooping again."

Wrzesniewski helps prepare business leaders of the future, but
like Michael Pratt, who opened the previous chapter, she seems dis-
inclined to join their ranks. On her last birthday, teaching responsibilities, research demands, and caring for her children and aging
in-laws left her no time to celebrate—no party, no dinner out. But
her husband, Anthony, had the good sense to buy her a gift. Ear-
rings? Flowers? Tickets to a Knicks game?

"I got a six-pack of nylon underpants from Target," she told me.
"Seriously, this is all I really wanted. All my underwear was baggy

[due to her recent pregnancy]. It's what I needed. And Anthony noticed!"

Wrzesniewski was raised to be grateful. She grew up outside Philadelphia in a family of truck drivers, line workers, and, in the case of one much older cousin, a blacksmith. Her father stocked cigarette vending machines and jukeboxes in bars before getting work at a refinery, and her mother worked nights as a nurse. Both her parents were active in their unions. Working opposite shifts, they rarely saw each other during the week, but both kept a sharp eye on their four kids. "My parents let us know that if we worked our tails off and got Bs and Cs they'd be proud," Amy said. "But if we took it easy and got an A-minus, they wouldn't be happy. For them effort was everything." Amy recalled scoring an 88 on a calculus test, and sharing her disappointment with her mother. "Another kid hardly studied and got a perfect grade," she said. "To me, that wasn't fair. My mother was horrified that I would say such a thing. She said, 'Think about the kids who studied hard—really hard—and got Cs. You're lucky. If you want better grades, get back to work.' That was my 'come to Jesus' moment. . . . From then on, hard work was my calling card."

Hard work brought Wrzesniewski a partial scholarship to the University of Pennsylvania, just as the new movement in positive psychology was taking hold there in the early 1990s. Freudians centered their attention on pathologies of despair—narcissism, paranoia, depression, schizophrenia. "Positive psychologists" (like Abraham Maslow, a father of the movement) looked in a more hopeful direction, to characteristics that predispose us to thrive: generosity, optimism, resilience, courage. In graduate school, Wrzesniewski was naturally drawn to this positive approach, but she harbored no illusions. "Growing up, I saw that work could bring great joy," she told me. "But it could also bring alienation and pain. I wanted to get to the bottom of that—to find out how the same work could be so positive for some, and could lead to such disappointment and pain for others."

Many of us can recall being nudged toward a certain life path by a family friend, a close relative, or a profound experience. For Wrzesniewski, the nudge came from *Habits of the Heart,* a collection of essays first published in 1985. In the 1996 edition sociologist Robert N. Bellah updates his book with this prologue: "Underlying [our anxiety] is the realization that for most Americans, growth of the global economy no longer means opportunity but rather 'downsizing,' 'reengineered jobs,' and the pink slip of dismissal. Yet through all these wrenching threats to prosperity there has been curiously little public protest about the changing rules of the economic game."

In the essays that follow, *Habits of the Heart* explores the inevitable tensions that arise from the nation's growing focus on individualism and its waning sense of community. As part of that exploration, it outlines the different ways people relate to their work: whether as a job, as a career, or as a calling. Those who claim to have "a job" see their 9 to 5 mostly as a means to an end, a way to support a life outside the job. These people tend not to express their ambitions, interests, or goals through their jobs, but rather look elsewhere to fill those needs. They also are less likely to judge themselves by the standards set by their employers. By contrast, people who see their work as a career are inclined to measure their self-worth in terms of occupational advance and achievement. They invest heavily in their jobs and see them as a reflection of their status and power. Finally, those who describe their job as a calling (or, as some put it, a vocation) see their lives and their work as spiritually inseparable. The "called" tend to focus less on financial gain or feelings of achievement than on the sense of purpose, mission, and community engendered by the work itself.

The phrase "being called" has a theistic twang, as in "being called to the church." But a calling need not evoke a higher spirit. Early-twentieth-century psychologist and educational reformer John Dewey characterized a calling as any activity that made life "perceptibly significant to a person." By Dewey's standard, a calling was not always socially relevant in the conventional sense: it described an attitude and disposition, the way one approached one's work rather than any particular occupation.

Intrigued by Dewey's theory, Wrzesniewski set out to test it. Her central question was this: Is the experience of being "called" a function of a particular type of job or, as Dewey implied, a function of the individual holding the job? To address this question she and her team at Yale surveyed two hundred workers at the university and a nearby health center: physicians, nurses, computer programmers, librarians, health educators, analysts, administrative assistants, and clerks. It surprised her that these workers had no difficulty sorting themselves out as having a job, a career, or a calling. Each seemed to have a pretty good idea of where he or she stood. And as it turned out, these assessments correlated not with the job itself but with the attitude and outlook of the individual doing it.

Consider, for example, the position of "administrative assistant." In the Wrzesniewski study, one-third of respondents employed in this role classified it as "just" a job, one-third as a career, and one-third as a calling. So, how did they differ? The "called" were not higher paid or more challenged than the others. They didn't have more autonomy or feel more respected or face more interesting challenges. What made the difference was the way the administrative assistants individually perceived and engaged in their roles, whether it be a job, a career, or a calling.

Wrzesniewki's own administrative assistant, a kindly woman who offered me lunch and homemade brownies, clearly considered her job a calling and admitted as much. In contrast, a younger assistant working nearby simply shrugged when I asked her for directions, and gave every indication that she considered her position "just a job." While these women had similar responsibilities, they seemed to have vastly different outlooks on what these responsibilities might bring them in terms of fulfillment. Wrzesniewski's research and that of others suggests that many workplaces are similarly divided, with about one-third of workers falling into each of the categories. For contrary to what many of us believe, individuals can feel "called" to almost any occupation. It's not the job itself, but how we approach it that seems to make the most difference.

Consider, for example, the work of a sushi chef. To a naive and clumsy amateur, spending long hours slicing fish into exquisite morsels may sound exceedingly dull. I suspect many of us cannot imagine concentrating on that effort and if forced to do so would approach it with dread—at best, as a job to be done. But many of us understand intuitively that this is a reflection of our attitude toward the work, not of the work itself. We know this because we've heard of sushi masters and their passions.

Jiro Ono, the eighty-five-year-old subject of the documentary *Jiro Dreams of Sushi*, is owner and head chef of Sukiyabashi Jiro, a ten-seat sushi restaurant wedged beneath a Tokyo office building adjoining the entrance to a metro station. Jiro arrives at his kitchen each morning as though at a threshold—for him, it's all about what's to come. In Japan he is an honored *shokunin*, an artist who pursues perfection through his craft. The honorific implies not only mastery but social consciousness; the shokunin has an obligation to do his best work for the betterment of all. When applied to Jiro this seems rather a stretch; the chef plies his skills for a tiny number of patrons willing and able to shell out hundreds of dollars for a twenty-minute gustatory jolt. Yet one could easily argue that Jiro is a positive force, in the sense that his tireless pursuit of transcendence moves others to pursue the same. Jiro seems not only fulfilled and satisfied by his work but utterly absorbed by it, a hero on his own terms. Clearly, he has found his calling.

Still, Jiro offers a potent example of how a calling can be a double-edged sword. Jiro is in some sense a tyrant, setting ironclad rules and demands that force others to comply with his standards. He insists that customers eat his sushi at its peak—immediately after it's prepared—leaving them no choice but to gulp down their $400 twenty-course meals in half an hour. Patrons who dare take a small bite of their sushi—rather than eat it whole—are reprimanded by Jiro's assistants, or in some cases by the master himself. In the film, even his sons seem to cower in his presence. Jiro's determination to become better and better can be seen as a form of narcissism, in that it rationalizes behaviors that would not likely be tolerated in those of us who are less revered.

Jiro has given everything to his work and gotten much in return, but it's difficult to know whether his sacrifices have made him truly happy. (For one thing, while he seems to have a wife, he apparently spends so little time with her that his sons barely recognize the relationship.) A calling, then, can pose risks to the called.

Psychologist Jeffery Thompson teaches at Brigham Young University, the nation's largest religious university owned and operated by the Church of Jesus Christ of Latter-Day Saints. Raised in the Mormon tradition, he knows his gospel, and also the dangers of unmet expectations. "If you believe you were put on this earth to fill some 'calling,' and for whatever reason you do not to do it, you might easily consider that a moral failure," he told me. The more "called" we believe ourselves to be to an occupation, Thompson explained, the more likely we are to tolerate and even overlook whatever hardships come with it. And while this acceptance of hardship can lead us to the pursuit of excellence, it can also lead us to unrealistic expectations and exploitation.

Thompson's seminal study, "The Call of the Wild: Zookeepers, Callings, and the Double-Edged Sword of Meaningful Work," co-authored with J. Stuart Bunderson, offers a poignant illustration. Zookeeping is not a lucrative occupation; in 2017 the average pay was reported as $11.95 per hour. This low wage comes despite a relatively high educational requirement: of the 1,201 zookeepers in Thompson and Bunderson's study, three out of four had at least one college degree. Still, few if any zookeepers thought they had hope of advancement or of being offered a substantial raise. And the job is anything but glamorous, as it mostly involves feeding and caring for ungrateful creatures under the clueless watch of a thankless public. As for status, most zookeepers agree that it is low. How low? One zookeeper recalled a nun ushering a flock of students past the cage he was cleaning with this warning: "Study hard, children, or you'll end up *like him*."

Nonetheless, the zookeepers largely reported themselves en-thralled with their work. In a word, they felt "called" to it. Many described feeling destined for the job, saying it was "wired" into their DNA. Most felt a deep obligation to care for animals that, in the words of one, had "basically given up their freedom to educate people." Some felt so driven to their vocation that they confessed they would do it for free. And many had done it for free, some vol-unteering for years before landing a paid position.

"It's no surprise, really, that they love their jobs," Thompson told me. "But loving your job is not always a good thing, at least not in the way that actually benefits workers. I love teaching at Brigham Young, and I don't mind saying so, but I've been warned to keep quiet about it so as not to get taken advantage of. It's great to be absorbed by your work, dedicated to your work. But there is a downside. Employers don't like to talk about that, because, frankly, they'd love it if we all felt 'called' to our jobs."

Some employers have gone so far as to hire consultants to de-sign an algorithm to sort out the "called" from other job candi-dates, on the logic that the former will happily tackle any task without argument or demands. Wrzesniewski herself has been of-fered the opportunity to design such a metric, and has politely—and firmly—declined to do so. "We're entering an age where there is more demand from people who want to work for an organization that stands for something," she said. "So organizations do a lot of window dressing, and some adopt postures that are essentially misleading. Not all of us needs a calling. What everyone needs is the opportunity to make meaning from their work."

Each spring, Wrzesniewski spearheads a two-day retreat of

scholars from around the world informally called the "Meaning Meeting." In 2004, when she initiated this tradition, only fourteen experts were invited. "Now [with so many more in the field] I have to turn people away," she said. "We have such a great time getting together, studying this puzzle that until fairly recently no one really wanted to talk about—that is, this counterintuitive idea of struggling to find meaning in work in a time when most people dislike their jobs."

The Meaning Meeting I was fortunate enough to attend was a shorts and T-shirt affair held in a leafy retreat in the Connecticut Berkshires. The plumbing was sporadic and breakfast was appalling (think still-frozen slices of Wonder Bread posing as "toast"), but few if any of the other attendees seemed to notice—they were an uncannily undemanding assemblage.

Sociologist Michel Anteby was the first up with a formal presentation. In his day job as a professor at Boston University's Questrom School of Business, Anteby favors Oxford shirts and lectures forcefully on such matters as "managing human capital." In the Berkshires he wore flip-flops and spoke movingly of the importance of what he called "invisible" work, in jobs like child care and garbage collection. At one time, these "under the radar" jobs held out the promise of autonomy—child care workers could decide which books to read their charges and when to put them down for a nap; garbage collectors could schedule their own breaks and grab a sandwich or a smoke when they felt the need. This gave people a chance to craft their jobs to their own purposes and in some cases make meaning of them. But thanks to our modern obsession with surveillance, Anteby said, even these modest efforts to take personal control have come under threat. Nanny cams are commonplace in homes and day-care centers, and something similar is happening in trash collection—in 2016, Waste Pro USA, a trash and recycling company, partnered with a wireless provider to buy and install 360-degree "video systems" in each of its 1,800 vehicles. On its website, the company explains: "The 3rd Eye camera technology Waste

Pro . . . offers the company unmatched access to what is happening in and around our vehicles at all times. . . . We use the information from the cameras to coach both positive and negative behaviors of the employees before accidents, injuries, and property damage occur." Similarly, it is increasingly common for retail stores, banks, restaurants, and other businesses in which workers interact with the public to use video surveillance in locations where security or theft prevention is important. It is also common at warehouses, and increasingly in offices, where employers claim to use cameras for "security purposes." And also, of course, at airports.

"Baggage screeners have it especially tough," Anteby told me. "They feel they are 'disappeared' into the woodwork, interchangeable, no more than a code number. The only way they can get noticed as individuals is to screw up. And that's what those surveillance cameras are about."

I had been through countless airport security checks, and found it hard to believe that TSA agents felt so beleaguered. While some seem bored, most appeared cheerful and even empathic. There was that TSA comradery, where agents josh among themselves and sometimes with passengers. But speaking with an actual TSA agent, I learned that these benefits are undercut by management practices that can take all the fun—and sense of purpose—out of the job.

Jason Edward Harrington spent six years working a bag checkpoint at O'Hare Airport in Chicago. A college graduate and fledgling freelance writer, he took the job assuming it would be temporary, but then, for some reason, it wasn't. Still, he said, if it was just the work, he might have hung on even longer. He enjoyed meeting passengers from all over the world, some of whom showed a real interest in him. What wore him down was a system built on a foundation of suspicion. His every move was followed and videoed, a practice the TSA claimed was for *his* protection. If, perchance, a traveler's iPad went missing, he was told, the tapes would prove that Harrington was not to blame. Harrington was on board with that, as laptops and iPads went missing nearly every day. But the problem, he told me, was that supervisors grabbed any opportunity to view the tapes to search for the slightest infraction—anything from gum chewing to trips to the bathroom. "If they trusted us, respected us, you could really enjoy the job," he said. "But they didn't. Our default was to try everything we could to get out of there—if not find a new job [the TSA workers he knew typically applied for new jobs *every week*], then at least get out of camera range on our shifts."

Electronic surveillance of employees, both directly through video cameras and indirectly via software, has grown rapidly across most industries, notably since the tragic events of 9/11. No one is sure why, but the most likely reason is the rising sophistication and declining cost of spy technology. Employees *are observed* because they *can be observed* by an array of increasingly sophisticated devices and techniques from DNA analysis to eye scans. Two of every three employers monitor employee website visits, and nearly half keep tabs of their employees' keystrokes. Twelve percent monitor employees' personal blogs, and 10 percent monitor social networking sites for clues to their employees' leisure time activities. Almost half monitor employees with surveillance video systems similar to those the TSA uses to ogle baggage screeners. And some companies feel entitled to stalk employees right into their private lives, for example through employer-issued cell phones that track them via GPS.

The company Humanyze, formerly known as Sociometric Solutions, has taken this "human analytics" approach one step further with what it calls "moneyball for business." Moneyball refers to Michael Lewis's lively best seller about the Oakland Athletics baseball team and its general manager, Billy Beane. The book—and its even more popular film adaptation—centered on Oakland's ingenious use of statistics to assemble a team of particularly gifted ball players. The scheme relied on objective data, such as individual on-base and slugging percentages. Humanyze uses a similar strategy to make business more efficient. But rather than relying on statistics, it gathers data directly by fitting employee ID badges with a microphone, location sensors, and an accelerometer. The avowed purpose of all this is not to spy on individuals but to tease out patterns of employee behavior and interaction that affect overall company performance. For example, there's the burning question of whether it's more productive to encourage employees to bring coffee back to their desks or to encourage them to gather around a centrally located coffee machine. Humanyze's data offers evidence that gathering around the coffee machine results in higher overall productivity.

This seems harmless enough, and it would be, were the world a different place. Roboticist Matt Beane, who once consulted with Humanyze, said engineers at the company worked very hard to make the process of monitoring employees transparent and fair and to ensure that personal data remained private. "But, unfortunately, there are implicit pressures to share the information with employers," he told me. And there is no legal barrier to doing so.

In his essay "In Praise of Electronically Monitoring Employees," MIT business scholar Andrew McAfee (whom we met in a previous chapter) unveiled a study of surveillance he had completed in collaboration with Lamar Pierce of Washington University in St. Louis and Daniel Snow of Brigham Young University. The researchers monitored the comings and goings of waitstaff at 392 casual dining restaurants scattered across the United States. Apparently, knowing they were being watched reduced employee theft by an average of $23 a week for each location; basically, not a whole lot. What was significant was that weekly revenue grew by an astonishing $2,975 per location, nearly $1,000 from drink orders alone. McAfee speculates: "As far as we can tell, performance improved simply because people started doing their jobs better. To oversimplify a bit, once the bad actors saw that theft was closed off to them as an option they realized that the best way for them to take home more money was to hustle more, take better care of customers, and generally be a better restaurant employee. And I imagine that once some people started acting that way the rest of the staff joined in; good behavior is contagious, just as misbehavior is."

McAfee did not mention whether he'd spoken to any servers. If not, perhaps he should have. The casual dining restaurants he observed included Olive Garden. Olive Garden is part of Darden Restaurants, Inc., the world's largest full-service restaurant conglomerate with over two thousand locations and roughly 148,000 employees in the United States alone. Darden is not known for its employee-centric labor practices. Starting in 2016, to cite one example, half of its US workforce were issued payroll cards in lieu of standard paychecks. This makes good business sense, as each card shaves about $2.75 per pay period off the company's overhead, saving Darden a total of as much as $5 million per year. But the cards make less sense for company employees. The cards come triggered with fees: 99 cents for using a card to pay utility bills, 50 cents if declined at a cash register, $1.75 to withdraw money from an out-of-network ATM, and 75 cents to check the card's balance. If employees lose their card, they must pay $10 to replace it. And that $10 looms large: Olive Garden pays servers as little as $2.13 an hour, plus tips.

The proposition that job performance improves when employees are constantly monitored, and thereby at least theoretically deprived of the opportunity to steal, is not a hopeful one. Moreover, it is not supported by the data from this or any other study. Another equally plausible explanation for the growth in restaurant revenue is that installing spy software was part of a larger commitment on the part of management to organize and streamline operations, arguably a good thing. Another possibility? That surveilled employees felt pressured to push customers to order more, arguably not a good thing. For while upselling customers may well pad the bottom line in the short term, the practice is not necessarily good for business in the long run, as few of us enjoy feeling pressured, let alone pressured to eat and drink too much. And it perhaps should go without saying that there was little consideration of the cost to low-paid employees of having to work under even more stressful conditions. Nearly every study of the practice suggests that surveillance vastly increases workplace stress, promotes worker alienation, lowers job satisfaction, and conveys the perception that the quantity of work one generates is more important than its quality. And there are other, equally damaging drawbacks. In a recent analysis aptly entitled "Watching Me Watching You," British anthropologists Michael Fischer and Sally Applin conclude that as commonly construed, workplace surveillance creates "a culture where . . . people more often alter their behavior to suit machines and work with them, rather than the other way around, and . . . this has eroded conceptions of agency." That is, the constant surveillance of employees diminishes their capacity to operate as independent thinkers and actors.

So, does it benefit employers to survey their staff? After all, in surveys, roughly twenty-three million workers openly admit to squandering at least an hour a day, at an estimated annual cost to employers of $85 billion. But is this cost real? Perhaps not. Psychologist Howard Weiss points out that not everything we do on the job should have a clear practical purpose. "I've found that 25 to 40 percent of our thoughts are off task during the day," he told me. "People feel guilty about that, and employers don't like it. But mind wandering might replenish you, and in the long run might allow you to work more efficiently."

So are we more efficient and productive on the job when we know we're being watched? That's hard to know, but the near-ubiquitous use of ever more sophisticated monitoring technology in the workplace reveals a dangerous erosion of trust. And there's ample evidence that workers who sense they are not trusted are less productive. When employers closely monitor our work, Wrzesniewski said, they hasten our alienation from it. They make it difficult for us to think independently and act proactively. And they make it nearly impossible for us to make meaning of our work. In fact, those of us who do "cheat" on the job often do so in retaliation for the very lack of trust surveillance implies: for example, TSA employees, Harrington told me, waste countless hours finding clever ways to evade the surveillance camera's roving eye.

Wrzesniewski's data supports her insight that we work best when we are trusted to perform the job in a way that *allows* us to make meaning out of what we do, rather than when we are urged to see the job itself as meaningful. "Our thinking about a job can be as misguided as our thinking about marriage," she said. "In the case of marriage, many of us think that there is only one soul on this earth who we can partner with. But surely that can't be the case. What are the chances of finding this one 'right' person, the right age, the right geography . . . what are the chances of finding someone just right who happens to be in your orbit? It's too much! Who could wait for that to happen? You create the relationship, taking the raw ingredients and making the most of them. And when it comes to jobs, too, this is a much more realistic approach. Rather than expect employers to give us that opportunity, we can craft our jobs to make them closer to the job that suits our purposes."

Wrzesniewski tripped over this theory of "job crafting" early in her career, while conducting an ethnographic study of twenty-nine hospital janitors. She wondered what, if anything, these janitors did to extract meaning from their jobs. Rather than speculate or rely on surveys, she and her colleagues spent months listening to and recording the janitors' individual stories. All the cleaners worked at the same hospital, and all had roughly the same duties. But not all of them felt the same way about the job. Indeed, their experiences of their work varied dramatically. About half disliked the job and described it as low-skilled. This half complained of abusive bosses, exhausting shifts, and dangers of every sort. In a word, they were disgruntled. The other half took a completely different view. They enjoyed the job and described it as highly skilled. In a word, they were satisfied. They had found a way to make meaning from work that the other half contended offered no opportunity for meaning.

The contrast in attitude between these two groups was so stark that Wrzesniewski found it hard to believe they were talking about the same job. Digging deeper, she found some essential differences, and again, none of these differences had to do with the job description. People in the first group did exactly what was required by management. They kept the hospital clean and tidy and kept their eyes and ears to themselves. The second group addressed the job in an entirely different manner. They, too, kept the hospital clean and tidy. But they also regarded patients as their wards, lingering by bedsides to commiserate and offer moral support. When cleaning a patient's room, they kept a watchful eye on heart monitors and notified a nurse if they noticed anything amiss. They cheered on the children and comforted the elderly. They understood they were cleaners and rarely if ever overstepped their bounds. But they also thought of themselves as healers. And the patients under their watch said they were grateful. "You would think organizations would pay attention to this," Wrzesniewski told me.

In fact, the hospital did pay attention, but not in the way she meant. The janitors were chastised, told to stick to their cleaning. To do more, they came to worry, was to risk losing their jobs. Wrzesniewski was saddened by this, but not surprised. "There was no way to monetize the value the cleaners were adding to the patient experience," she told me. "And the bottom line is paramount. I've never seen an organization that sees worker dignity as a terminal value."

Psychologist Abraham Maslow, creator of the hierarchy of needs paradigm, confided in his diaries that he saw his theories as a compromise, a way of threading a path through delicate institutional hierarchies without treading on ideological toes. His goal was not to help workers directly but to help employers create an environment where the needs of the individual were naturally aligned with the demands of the organization. For Maslow and many of his twentieth-century contemporaries, this was a win-win strategy— when employees are happy, they reasoned, businesses thrive and workers benefit. And to some extent, they did, back then. But today efforts to align the goals of institutions with those of workers are far more complicated, and fraught.

As we've seen, at the close of World War II and for roughly three decades to follow, productivity and wages grew nearly in tandem in the United States. Government, business, and labor, though not always in agreement, collaborated in an effort to keep workers happy and the economy moving smoothly. Labor, management, and shareholders all profited as output grew, and executives, even chief executives, pocketed what seemed more or less their rightful share: in 1965 the CEO-to-worker compensation ratio was a quite reasonable 20 to 1. But early in the 1970s, the power relationship between employee and employer began to shift. Though productivity continued to rise, wages stagnated and profits and executive compensation soared. Numbers tell the story.

Between 1973 and 2014, productivity grew 1.33 percent *each year* while the yearly growth in median hourly compensation was a meager 0.20 percent. During that period only about 15 percent of productivity growth translated into higher hourly wages and benefits for the typical American worker. What this meant was that most of the benefits of the nation's growing productivity were siphoned to shareholders and into the C-suite. By 2013, the CEO-to-worker compensation ratio stood at 295.9 to 1, far higher than it was in the 1960s, 1970s, 1980s, or 1990s. Likewise, from 1978 to 2013, inflation-adjusted CEO compensation ballooned by an incredible 937 percent, an increase of more than double the stock market growth and what seemed like light-years beyond the 10.2 percent growth in a typical worker's compensation over the same period. By then, the gulf between labor, shareholders, and executives had widened into a chasm. The problem, as framed recently by Princeton University political philosopher Elizabeth Anderson, is that "the amount of respect, standing, and autonomy" workers receive does not depend on their essential humanity but is "roughly proportional to their market value."

So what happens to our sense of self when our market value

withers? At the Meaning Meeting, psychologist Sally Maitlis of the Saïd Business School, University of Oxford, addressed this question obliquely through the life stories of forty performing artists she had followed over the course of nearly two years. Half of these artists were professional dancers, the other half professional musicians. And all of them because of illness or injury had been forced to abandon jobs they loved. "These were people who had devoted their entire lives to their work, who *were* their work," Maitlis told me. As one horn player lamented: "I defined my whole life by this piece of metal and what I could do with it."

Maitlis spoke to each artist twice, with eighteen months between interviews. From what she described of these conversations, it's hard to imagine individuals more forcefully called to their vocation or more devastated at the prospect of its loss. Not only did their responses to her questions surprise her, they sharply contradicted what she and other experts had come to believe about work and its centrality in our lives.

What Maitlis discovered was that artists who felt *most* passionate about their former careers in symphony orchestras or dance companies were the least likely to recover from their loss. After being sidelined by their injuries they grew frantic, dashing from specialist to specialist in pursuit of a cure. They spent endless hours surfing the web for remedies and complained ceaselessly to loved ones. At least one artist confessed to thoughts of suicide. Like the "broken" factory workers of Marienthal, they saw no life for themselves beyond their jobs.

By contrast, those artists who expressed *less* passion for their jobs in dance companies and orchestras fully recovered from their loss, some triumphantly. It's not that these artists didn't love their work or feel strongly about it—of course they did. Most of them had devoted their life to their art. But as Maitlis explained it, these seemingly "less passionate" individuals had uncoupled their job identity from the core of their work identities. Their relationship to their work was not defined by their job. Rather, they had internalized their devotion, and it remained part of who they were even when their career was gone. Although no longer able to play his instrument, a trumpeter maintained a devotion to music that transcended his need to perform. "So I'll go back to my original love," he told Maitlis. "I'll go back to being a dedicated listener." Listening did not constitute a career, of course; for that, he became a teacher. But he remained active and engaged in his field and by exercising that connoisseurship sustained a sense of meaning and purpose. He and the other artists who continued to flourish once their careers were gone had found ways to make meaning of work that did not manifest in a job. Channeling their artistic drive in new directions, they created meaning from a genuine engagement with the art itself. They prevailed by finding new ways to reignite the passion for which *the job* they had once held constituted only one of many possible outlets. The job was gone, but the work—and the meaning made from the work—would always be with them.

Maitlis believes her findings have implications that extend well beyond the artist's realm, to almost any occupation or vocation. She said that flourishing in a global economy requires us to see ourselves independent of our jobs while maintaining a strong grasp of our work identity. She admits that's not always easy, particularly given today's pressures to be "the best" at what we do.

"Employers demand that we give our all, that we 'become' our job," she told me. "And as employees we are expected to achieve excellence by specializing in a very narrow domain. We are only as good as the service we can provide. But that is a very precarious setup. One day you are everything—at the top of your game. The next you are laid off or demoted and you are nothing. And if— thanks to your former job—you are too specialized to apply your skills elsewhere, you lose your entire work identity. Psychically, this is a terrible thing."

Where we find meaning and how we make meaning of our work is a deeply personal matter. Acknowledging this offers us a sense of liberation, the freedom to untether our very human need for a sense of purpose in our vocations from our very practical need to earn a living. While it's healthy—even essential—for us all to strive to make meaning from our work, not all of us can make meaning from our jobs, nor should we be expected—or driven—to try to do so.

For me, as for many others, this message hits close to home. My father, a pediatrician, was good at his job, but it was not the job that he turned to for meaning. His passion was not people (whom he often failed to understand) but plants, and his unrequited aspiration was to design and manage a marvelous garden. The assumption—the imposition—that he put nearly all his focus and energy into his "meaningful job" was a heavy burden, one that ultimately brought an aching disappointment that he never completely escaped.

As I've said—and will say again—my intent is not to offer easy answers or pat solutions, for in matters of work and its prospects, there are none. But I hope I've convinced you that as good jobs grow scarcer our response should not be to try to "create" more "meaningful jobs," but rather to expunge the idea that "job creators" are also "meaning creators."

Clearly, there is no end of work to be done, and the world would be a far better place were each and every one of us able to indulge our natural inclination to do it. Our most obvious challenge is creating new and better twenty-first-century jobs. Our challenge is also to reform an aged economic system based on twentieth-century metrics that overlooks and under-rewards vital work from which we ourselves can make meaning. We cannot rely entirely on jobs or the promise of jobs to sustain the nation's psychic buoyancy. On the contrary, as we've seen, reimagining work for the twenty-first century requires us to find ways to generate the psychological, emotional, and economic benefits of work *outside* a traditional employment context. This won't be easy, but it will be exhilarating, and the starting point to me is clear: our schools.

Part III

Learning to Labor

Education is not the filling of a pail,
but the lighting of the fire.

—W. B. YEATS

A CHILD'S WORK

Two ideals are struggling for supremacy in American
life today: one the industrial ideal, dominating thru the
supremacy of commercialism, which subordinates the
worker to the product and the machine; the other,
the ideal of democracy, the ideal of the educators, which
places humanity above all machines, and demands that
all activity shall be the expression of life. Those two ideals
can no more continue to exist in American life than our
nation could have continued half slave and half free. If
the school cannot bring joy to the work of the world, the
joy must go out of its own life, and work in the school
as in the factory will become drudgery.

—MARGARET A. HALEY, PRESIDENT OF THE
NATIONAL FEDERATION OF TEACHERS, 1904

When our daughter Alison was eight years old, her father and I were
summoned to her school for a conference. This was not the first
time we'd received such a call. Years earlier we'd been warned that
Alison's refusal to nap was a "nontrivial" violation of preschool
protocol. Still, we were fairly certain that naps were not required of
third graders. Arriving early for our appointment, our knees poked
high above the tiny grammar school desks, we feared the worst.
The teacher, bless her, got right to the point—there was a problem,
and once again, a "nontrivial" one. Our daughter, we learned, was
a showboat. She rushed through her problem sets to make time to

help other kids with their problem sets. If we thought that was no big deal, we were mistaken. Alison needed to "buckle down" and fast. Third grade might seem like a cakewalk, but there was middle school to consider and high school and then—looming large—college. Our daughter's very future rested in our trembling hands; it was on us to pull her back from this feckless detour and set her firmly on the path to success.

I left the meeting deeply conflicted.

I was proud of my girl and her generous spirit, and secretly pleased that other kids trusted her to help them. But what if her teacher was right? What if—at age eight—she was already foreclosing her future? In the end, I caved. I didn't exactly transform into Tiger Mom, but I did caution Alison that while helping other kids was nice, looking out for her own interests was smart. And she needed to be smart.

I know I was wrong to let fear trump my daughter's inclinations and my own values. But it's easy to forget that back then, in the mid-1990s, the nation itself was afraid. A decade earlier President Ronald Reagan's National Commission on Excellence in Education had sounded the alarm: "Our nation is at risk because our once unchallenged preeminence in commerce, industry, science and technological innovation is being overtaken by competitors throughout the world." Pretty frightening. The perceived threat came mostly from Japan, then an economic and technological juggernaut. Americans were terrified that the Japanese would eat our lunch (meaning our jobs) if our country (meaning our kids) didn't wise up. The business-sponsored Committee for Economic Development fanned the flames, pointing out that American children were ill equipped for the work of today, let alone the work of the future. Here's a taste of their 1985 report, "Investing in Our Children":

> Employers in both large and small businesses decry the
> lack of preparation for work among the nation's high

school graduates. Well over one-quarter of the nation's youth never finish high school. Many who graduate and go on to higher education need remedial reading and writing courses, which about two-thirds of U.S. colleges now provide. Nearly 13 percent of all seventeen-year-olds still enrolled in school are functionally illiterate and 44 percent are marginally literate. Among students who drop out, an estimated 60 percent are functionally illiterate. In contrast, Japan, America's most important competitor, has the highest rate of high school completion and literacy in the world, close to 100 percent. Japanese students study more and learn more.... In science and mathematics, Japanese test scores lead the world.

Oh, those wily Japanese! Their cars were snazzier, their food was healthier, and now their children were smarter! Casting the nation's educational "crisis" as an *economic* threat helped pave the way for titans of industry to reclaim their place as legitimate thought leaders on schooling, a topic about which many of them seemed to know very little. Prominent among these thought leaders was IBM chief executive Louis Gerstner, a former Nabisco executive whose business triumphs included elevating the cartoon mascot "Joe Camel" to national icon status (thereby luring children to the cigarette brand) and yanking two multinational companies back from the brink of insolvency by—among other things—firing thousands of employees. Gerstner had no experience or training in education, he confessed to a special meeting of Congress, but had "spent a lot of time" on it and had "the scars to prove it." Apparently, the scars were enough.

In 1996, Gerstner hosted the National Education Summit at IBM's conference center in Palisades, New York. In attendance were forty-one governors and forty-nine executives, almost all of them white and male, representing the nation's largest corporations. While there was also a small contingent of education "experts" in attendance, students, student advocates, and teachers were barely represented, and therefore easy targets. The slings, arrows, and pop culture references flew. "Too often we seem too willing to accept underachieving standards suitable only for a Beavis, a Butthead, or a Bart Simpson," Nevada governor Bob Miller carped. "The nation's governors and CEOs are fed up with passive acceptance of mediocrity." (It went unmentioned that most of those governors and CEOs were products of the very educational system they decried.)

This was the second National Educational Summit. The first, in 1989, was a landmark event, an acknowledgment that tens of thousands of school districts—and fifty states—could not without national leadership hurdle the challenges spelled out in *A Nation at Risk*. Organized by President George H. W. Bush, the event included forty-nine governors (and *no* CEOs) who agreed upon a concise list of eminently sensible goals, among them that all teachers be competent to teach, that most Americans graduate from high school, and, intriguingly, that all schools be certifiably free of drugs, alcohol, and guns.

Spearheaded by the standing president of the United States, the first educational summit was aspirational, an opportunity for state representatives to come together to seek support and common ground. In the words of Harvard education professor Jal Mehta, it reflected a "'Field of Dreams' optimism. If we built the goals, then schools would meet them." Spearheaded by the standing CEO of IBM, the second summit was no Field of Dreams. Its report concluded: "The primary purpose of education is to prepare students to work successfully in a global economy." The implicit threat was barely veiled: if schools failed to rise to this goal by setting and enforcing strict academic standards, customers (parents) would be set free to take their business (children and tax dollars) elsewhere (private and charter schools).

The educational community observed all this with growing unease. Thomas Good, a professor of educational psychology at the University of Arizona, gave voice to their concerns, writing: "Recent policies for transforming American schools have been developed with little regard for research evidence.... Proposed policies are seen by many educational researchers as incomplete and unlikely to work." Making matters worse was a lack of clarity on what these policies should be. While CEOs proclaimed that America's children must be made "ready for work," what they meant by "ready" was anyone's guess. Meanwhile, there was the question of who would fund these "reforms." As educational economist Norton Grubb told me, "There was no point in advocating higher standards without allocating the resources to achieve them."

While it's become customary to conflate education and job preparation, America's founders saw education as essential not for the training of workers but for the preparation of citizens. In the 1770s, Thomas Jefferson drafted "A Bill for the More General Diffusion of Knowledge," which began: "Those entrusted with power have, in time, and by slow operations, perverted it into tyranny; and it is believed that the most effectual means of preventing this would be, to illuminate, as far as practicable, the minds of the people at large." Jefferson proposed that public schools be built and paid for by the state and that "reading, writing, and common arithmetick" be taught there to "all the free children, male and female." With the notable exception of slaves, Americans were in fact remarkably well educated by the standards of the time. As one observer wrote in 1800, "No country on the face of the earth can boast of a larger proportion of inhabitants, versed in the rudiments of science, or fewer, who are not able to read and write their names, than the United States of America. This general distribution of useful knowledge and competency shared by almost every individual is the best security of moral virtue and the finest pillar of republican government."

And yet, little of this "useful knowledge" was passed down by trained teachers, as not all that many Americans spent much time in the classroom. Ben Franklin left school at age ten to work in his father's candle-making business, and Abraham Lincoln reckoned that an "aggregate of all" his formal education "did not amount to one year." (Lincoln once joked that "little qualification was ever required of a teacher. . . . If a straggler supposed to understand Latin happened to sojourn in the neighborhood, he was looked upon as a wizard.") Suffragist Elizabeth Cady Stanton, who taught her own six children at home, condemned the teaching profession as "a pool of intellectual stagnation."

Eventually, though, formal schooling caught on. Over a period of rapid industrialization between 1890 and 1920, education through elementary school was made compulsory in every state, and high school attendance soared from roughly 10 to 50 percent of the population. Still, not all Americans agreed that formal education was necessary, or even desirable, especially for the urban poor. Prior to the child labor laws of the late 1930s, students in rural regions graduated in significantly greater proportions than did city kids. School attendance was lowest in the *most* industrial states, where the lure of factory wages seduced children away from their studies the day they were old enough to snare a work permit.

The Great Depression brought laws ending child labor nationwide, not necessarily to protect young minds, but to relieve the intense competition for scarce jobs. In 1938, President Franklin Delano Roosevelt signed the Fair Labor Standards Act, placing limits on most forms of child labor outside agriculture. This left many American children, especially city kids, with little reason to avoid school, and their parents with every reason to encourage them to attend. The shift toward mass education transformed a nation of rustic one-room schoolhouses into a nation of "school systems" directed at the needs of a bustling industrial economy.

With the rise of industry, public schools became focused on job readiness. (Education for its own sake was reserved for elites, most of whom sent their children to private schools.) Ellwood Cubberley, dean of the Stanford University School of Education from 1917 to 1933, described public schools approvingly as "factories in which the raw products [children] are to be shaped and fashioned into products to meet the various demands of life." Theodore Search, president of the National Association of Manufacturers, heartily endorsed this view, declaring the prime product of public education to be "skilled hands and trained minds for the conduct of our industries and commerce." Reverend Frederick T. Gates, adviser to John D. Rockefeller Sr., whose General Education Board funded public schools with millions of dollars, extolled a "country school of tomorrow" where "the people yield themselves with perfect docility to our moulding hand. . . . We shall not try to make these people or any of their children into philosophers or men of learning or of science. We are not to raise up from among them authors, orators, poets, or men of letters. We shall not search for embryo great artists, painters, musicians. Nor will we cherish even the humbler ambition to raise up from among them lawyers, doctors, preachers, politicians, statesmen, of whom we now have ample supply." By the early twentieth century, many public schools were unabashedly hierarchal, with the mostly female teachers lorded over by the mostly male superintendents acting as de facto CEOs.

Yet, despite this push by industry to "train up" the masses for factory jobs, a "mass production" model of schooling was not universally embraced. Indeed, in some rural areas this model was impractical if not preposterous, as most adults earned their living from the land and expected the same of their children. Meanwhile, many forward-thinking reformers argued that education was not about turning children into industrial fodder but about guiding them across a threshold of independent thought. And yet, the myth of the school as factory remains. The charge that American schools did once and continue to treat students like so many widgets on an assembly line has become the stuff of rousing TED talks and the basis for public policy on both sides of the aisle. Here's the view of Obama administration secretary of education Arne Duncan: "Our K–12 system largely still adheres to the century-old, industrial-age factory model of education. A century ago, maybe it made sense. . . . But the factory model of education is the wrong model for the 21st century." And here's Trump administration secretary of education Betsy DeVos speaking in Texas in 2015: "It's a battle of Industrial Age versus the Digital Age. It's the Model T versus the Tesla. It's old factory model versus the new Internet model. It's the Luddites versus the future."

As anyone who has stepped foot in an actual factory knows, few if any American schools are modeled on factories, and not many actual teachers are Luddites. Indeed, the most factory-like elements—strict standards and rigid assessment tools—are the very things promoters of so-called educational reform declare we need "more" of to meet twenty-first-century demands. Here's DeVos again:

> We must open up the education industry—and let's not kid ourselves that it isn't an industry—we must open it up to entrepreneurs and innovators. . . . We are the beneficiaries of start-ups, ventures, and innovation in every other area of life, but we don't have that in education because it's a closed system, a closed industry, a closed market. It's a monopoly, a dead end. And the best and brightest innovators and risk-takers steer way clear of it. As long as education remains a closed system, we will never see the education equivalents of Google, Facebook, Amazon, PayPal, Wikipedia, or Uber.

DeVos's characterization of public education as an "industry" ripe for disruption is consistent with that of corporate school reformers on both sides of the political aisle. Prominent among their claims is that more formal training—especially in math and science—is key to success in the digital age and that schools must be prepared to deliver this training with ever greater rigor and efficiency. But while this seems sensible, it's not enough—for the relationship between education and work is less linear than these advocates acknowledge.

In their important and widely praised book *The Race Between Education and Technology*, Harvard economists Claudia Goldin and Lawrence Katz offer an insightful analysis of the coevolution of educational attainment and income growth in the United States from 1890 to 2005. Though I'm not quite sure it was the authors' intention, their insights remind us that more education per se is not necessarily the cure for our nation's work disorder. For they point to what seems a cruel irony: namely, that the market value of higher education is greatest when the opportunity to become highly educated is scarcest.

To clarify this principle, it helps to take a look back to a time when very few Americans had much formal education: in the late 1800s less than 6 percent of Americans had a high school degree. That degree was valuable. Clerks with a high school degree earned nearly 1.7 times as much as did those without one. Degreed managers fared even better, earning nearly 2.4 times as much as did managers with no degree. Naturally, this wage differential encouraged more Americans to complete high school, and they did. And true to the principle of supply and demand, as the number of graduates rose, their wage premium fell. In the late 1920s, as high school attendance soared and nearly 30 percent of Americans had a high school degree, clerks with a degree earned only slightly more than did their non-degreed colleagues. Once education was no longer scarce, the market value of education declined, and a high school diploma was no longer considered a "golden ticket" to prosperity.

This makes perfect sense—things that are or seem scarce in relation to their demand, like gold and truffles and dermatologists, are pricey. Things that are or seem less scarce in relation to their demand, like wood pulp and saltwater and writers, are far less so.

So why, throughout the first nine decades of the twentieth century, did the rise in average educational attainment coincide with a dramatic reduction in income inequality? The quick answer is that while the rich often got richer, so did many other people. This was due in part to the rise of labor unions that fought hard to ensure that even low-skilled workers earned a living wage. But it was also due to the more subtle and perhaps counterintuitive factor we've already touched upon: the relative decline in the market value of education as more people acquire it. Roughly put, technology brought an increased demand for educated workers, but that demand was consistently outpaced by the number of people prepared to meet it. As a consequence, wages for white- and blue-collar workers rose nearly in tandem. As economist and Illinois senator Paul Douglas forecast in the 1920s: "Gradually, the former monopolistic advantages are being squeezed out of white collar work, and eventually there will be no surplus left."

The Gilded Age of the late nineteenth century brought a new class of capitalists, and an unprecedented concentration of wealth that many observers of the time found alarming. In response, the government pioneered a very progressive estate tax on large fortunes and a progressive income tax. As a result of these taxes and other reforms and factors from 1910 through 1970 inequality declined, but since then has made its steady creep higher. Economists Katz and Goldin attribute this rise in income inequality to an "educational slowdown," a decline in educational attainment that continued into the early 2000s. They reasoned that a lack of education made it difficult for many Americans to find and sustain good jobs in a global economy that, they and many others contend, demanded ever more sophisticated skills, in particular computer skills. They suggested as remedy more public investments in schools and teachers and new policies to enable more young people to complete their education at the highest level possible.

Few challenged or even questioned these assertions, for two reasons. First, they came from a pair of Harvard economists of great renown and stature. Second, public education has throughout our history been both our crowning glory and our whipping boy. While Americans generally agree on the value of education, the claim that the US educational system has failed to stand up to the demands of the high-tech economy holds enormous appeal, especially to leaders in the business community who have for generations bemoaned the nation's "poorly educated" workforce. The charge that it is the poor quality of the American educational system that is to blame for the very un-American disparities between rich and poor is particularly attractive.

To be clear, I agree with Katz and Goldin that investments in higher education are and have always been critical, for any number of reasons. But while education and plenty of it is vital, it appears to have a limited impact on income inequality, because in recent years, the challenge of educating most of our citizenry through high school and much of it through college has been met. In 2007 high school graduation rates started to rise, and in 2015 they topped out at 91 percent of adults ages twenty-five to thirty-four. Yet, rather then declare victory, many pundits set their sights higher, on college attainment. President Obama went so far as to call a college degree an "economic imperative that every family in America has to be able to afford." Americans strove hard to rise to that challenge: at this writing, a record 33.4 percent of Americans hold at least a bachelor's degree. With the exception of South Koreans, more of us attend college than do citizens of any other nation, and we pay heavily for the privilege. We make that financial sacrifice because we believe—and have reason to believe—it will enhance our value in the workforce. And few of us question that belief. But let's reopen that question and think back to the clerks of the early 1900s. As more clerks acquired a degree, its financial value *to them* declined. (I'm not suggesting that the actual value of the degree declined, or that its value to society declined, but only that its relative monetary value to the holder declined.) In similar fashion, as the number of college-educated Americans grows, the average market value of a bachelor's degree to its holder has since the start of this century been in steady decline.

Again, this is not to suggest that education is not desirable, even essential—I've encouraged my own children to acquire as much as they can stomach, but not because I believe it will necessarily enhance their employability or "market value. Yes, degrees from a handful of elite colleges and universities are associated with a significant lifetime earning premium. But it's important to distinguish between association and cause. Does an elite education per se increase earnings, or is it that students who pursue an elite education are simply more likely to be high earners? Social scientists took a hard look at that question and found that after differences in ambition and motivation are controlled for, the lifetime earnings of graduates of elite and nonelite institutions are about the same. Ambitious, driven students are more likely to attend elite institutions, and it is these personality traits—not necessarily the institution they attend—that better predict success. One surprising bit of supporting evidence is that the selectivity of the colleges from which applicants are *rejected* is twice as predictive of their future incomes as is the selectivity of the college from which they graduated. While it's impossible to know why this is the case, some speculate that the traits motivating a student to apply to a top-tier school—in particular self-confidence—correlate with traits that predict job success.

So in the case of higher education—even elite higher education—it's unclear whether the critical factor behind success in the workplace is the education itself or something else signaled by that education. Given that no experiment can be done to test that question, there is no certain answer. But what is certain is that any child born into wealth has a substantial advantage in accessing advanced education of any sort, and especially an elite education. In one well-documented study, children from families in the top quintile of income were *seven to eight* times more likely to attend a highly selective college than were children from families in the bottom quintile. Disturbingly, black and Hispanic students were significantly less likely than white and Asian students to attend elite colleges *even when family income was controlled for.* That is, students from wealthy black and Hispanic families had a lower chance of attending an elite college than did students from middle-class white families.

It's no secret that higher education comes at a price that is increasingly out of reach for middle-class Americans, even at public institutions. Since the 2008 recession, many states have slashed education funding, and the cuts have spurred public universities to seek nonresident students, who pay roughly 150 percent the amount paid by in-state students. In 2017, an astonishing 59 percent of the freshman enrolled at the University of Alabama hailed from out of state, making the university one of ten state "flagships" where a majority of students came from families that did not pay taxes in that state. This stampede of out-of-state students forces out untold numbers of in-state residents, who are left to search elsewhere for an affordable education. And, unfortunately, community colleges do not offer a surefire refuge.

In recent years, Sallie Mae has reported a jump in community college attendance by students from families with substantial incomes—42 percent of students at two-year colleges who depend on family support come from households with incomes of $65,000 or more, and fully 17 percent from families with an income of $100,000 or more. This influx of higher-income students has resulted in some low-income students, most of whom attend college part time, getting closed out of classes. Some of the poorest have been lured to for-profit colleges, until recently the fastest-growing sector in higher education. Incredibly, nearly half of all dependent students at for-profit colleges come from households with less than $30,000 in annual income. The graduation rate at for-profit institutions is extremely low—only about one in four entering students manage to earn a diploma within six years of entrance. In 2015, roughly 47 percent of all student loan defaults involved for-profits, and for-profits consumed one in four federal student aid dollars.

Clearly, Americans make enormous sacrifices—financial and otherwise—to attend colleges and universities, and for good reason: the higher education "earnings premium" is such a staple of public discourse that we've come to take it for granted. But is it real? The short answer is "It depends." The *average* incomes of those who graduate from high school and college are substantially higher than the *average* incomes of those who don't. But averages aren't always meaningful and in fact can be deceiving. To illustrate, let's have a look at what statisticians sometimes refer to as the "Bill Gates effect."

The "Bill Gates effect" comes into play in calculations by which outliers are included in the determination of averages. For example, let's say it's Friday night, and ten friends gather for drinks and darts at Joe's Bar and Grill. (For the purposes of this exercise, let's agree that these ten are the only patrons in the bar that night.) The annual income of these friends ranges from $25,000 for Tom, a budding musician, to $65,000 for Susan, an accountant. Let's say their average income is roughly $43,000. (The average is calculated by adding together everyone's income and dividing it by the number of people—in this case, ten.) At 10 p.m. Tom is just getting started, but Susan decides to call it a night. As Susan leaves, Bill Gates walks in the door and joins the fun. Suddenly, the "average" income in that bar soars from $43,000 to hundreds of millions of dollars. Naturally, the entry of Bill Gates into the bar does not raise the actual income of any patron. So, in fact, the *average income* of this group offers no real indication of the financial well-being of any one of the old friends now enjoying free drinks, thanks to Bill Gates.

In the above case, Bill Gates is the outlier, not only the richest person in the bar but one of the richest people in the world. In the case of education, elite graduates of elite institutions are the outliers not only of college graduates but of college graduates with gold-plated credentials. It's not uncommon for graduates of the top fifty or so state and private colleges and universities to enjoy incomes three to four times those of graduates of institutions ranked just a step or two below. This relative handful of "winners" skew the average, but they do not represent or improve the fortunes of the vast majority of college grads, who may or may not find success. The bottom line is this: higher educational attainment generally correlates with higher incomes, but it is not necessarily the cause of those higher incomes. And here's a bit of evidence that suggests that a college education may not be the powerful driver of fortunes it once was: since 2000 the wage gap between workers with at least a college degree and those with only a high school degree has slowed to a halt, with the bottom 25 percent of college graduates earning on average no more than do high school graduates. As we've noted, college dropouts do even worse, often earning less than high school graduates. From this it appears that college attendance that results in no degree may present a serious risk to vulnerable low-income students. College attendance can actually serve as a roadblock, saddling young people with debt while having little effect—or even a negative effect—on their lifetime earnings. (Student loan debt in the United States had soared to $1.36 trillion by September 2017, and it appears that roughly 22 percent of borrowers are having great difficulty repaying it.) Rather than offering promise, for some, education and its demands loom as a threat.

In the course of researching this book, I encountered many surprises, but none more counterintuitive than this: a college degree of almost any kind is worth not more but *less* to people born poor. Yes, you read that right: a college degree is—on average—of less value to the less privileged than to the privileged. This unexpected and startling revelation was made by economists Tim Bartik and Brad Hershbein of the W. E. Upjohn Institute for Employment Research, while they were scouring the Panel Study of Income Dynamics (PSID). Since 1968 the PSID has conducted yearly or biyearly interviews with eighteen thousand individuals from five thousand families around the United States to track their employment status, income, financial holdings, expenditures, health, and education. Through this unique instrument, Bartik and Hershbein were able to follow the life trajectory of children born into poor, middle-class, and wealthy families. They sorted high school graduates from college graduates in these socioeconomic groups, then compared the average earnings of each of these groups as they aged, from twenty-five to sixty-four. What they found was that a college degree did not benefit all subjects equally. Middle-class adult degree holders raised in middle-class families earned 162 percent more over their careers than did adults raised in middle-class families who did not have a degree. So for people born into middle-class families, a college degree appeared to be a wise investment. But for those born into poverty, the results were far less impressive. People born poor who managed to get a degree earned only slightly more than did those born middle class who did not obtain a degree. And over time, even this small "degree bonus" ebbed away: in middle age, college graduates who started life poor had on average *lower* incomes than did nondegree holders born into the middle class. The scholars conclude: "Our key finding is that the proportional increase in career earnings from obtaining a bachelor's degree, relative to a high school diploma, is much smaller for individuals from lower-income families compared to those from higher-income families. . . . Individuals from poorer backgrounds may be encountering a glass ceiling that even a bachelor's degree does not break."

This phenomenon is not unique to the United States. As noted earlier, South Korea is the world's largest producer of college graduates per capita, and at last count, over 50 percent of the total unemployed population in South Korea have college degrees. There, the "education premium" seems no longer to apply: the average lifetime earnings of college graduates in South Korea have recently sunk below those of high school graduates.

Once again, this is largely a matter of supply and demand: workers generally command higher wages when their demand exceeds their supply. The most recent statistics show that roughly 35 percent of the US workforce and 37 percent of young adults hold a bachelor's degree, a huge leap forward by almost any measure. Unfortunately, according to the US Bureau of Labor Statistics, fewer than 20 percent of US jobs require a bachelor's degree. And while the jobs of today are not necessarily the jobs of tomorrow, consider this: the Bureau of Labor Statistics predicts that in 2026 at least 64 percent of jobs will require no education beyond high school, compared with 25 percent of jobs that will likely require a four-year college degree.

Our real education "mismatch" may be of a sort many of us prefer not to consider—that we are educating our citizens for jobs that simply do not and will not exist. If so, the so-called college degree premium may really be a "no-college-degree" penalty—that is, it's not that a degree per se gives us the leverage to build a better working life, it's that not having a degree decreases whatever leverage we might otherwise have. This distinction is no mere semantic quibble. It is key to understanding the uneasy and growing chasm between educational attainment and employment. For many if not most of us, it's not our education per se that determines our employment trajectory so much as where that education positions us in relation to others.

So what role does education—or the lack of it—truly play in employment? That's a complicated question, and to many people a painful one. Anyone who has looked for a job in recent years, or knows someone who has, is aware of what economists call "credential creep." At this writing, nearly half of all recent college graduates are underemployed in the sense that they are employed in functions for which a college degree is not required. A casual glance at almost any online job site suggests that a college degree has become a vetting mechanism, a way to quickly exclude a category of applicant that—perhaps not incidentally—includes a large fraction of the traditionally underserved. The number of restaurant servers with college degrees grew by 81 percent from 2000 to 2010 according to US Census Bureau figures, while janitors with college degrees rose by 87 percent. Burning Glass, a company that analyzes employment notices, reported in 2015 that 65 percent of postings for executive secretaries and executive assistants called for a bachelor's degree, a credential held by only 19 percent of those *currently* employed in these roles. There's a solid chance that the young man or woman inspecting your rental car for dings will be paying off his or her college loans for years to come: with the exception of military veterans, Enterprise Rent-A-Car requires all its rental agents to have both a college degree and experience. Over half of all Uber drivers hold at least a bachelor's degree. And this trend shows no signs of reversing. The Bureau of Labor Statistics reports that of the ten occupations projected to have the most job growth through 2026, only one—registered nurse—requires a college degree and six—personal care aides, restaurant waitstaff, janitors and cleaners, general laborers, home health aides, and food preparers—do not technically require a high school diploma.

Most Americans who attend college do not attend selective colleges for the very reason that most American institutions of higher learning are not selective—the vast majority of colleges and universities report accepting at least one of every two applicants, and many accept nearly all applicants. This implies that many students who are not truly college ready are admitted, an implication made real by the fact that 68 percent of those who attend non-selective colleges fail to graduate. College dropouts, even those with two or three years of post–high school education, enjoy little if any of the so-called college premium. On its face this makes no sense: after all, it's not the sheepskin that should enhance job opportunities and performance but the knowledge and abilities that the sheepskin represents. Under this logic, real-world success would correlate with the number and quality of courses a student has completed, not with degree attainment per se. But this is decidedly not the case. The Bureau of Labor Statistics reports that college attendees who fail to graduate actually have lower earning prospects than do those who have no college at all. The fact that college attendance has the potential to *decrease* lifetime earnings suggests that college-level knowledge is not necessarily what employers require. Instead, it is likely that at least some employers are using a college degree as a sorting mechanism, and not an unbiased one. Since students from high-income families are eight times as likely to earn a bachelor's degree by age twenty-four than are students from low-income families, this sorting process almost inevitably discriminates against low-income job applicants and contributes to—and perpetuates—the nation's income gap.

In his landmark 1977 study *Learning to Labor: How Working Class Kids Get Working Class Jobs*, British sociologist Paul Willis relates the true story of a group of teenage boys growing up in a place he called "Hammertown," a hardscrabble factory town where workers far outnumbered opportunities. He wrote that the "lads" rebelled against school authorities, believing that their future lay not in books or office jobs but in the blue-collar work of their fathers. These "lads" were scornful of what Willis called the "work hard, move forward" educational system they believed would bring them at best a humiliating low-wage desk job. These students did poorly in school, and most of them dropped out. They failed not because they were lazy or dimwitted but because the standards of educational success of the time were proscribed by a system geared to satisfy the demands of employers rather than to build on individual capabilities, values, and strengths.

Willis writes, "Prevented [by the school] from pursuing alternative flowerings of their capacities or subversive courses of growth, credentialism enslaves their powers and seeks to trap them in the foothills of human development. . . . The proliferation of qualifications is simply a worthless inflation of the currency of credentialism, and advance through it, a fraudulent offer to the majority of what can really mean something only to the few."

The key here is the final phrase—the "fraudulent offer to the majority of what can really mean something only to the few." The "lads" had grown up in a culture built on a working-class repertoire of practical knowledge, life experience, and street smarts, all of which had become devalued. What they objected to was not education per se, but education that had become a proxy for inherited privilege rather than a scaffold on which to construct a life of privilege.

As we've seen, today more than a third of all Americans between the ages of twenty-five and thirty-four have a college degree, and 70 percent of all high school graduates have at least some college experience. Hence, Americans have more formal education than ever before, while at the same time average incomes have all but flattened and poverty rates remain stubbornly high. How to account for this apparent paradox? Jeannette Wicks-Lim is a labor economist at the University of Massachusetts at Amherst who specializes in issues of poverty and race. She explained that through much of our nation's history education was indeed key to economic advance; for example, a well-educated farmer or tradesperson or clerk was better able to adapt to new technologies. But today the demand for a relatively small number of highly trained specialists—especially in the tech and financial sectors—has led to the overselling of education as a prerequisite of employment. "The percentage of Americans making $10 or less has remained constant for three decades—it's stuck at 25 percent of the workforce," she told me. "This despite the fact that our workforce is about twice as productive as it was in 1980, when only 40 percent of Americans had any college experience, and only one in six had a degree."

Here's how dramatically things have changed: If you were born in 1940, it's highly likely—better than nine chances out of ten—that your lifetime earnings were greater than your father's. But if you were born in 1985, you have only a 50 percent chance of exceeding your father's lifetime earnings. Most of this change is due not to any educational deficits; on the contrary, the younger you are, the more likely you are to have a college degree. Rather, the bulk of this change is due to an unequal distribution of economic growth. In his magisterial history of economic inequality, *Capital in the Twenty-First Century*, economist Thomas Piketty concludes that among a number of possible factors underlying income disparity, "the educational factor does not seem to be the right one to focus on."

Of the many ways we Americans manifest our boundless optimism, a commitment to universal education ranks near the top. It should remain there. Preparing young minds is a vital exercise, one we must continue to pursue with vigor, creativity, and humility. But the insistence that more education on its own necessarily enhances earning prospects is not only wrong, it's cruel, saddling too many of us with unrealistic prospects and crippling debt.

Business-backed education "reformers" have every right to make their needs known and to advocate for them through their lobbies and foundations. They have every right to participate in public debates and discussions and to give voice to their collective desires and needs. They have every right to exert their influence and to push for their interests and those of their stockholders and supporters. But they should never be mistaken for impartial arbiters of public policy aimed at shaping how America learns to labor. For that, we must turn our attention elsewhere.

MIND THE (SKILLS) GAP

When demand is constraining an economy, there is little to
be gained from increasing potential supply.

—LARRY SUMMERS

A year or so after they were married, Leroy and Susan lived with
their infant daughter in her great-grandmother's house in Chicago's Roseland district, a subprime patch of real estate on the
city's South Side stretching well beyond the reach of the elevated
train service. Roseland had once been a prosperous place, home to
thousands of steelworkers. But those factories were long gone, and
with them the prospects of residents like Leroy and Susan who had
reason to believe that their life would be better were it to include a
functioning kitchen. For that, they needed work. And for the last
year or so, work didn't seem to need them.

They'd heard the promises of politicians to bring the "jobs
home." But neither Leroy nor Susan took those promises seriously.
No matter what they saw on TV or read online, they were fairly sure
factory jobs weren't coming back. Actually, they were too young
to think of factory jobs as anything but over. The last factory in
their neighborhood—the old Sherwin-Williams paint plant—had
been closed for more than twenty years. And they didn't know any-
body who worked in a factory, so factory work had never figured
in their life plans. They were educated and had skills. Leroy had

a high school degree and years working construction, sometimes managing the projects. Susan had a GED and a pile of credits from a community college. They sought out almost every position posted for which they qualified, including entry-level jobs at Sears, Walmart, and Target. Mostly they applied online, as required. They sometimes found this process intimidating, but not for the reasons some employers claim. They had no difficulty reading and understanding the questions, no trouble doing the math, no trouble operating the computer—there was no "digital divide" keeping them from a job. It was the subtext that stumped them. Here are a couple of questions on a Target job application:

> "Do you think your parents are proud of you?"
> "Have you ever applied for food stamps?"

What is the "correct" answer to questions like these? If you suggest that your parents are "proud," does that make you seem confident or arrogant? If you admit to using food stamps, does that make you sound sensible or unworthy? Leroy and Susan simply could not crack that code.

Some of us might have theories as to why people like Susan and Leroy fail to get a foothold in the digital economy—notably, that they lack the proper attitude and/or education and/or skills. But few of us base these judgments on direct observation or evidence. Among the few who do, Johns Hopkins University sociologist Kathryn Edin stands out, and, I guess you'd also say, apart.

Edin bears an uncanny resemblance to Ellen DeGeneres—blue eyes, lightly tousled blond bob, a guileless, all-American grin. And like Ellen, she was raised with religion. She grew up in rural Staples, Minnesota, where she spent her spare adolescent hours at a local trailer park, scouting fresh recruits for the Sunday school at Evangelical Covenant Church. It was a small and very poor church, she told me, where "you didn't have to clean up to show up." Her mother drove the Sunday school van.

Kathryn played the bass drum in the Staples High School marching band, squinting through "inch-thick" glasses. She was chosen by the Rotary Club to represent Ireland in the Model United Nations. After graduating from high school, she left Minnesota for Chicago to study social work at North Park, a Christian college popular with first-generation Swedish immigrants. Kathryn was second-generation and a good Lutheran. She marched barefoot around campus on snowy evenings to emulate St. Francis of Assisi. She earned extra credit tutoring kids at Cabrini-Green Homes, a 3,600-unit public housing project notorious for gangs and seemingly random murders. And after getting her social work degree she took a job, as she knew she was supposed to. Then she had second thoughts. "The graduate fellowship Northwestern offered paid better," she recalled. "So I took it."

Edin searched hard at Northwestern, seeing what other scholars declined to see. Funding and status at the time gravitated toward data analysis, and it was on data that most poverty experts focused. But Edin turned her attention beyond data and listened to people's stories. And given her personal history and experiences, what she heard did not really surprise her. "Poor people," she told me, "are pretty much like the rest of us."

Edin's dissertation, "There's a Lot of Month Left at the End of the Money," had all the pathos of a country-western ballad. An ethnographic account of twenty-five Chicago families struggling to get by on public assistance, it pretty much shattered the myth of the "welfare queen." Of the many families Edin got to know personally, few received a government subsidy large enough to cover the basics of food, rent, and utilities. Most earned extra money off the books—cleaning houses, picking through garbage to collect bottles and cans for recycling, and—if they saw no choice—selling drugs and/or sexual favors. Parents, mothers mainly, did what it took to make ends meet while raising their children as best they could, which was not always the way they wished they could. Edin's dissertation ended on this plaintive note: "Of the welfare clients I observed, most work as hard as their middle-class counterparts." The difficulties of the very poor, she argued, stemmed not from a reluctance to work but from something very close to the opposite: a system that undermined their every effort to do so.

Edin has empathy for her subjects, and affinity. She has two adopted daughters, young women of color whose biological mothers loved them but were in no position to care for them. Experiencing this and other things has led Edin to doubt easy assumptions and to seek deeper truths. She's spent years listening to mothers and fathers in the poorest neighborhoods of Chicago, Boston, Charleston, San Antonio, Baltimore, Philadelphia, and Camden, New Jersey. And while these people differed in many ways, they had one thing in common: every one of them was praying for good work.

"In America, work is about citizenship," Edin said. "Without work, you're not really considered a citizen."

Edin gives a lot of public talks, and she often begins by asking audience members how many Americans they think get Temporary Assistance for Needy Families, the government subsidy we know as "welfare." While observing one of these events, I heard someone shout out "54 percent." Edin agreed that political rhetoric made that estimate sound reasonable. But it was way, way too high. The actual figure was less than 1 percent.

"Welfare is all but dead in America," Edin told me. "Poor folks are trying so hard to hang on to the edge of a labor market, a market that does not offer enough jobs. And the quality of the jobs has become so fundamentally degraded.... The majority of households living in poverty include at least one adult with a job. What this tells me is that something is very wrong with work."

For more than a quarter century, the nation's largest antipoverty scheme has been the Earned Income Tax Credit (EITC), a subsidy put in place in 1975 aimed at low- to moderate-income *workers* to offset the payroll tax, and rising food and energy costs. Beneficiaries of this government largesse must have a job. Many people consider that a good thing, and it can be: the Internal Revenue Service reports that the EITC lifts six million Americans, half of them children, out of poverty every year. And as a tax refund, the EITC does not carry the stigma of welfare. But because it arrives only once a year during refund season, it often comes too late to help struggling families, many of whom go into deep debt while waiting for the check to arrive. Even more problematic is that the government leaves recipients no choice but to take any job they can get, including the sort of precarious, low-wage gigs that made and keep them poor. Many nations insist that families have a bit of lee-way when the children are still in diapers, but the United States is not one of them. We require most every able-bodied parent to sing for his or her child's supper, even when that supper is a bottle of in-fant formula. And we built this requirement on the fantasy of the wide availability of stable, living-wage jobs. Edin calls this wishful thinking "toxic alchemy."

The EITC forces people to take jobs they might otherwise prefer not to take for reasons with which many of us would sympathize— for example, a lack of affordable day care. And like most policies that increase the labor supply, the EITC is as much a subsidy to employers as it is to workers. Because it incentivizes more people, no matter their skills, to accept any job they can get, it reduces the need for employers to create better jobs, or to open up better jobs to people closed out of them, people who may lack credentials or a certain pedigree but who, like Susan and Leroy, are willing and able to work. "The idea that a lack of skills is preventing many people from working their way out of poverty is wrong," Edin said. "'Skills' is a smokescreen for other things."

Randall Collins prefers to substitute the word *scam* for *smoke-screen*. Professor emeritus at the University of Pennsylvania, Col-lins is one of the nation's most eminent sociologists, and a keen observer of human nature. Among his earliest memories is living in Berlin, where his father worked as a foreign service officer, at the end of the Second World War. It was then that he learned that many things are not what authorities claim them to be. "There's nothing like the diplomatic world for this stark contrast between what happens on the very formal idealized front stage and what happens backstage," he said.

Collins pointed out that employers have bemoaned the quality of the American worker since the dawn of the industrial age. Indeed, in the late 1800s, Frederick Taylor based his influential theory of "scientific management" on the assumption that some workers were barely human. As Taylor saw it, "One of the very first requirements for a man who is fit to handle pig iron as a regular occupation is that he shall be so stupid and so phlegmatic that he more nearly resembles in his mental make-up the ox than any other type."

While it's no longer acceptable to compare workers to farm animals, it is acceptable—even typical—to insist that not enough of us are up to the stringent demands of work in the digital age. Americans are so lumpish, the theory goes, as to constitute a sort of stumbling block to innovation that would otherwise boost the economy and—ultimately—create more jobs. By this reasoning, workers are all but unemploying themselves by not rising to the opportunities progress has granted.

This "skills gap" argument is a particular favorite of politicians and business leaders. When asked why his products were not manufactured in the United States, Apple CEO Tim Cook famously responded: "It's skill . . . the US over time began to stop having as many vocational kinds of skills." Cook's view was backed up by data from corporate lobbyists: namely, a 2011 survey conducted by the National Association of Manufacturers (NAM), an industry organization that lambasted the Obama-era labor regulations as "job killers." The NAM reports that 74 percent of manufacturers cite "a lack of skilled production workers" as a significant "negative impact" factor on their bottom line. This "skills gap" finding was so widely quoted that it became a sort of cultural meme. But other than the say-so of employers, there was little if any evidence to support the vague and slippery claim.

"Decades ago, critics complained that Americans were too stupid to work in factories," Collins said. "Now, they complain that Americans are too stupid to work in retail stores or warehouses, or write code. There's just no end to their griping, and very little evidence that it's justified."

Given the attention lavished on the "skills crisis," it seems remarkable that actual data linking skill demand with hiring became available only in 2016, thanks to the efforts of Paul Osterman of MIT and Andrew Weaver of the University of Illinois. The researchers focused on manufacturing in part because manufacturing firms, along with the NAM lobby, were among the loudest voices on the issue. In their seminal study "Skill Demands and Mismatch in U.S. Manufacturing," the economists surveyed companies to find what—if any—skills were truly lacking in the US manufacturing sector. They asked each firm the following questions: What skills do you demand of your production workers? What is the incidence of hiring difficulties (potential skill gaps)? What factors, including skill demands, predict these hiring difficulties? And what stories about skills and skill gaps are consistent with the observed patterns?

Of the 2,700 manufacturers surveyed, 903 responded. Roughly three-quarters of these companies reported that their core production staff were required to have basic reading and math skills, and 62 percent of companies required basic word processing and Internet search skills. No companies required skills that exceeded the grasp of a respectable high school graduate, or, for that matter, a good many high school dropouts. And here's the kicker—63 percent reported having no vacancies at all, and more than 76 percent reported having no long-term vacancies. Only 16 percent cited "lack of access to skilled workers" as a "major obstacle to financial success." But it was not sophisticated "digital age" skills that this 16 percent were after—there were plenty of applicants who could program computers and engage in critical thinking. What was in relatively short supply were employees willing to take on low-paid jobs requiring only the most basic skills—reading, writing, and math on a junior high school level. The problem was not that workers lacked skills but rather that employers could not find enough workers with even the most basic skills willing to take their low-paid jobs.

Osterman and Weaver do not discuss the reasons for this difficulty in attracting low-skilled workers, and it remains something of a mystery. But I believe I found at least part of the answer in Brodhead, Kentucky, a small town at the head of the Dix River about an hour's drive from Lexington. I went there to visit Bobby and Tammy Renner and their four grown children, one of whom, Robert, we'll meet later on, in chapter 10.

When we met, Bobby and Tammy were both forty-nine years old and juggled tough jobs—Tammy as a health care aide at a rehabilitation facility for mentally challenged adults, and Bobby as a laborer at AGC Flat Glass in Richmond. Tammy worked the 11 p.m. to 7 a.m. shift, and though her charges should have been asleep at that time, they often weren't. "One night a patient hit an aide on the head with a chair, and she had to be hospitalized," she told me. "That aide never came back. I believe we should get hazard pay, but I wouldn't dare say that to my supervisor. I need this job."

Bobby worked twelve-hour shifts at the glass factory—4 a.m. to 4 p.m. four days a week. He preferred this schedule, as it freed him up one weekday to care for his beloved granddaughter, whose photos pretty much dominated Bobby's Facebook page. Bobby had worked the job for nineteen years, and he was proud of his near-perfect attendance record. He was also proud of his wage of $18 an hour, more than he could imagine pulling down anywhere else. "We don't want unions," he told me over coffee in the family kitchen. "If the unions came, management would just pick up and move to Mexico." I asked Bobby if his boss had trouble finding workers, and he said yes, sometimes. Part of the reason, he said, was that the job was very hard on the body. He then paused to thank Jesus that at his advanced age he was still able to handle it. After a minute or two, I asked, why don't younger people apply? "Some folks are born lazy, and that's a fact," he said. As for the others, well, "They know they can't pass that drug test."

Hauling and packing glass can be dangerous, made all the more so if an employee is high. That risk is significant: Kentucky is one of the top five states for death by drug overdose. And while many states have laws that regulate or prohibit drug testing in the private sector, Kentucky employers are free to implement testing policies at their own discretion.

Not everyone approves of the practice, especially since evidence of drug use can linger in urine and hair for days or even weeks, meaning that recreational use of marijuana on the weekend may disqualify an otherwise qualified job candidate. In Kentucky, one man I met at a café summed up a common objection: "Coming to work drunk, now that's a problem. But smoking a joint on the weekend? Whose business is that?"

Drug testing of employees has its roots in the experience of the world's largest employer, the US Department of Defense. In 1980, 27 percent of surveyed military personnel admitted to illicit drug use in the previous month. This alarming finding prompted the military to start testing, and five years later illicit drug use by DOD employees dropped to 9 percent. This success moved President Ronald Reagan to sign the 1986 Drug-Free Workplace Act, requiring that all federal employees refrain from illicit drug use both on and off the job, and mandating testing to make sure they did. By the mid-1990s tests were routine at more than 80 percent of all US companies. When illicit drug use started to decline through the early 2000s, workplace testing declined with it—only to rise again in the early 2010s. Today, nearly half of all US companies, including most Fortune 500 companies, require candidates to pass a drug test as a condition of employment, and their employees to submit to random drug tests while on the job.

Applicants failing to pass drug tests are seen as a serious obstacle to filling job vacancies. A few small companies around Kentucky have gone so far as to welcome recovering drug addicts to join their firms, even offering them paid time off to gather in support groups. So, in Kentucky at least, the gap is not in skills so much as in sobriety.

While AGC Glass and similar employers may not be what most of us think of when we think of the future of work, perhaps they should be. Paul Beaudry, the outspoken Canadian economist we met in an earlier chapter, put it starkly: "New technology tends to be biased *against* most cognitive tasks. Perhaps this will change in the future. But for now, there is no indication that technology is making jobs more demanding, and every indication that it's decreasing the need for skill."

Consider banking, an industry sector that demands both a good head for numbers and strong customer service skills. In 2013, Wells Fargo opened its first high-tech "neighborhood bank" branch in Washington, DC, featuring an array of fancy ATMs called "Store Teller Machines" (STMs). The STMs "memorize" customers' preferences and conduct roughly 80 percent of banking transactions. Service representatives are also there to help customers navigate the technology—for example, to deposit a check in the STM. If customers require a more complicated transaction, such as instruction in how to apply for a loan, the rep links them via technology to the appropriate specialist.

Thanks to STMs and related innovations, the banking sector is cited by some as paradigmatic of how technological progress eliminates old, lower-skilled jobs and creates new, higher-skilled jobs that pay better. And customer reps do in fact earn slightly higher salaries than do traditional bank tellers. But the reps aren't actually replacing the tellers, whose central function—cash handling—has been largely absorbed by ATMs and online banking. Rather, the reps use technology to decrease the need for other higher-skilled employees, like loan managers. Experts predict that the demand for skilled bank employees will continue to decline well into the future.

Okay, but what of the high-tech sector? Certainly, it seems it and related industries have a near endless demand for new employees. After all, in the summer of 2011, when unemployment hovered at a staggering 9.1 percent, New York senator Chuck Schumer and Texas senator John Cornyn opened a subcommittee hearing on immigration with a call to staple a green card to the diploma of every foreign graduate of an American university with a degree in science, engineering, or math. "As we all know," Cornyn said, "there is a scarcity of qualified people for many jobs, particularly those in high technology." The *New York Times* went on to call for colleges and universities to increase by ten thousand the seventy thousand or so engineers graduating annually from US institutions. Microsoft Corporation—one of the nation's largest employers of foreign citizens on temporary H1-B visas—requested that an *additional* twenty thousand visas and green cards be granted to qualified foreign graduates and that funds generated by those visas be applied to educate still more Americans in STEM disciplines.

Ron Hira, professor of public policy at Howard University, has for years been a sharp observer of these events. A native of India, he immigrated to the United States with his family as a child. Given his background, one might assume that he is sympathetic and supportive of foreign engineers and scientists immigrating to the United States, and he is sympathetic and supportive. But he is also frustrated over public pronouncements of a STEM "skills crisis," which he decries as a cover for self-interested parties to overproduce graduates, abuse the visa system, and outsource jobs. Even in electrical engineering—an occupation at the heart of high-tech innovation—US employment declined to about 324,600 in 2016, down from about 385,000 in 2002. Overall, the supply of STEM graduates, he told me, is two and perhaps even three times larger than demand, forcing many experienced engineers to seek jobs at the margins or even outside the science and technology sector. "We're not seeing indicators of a talent shortage, such as a significant increase in salaries, outside of some very confined specialty areas," he told me. Hira recalls once sitting through a congressional hearing on immigration, horrified as Microsoft Corporation's chief lawyer complained of a scarcity of qualified engineers. "That was about the same time Microsoft laid off five thousand employees," he said. And this disconnect is not just in computer science and engineering but in math, chemistry, biology, and other STEM fields. Not long ago a blue-ribbon panel of top scientists cautioned: "The training pipeline produces more scientists than relevant positions in academia, government and the private sector are capable of absorbing."

Economist Paul Krugman once coined the term *zombie idea* for beliefs that have been "repeatedly refuted with evidence and analysis but refuse to die." The skills gap is one of these zombie ideas, a meme so virulent that it has, as Krugman quips, "eaten our brains." To recognize this, we need only ignore the pundits and open up our minds. For when it comes to skills, Americans have a long history of rising to the occasion. During World War II, hundreds of thousands of critical positions went vacant as skilled workers got called into military service. The nation bridged that very real "skills gap" with some very real job-training programs. By the war's end, about 1.75 million Americans had been certified in Training Within Industry, a program designed to quickly equip civilians to fill essential roles at thousands of worksites across the country. The National Youth Administration trained young women, many of whom had never before held a job, to be electricians, welders, photographers, machinists, and radio repair specialists. Similarly, throughout the dot.com boom—the speculative investment boosting Internet companies between 1995 and 2000—Americans scrambled to gain the knowledge and skills they believed would bring them challenge and prosperity. Applications to computer science and engineering programs soared, as did enrollments. Somehow, Americans *could* do the math. But starting in roughly 2004, this pattern reversed, not because Americans became stupid but because job prospects changed. Unemployment for bachelor's-degreed computer scientists and electrical engineers at the time leapt to 6.2 percent, exceeding the general unemployment rate of 5.7 percent. Smart students preferred not to invest their hopes, efforts, and intellectual capital in sectors that—no matter the hype—dumped workers at the least provocation, sometimes only to replace them with cheaper workers, whether they be domestic or from abroad.

Americans tend to be rational actors, and we tend to follow the money. In recent decades, finance, insurance, and real estate have been juggernauts—growing from roughly 11.2 percent of GDP in the 1950s to more than 20 percent today. So it should come as no surprise that the most popular college major overall is business, and the most popular major at elite colleges and universities is economics. Elite graduates of these programs are attractive not because they are innovators or risk takers, but because they have demonstrated a willingness to focus their energy and time on their employers' explicit goal of making large sums of money. As one Harvard Business School professor told me, "We teach our people to squeeze the orange harder, not to grow a new sort of tree."

Peter Cappelli, professor of management at the Wharton School and author of *Why Good People Can't Get Jobs*, explained that employers seek candidates who can be "plugged" into the organization and can immediately "play" whatever game management requires. This "plug and play" strategy is favored because it vastly reduces the need for employee training. But this practice makes workers vulnerable to layoffs when the skills they have mastered grow outdated. "This is why the long-term unemployed have such difficulty finding work," Cappelli told me. "It's not because they can't do the job, it's because they *aren't* doing the job right now. There are plenty of people graduating with the appropriate degree, but many of them are green, they lack experience. And generally employers want at least two or three years of experience—they want people trained, but they don't want to train them."

The real story behind the so-called skills gap, some suspect, is the desire of businesses big and small for an an oversupply of talent that results in more competition among workers for any particular position, and thereby less need for employers to offer concessions to lure them. While this theory is difficult to prove, it is supported by ample circumstantial evidence. Roughly four million jobs are posted online every month, and an average of 245 candidates apply to each listing. Some employers complain that few if any of these 245 candidates are qualified. This may be true in some cases, perhaps in some glass factories in Kentucky. Yet the Federal Reserve reports that the number of jobs listed as available by employers typically vastly exceeds the number of actual job openings calculated by the Bureau of Labor Statistics. Some human resource professionals call these fake openings "ghost jobs."

A ghost job is born when a company posts a position for which it is not actively seeking candidates. Why would employers do such a thing? There are a number of reasons. For example, they may post in an effort to snag an elusive "unicorn," that rare superstar coder or marketer or "creative" who is not actually looking for a job but might make a move if offered the right incentives. Because there is no actual "opening" to fill, unicorn hunts can go on for months, even years, with no hires. Employers may also post fake openings to amass a large pool of résumés to which they can turn later to avoid having to pay a recruiter when an actual position opens up. As well, employers may post fake openings to signal their success to investors, media, and customers. Being in a position to hire, or appearing to be in that position, implies expansion, or at least implies that the company is not laying off workers or shrinking by attrition.

Where I live in New England, MathWorks, a maker of technical computing software, offers an example of a company that once posted job openings that didn't appear to actually exist. The company was famous around town for its public radio announcements of "more than two hundred job openings." Oddly that exact phrase—"more than two hundred"—remained fixed year after year. Many of us wondered how this was even possible. MathWorks is a highly reputable firm known for its first-rate products and services. With Harvard, MIT, Tufts, and dozens of other lofty universities within an hour's driving distance, why was this excellent company unable to find the qualified workers it seemed so eager to hire? One MathWorks employee involved in the hiring process leaked what seemed like a plausible answer. "Do not be frustrated if you do not get into MathWorks," he wrote some years ago on Glassdoor, a popular job website. "MathWorks gets a huge number of applications, and it rejects almost any applicant for no clear reason."

No clear reason. Susan and Leroy—the struggling married couple who introduced this chapter—know all about that. They do have high school degrees, focus, and skills. They spent months crafting job applications, consulting with friends to refine their message, making every attempt to convey their intention to work hard and well. And eventually their persistence paid off. Leroy got a thirty-hour-a-week job at a supermarket that paid $8.50 an hour. He was grateful for the job, but it came with no health insurance, and for every dollar he made, the family's food stamp allowance was cut by 30 cents. Things were better, but not good enough. Susan, too, needed a break. So she was thrilled to get a text message from Goodwill Industries inviting her in for a job interview. It was the first response to an application she'd received in over a year.

When the big day came, Susan dressed in her best, a long-sleeved white shirt tucked into trim black slacks. She paid special attention to her shoes—shoddy footwear, she'd heard, signaled poverty of the sort that might distract from her better qualities. She typed Goodwill's address into Google Maps to get directions, dropped her baby off with her grandmother, and hurried to the bus stop. It was a long ride across town into unfamiliar territory, and she inadvertently exited the bus prematurely. She walked the final thirty blocks in one-hundred-degree heat, arriving just in time but wilted, her shoes scuffed. She apologized for her appearance and carried on with the interview. She thought it went quite well. And for the first time in a year, she was hopeful. Every sign was good. A week later, still optimistic, she spotted the job relisted on the Goodwill website. No explanation, no rejection letter, not even an email. But then again, she didn't expect to hear back. Goodwill had so very many people to choose from . . . more good people than good jobs, for sure.

If there is a gap in the working landscape, it is perhaps less one of skills than of opportunities, a reflection of the yawning income disparity that is a hallmark of our age. Lacking economic power and without union representation, many workers have little *political* power with which to leverage their very real skills. This problem was made abundantly clear to me—as was one approach to a solution—while touring 99 Degrees Custom, an apparel company based in the postindustrial city of Lawrence, Massachusetts. Lawrence, which we'll revisit in a later chapter, was the site of the Bread and Roses strike of 1912, when thousands of textile workers—most of them female immigrants—waged a two-month campaign for an improved wage and against all odds won the fight. It's no coincidence that 99 Degrees Custom is situated in the historic mill complex where the strike began. The company was founded in 2014 by Brenna Nan Schneider, a self-described "social entrepreneur" who cut her teeth in her family's manufacturing and design business in the Pocono Mountains region of Pennsylvania. An honors student, she played varsity tennis, served in student government, acted in the school play, volunteered on the yearbook and homecoming

committees, and cofounded a nonprofit called Children Helping
Anyone in Need. She planned on a career in public service but after
college decided to earn an MBA to return to a life in business. She
founded 99 Degrees Custom with the hope of making it a bridge
between the city's struggling workforce and opportunities in advanced manufacturing. "I envision a future of inclusive innovation," she told me.

As implied by its name, 99 Degrees Custom is a "mass customization" company that fills special orders from larger clothing
brands, some of them novel designs—like "smart" running tights
embedded with sensors to monitor body temperature, heart rate,
and running cadence. The day that I visited, most of the company's
fifty largely immigrant employees were busy at workstations absorbed in the many complex tasks involved in shaping, cutting, and
sewing custom-designed apparel—gym shorts, T-shirts, running
jackets, hand warmers, and other pieces made both for the military
and for companies like West Elm and Nike. I was warned not to
take photos of the prototypes or of the high-tech equipment used
in their fabrication. As I watched the seamstresses and machine
operators working with dexterity and skill, it did not surprise me
that several had decades of experience, some working with famous
designers. What did surprise me was their wage.

"Twelve dollars an hour with benefits is pretty much the best I
can offer," Schneider said, shaking her head. "I'm not comfortable
with this, because there is no greater motivator for me than to push
the industry forward. And believe me, I'm not getting rich. I'm
barely covering my costs. Our operators are manual workers in a
capital-intensive world—basically, they are high skill and low wage.
Vietnam makes some very high-quality clothing, and we also compete with Myanmar, Bangladesh, Mexico. Most consumers won't
pay more for American made, at least not much more. We have to
compete in a global market, which means we have families living in
poverty and jobs that are being created that keep them in poverty."

Schneider continued: "How do you change that? We are investing in the advancement of our own employees, creating a workforce that is ready for the future. We use machines to do the low-skill, repetitive work and free up our team to focus on quality and innovation. We produce products in synch with demand so that companies don't have to hold on to inventory and also can be more responsive to consumers who increasingly are looking for individual expression. And we are beefing up the technology so that each employee can do more in less time." When I pointed out that this would also result in fewer jobs over time, Schneider agreed. But, she added, these would be good jobs, and perhaps if Americans were willing to see themselves chiefly as workers rather than consumers, there would be more of these *good* jobs. "Our challenge—our opportunity—is to couple the best of technology with the best of our people," she told me. "That is, to empower our employees to think independently, as entrepreneurs and engineers, and to compensate them to do so. I believe that is the future of work not only here in Lawrence, but other cities around the world. And it's up to us to build—and support—that future."

THE THOUSAND-MILE STARE

Through the whole of his life he [the poor man's son]
pursues the idea of a certain artificial and elegant repose
which he may never arrive at, for which he sacrifices a real
tranquillity. . . . It is this deception which rouses and keeps
in continual motion the industry of mankind.
—ADAM SMITH

Adam Murka's eyes filmed with tears as he recalled hearing the news. It was summer of 2009 when word came that the General Motors Assembly Plant in Moraine, Ohio, was shutting down, probably for good. Plant closings were an old, familiar story, but this time it was personal. Murka's family worked at that plant—his aunts and uncles, his stepfather. Those relatives not directly on the GM payroll were likely to work down the street at Delphi, making parts for GM vehicles. Adam said he and his buddies visited the plant frequently, on school field trips or just for fun. They'd hang out, goofing around together until the grown-ups punched out, strolled through the gates, and—one by one—drove them home to supper. "This plant formed the fabric of our community," he told me. "Everyone knew someone who worked there, and when those three thousand jobs were lost, everyone felt the pain."

Adam was twenty-eight years old when we met several years later, but his tweed jacket, tie, and worried look made him seem a good deal older. As we approached what remained of the Moraine facility he pointed out landmarks. What did it look like? "Ghost town" isn't quite right. Ghost compound maybe, or ghost ranch. It spanned 4.1 million square feet, an area of more than nine football fields. I could imagine it parching into desert, tumbleweed clinging to the barbed-wire fence. There was no sign of life, not even a security guard. The gates weren't padlocked, so we drove straight through, parked near a loading dock, and got out to take a look around.

"A few years ago those lots were filled with trucks and cars," Adam said, nodding toward an expanse of blacktop that merged with the horizon. "That's where the employees parked. It was acre upon acre of vehicles. If I gave you a dime for every foreign car in those lots and you gave me a nickel for every American-made car, you'd have gone broke fast."

Back then, Adam drove a Chevy Blazer, but no more. Today his ride was a Honda Civic. He's got nothing against American-made automobiles; it's just that he isn't sure what *American-made* means anymore. Certainly not made in Moraine. He told me that when the plant closed, locals rallied to hold back the scrap dealers from dismantling the buildings and selling them off ton by ton. They managed to scare off the dealers, but the victory was bittersweet. Picked over and stripped of their value, the buildings stood like empty husks, a stark reminder that good union jobs are largely a thing of the past in this corner of Ohio.

When GM closed Moraine, 2,170 hourly employees lost their jobs. But that wasn't the half of it, Adam said. Another 10,850 job cuts followed, for a total of 13,020 jobs lost in and around Moraine. Like a row of dominos, jobs continued to topple through GM's supply chain: to name a few, DMAX laid off 645 workers; Jamestown Industries laid off 80 workers; Johnson Controls laid off 130 workers; PMG Ohio laid off 70 workers; Plastech laid off 88 workers; four Delphi plants laid off 2,120 workers; Tenneco laid off 118 workers; and EFTEC—supplier of adhesives, sealants, coatings, and application equipment for the automotive industry—laid off 83 workers. Almost overnight, 33,024 jobs were gone thanks to the shuttering of one GM assembly plant.

Moraine made trucks and SUVs—Chevrolet Trail Blazer, GMC Envoy, Envoy Denali, Isuzu Ascender, and the most expensive Saab ever built, the 9-7X. The plant held eleven national awards for quality and efficiency, thanks to a workforce that was as proud as it was loyal. Many employees arrived there fresh out of high school, and most, it seemed, had no intention of leaving before their grandchildren were ready to take their place. When the last truck rolled down the assembly line two days before Christmas, the line workers walked behind it in noisy solidarity like mourners trailing a casket at a New Orleans funeral. After hugging and shedding tears, they punched out one last time, walked out the door to the snow-damp parking lot, got into their company-subsidized American-made vehicles, and drove off to . . . who the hell even knew?

"You know what depression looks like?" Adam asked. "It's not looking down at your shoes. It's that thousand-mile stare. People here had that stare. It felt like a death in the family, but not just your family—in everybody's family." When Adam told me this, I thought of Marienthal, where so many men walked slowly and lost track of time. When I asked Adam about that, he nodded. "Time, right, lots of folks thought there was just too much of that."

Like Amy Cotterman, whom we met earlier, Adam lives and works in Dayton, the city where he grew up and a place for which, like her, he harbors tremendous hope. He walked me through the historic Oregon District with its smattering of boutiques, fancy coffee shops, and taverns. A mural stenciled across a brick building read "Dayton Inspires." We drove past the sweeping campuses of University of Dayton (Adam's alma mater), Wright University, and Wright-Patterson Air Force Base. But all that seemed far away as we stood looking around Moraine.

General Motors was once Ohio's largest employer, with twenty-six thousand jobs. Today, no single American manufacturer can begin to make that claim. The Dayton economy has modernized and diversified, with companies, foundations, and universities. Attracting a new sort of businesses, Adam told me, is key to turning the city around, and he works hard to help make that happen.

Adam cut his teeth in Washington, as communications chief for Republican congressman Mike Turner. But he found politics disheartening, and he returned to Dayton to sign on as director of communications at Sinclair Community College, a place, he thought, that would offer him a far clearer vantage from which to foresee and help shape the future.

For millions of Americans, community colleges do hold out a lifeline, the opportunity to build and hone skills they hope will start—or jump-start—a working life. Some years ago, President Obama extolled community college as key to boosting the nation's annual production of college graduates to his goal of five million by 2020. With over forty thousand students, Sinclair Community College was on the front lines of that effort.

The reach of the college is astonishing: one of two Montgomery County residents has sampled its offerings, and many have left with a certificate or degree. Near the end of one memorable commencement ceremony there, a new graduate rose from his seat to announce he'd spent thirty-two years completing his associate's degree. The audience roared its approval. This was in 2012, when Ohio was on the rise. Moody's Investors Service had upgraded the state's outlook from negative to stable, and there were predictions that the state's employment rate—already above the national average—would continue to improve. Not everyone believed that the state's three hundred thousand manufacturing jobs were coming back, but many looked to Sinclair to help them make the best of any new opportunities.

Sinclair was more than ready for the challenge. The college comprises twenty concrete Brutalist structures sprawled across a campus designed for high traffic and low maintenance. The buildings are linked aboveground by enclosed elevated bridges and walkways, and belowground by basement tunnels. The architect, Edward

Durell Stone, was perhaps most famous for his design of the Kennedy Center for the Performing Arts, a structure compared to "a glorified candy box" and "a great white whale washed ashore." Sinclair, by contrast, might pass for a high-class minimum-security prison, were that prison to have doors that swung both ways.

In matters of curriculum, Sinclair has things you might expect in a community college, like courses in dietetics and emergency response and criminal justice and hotel management and nursing. And it has things you might not expect, like "Introduction to Unmanned Aerial Systems." As are many community colleges, Sinclair is betting big that drone designers and operators will be in great demand going forward, not just by the military, but in a broad range of civilian applications such as environmental monitoring, disaster response (fires and floods), and agricultural and scientific research. Adam took me to the Sinclair UAV lab and handed me a recently purchased drone. It was ebony, the size (though not the shape) of a coffee table, light in the hand, and with the look and feel of a toy. Sinclair had invested heavily in every aspect of UAV operations and had federal clearance to pilot drones over an airport in nearby Springfield. "For every drone that goes up you need a dozen analysts on the ground to handle the data," Adam told me. "That's a lot of good jobs." Not as many as GM and Delphi, he cautioned, but a start.

That evening at dinner, Adam introduced me to Steven Johnson, president and CEO of Sinclair since 2003. Johnson arrived late and, waving away a menu, confessed that he had earlier wolfed down three slices of pizza at a student event. Six feet seven inches tall, with a tightly trimmed salt-and-pepper beard, Johnson is soft-spoken and intense. Anointed one of the "top leaders of the decade" by the *Dayton Business Journal*, he was—and likely still is—the highest-paid government employee in the county. After spending a few hours with him, it was absolutely clear to me that he had earned that distinction.

Johnson began by offering me a brief history of the college, pointing out that Sinclair was founded in 1887 for men like his grandfather, a peasant farmer who immigrated to the United States from Norway some years before World War II. "People were coming here from all over Europe, people who didn't speak English well," he said. "They needed to learn. There were industrial jobs and these immigrants needed Americanization to get them." (By *Americanization* he meant the basics—the ability to get to work on time, get through the routine, and leave without making trouble.) In those early days, the entire student body fit into two rooms at the Dayton YMCA, fifty-five men gathering after finishing up their day jobs as ditchdiggers or farmhands to learn bookkeeping and mechanical drawing. Photos from the period show a windowless room festooned with American flags and men of various ages in dark suits staring stiffly at the camera. In 1948 what was then known as "YMCA College" was rechristened Sinclair College in honor of deceased YMCA secretary David A. Sinclair. A quarter century later, the college moved to its current home, a sixty-five-acre wedge of urban renewal on the western edge of downtown Dayton, just minutes off the interstate. Convenience, and plenty of parking space, seemed to be central features.

"For many of us, college is one of the few things you do only once—you go when you're eighteen, stay until you're twenty-two, and never go back," Johnson said. "But that model doesn't work for everyone. Sinclair is a place you can come back to again and again for the rest of your life—to refresh, retrain."

Sinclair is unusual in that its primary strategy is to train students up as a sort of bait—that is, to prepare people for jobs that might be on the horizon and then hold out this trained workforce to lure employers to the greater Dayton area. Rather than "Build it and they will come," the logic is "Train up and they will come." When I visited, Deb Norris, an MBA with decades of corporate experience, worked as Sinclair's senior vice president of workplace development and corporate services. (Later, she left Sinclair to start her own consulting firm, with a focus on the drone industry.)

Norris collaborated with city representatives to pitch directly to industry—Caterpillar, WilmerHale, Payless, and other companies looking to expand or move their operations. "There is a huge possibility for job growth in manufacturing," she told me at dinner. "But it's not going to happen through long runs of standardized products on production lines. You've got to look at the nature of the work and how it's changing. GM workers were pulling down $40 an hour with a very low skill set. That won't work anymore. Employees need to be flexible, nimble, more open to innovation. You don't just walk out of high school and march directly into an advanced-manufacturing facility."

The phrase *advanced manufacturing* is so commonly used—by politicians, economists, and business leaders—that it's easy to assume that it means the same thing to everyone. It doesn't. Rather, the term is relative, meant to suggest a new sort of manufacturing that requires technology-related skills that the old sort didn't. After the financial meltdown, Sinclair's enrollment swelled with factory and IT workers eager to retrain for what everyone hoped would be new opportunities in the advanced-manufacturing sector. Daryl Curnutte, program manager of Sinclair's Tooling and Machining Program, was ready for them. "I told my students then and I tell them now that they can't expect to get paid well for doing a job just anyone could do," he said. Curnutte told me there were plenty of jobs, "but the skill set required is pretty technical." When I asked what he meant by that, he invited me to visit one of his classes to see for myself.

I arrived to find fifteen mostly male students working heads down on their capstone project: a measuring device that required them to machine and assemble about a dozen different components. It was precise, painstaking, and highly skilled work. "About 90 percent of these people had never done this sort of thing before coming to Sinclair," Curnutte told me as we surveyed the room. "We take our time, build them up from the bottom up," by which he meant the students, not the measuring devices. When I asked what positions these students were training for, Curnutte outlined three options: operator, programmer, and tool and die maker. Operators load and unload the milling machines that make the parts and do quality control on the final product. Programmers write the computer code that guides the milling machines. (Curnutte explained that programmers are falling out of demand because the newer milling machines are so easy to program that even operators can manage the job.) Tool and die makers machine by hand the nonstandard high-precision parts used in medical, aeronautics, and other highly specialized industries. Curnutte himself has a side business in tool and die and reckons that fewer than 20 percent of his students will rise to his level. "Tool and die maker is the top," he told me. "Most of them are not going to make it to the top."

In 2017, a highly experienced tool and die maker in Ohio earned on average $23.81 an hour, just short of $50,000 a year; above the national average of $46,119.78 a year, and well above the median wage of $29,930.13. To get some idea of what's required to earn this above-average wage, I checked out recruitment notices. Below are the requirements listed for a tool and die maker with a minimum of five years' postapprentice experience posted by a company in Georgia, where wages tend to be lower than in Ohio. This job offered an annual salary of $40,000.

Job Duties:
- Share knowledge by assisting in training members in the proper methods and techniques.
- Take action to meet or exceed customer quality, cost and delivery expectations and achieve operational goals.
- Work with Tooling Engineers and drawings to recommend design changes and improvements when necessary.
- Fabricate, repair and maintain all dies, fixtures, jigs and other tooling items required for the proper running of equipment.
- Design and create tools.

- Assist in preventative maintenance program for tooling.
- Project work as needed.
- Follow standard work for tooling duties; suggest and document improvements to standard work.
- Participate in activities as appropriate to ensure the success of the organization.

Working Conditions:

- Seasonal fluctuations in temperatures and humidity.
- Dust, fumes and noise are commonplace.
- Work with chemicals associated with a repair or clean-up operation.
- 12 hour shifts and change of shift or hours worked if requested with reasonable notice.

Physical Conditions:

- Work up to 12-hour days with continuous standing and/ or motion on a concrete floor.
- Lift and carry up to 50 pounds (for up to 10 feet) on a continuous basis.
- Frequent use of hand, arms, legs and/or back in a push/ pull motion up to 25 pounds.
- Use of abdominal and lower back muscles to support part of the body frequently or continuously over time without "giving out" or fatiguing.
- Continuous movement of hand, hand together with arm, or two hands to grasp, manipulate, or maneuver raw materials through machine processes.
- Continuous coordinating of two or more limbs (for example, two arms, two legs, or one leg and one arm).
- Continuous and repetitive use of wrists, hands, arms, and legs including bending, lifting and gripping.

- Continuous movement at the waist, back, hip and knees including bending, kneeling, squatting and twisting.
- Frequent reaching and lifting up to 15 pounds at and above the shoulders.

Curnutte's students may well have been capable of strenuous, repetitive physical activity, but not all of them looked ready for it. Several had been laid off at the General Motors assembly plant in Moraine and hadn't held a job in years. Some had kids who were old enough to be tool and die makers themselves. One former GM employee who was about to graduate told me that he had already nailed an entry-level job as a machinist. He said the position didn't pay nearly what he had hoped—the starting wage was $10 an hour, less than a quarter of his former wage. He'd been told that the pay would likely increase over time, and he didn't find that terribly cheering. "I'm forty-six years old," he told me. "I don't have that much time."

The concept of transforming former factory workers, construction workers, and others eclipsed by automation is hardly a partisan one: politicians on both sides of the aisle seem to favor it. "Many businesses are struggling to find and hire qualified employees," Virginia Republican representative Dave Brat told the House Small Business Committee in 2017. "Dozens of business leaders tell me all too often that they can't find a qualified skilled workforce to fill job vacancies." And Hillary Clinton, at a 2016 campaign event in Hatfield, Pennsylvania, where she met the owners of K'NEX, a family-run toy manufacturer, spoke of the "more than one million" open jobs in America right now that aren't being filled for lack of skills.

Just how either Representative Brat or Secretary Clinton knew this is not entirely clear, for there is no reliable measure of the number of job openings in the United States. Rather, as we've seen, there are estimates of job openings based on representations made by employers. For example, here is Apple CEO Tim Cook once again explaining why Apple has no choice but to manufacture overseas: "The US, over time, began to stop having as many vocational kind of skills. I mean you can take every tool and die maker in the United States and probably put them in the room that we're currently sitting in. In China, you would have to have multiple football fields."

The room Cook inhabited must have been cavernous, for at the time of his speech, according to the Bureau of Labor Statistics, there were nearly half a million tool and die makers in the United States. What was actually in short supply was demand for their services. Forty percent of tool and die firms had folded since 1998, and employment in the field had shrunk by more than half, thanks in part to the outsourcing of companies like Apple. Automation had also taken a toll. As one Wisconsin company promised in its promotional literature: "Our tooling department runs with 'lights-out' (24-hour) operation to ensure that your deadlines are met." Not many human tool and die makers, no matter how skilled, can work in total darkness.

Community colleges make no secret of their purpose—most are designed to prepare students for a life on the job, not a life of the mind. And for some, that seems to work quite well. A quick glimpse of the website of almost any community college offers glowing testimonials of graduates whose lives were changed—and in some cases even saved—by their experience. Those testimonials are real, and many of us know people for whom community college was a stepping-stone to a satisfying working life. Some of us are that person. But these success stories are the exception, not the rule, for those who attend.

On paper, community college graduates seem to benefit financially: the most recent data shows the median income of high school graduates ages twenty-five to thirty-four working full time to be $30,000, while comparable graduates of community colleges earned a median of $34,970. But there's a catch—in fact, two catches. Here's the first: fewer than 40 percent of community college attendees graduate within six years, and one in four drop out after just one semester. And here's the second catch: in the most recent data, only 66 percent of community college graduates were working full time, implying that the median income of all graduates—including those who worked part time or not at all—was substantially lower. To further complicate matters, even this wage differential was skewed. Community college graduates are on average older than high school graduates, and some graduate in specialties like fire science and criminal justice that offer a leg up into well-paid unionized public service jobs. (According to the most recent figures, firefighters earn an average wage of $46,870 and police officers $60,270.) Again, this is the Bill Gates effect in action: these high-earning public service workers skew the averages.

Community colleges can be extremely helpful, especially for those who enroll either to earn a specific credential (such as certified nursing assistant), to master a specific skill (such as culinary arts), or to gain access to a four-year college. Any of these approaches can work, and often do. But for people like Susan, whom we left in the previous chapter, the cost of attending community college—two years of lost or reduced wages and associated transportation, textbooks, child care, and other expenses—can tip the balance, causing them to leave school with no credential, possibly in debt, and with no prospect of a good job.

Steven Johnson understands all that, but it doesn't daunt him. "We're not Sarah Lawrence, not Wellesley," he told me. "We're trying to help people get enough education to make something of themselves, people who are financially limited, academically limited, logistically limited. You've heard of 'just-in-time' manufacturing? This is 'just in time' education."

The problem with this well-meant argument is that manufacturing and education have almost nothing in common. Few people—no matter their inclinations or abilities—have the time and/or resources to return to college on a regular basis to "tune up" their skill set. And even for those few, no college—not even Sinclair— is really designed to cater to "just in time" job market demands.

Trace Curry, a twenty-three-year-old from Richmond, Virginia, was one of several "model students" I met at Sinclair. Curry was a sparkling facet in the jewel of Sinclair's crown—the Unmanned Aerial Systems (UAS) certificate program. A few years earlier, the Association of Unmanned Aerial Vehicle Systems had predicted that Ohio would be awash in 2,700 new UAV-associated jobs by 2025, of roughly 100,000 new jobs created nationally. Almost immediately, Sinclair invested heavily, pumping millions of dollars into UAV-related training programs. Trace Curry was a one-man cheering squad for the effort, featured in flattering portraits of Sinclair in *Time* magazine and Bloomberg Technology, among other outlets. Yet when I called him after graduation, Curry was at loose ends, working as a parking garage valet. He said his long-term goal was to work for NASA, but for now he was hoping to nail a job as a luggage screener for the Transportation Security Administration.

"I would love to have a job in the UAS field, but the TSA is steady, and reliable, and that's what I need," he told me. "Also, UAS is moving so fast—and employers don't want to send you back to school . . . so I feel like my skills are already obsolete." He may be right—in early 2018, the University of North Dakota alone had two hundred students enrolled in its UAS degree program. As of now, there is no way to know whether those graduates will get jobs and, if they do, what sorts of jobs. But what is sure is that the competition for those jobs will be fierce—in the summer of 2016, the first time it was offered, more than 13,700 people flooded in to take the commercial drone licensing test under new US regulations. By the fall of 2017, roughly sixty thousand people had obtained remote pilot certificates, meaning they were eligible to pilot commercial drones. Despite industry claims that their services were in booming demand, the average salary for drone pilots had leveled out at roughly $30,000. The reason, according to a leading drone industry website, is that "there are a lot of people who know how to fly drones."

Job-training programs, whether in or outside of community colleges, have been popular for generations. In response to a 3.5 percent drop in "goods-producing industries," President John Kennedy signed the Manpower Development and Training Act of 1962, directed at workers who had lost their jobs to automation. The act was the first of a series leading to the Job Training Partnership Act (JTPA) of the early 1980s. In an era of deregulation and cuts in antipoverty efforts, job training and retraining enjoyed widespread support among politicians for offering a "leg up" to the poor rather than a "handout." Their argument was that unemployment and underemployment were a reflection not of a systems failure, that is, a shortfall of good jobs, but of the failure of individuals to keep up with the changing demands of the marketplace.

But these arguments crumbled under the weight of evidence. In 1993, the Labor Department released a study that concluded that low-income out-of-school young men who graduated from the JTPA program actually had 10 percent lower earnings than did men from a similar demographic who never participated in the program. A more recent study, reported in 2012, concluded that in comparison to job seekers without special training, those with training showed similar employment histories but with somewhat lower earnings. If anything, job training seemed to limit, not expand, employment prospects. One of the most serious problems was the training of too many people for a particular job category, and thereby lowering the wage in that category by flooding the market.

Sinclair had put its faith in drones. But Richard Stock, an economist at the University of Dayton, told me that "no one seriously believed" that the UAS industry would stimulate substantial job demand in the larger Dayton region and that speculation to the contrary was aspirational, not based on evidence. "Don't get me wrong, Sinclair is a model, but even a model college can't figure out what jobs demand will be," he told me. "Sinclair and other colleges have many training initiatives trying to respond to interests of very small industries." While there are and always will be periodic shortages of labor in certain industries at certain wage levels, devoting public resources to "just in time" training for any particular job seems at best a gamble.

In the fall of 2016, the Moraine plant officially reopened to great fanfare. Various press reports described the refurbished 116-acre facility as a "showcase" and a "symbol of industrial rebirth." Hundreds attended the ribbon cutting, including notables from the automotive industry, a US senator, a US congressman, and Lieutenant Governor Mary Taylor. Clearly, Dayton was back in the "making" business. But it wasn't General Motors or another American company that threw the party. It was China's Fuyao Glass Industry Group, the world's leading manufacturing company specializing in automotive glass. The Moraine factory was the centerpiece of Fuyao's American operations, poised to build four million windshields annually, roughly 30 percent of all the windshields made in or imported into the United States each year.

Cho Tak Wong, Fuyao's founder and chairman, said he was "investing in America" and hoped to revitalize both Ohio and the US auto industry. "Today's grand opening in Moraine is the culmination of a monumental undertaking by Fuyao and our partners," Cho announced at the opening ceremonies. "We are proud of our work in Ohio, in the heart of the US auto corridor, and are highly committed to supporting the growth of the North American automotive market. Fuyao China currently supplies around 70% of the Chinese auto glass market, and through close work with our OEM partners, we believe we will replicate this success in North America."

Raised in crippling poverty during China's Cultural Revolution, Cho is a self-made billionaire with little patience for red tape or regulation. He spent two years and half a billion dollars renovating the GM assembly plant, his company's single largest investment in the United States. Ohio courted these attentions with one of the largest incentive packages in state history. The reason was this: Cho had promised 2,500 and maybe even 3,000 good jobs. Sinclair Community College was called upon as a partner to help round up qualified candidates to recruit for these positions, and Steven Johnson pledged to hold as many campus recruitment events "as it takes" to get them filled. JobsOhio, a nonprofit corporation that promotes job growth and economic development in the state, also rolled up its sleeves. Like so many struggling cities around the country, Dayton would do almost anything to land jobs.

Jane Dockery is associate director of the Applied Policy Research Institute at Wright State University in Dayton, where she focuses on regional economic development. "We'd done a study of GM workers, tracked them over a period of two years, and it wasn't pretty," she told me. "Some were working in retail, at places like Cracker Barrel. But a lot were not working at all. The unemployment numbers just don't show you what's really going on—people working minimum wage or part time, people who had simply given up. We knew there were a lot of people out there who needed something better."

Fuyao was supposed to be that something better. But the talent search did not go as smoothly as hoped. Sinclair College and JobsOhio processed an initial 3,299 applications for the position of production associate, which was described to me as a euphemism for "generic factory worker." Of those 3,299 applicants, 65 were rejected because they declined to work nights and weekends, and 9 because they lacked a high school diploma or GED. But a whopping 482—all of them high school graduates and not a few Sinclair graduates—were rejected because they failed to pass an eighth-grade-level math test. For most rejected candidates it was apparently not a lack of skills but a lack of basic knowledge that was holding them back.

JobsOhio rushed to arrange remedial classes and tutors, but it was not certain whether these applicants would be given a second chance. Ultimately 1,209 semifinalists were scheduled for interviews, and of these, 205 were offered a ninety-day temporary appointment with Staffmark, a staffing company based in Cincinnati. Of these, the ones who managed to make it beyond the three-month probation period were welcome to apply for a permanent job, at a wage of $12.60 an hour, according to Dockery. This was roughly $2.65 an hour less than was typical for production jobs in the region.

In the spring of 2017, Fuyao's Dayton operation was reported to have two thousand employees and was Ohio's largest Chinese-owned manufacturing operation. It's unclear how many of those employees were Americans, but it is perhaps telling that the company states in job postings that "languages spoken commonly in the workplace are English and Mandarin." A former manager filed a lawsuit claiming he was fired in part because he was not Chinese. Rank-and-file employees complained that the Chinese management had little interest in training, sharing responsibility, or even interacting with American employees, and management complained that American workers did not work hard or fast enough. In the fall of 2017 the Occupational Safety and Health Administration fined the company for serious safety violations. The company was hit with an angry campaign led by the United Automobile Workers (UAW) and, according to a document filed with the US Labor Department, shelled out $747,410 to an Oklahoma-based consulting firm that specialized in "union avoidance." Fred Strahorn, the Democratic minority leader of the Ohio House of Representatives, summed up the situation at a luncheon meeting. Fuyao's employment policies, he said, felt a "little bit like a 'hostage situation.'"

Clearly, Sinclair Community College had played no role in creating this "hostage situation," nor has the college any intention of educating students for bad or nonexistent jobs. On the contrary, Sinclair remains a model institution: well integrated into the community, fairly priced, and responsive to individual student needs. But the fact that Sinclair is among the best community colleges in the nation makes the point all the stronger—that is, the danger of responding to "industry demands" to calibrate what we learn or teach our children.

"I think if I were a former GM production employee, and all I could get were offers at the glass plant, I'd be done with working," Dockery told me. "Our local employers are competing in a global market, and we strive to train people for whatever job they may offer. So, like it or not, they want us to help people compete at the level of lowest common denominator. The community colleges see themselves as the economic development arm, that they should be 'preparing' people for jobs, and telling companies they have training in place. But what jobs, exactly? There are better jobs, and jobs that pay better, but from what I can tell there really aren't that many of them. In a global economy, there is so much pressure on the bottom line, and even though the economy has improved, we haven't found our way, at least not here in Ohio. I don't think we should be 'training' people for jobs that don't exist, and might not exist. In fact, I'm not sure community colleges should be in the job 'training' business at all. Maybe what community colleges should be doing is what colleges were designed to do—encourage critical thinking and inculcate lifelong learning. You know, we can't predict the future, but we can prepare people to help shape it."

WHEN THE SPIRIT CATCHES YOU

Our students are very well prepared to see where work
stops being a good and becomes an evil.
—LYLE ROELOFS

Robert Renner is the son of Bobby and Tammy Renner, the couple
we met earlier in Brodhead, Kentucky. You might recall that Bobby
Renner works in production at an American auto-glass company.
You might also recall that at age forty-nine Bobby wondered how
long his luck would last; he suffered from back pain, and there was
no telling how long he could keep up the pace at the factory. Also,
he feared that someday the factory would move to Mexico. "You
never know about your health, and with a factory job, you have to
depend on God for everything," he said. "I'd like my son Robert to
have more of a choice."

Robert was twenty at the time, a student of mechanical engineering. Poised and well spoken, he had only good things to say
about his parents, his mentors, and his formative years at Rock-
castle County High School, where he showed an interest in automotive technology and English literature. After signing on with
Upward Bound, a readiness program for first-generation precollege
students with a special focus on science and math, he developed an
interest in those things too.

Upward Bound arranged for Robert to visit Berea College,

where both of his older sisters had studied and one had completed a nursing degree. Those odds sounded good enough to Robert, and throughout high school he spent six weeks every summer preparing to attend. He took math and science classes, met with his tutor regularly, and joined fellow students on field trips to places like Emory University in Atlanta and the Holocaust Museum in Washington, DC. When he graduated from high school, Berea kept its promise and took him in—for free.

Robert was lucky, but not in the way you might think. All students at Berea College pay little to no tuition, and like Robert, few if any can afford to pay. Even the foreign students arrive without silver spoons, from places like Afghanistan, Turkistan, Vietnam, and Moldova, the tiny nation wedged between Romania and the Ukraine that was home to a Berea computer science major who dazzled me with her mastery of American history and politics. In fact, none of the students I met at Berea failed to dazzle me. Though not many had a particular job in their sights, like Robert, all of them seemed to know their own strengths and how best to apply and build on them.

As you've likely guessed, Berea College has always stood apart. Founded by abolitionists in 1855, it has a long and distinguished history of keeping its door open to minorities, to women, and particularly to the poor. With roughly 1,600 students, it is the largest member of the Work Colleges Consortium, comprising eight liberal arts colleges—all but one in the South—that promote the fluid integration of work, learning, and service. Work College students perform most on-campus tasks from accounting to food service to tutoring and counseling other students. Boone Tavern Hotel, where I stayed, was manned by Berea students, as was the farm where the hotel restaurant got the eggs for my breakfast. Through work Berea students hone skills and their labor lowers operational costs, though not always significantly, as student workers are paid for their efforts and are carefully supervised by faculty and staff.

Berea students are graded on their work performance just

as they are on their academic performance, and failure in either sphere can result in suspension. Labor is not auxiliary to their education, it's integral, meaning that students confront the purpose of work every day, and also its consequences. "Our students are very well prepared to see where work stops being a good and becomes an evil," Berea president Lyle Roelofs told me.

In 2017, *Washington Monthly* declared Berea the nation's "top liberal arts college" for the third year in a row. The announcement prompted a flood of inquiries from other college administrators, so many that Roelofs joked he was tempted to write a book entitled *How Harvard Can Become the Berea of the North.* A physicist, Roelofs is the first scientist to lead the college, and, like the college, he is in many ways unexpected. Tall and patrician, with a Fitbit bracelet circling his wrist, he told me his hobbies included knitting, most recently a tiny cap for a new grandchild. A midwesterner by birth, before coming to Berea he was provost at Colgate University, an elite private institution tucked away in leafy Hamilton, New York. The total estimated annual cost of attending Colgate—tuition, room, board, and assorted expenses—was in 2017 nearly $70,000. The total estimated yearly cost to students of attending Berea was just north of $2,500.

Roelofs likened Colgate and similarly elite private colleges to a genetic trait passed down through the generations. "I was at Colgate for eight years, educating the seventh generation of the Colgate family," he told me. "We don't have those sustained relationships at Berea ... because the children of successful graduates are not eligible to attend." He added that his current position was the "ultimate reward," meaning he no longer felt the obligation to pander to moneyed interests. "We have no sense of perpetrating privilege of the top 5 percent, because we don't depend on the top 5 percent for support," he told me. Berea skirts this dependency thanks to its roughly $1.2 billion endowment, nearly $700,000 per student, placing it in the top twenty best-endowed colleges and universities in the nation. Less than a third of this endowment was donated by alumni. When I asked Roelofs how he and previous presidents managed to pull this off, he laughed. He'd heard this question so many times, he said, that his response was almost a reflex. "Our donors deeply believe in and support our mission," he said. "Being unique makes it relatively easy to raise funds."

Among those donors, I was told, was an African American couple who fifty years ago stopped for the night at Boone's Tavern Hotel. They were warmly welcomed, and the next morning, before checking out, they informed the innkeepers that if they ever acquired a million dollars, they'd donate it to Berea College. The rest, apparently, is history.

Berea students come from households with a median income of $29,000, and, like Robert, most represent the first generation in their family to attend a four-year college. Typically, the road leading them to Berea has been very rough. Though no one was looking for pity, or even sympathy, several students whom I spoke with teared up while sharing their stories. "The students who come here are the key ingredient to keeping the family together," Roelofs told me. "Dad might be dead or in jail, the siblings drug addicts, and the mom on welfare. The one person who can make a difference is this kid, and we're telling that kid to join us and leave his or her family behind. Not everyone can handle this."

Roelofs told me of a rising junior who committed suicide. "I went to his funeral. It was in a small church in southern Ohio, and the striking thing I learned there was what a different world the rural poor inhabit. There was no sense that the young man might have needed help, and certainly not psychiatric treatment. To these people it was 'God's time to call him home.' They accepted it."

In his blockbuster memoir *Hillbilly Elegy*, Yale-educated attorney J. D. Vance delivers a stirring account of what passes for life in eastern Kentucky—crime, drug addiction, spousal and child abuse. As one Appalachian-born observer wrote, "In the rise of Donald

Trump, [this book] has become a kind of Rosetta Stone for blue America to interpret that most mysterious of species: the economically precarious white voter." Vance, who was raised in the region, makes the extraordinary claim that these people "purchase homes we don't need, refinance them for more spending money, and declare bankruptcy, often leaving them full of garbage in our wake. Thrift is inimical to our being." While Vance likely employs the pronoun *we* to demonstrate his solidarity with "those people," it seems to me that *Hillbilly Elegy* is not a Rosetta Stone but a mirror, reflecting a growing disdain for what many of us fear is an increasingly disenfranchised and dysfunctional working-class "culture" all but devoid of compassion and common sense. But from what I saw in eastern Kentucky, this is a misleading generalization. Bobby Renner, for one, is an Evangelical Christian and a supporter of Donald Trump. He is suspicious of government and scornful of "welfare cheats." But when we spoke he voiced great sympathy for the truly poor, especially those who for whatever reason were unable to earn a high school degree. He supported universal health care and free or subsidized public education through college. (And far from being "unneeded" and "filled with garbage," his house is much needed, and filled with his aged parents, his wife, his daughter, and an adored granddaughter.)

If Appalachians—and other working-class Americans—are constrained, it is less by their culture than by a socioeconomic system that presumes they can—and even must—rely on a twentieth-century-style job to satisfy their twenty-first-century needs, material, psychological, and spiritual. Berea College recognizes the folly of this logic and strives to rise above it. Unlike community colleges focused on training students to anticipate and meet the demands (whether real or hypothetical) of industry, Berea takes the long view, carefully preparing graduates to cope with the vagaries of a quixotic global economy. This means that some students—like Robert—work toward becoming a professional in an existing institution, while many others work toward building something entirely new.

"The future is by definition uncertain and we don't have a crystal ball," Roelofs said. "But we have a basic faith that liberal arts education is a liberating education. Our goal is to graduate people who can think and understand how other people think. And that knowledge, we believe, will serve them well no matter the work they pursue."

Appalachia has since its settlement teetered on the edge of solvency. Eastern Kentucky in particular has a long history of poverty and crime—meth lab busts are perennial newsmakers, as are reports of drug trafficking. (Just months after my visit, a Berea pharmacist was convicted of money laundering and illegally dispensing hundreds of thousands of prescription pills and thousands of boxes of pseudoephedrine.) In the early twentieth century, Appalachians became, as one observer put it, "putty in the hands of the Eastern capitalists" who shaved the trees off mountains to better strip them of coal. After the coal was gone, companies fled, leaving the land denuded and the locals to cope with the scars of pollution and poverty.

Mining culture cuts deep in this region, where locals donned hard hats to brandish "Trump Digs Coal" banners at rallies. Roughly 70 percent of Kentucky's electricity is coal generated (until recently it was 90 percent), and unlike a lot of other states Kentucky has no mandate to reduce the use of coal. Coal all but built the state's economy and gave it some of the cheapest energy in the nation. But soon after Trump's election it became clear that efforts to roll back environmental protections or otherwise deregulate the industry were unlikely to have much impact on jobs: in 2017 there were fewer than 50,000 coal miners in the nation, down from a peak of more than 250,000 in 1980. In Kentucky, fewer than 7,000 miners remained.

Roelofs sees the decline of coal as a "great opportunity" for Appalachia to reinvent itself around sustainable industries, like agriculture and forestry and especially renewable energy—hydro, wind, and solar. While thanks to automation, mining operations need fewer workers, renewables need more: construction workers, skilled tradespeople, and engineers. Economist Robert Pollin and his colleagues at the Political Economy Research Institute (PERI) at the University of Massachusetts once estimated that a transition to renewable energy would create 2.7 million new jobs nationally—an average of 12.6 jobs per $1 million in investment, compared with an average of roughly 10.6 for oil, gas, or coal. The labor necessary to retrofit and improve infrastructure would add another 14.6 jobs per $1 million in investment. That's a lot more jobs for the buck than the fossil fuel industry can muster.

In April 2017, a Kentucky coal company announced it would build the state's largest solar farm atop a mountain denuded by strip-mining operations. At the time, it was uncertain how many jobs the solar installation would generate, but the plan was to employ former coal miners in every step of the operation. The hope was to direct public focus away from a dying industry that was hemorrhaging jobs into a twenty-first-century industry that could arguably create jobs. But advocates of these and similar efforts were quick to insist that Kentucky should never turn its back on its past.

Peter Hackbert, who holds a chair in entrepreneurship and management at Berea, has for decades studied eastern Kentucky and its tortured relationship with coal. "Miners and their families backed Trump because he promised to bring back what they once had—high-paying jobs for people with just a high school degree," he told me. "We know those jobs are history. But rather than confront this with hopelessness and despair, we're trying to uncover new possibilities and opportunities."

One strategy is to leverage traditional culture—visual, musical, culinary, literary—to stimulate economic development. To skeptics, this vision may sound utopian, but it's far more practical than they might assume. On a national scale, arts and crafts play a major role in the economy, generating nearly $729.6 billion annually and employing five million people. Surprisingly, these benefits are far greater than those brought by either the construction industry or the transportation and warehousing sectors. And for every hundred jobs created directly in the arts, sixty-two more jobs blossom in retail, information technology, manufacturing, hospitality, and food service. Historically these job-creating effects, both direct and indirect, have accrued mostly in urban centers. It's hard to imagine Dallas, New York, Chicago, Boston, Philadelphia, Washington, Los Angeles, and other major cities stripped of their art museums, theaters, concert halls, and craft and food fairs, and easy to see the thundering impact these institutions and activities have on their bottom lines. (The Center for an Urban Future estimates that the "cultural industry" is responsible for 150,000 direct jobs in New York City alone, and a huge driver of tourism that creates many more jobs.) Hackbert is convinced that digital technology will boost the reach of eastern Kentucky and other sparsely populated regions and position them to leverage their cultural heritage to greatly expand their creative economy.

The rise of the creative economy is not without controversy. In some cities so-called creatives working in finance, technology, the arts, and other sectors have shouldered out "outmoded" industrial and manufacturing workers. This leads to polarization, with high-paid newcomers luxuriating at the top and onetime blue-collar workers stranded in low-wage service work. Essentially, the working class becomes the servant class to the "better educated" or "more talented." For example, on a visit to Detroit, it was impossible not to notice that Quicken Loans, the nation's largest mortgage vendor, had all but taken over the city's financial district. The company's thousands of young professional employees, many if not most of them from outside the Detroit area, had swamped the real estate market, raising rents and forcing locals out.

Avoiding this problem requires completely rethinking development strategies to build on the skills and strengths embedded in local and regional culture. Berea mayor Steven Connelly is a vocal advocate of this ground-up strategy. An attorney by trade, Connelly was born and raised in Berea, his parents having met at the college. After military service and a side trip to the University of Kentucky to earn his law degree, he returned to Berea in the 1980s to raise his own family. His loyalty to the region, though absolute, does not cloud his awareness of its challenges.

"We smoke, we're obese, we have heart and dental disease," he told me. "And our two biggest drawbacks are huge: lack of education and lack of resources. When I became mayor in 2003, it was fairly clear to me that every county in this state was going to have to reinvent itself. Each place has its own assets, and you have to figure out how to manage them. Eastern Kentucky has very little flat land, we're a mountainous region. That defines us. Those mountains were raped by mining and timber companies, the wealth removed and the heritage drained out of the local people by landlords and corporations. That's our liability. But we have an asset. Berea City played a significant role in the handicraft revival movement of the 1890s, and as the rest of the country moved into the industrial age, we worked at preserving our craft skills—weaving, woodworking, glass blowing, pottery, musical instrument making. We have a 125-year history of being intimately tied to the craft movement, as we are today: we are the folk arts and crafts capital of Kentucky. We believe we can build on that in a number of ways. In fact, we already have."

Berea's boast—"Where art's alive"—is easily verified by a stroll around the town's College Square with its charming coffee shops, boutiques, and craft emporia. A highlight is the studio of Warren A. May, a world-renowned woodworker who carves tables, chests, and Kentucky mountain dulcimers from cocobolo rosewood. About a mile or so from the square, not far from the headquarters of the Kentucky Guild of Artists and Craftsmen, is the Artisan Village District, a warren of studios and galleries. I stepped into Music Makers, where Randall Conn, his wife, Regina, and their adult son were just finishing up lunch. Randall and his son specialize in the building and repair of string instruments—guitars, banjos, fiddles, mandolins, stand-up basses. At my request,

Randall grabbed one of his gourd banjos and picked a few chords, not mentioning what I already knew: that he and his band had played at the Grand Old Opry, among other venues. From the look of his studio, scattered with instruments in various stages of repair, business was fair to good. But Randall and his family don't depend on music making or instrument making and repair for their entire income. "Randall's a craftsman," Regina told me, casting a proud eye toward her husband of over thirty years. "He makes things. And one of the things he makes are custom wood floors. He goes all over the world, consulting, and overseeing installations." One such installation, in the SoHo district of Manhattan, apparently cost the owner $100,000, nearly three times what the average Kentuckian earns in a year. "It's a darn good thing that Randall likes to travel," Regina said.

Randall, who looked well beyond fifty, said he relied mostly on word of mouth for his business and had no need to truck with the Internet. "I'm busy enough," he told me. Justin Burton, a twenty-four-year-old craftsman whose studio was just a few doors down from Randall's shop, takes a different view. He peddles his wares on Amazon and eBay, and maintains an impressive website. Justin grew up in Russell Springs, a town of roughly two thousand in central Kentucky. His father worked for underwear maker Fruit of the Loom, once the state's second-largest employer after General Electric. That surprised me. Like many city dwellers, I considered the loss of factory work as a mainly urban problem, hollowing out former showplaces like Detroit, Chicago, Baltimore, and Buffalo. But as I later learned, rural manufacturing—textiles, pulp and paper, refineries, food processing—is especially vulnerable to global competition and automation. In 1988, Fruit of the Loom left Kentucky in pursuit of cheaper labor overseas, and Burton's dad lost his job, as did many others. In recent decades, nearly half of all rural jobs lost to displacement have been manufacturing jobs, compared with about one-third in the nation as a whole.

Justin's father never fully recovered from the factory closing. He tried selling used cars and other things, but eventually drifted away from his family, leaving his son at sea. Justin was deeply hurt but also hopeful. He knew he wanted something different from what his father had, but he wasn't sure what. "There is a factory in my town, but I call that 'last ditch' because it's filled with meth heads," he told me. "Do you know how dangerous it is to mix meth and factory work?" In Russell Springs, Walmart was the largest steady employer, followed by the local hospital. Walmart held no appeal, and the hospital, well, he didn't see himself as a healer. "Hospital jobs are the new factory work," he said. "I didn't want that." He didn't go for job training, because where he came from, most people didn't train for jobs, they simply did them and hung on until the job gave up on them. Determined to break away after high school, he enrolled in Berea, the one college he knew he could afford.

Justin loved Berea, the campus, the people, and the study of archaeology. That objects thousands of years old could still exist intrigued him, as did the stories they told. All the talk of "material culture" got him thinking, and he started poking around the Berea crafts program, looking for a niche. And one day, he happened upon the broom making studio.

Broom making is an ancient and venerable craft, but Burton didn't know that at the time. What attracted him was its earthiness and simplicity. As an apprentice, his first job was sorting and measuring broomcorn, a variety of sorghum used to make bristles. (Berea College tried—and failed—to grow broomcorn on its working farm and now imports the plant from Mexico.) Sorting and measuring broomcorn was tedious work, but Justin persisted, and over a six-month course advanced to braiding and assembling entire brooms. That he was able to make such beautiful, useful things had never occurred to him before, as no one in his family was particularly handy or artistic. He'd grown up in what he called "Walmart culture," where people lived with cheap, poorly made objects not because they preferred them but because they believed they had no choice. For some reason, broom making felt like a liberation from a life of second best. After graduation, he purchased an antique bundling machine from a dead broom maker's widow and turned his hobby into a business, the Broom House.

You may laugh, and I get it: broom making? Yeah, okay, but hand-made brooms were once big business. Some decades ago, Berea College sold as many as 150,000 brooms a year, painstakingly crafted by students and workers from the neighboring communities. Of course, broom making by hand is today almost vestigial, practiced mostly by elderly masters. "I'd guess that there are fewer than one hundred broom makers left in the entire country," Justin said. "And I'm one of them. I've been in this business for four years, and I'm sticking with it. My goal is to sell fifteen hundred or maybe two thousand brooms this year. Turns out, a lot of people want something with a story behind it. I tell them that if they hang one of my brooms on the wall—rather than hide it away—it will be ready whenever they are [presumably for sweeping, or for storytelling]. Also, they'll save closet space."

Justin custom-makes brooms for birthdays and weddings. He has buyers from around the United States and from Germany, France, the United Kingdom, Australia, and Japan. He leads work-shops, gives lectures, and sells his brooms at craft fairs, of which there are plenty. ("Craft fairs are like cockroaches," he told me. "When you see one, you know there are fifty more hiding some-place.") And he dreams of one day seeing his brooms displayed in museums. "I'm really curious to see where my brooms end up in ten or twenty years," he said. "I feel like I'm making material culture for the future."

Justin is not banking on a narrow skill set to pave his way to a prosperous and meaningful life. He's nimble, open to change, and determined not to be typecast. He has not plotted out his life's career. Yes, he's grown the requisite craftsman's beard and tied his hair back in the requisite craftsman's ponytail. He's called upon a few friends to grow broomcorn for him so he'll never be in short supply. But he's also planning to get a master's degree to pursue a side interest in arts preservation. And who knows, he said, one day he just might try his hand at something completely different—like, maybe, accounting.

"Anyone who wants to stick around this area knows they've got to do more than one thing," he told me. "Because there is no more 'one thing.' [President] Trump said he was going to bring back mining jobs, but we know how that works—it doesn't. There is no way in hell he's going to bring back even one job. Mining is automated, and getting more automated—it takes one miner to do the job it once took one hundred miners to do. Anyway, not everyone was a miner. My grandfather was a truck driver, and that's still a really big job around here. I probably know twenty, maybe twenty-five truck drivers. But those jobs are going to go, too, with self-driving vehicles. Automation, there's nothing you can do about that. So the jobs are just not going to be there. The way I see it, there are two possibilities—we can pay people to sit around and do nothing, or we can help them do something. I don't think many people want to sit around, and I don't think it's good for the country to have a lot of people sitting around. So we've got to find something for them to do. We still need the trades, like plumbing—I'd love to watch a robot try to do that, wouldn't you? And the liberal arts, humanities, crafts. That's work only humans can do."

Appalachia is rich in a tradition of making things. But with a population of under five million people, the region falls short in market demand. This is especially true in Appalachian Kentucky, where nearly a quarter of the population lives below the poverty line. Exports are an economic imperative here, and broadband Internet access is key. Low-income households are far less likely than wealthier households to have broadband, especially in rural areas like Appalachia. Microsoft, among other companies, is working to close that digital divide. But broadband access does not automatically engender sustainable employment opportunities. For example, call center jobs enabled by the Internet offer little stability: in recent years, hundreds of thousands of these jobs have vanished from low-income US communities, most of them transferred to lower-wage nations like the Philippines and India.

"We can't rely on old ideas—like call centers, we must create value around new possibilities," Hackbert said. "The most exciting enterprises are making it up as they go along, they're comfortable with ambiguity and uncertainty." As an example, he singled out a business in Hyden, Kentucky, a mountain town of fewer than four hundred souls, perched tight along the middle fork of the Kentucky River.

Hyden burst briefly into the spotlight in the winter of 1970 when a coal dust explosion just four miles from town killed thirty-eight miners. Word got out that it was the worst mining disaster in forty-five years, and the story spread. The lone survivor, conveyor belt operator A. T. Collins, was blown sixty feet out of the mine and into the road. He spent two weeks in Hyden Hospital, soon to be the new home of the other thing Hyden is famous for: the Frontier Graduate School of Midwifery.

Midwifery plays a vital role in rural Kentucky, a region where physicians have never been plentiful. The Frontier school was founded in 1939 by the Frontier Nursing Service as part of a demonstration project focused on the care of mothers and children. FNS founder Mary Breckinridge, the mother of nurse-midwifery in the United States, located her operation in the eastern Kentucky mountains, "in the heart of a thousand-square-mile area covering parts of several counties, where some 15,000 people lived without benefit of one resident state-licensed physician."

When FNS got its start in 1925, it secured staff in one of two ways: by sending American nurses to Great Britain for midwife training or by importing trained British nurse midwives to Kentucky. The midwives roamed the region on horseback, delivering babies and health care of almost every sort. But at the start of the

Second World War, most of the British nurses felt the call to return home and it was no longer possible to send American nurses abroad for training. Rather than cut back on its services, FNS opened the school and enrolled its first class, training its own midwives, who now had the luxury of traveling the region by Jeep rather than horse. The school has been in operation ever since, training nurse midwives and nurses from every state and from around the world. Considered one of the finest institutions of its kind, it is also, as Hackbert suggested, comfortable with ambiguity and responsive to technological change. In 1989, it became the first graduate school of nursing to engage in distance learning, and in 2011, in partnership with several other institutions, it went entirely online. "Frontier Nursing was there for the people of the mountains," Hackbert said. "And it could have stopped there, and survived. But to flourish, it needed to reinvent itself for the digital age. And when the college flourished, the entire region benefited."

Graduate nursing candidates complete the bulk of their studies from a distance, but are also required to gather in Hyden several times during the course of their training. Hyden mayor Carol Graham Lewis Joseph told me that FNS has long been one of the town's largest private employers, attracting students, graduates, and other visitors to local businesses: restaurants, hotels, campgrounds, and craft shops. When I asked if all of this had any real impact on the people in Hyden and the surrounding county, she laughed. "Of course it does. People might not make a lot, but they don't need a lot. My first husband put himself through college making rocking chairs. And he also put me through graduate school. If we'd had Internet back then—like the nursing school does—he would have made even more money. This area is beautiful, and everyone I know who left wants to come back. What we seem to be missing is work . . . but you know, it's all around us. There are so many people here who have talent—quilters, blacksmiths, potters. We have gorgeous parks, trails, wild horses. We believe tourism is the next big thing.

You tell people to come see us and I promise you, they will not be disappointed."

Nurses who get the bulk of their training via the Internet, supporting craftspeople who make things the old-fashioned way and sell them to the world online: this unlikely cycle is precisely what Hackbert had in mind when he described the process of reinvention. Justin Burton was just one of many young people I met in Kentucky who saw themselves as part of this cycle. The opportunity to use their hands as well as their heads—in craft workshops, breweries and distilleries, small farms, specialty food production, sustainable forestry, and the trades—seemed a hopeful alternative to low-wage service jobs in hospitals, factories, and call centers. David Tipton, Berea's dean of labor, said that regardless of the short-term success of these and similar efforts, over the long term they are a critical part of the essential task of reinventing work in the region. "Jobs are just jobs," he told me. "If you cultivate a certain skill, and there are no jobs related to that skill, well, you're just out of luck. So the most important thing we hope to teach our students is flexibility, of being a lifelong learner, of creating their own opportunities."

Tipton, a Berea graduate, is a sterling example of what he speaks. In addition to his duties at the college, he cultivates a small organic farm, and boasted that this season's bumper crop of eight thousand pounds of potatoes brought a healthy dollar a pound. In Kentucky, that amounted to what the average service worker earned in four or five months. Hypothetically, those eight thousand pounds of potatoes, in combination with growing other farm products and engaging in a few other moneymaking activities like teaching yoga (which he once did professionally), could, Tipton said, provide sufficient income to keep a roof over his family's head, and food other than spuds on the table. And in Kentucky, that means a sense of security and independence.

"I had a friend who chose to be a blacksmith," Tipton told me.

"He doesn't make buckets of money, but his life is sustainable. He has a family, kids. And he's one of the happiest men I know. We have students who are learning to log with horses. There's been an explosion in truck farming [small mixed farms], and a lot of our students are interested in that. Will they end up making their living that way? We don't know, but worrying is not where we put our energy. They are obviously going to have a lot of opportunities, not all of which we can anticipate. Our purpose is not to link students to any particular job. Our purpose is to prepare them for a life in a world where almost nothing is certain."

Listening to this, my thoughts turned to a book I'd recently read about Finland, a once-impoverished nation where very little has ever been certain and where good work has never been taken for granted. Like Kentucky, Finland has a challenging geography, a sparse and sprawling rural population, and a rich tradition of crafts and culture. I'd learned a lot about work and how it was changing in Kentucky. I decided to go see for myself whether Finland, too, had any lessons to share.

Part IV

Thinking Anew

The highest reward for a person's work is not what
they get for it, but what they become by it.

—JOHN RUSKIN

THE FINNISH LINE

Problems cannot be solved at the same level of
awareness that created them.
—ALBERT EINSTEIN

So . . . allow me to guess what you are thinking: "Finland and the
United States are not the same!"

Agreed!

Finland is a Nordic country, with roughly the population of
Colorado, and roughly the acreage of New Mexico. It has no Dis-
neyland, no Grand Canyon, and no Times Square. In Helsinki,
the capital city, pedestrians wait patiently for traffic lights to turn
green, even when there is no traffic. Every year the Finnish town
of Sonkajärvi hosts the World Wife-Carrying Championships and
the winners are almost always . . . wait for it . . . Finns! The national
sport is a dysfunctional cousin of baseball called *pesäpallo* in which
a strike is known as a "wound" and when you're out, "you're dead."
Finns not only anthropomorphize reindeer, they smoke and eat
them. As for Finnish humor . . . here's a sample: "Two brothers get
together for a fishing weekend at the family dacha, three hours
north of Helsinki. For three days and nights they fish, eat, and
sleep in silence, exchanging not a word. On day four the younger
brother musters his courage, clears his throat, and, with tears in
his eyes, blurts: 'My wife is leaving me.' The older brother stands

mute for several minutes, and finally responds: 'Are we here to fish,' he inquires, 'or are we here to talk?' "

So yes, Finns in many ways are not like us. But that does not mean that Finns and Americans have nothing in common. Consider, for example, our guilty pleasures. When last I looked, the longest-running dramatic series on American television was *Days of Our Lives*; in Finland the contender for that title is the equally soapy *Salatut elämät* (Secret lives). Other Finnish favorites include *American Idol* (Finnish edition) and *Dudesons*, a show that features four scruffy "dudes" with a proclivity for swatting one another in the crotch with a baseball bat. The Finns smoke nearly as much as we do and imbibe even more alcohol. They have a weakness for fast food and sweets. They give birth out of wedlock and divorce one another at an astonishing rate. And very much like us, the Finns struggle mightily to adjust to globalization: at this writing the Finnish economy still struggles to gain purchase in the wake of the financial crisis.

Finland has never been the exclusive, homogeneous Nordic refuge so many assume: it has a substantial Swedish-speaking minority and an indigenous population of Sami people (more familiar to us as Lapps or Laplanders). Further complicating things, the population of foreign-born Finns nearly doubled between 2000 and 2010 and continued to climb to more than 6 percent of the population by 2018. In Helsinki, the nation's capital, nearly a fifth of children are foreign born. Not all Finns approve of this intermingling, and some bitterly resent it. But most—even most members of the politically conservative True Finn Party—seem to welcome this influx of outsiders. Perhaps that's because the nation's history of isolation was no picnic.

Finland was until the 1960s the Appalachia of Europe, a poor agrarian backwater best known for high rates of both alcohol abuse and domestic violence. With few natural resources beyond lumber and few notable exports beyond wood, paper, pulp, and a scattering of minerals and plants, the country did not have much to offer in trade. A third of the country lies above the Arctic Circle, where in winter the sun stays below the horizon for two full months—the polar night is fifty-one days long. Three-quarters of Finland is shrouded in forests, leaving most Finns to huddle in and around a small handful of cities, Helsinki being by far the largest.

It gets worse. The Finnish language is unrelated to other Indo-European languages, and few people other than Finns bother to learn it. Aside from peat, the country had little in the way of domestic sources of energy and no choice but to import all of its coal, natural gas, and oil, as well as the uranium used for nuclear power. For decades it directed what exports it had to the Soviet Union, which in turn sent it food and petroleum. After World War II, the economy rapidly industrialized, urbanized, and assumed an upward trajectory. But when the Soviet Union collapsed in 1991, Finland lost a critical export market and fell into the deepest recession endured by any industrialized country since the 1930s. Unemployment peaked at 18.5 percent, and stock market and housing prices dropped by half. Adding insult to injury, Finland was designated the "world leader" in teen suicides. Cold, dark, and isolated, Finland was the punchline in some sort of cosmic joke, a place where people were born but where almost no one arrived voluntarily.

To get a feeling of what the Finns themselves thought of all this, here is a snippet from a traditional folk song, titled "I Am a Finn":

> *Life here is hard work*
> *And it rarely comes with any luck*
> *This is something only a Finn understands.*

Charles Darwin wrote that "in the long history of humankind (and animal kind, too) those who learned to collaborate and improvise most effectively have prevailed." Given little choice, the Finns eventually took Darwin's advice to heart. Fiercely egalitarian, they gradually adopted measures to benefit the majority over the chosen few. They voted for dramatic increases in public services like education, unemployment supports, and health care, as well as infrastructure, and research and development. Over time, this sure, steady investment in human capital turned what was once an isolated, energy-starved, linguistically challenged backwater into one of the most productive and innovative nations in the world.

In the 1990s, Finland rose as a high-tech powerhouse, with Nokia at the lead: the company was responsible for roughly a quarter of all exports. Labor productivity soared, and average incomes grew. In 2010, Finland ranked first on *Newsweek*'s list of the world's best countries and was named second-happiest nation (after Denmark) by the Gallup World Poll and the Organisation for Economic Co-operation and Development. In 2016, it was crowned first in quality of life, defined as "the capacity of a society to meet the basic human needs of its citizens, establish the building blocks that allow citizens and communities to enhance and sustain the quality of their lives, and create the conditions for all individuals to reach their full potential." In March 2018, the United Nations declared it the world's "happiest country."

Finland is a highly industrialized free-market economy, and it's possible to get very rich there—Antti Herlin, chairman of KONE Corporation, a Finnish elevator and escalator manufacturer, is a billionaire several times over. The nation has no federally set minimum wage, and taxes are by US standards reasonable—indeed, the Finnish government announced a 4.5 percent *decrease* in the corporate income tax rate in 2013. Yet the standard of living in Finland is among the highest in the world. Most working Finns are covered by legally binding collective agreements specifying pay ranges by sector—physicians, teachers, janitors, and home health aides are all similarly covered—agreements that were sanctioned by industry and government, working together. As a consequence, in Finland the phrase "working poor" has little resonance—not everyone in Finland is middle class, but no working person need fear losing a home, health care, or education for his or her children.

The Finns do not mince words. Their self-avowed national character trait *sisu* translates roughly as "perseverance in the face of hopelessness." They tend to face challenges squarely, and with great humility and compassion. Many American economists seem to believe that given some gentle prodding, the free market will create good work for all who deserve and earn it. For them, it's a matter of people rising to the demands of the global economy. By contrast, the very first economist I met with in Finland scoffed at the notion that most citizens should or could conform to the new realities. Rather, he and his colleagues argued that no nation can flourish unless society itself supports opportunities that suit the needs, abilities, and talents of all its citizens. The Finns do not rely on the promise of upward mobility to defend low wages but rather treat almost every job as an end in itself, independent of where it may or may not lead. In Finland, the adage "A fair day's pay for a fair day's work" is no joke.

In Helsinki, dining at a family-style restaurant one evening, I remarked on the skill and graciousness of a server, who, like most Finns, spoke perfect English. My dining companion, a businessman, looked amused. He'd been to similar restaurants in the United States, he said, and noticed that the servers were sometimes, hum, could he say not quite prepared? He explained that in Finland waiting tables is a valued trade for which people are fairly compensated. "We believe that if you can afford to eat in a restaurant, the person serving you deserves the same opportunity," he said.

This seemed sensible to me, and I wondered if other Americans might not agree. After all, the US Bureau of Labor Statistics recently crowned "food services and drinking places" the nation's fastest-growing employment subsector, surpassing construction and manufacture. And unlike mining or manufacturing or IT, restaurants don't cluster in just a handful of regions but are spread across the nation, serving local economies from Austin to Little Rock. In recent decades, restaurant work has grown as part of the

fundamental shift in all work—that is, away from mass manufacturing to service. Indeed, between 1990 and 2008 nearly 98 percent
of all new jobs, 27.3 million in total, were "nontradable," meaning
jobs in sectors such as health care and teaching and food service
that cannot be outsourced. In the developed world, nontradable
work, basically service work, is the work of the twenty-first century.
And unlike some American politicians, the Finns are ready to face
that undeniable fact.

The Finns fear idleness, both for themselves and for others,
and bolster the unemployed with funds, counseling, and in some
cases temporary positions to help keep them solvent and optimistic throughout their job search. Several government agencies coor-
dinate "occupation-oriented rehabilitation" that includes making
special accommodations for disabled workers. The nation's "youth
guarantee" offers everyone under the age of twenty-five and recent
graduates under thirty either employment, an opportunity to further their studies, or some form of on-the-job training within three
months of becoming unemployed. And this steady investment in
human capital actually begins much earlier, with state-supported
prenatal care, child care, and education up to and including a doctoral, medical, or law degree.

Finland's exemplary school system is famous for launching students to the top of international academic assessments. That's old
news. Most of us have heard of the so-called Finland Miracle. But
I wondered what role, if any, this and other social investments had
played in the country's transformation into an innovation hub, a
nation known for churning out extraordinary numbers of both visionary video game designers and world-class symphony conductors. And I wondered, too, whether this quirky Nordic nation could
realistically serve as an incubator of ideas and practices that could
be adopted in the United States.

My first stop was a visit to Pekka Ylä-Anttila, then head economist at ETLA, the Research Institute of the Finnish Economy.
Ylä-Antilla greeted me in what I came to regard as the customary

Finnish fashion: with cakes, coffee, and a fully loaded PowerPoint presentation. Clicking steadily through the charts and graphs, he landed heavily on one central point: Finland's commitment to its *human* capital. "We are a small nation, so we can't afford to lose anyone," he said, filling my cup. "Our economy is R&D driven, so we really care about our labor force. We have the highest proportion of researchers to workers in the world, and one of the highest rates of innovation. Part of the reason for that is that we have worker protections—without protections, workers won't take risks, but to innovate, they must take risks. Every single person living in this country, no matter where he or she is from originally, has the potential to make a contribution, and we do everything possible to help them fulfill that potential." Finland is less focused on predicting and preparing individuals for particular jobs, he continued, than on helping citizens acquire the knowledge, tools, and resources to chart their own course in a fickle and unpredictable world economy. "It's important to stop thinking industry by industry—biotech, nanotech, IT," he explained. "If you can digitize work, which we can, it can go anywhere. So there's no point in a country trying to specialize in any one industry. We think it's more effective to encourage people to become generalists with the capability and internal resources to invent work for themselves, and the work of the future."

All this sounded fine in theory, but how, I wondered, was Finland preparing its young people to *invent* the work of the future? And what if any lessons could citizens of larger and more diverse nations take away from this process? To find out, I contacted the miraculously efficient Finnish Consulate General and asked for help in arranging visits with entrepreneurs, social scientists, union representatives, and at least one public school to which Americans could realistically relate. Days later I was in a Helsinki cab plowing through late winter drear on the way to Kallahti Comprehensive School in the sprawling Vuosaari district.

Vuosaari borders the Baltic Sea, and I'd read that in some neighborhoods it's scattered with charming beach villas. But I spotted no beach villas, just block after block of squat government-subsidized apartments. It is in these dowdy complexes, the cabdriver told me, that the immigrants live. When the Soviet Union collapsed and Yugoslavia broke apart, Russians and Slavs flooded Finland, many settling in Vuosaari, the easternmost stop on the Helsinki metro. Joining them were Somalis who were living in Soviet territory at the time of the collapse, whether to attend university or to seek refuge from the Somali civil war. Today, so many Somalis live in Vuosaari, the cabbie told me, that locals renamed the main street "Mogadishu Avenue." There are also Turks, Kosovo Albanians, Thais, Bangladeshis, Estonians, and Congolese. "It is like the UN," he said. "But without the diplomats."

We arrived at Kallahti Comprehensive to find what appeared to be the school's entire multiethnic constituency, five hundred strong, spilled across the playground, also like the United Nations, but in miniature. Hoofing soccer balls, gossiping, sneaking smokes—none of the kids seemed fazed by the freezing drizzle. (I was later told that failing a deluge or well below zero temperatures, all but the oldest students are required to spend fifteen minutes of every hour outdoors.) The single identifiable adult, her chest banded with what looked like a crossing-guard vest, gently directed me inside to a small conference room, where the now-expected coffee, pastries, and presentation were waiting.

Vice Principal Kimmo Paavola took my coat, hung it up to dry, and apologized for being "distracted." Apparently a seventh grader had been "struggling with his studies," so early that morning Paavola had convened with the boy, his parents, his teachers, a school psychologist, a social worker, and two other specialists. The eighty-minute powwow culminated in the young man's diagnosis as a "sufferer of low motivation," a condition the educators took quite seriously. The first step in such cases, Paavola told me, is to enroll the underperformer in a small group workshop led by a social worker to "try to motivate him in life." Motivating tactics might include anything from one-on-one tutoring sessions to free tickets to a professional hockey game. Also, there is compulsory family counseling and individual counseling of each parent. If and only if these and other "motivators" fail, the student may be transferred to a special needs class, but—Paavola insisted—this happens rarely and always as a last resort. More than 30 percent of Finnish students experience some sort of intervention in the course of their education, but only a tiny fraction are designated "special needs," a label the Finns regard as stigmatizing and generally counterproductive.

"Many of our students are immigrants, struggling with two cultures," Paavola said. "Their parents have no time and no money, some are depressed or struggling with alcohol. The teachers here relish the challenge of finding a way to support the child even when he doesn't get the support he needs at home. That is our calling, to support people in their lives."

When he was a high school student, Paavola dreamed of becoming a phys-ed teacher, and at forty he looked the part—tall, muscular, head shaved for action. But fewer than one in ten applicants is admitted into Finland's eight highly competitive teacher preparation programs—the Ivy League of Finland—and Paavola did not make the cut. So he put his dream on hold, studied physiotherapy, and, for reasons that were not entirely clear, snared a job as a peacekeeper for the United Nations. "I took care of adult guys in Lebanon and Macedonia," he said. After two and a half years abroad he returned to Finland and was admitted into a four-year program in primary school studies. Then he got a master's degree in teaching. Yet despite his international experience, his multilingualism, and his degrees, he wasn't considered a strong enough candidate to gain admission to a secondary school teacher training program or to be a secondary school teacher. "Frankly, the teachers here were better students than I was, and better scholars than I am," he said. "As a school leader, it is my job to take care of them, to give them the resources they need. People need the collegial support, and that is what I'm here for."

Okay, I'll admit that last comment sounds a bit surreal. But I've triple-checked my notes, and that is precisely what Vice Principal Paavola told me: that his duty was to serve the needs of his faculty, whose challenge was to serve the needs of their students and their students' families. No complaints and no excuses. As a parent, as a teacher, I had to stop for a moment and let the significance of this sink in.

Paavola leads me upstairs to a classroom to observe one of his "better scholars" in action. We arrive on tiptoe at teacher Sanna-kaisa Essang's classroom to find two dozen seven-year-olds, some sitting at their desks, some sitting *on* their desks, and one lying on the floor beside his desk. Teacher Essang, an almost translucent blonde in a wraparound skirt and high-tops, speaks in a soothing whisper, forcing the kids to lean in her direction. They are shoeless (to protect the carpets) and in some cases sockless (by personal preference). One boy wears earmuffs ("just for fun"), one girl a hijab, the Muslim headscarf. Essang, who has a master's degree in multicultural education, has taught here for seven years. She informs the class that because of "today's guest" part of the math lesson will be taught in English. They smile. More than half the kids are foreign born, yet all are nearly fluent in Finnish and most seem to understand at least some English, the formal teaching of which—along with French—begins in third grade at this school. Swedish is compulsory and begins in seventh grade, optional German in eighth grade. All students are expected to be fluent in at least three languages by the completion of ninth grade. I'm told these first graders are already familiar with bits of algebra, geometry, and statistics. Today, they are mastering measurement.

Essang hands each child a paper tape measure—measure your desk, she says, your nose, one another, anything you want. A mini-riot ensues, and as we step back to enjoy the show Essang tells me how privileged she feels to have such an "exciting" class. "We have kids from Brazil, Bangladesh, Estonia, the UK, Somalia, and four from Russia," she told me, adding that 35 percent of her students are recent immigrants. "The Russian kids all speak together in Russian, and this excludes the other kids, so I try to make them keep it to the fifteen-minute recess period. Otherwise, they are to speak English or Finnish." After ten minutes or so, she calls the class to order, and asks the kids what they've discovered. There are no wrong answers, but there are funny answers. "So your nose is a hundred *centimeters* long?" she teases, pulling the tape measure from her nose to the floor. Giggles all around. "The room is a hundred *millimeters*? Okay, let's check again. Get your measuring tapes ready!"

On the blackboard is a rainbow, each color representing a reward for good behavior, not for individuals, but for the group. "Movie day, computer class, toy day, from all seven colors, the class chooses together," Essang told me. "This seems to be working really well." Exiting the building for recess, I ask Essang whether she has a teaching philosophy. "In our district lots of students are coming from broken families, so I feel that they need something stable in their lives, and someone they can trust. I encourage them to be who they really are . . . and once I've gained their trust, then they can learn."

The students at Kallahti Comprehensive School seemed by American standards less like disadvantaged immigrant kids than like precocious attendees of an elite progressive school. They were unhurried and unpressured, encouraged to think independently and to speak their minds, as though their thoughts really mattered. Later in the day, I watched an older group—fourteen- and fifteen-year-olds—bake and frost a cake in a home economics class, where I was told they also learned "laundry" and "money." This course, too, is required of all, and is taught almost like a chemistry lab, the instructor pacing the room critiquing knife technique with scientific precision. I asked one student, who mentioned she was born in the Congo, if she spoke French. "Of course," she said, eyebrow arching. "I speak French and also English, Spanish, Finnish, Swedish, and Swahili." So, I asked, will languages be your specialty? "No, physics." I learned later that this young woman's family had fled Africa for their lives and were cobbling together new ones in one of the government-subsidized housing units I had seen on my drive to the school.

Before I left Kallahti, Paavola walked me down to the Baltic shore, where the kids sometimes go for a nature break. It was bleak and beautiful, blissfully free of both housing projects and beach villas. As we walked he cautioned me that the school was not yet what he hoped it would become. "In past years, we've been a little behind the national average," he said. "I am hoping for average results next year. We always try to improve." To American ears this point-blank humility sounded as foreign as Finnish.

Some grumble that Finland's success is due to sheer luck, a function of its small size and Nordic homogeneity, as if each and every Finn were a Ralph Lauren vision of a fur-covered Viking. But with its public housing, bleak streets, and high unemployment, Vuosaari is no fantasyland. And neighboring Norway, also small and Nordic, doesn't do nearly as well as Finland in national tests. So it seems small size, ethnicity, and geography are not the whole story.

So what's Finland's "secret"? Leo Pahkin, counselor of education on the Finnish Board of Education, had this to say: "There is no secret. We take care of every student because of this calculation: it costs too much not to help people early, because later they will need to work for society. It's that simple."

Harvard University educator Tony Wagner, author of *The Global Achievement Gap*, said that Finland's success comes down to fear, or rather the lack of it. Wagner has spent a good bit of time in Finland, but much more time visiting schools around the United States. And the difference, he said, is stark. "I was at a school in Douglas County, Colorado," he told me. "I asked an auditorium full of students what they wanted most going forward. I'll never forget how one young woman responded. She was a high school senior, I believe. She said, 'I want to get rid of fear in my learning.' And that's what the American educational system has done to many students, made them afraid to learn by punishing them for taking risks that might lead to the 'wrong answer.'"

Wagner told me that the Program of International Student Assessment (PISA), in which Finns excel, measures not just what students know but what they can do with what they know. He said this is something that many American students, in their rush to get the "right" answer, rarely get a chance to consider, let alone practice. The Finns don't rank their children by aptitude or their schools by performance, a custom that one Finnish educator told me would be "unthinkably cruel" and that others dismissed as a "foolish waste of time and emotional energy." Rather, they take the view that encouraging students to muster the courage to ask questions, sometimes questions teachers cannot answer, is the best approach to prepare them for an uncertain future.

So, I wondered, what does all this mean for work? Apparently, the Finns were wondering too. The year of my visit, Helsinki had been designated the World Design Capital, an honor bestowed on "cities that have used design as a tool to reinvent themselves and improve social, cultural and economic life." Marimekko socks and Artek coffee tables don't exactly scream "reinvention," but the ever-practical Finnish government stretched the designation to include the "redesign" of the nation's "work practices." In surveys, many Finns reported feeling frazzled and burned out on the job. They felt out of control and overwhelmed, unable to be as creative or productive as they believed they could be. To sort out what actions might be taken to remediate this, the government engaged the services of Pekka Pohjakallio, then a partner and CEO of Helsinki-based 925 Design, a consulting firm with the avowed mission of "rethinking" work for the twenty-first century.

When we first met, Pohjakallio—a tall, square-jawed man—wore owlish glasses and a mild, slightly disengaged look that belied his intensity. Prior to cofounding 925, he told me, he'd spent most of his career at Nokia, the iconic success story underlying Finland's modern economy. When he started there in 1991, Nokia was among the most valuable technology firms in the world, and Pohjakallio soared there, moving from project manager to vice president of "Concepting and Innovation." He attributes this success to what he called "work heroics." Meetings and e-mail consumed him, and he often worked through the night and on weekends. Yet he was never quite sure why he was putting in so much effort.

"My parents are both retired teachers," he told me. "When they asked me what it was that I did at Nokia, I found it very hard to explain. I thought, well, if I can't explain it, than I guess I'm not sure what it means. Yes, I know I was having an impact on Nokia's net sales. But on any given rainy day in November, I couldn't relate to that—to the sales figures. It wasn't enough. Still, I had difficulty making a change. Even when I'd given my notice to leave the company and was no longer part of the inner circle, I couldn't stop checking my e-mail compulsively. If I wasn't part of things, I felt bad. It was almost a sickness." A sickness, Pohjakallio's research later confirmed, afflicting workers of every variety.

For Pohjakallio, the government-sponsored study was an ideal opportunity, not only to understand the nation's work malaise, but to gain insight into his own. He and his team interviewed 1,100 employees at ten workplaces, including a pulp and paper mill, a mining technology company, a debt collection agency, and an IBM outpost. "We didn't just talk to them, we spied on them for days," he told me. "Everybody seemed to be in a great rush all the time, but no one was quite sure where they were rushing to. And computers were not making things better, they were making things worse. It was so easy to book meetings by e-mail, there were endless numbers of them." (One beleaguered IBM employee had fifty meetings scheduled for a single day!) Almost all the workers spent much of their time simply reacting to stimuli—e-mails, text messages, phone calls. Unsure of what exactly was expected of them, they believed the best way to prove their worth was by demonstrating stamina defined as long hours on the job. At the end of the day, not many had much to show for their labors.

"We saw that many people work really hard all week and then are exhausted on Friday and don't really know what they have achieved. When this happens, they tended to compensate for this feeling of loss by working more. They asked themselves, 'What did I do?' and then reassured themselves by thinking, 'I don't know but at least I worked a lot.' We decided that is crazy."

As you'll recall from earlier chapters, each of us make meaning from our work in our own way. But in many work environments, the making of meaning has become difficult or even impossible. The constant distractions undercut whatever "flow" we strive to achieve, and the constant surveillance undermines our sense of control. Pohjakallio described a "hacker" mentality, whereby employees are encouraged to act now and think later, if at all. "Most people have job descriptions that don't really translate into anything tangible," Pohjakallio said. "So they don't really know what's most important in their job. Anything that comes their way is as important or even more important than what they are doing now. So they flit from thing to thing, often with little opportunity to focus, or to do one job correctly."

In the IT industry, for example, "Ship product now" is more than a slogan, it's key to the sector's culture, trumpeted prominently in the media and in in-house newsletters urging employees to "move fast and break things." This "Code wins arguments" ethic may seem to put power into the hands of the doers, at least temporarily, but it does little to help employees make meaning of their work. Some employees enjoy the intensity of such environments, and some are even captivated by it, but when asked, not many can quite put a finger on what, exactly, all this Sturm und Drang really adds up to, or even means.

As we've seen, this "Do now, think later" strategy is not exclusive to IT, but has become pervasive even in fields like journalism and medicine, where increasingly workers are judged not by the depth of their thinking and the weight of their judgment, but by their productivity, as measured by "content" in the case of journalists, and by "caseload" in the case of medical professionals. Many of these "knowledge workers" are left to wonder what real value they offer beyond corralling customers in service to their employers.

Some organizations try to maximize productivity and encourage "disruptive" innovation by gathering workers in teams. But among the Finnish group's most striking conclusions is that our faith in the power of teamwork may be misplaced. Indeed, studies stretching back decades reveal that brainstorming rarely leads to novel solutions, and in fact can discourage innovative thinking. Rather, peer pressure tends to funnel team members into the very same stream of thought preordained by parameters set by the meeting organizers. Many of us have experienced this frustrating "groupthink" in our own jobs, where any truly novel idea is pushed to the side by a rush to reach a consensus that comports with management goals.

True innovation bubbles up most often when the brain is relaxed and deep in thoughts beyond the particular problem at hand—that is, when we seem to be the least productive. And to be clear, ideas are not in themselves "disruptive." What's disruptive is the implementation of the ideas, a process that is every bit as creative as generating the idea itself. Pohjakallio said many organizations are so obsessed with generating the next new thing that they fail to implement the ideas they generate.

"Reflection is what makes most of us more efficient, not less," Pohjakallio said. "But we are given no time for reflection because it's impossible to measure, and impossible to bill against. We are constantly fixated on the ends, not the means, and that holds us back. If we really knew what was valuable, many of us might easily be able to accomplish what needs to get accomplished not in ten or twelve hours a day but in four."

As example of a better approach, Pohjakallio cited Helsinki's elite ice-hockey team, Jokerit. He and his colleagues interviewed coaches and managers and spent hours in the locker room observing and speaking with the athletes. "Ice hockey is not like most businesses," Pohjakallio said. "It's very clear on each player's role and responsibilities. Managers pay close attention to everything the players do—eating, sleeping, everything. You play two games a week, some home, some away. You need to be fresh, alert. Players cannot be consumed by overwork. For athletes, the point is to focus on working well, not long. So every step in the process is thought out carefully. It's not about billable hours, it's about achieving peak performance."

For professional atheletes the goal is clear, as are the rewards of hard work and persistence. But professional athletes are pampered elites, and it's reasonable to question whether lessons learned from their experience might be fairly applied to us. It would be great if our employers regarded us as unique assets, but to be honest, few of us are unique assets. As far as our employers are concerned, most of us are commodities—not interchangeable, exactly, but also not irreplaceable. I told Pohjakallio of the work of Canadian organizational psychologist Paul Fairlie, whom I'd spoken to months earlier. Fairlie said that job satisfaction had been slipping for decades in North America and Europe and that many people appear to be psychologically withdrawing from their jobs as an "important life pursuit." But here's the thing: according to Fairlie, studies indicate that only 8 percent of "life longings" are job related. (How he arrived at that precise number I do not know, but I'm using it here for the purpose of argument.) "Ninety-two percent of what humans want has nothing to do with paid work," he told me. "So if employers can help their workers find meaning in other ways, not just their job, that's easily a big plus."

Pohjakallio made his living as a workplace guru, so he was not eager to promote the idea of employers helping workers to find meaning outside the job. But he reluctantly conceded that he knew

just such an employer, and a very good one: Snellman, a meat production company in the north of Finland. Snellman is known for
its succulent sausages, a Nordic dietary mainstay. Earlier that year,
Pohjakallio and his team had interviewed dozens of employees at
Snellman and were stunned at how sharply the experience of those
workers contrasted with the experience of workers in other sectors,
especially IT. At Snellman, employees were encouraged to bring
their entire selves to the workplace, but not for the usual reasons.

"One Snellman employee we interviewed had studied philosophy and languages at university, and was very sophisticated,"
Pohjakallio recalled. "And it was quite clear that he enjoyed his job
making sausage. So I asked him what it was about the job that was
so satisfying. He told me: 'This company has changed the quality
of the sausage eaten in this country, and I'm part of that. Also, I
can get better every day here.'" Pohjakallio noted that the employee
did not say he was working his way up the job ladder, but simply
that he "got better," implying that he was learning and growing
not only on the job but in his life. Apparently, Snellman was doing
everything it could to help make that happen. "It's quite a special
company," Pohjakallio said.

Snellman got its start in a basement run by five brothers living in
a small town on Finland's northwest coast. But unlike most start-
ups, after more than six decades it is alive and thriving, renowned
for the quality of its products and its loyalty to its customers. That
loyalty also extends to its staff. A company promotional video captures workers pumping iron in a well-equipped on-site gym. The
workout room is similar to those found at the sort of American
companies that hope to capture employees in a ersatz "home away
from home." But Snellman is different. The video follows one employee as he leaves the gym, exits company headquarters, mounts
a bike, and pedals off to his actual home for an early dinner with
his actual family. Quite a contrast from companies that use gyms
and other perks to tie workers to the workplace. And I learned that
Snellman goes beyond "skills training" to offer on-site college-level

courses in languages and law. Far from urging employees to "move fast and break things," the company encourages them to move cautiously and invest in themselves. The message seems to be not "Give us your all and our company will make meaning for you," but rather "Our company will provide the income, support, and stability to allow you to make meaning for yourself."

"This company understands people," Pohjakallio told me. "And it understands that the work/life balance is an expired concept. The word *balance* to me implies conflict; the idea that there is this wonderful thing called life, and this awful thing called work that interferes with life. But that's not relevant anymore. Let's forget the work/life balance, because it almost always results in guilt, the feeling that we're always in the wrong place, be it at work or at home. Let's take away time as a measure of accomplishment; all that pressure doesn't make us more productive or creative, it leads to madness."

Snellman is hardly a hotbed of innovation. But it is very much a twenty-first-century employer, with more than two thousand direct employees partnering with more than 2,100 Finnish farmers. Pohjakallio pointed out that Snellman and similar companies employ far more people than do the vast majority of high-tech firms, and therefore that the lessons they teach might have a far wider application.

"A business that makes great products and takes care of its people and their families, where quality and trust are number one, that's the sort of company we can learn from," Pohjakallio told me. "I remember in particular an interview there with an employee, a typical Finnish guy, who told me that for him a feeling of security was everything. He said: 'This is a very good place for a small person to be.'"

Most of us, Pohjakallio said, are small people, not in the sense that we are lesser than others, but in the sense that we find satisfaction and purpose in small, steady accomplishments in our work rather than being saddled with vague and grandiose expectations.

"In the US, Mark Zuckerberg seems to work all the time and demands the same from his workforce," Pohjakallio said. "But he is not the role model of future business leaders. The CEO of Snellman, well, yes, maybe he's the one we should be looking up to. Work cannot be measured in hours spent, it must be measured in things accomplished, and accomplishing those things and making meaning of them takes thought. Our advice to companies is to give people the time and space to think, and to trust them. And we think what we have learned here, in Finland, can be applied anywhere around the world."

I thanked Pohjakallio for his insights and headed off to meet with Tommi Laitio, Helsinki's director of youth affairs. Laitio, who was thirty-five at the time but looked half a decade younger, greeted me in his bunker-like office, bundled into a thick wool sweater to ward off the chill. He made no apologies for the setting of his thermostat, though he did hint that frugality is all but embedded in his DNA. "My mother came from a family of six, with only two pairs of boots among them," he said. Laitio's parents grew up together in a one-company town, the company being a foundry that no longer exists. "When the cast-iron factory closed, that city died, and people there had no recourse," he said. A generation later, when Nokia lost its footing, Finland as a whole felt something similar, though not for long. Though fiercely capitalistic, Finland learned quickly that it could not rely for its working future on the largesse of private enterprise.

In January 2017, Finland became the first EU nation to pay two thousand unemployed citizens a basic monthly income of roughly $687—no strings attached—in a unique social experiment aimed at reducing poverty and, ultimately, unemployment. The two-year trial was meant not to incentivize sloth but to determine whether a guaranteed basic income would prompt unemployed people to work in a different way—to take more risks and maybe even innovate. After the first year, a few unofficial findings started to leak out. (At this writing, the official findings were not yet available.) It seemed that the payments had, at least in some cases, motivated positive change. Some beneficiaries had ramped up their volunteer work; others were employed part time or had found full-time jobs. One participant (who had two master's degrees and had been unemployed for nearly two years) said the payments gave her the freedom to take a part-time job she loved and greatly reduced her stress. And since all participants continued to get benefits no matter their employment status, some were using the extra income to start a side business. One father of six crafted "shaman drums" (sometimes used in traditional Lapland ceremonies) and sold them for nine hundred euros apiece. He also carved out space in his home to run an Airbnb catering to artists. As a British commentator described it, the payouts were not enough to pull the man and his family completely out of poverty, but they were enough to "remove the fear of utter destitution, freeing him to do work he finds meaningful."

I told Laitio that it seemed to me that such a scheme would be unpopular in the United States, where we prefer to allow market forces to sort things out. Laitio, who had lived in the United States, chuckled. "The Miracle of Finland is really no miracle," he told me. "Americans trust the markets. Finns trust the government, which means we trust each other. When you trust each other, you can do so much more."

Finland's modern success story was built on an extraordinary level of social trust, the glue that binds citizens together in common cause. When social trust is low, businesses stall in contract negotiations and litigation, and government gets mired in ideological infighting. When social trust is high, both business and government are able to more nimbly respond to change.

Harvard sociologist Robert Putman brought this issue to wide public attention when, in 1992, he reported that the proportion of Americans who claimed limited or no trust in the government had risen steadily to a troubling 75 percent. Putman found that Americans of the time not only voted far less frequently than did the previous generation but also were less engaged in educational, religious, and political organizations. In more recent surveys, nearly two-thirds of respondents said they distrust the news media, sales clerks, other drivers on the road, and people they met while traveling. Experts ascribe this to any number of factors, with the most likely culprit being the nation's dramatic economic inequality. Trust levels were highest in the 1960s, when income disparity in the United States was at historic lows. Trust levels declined as the gap between rich and poor broadened through the 1980s, 1990s, and 2000s. In 2017, with income inequality at historic highs, a mere 18 percent of Americans trusted the federal government to "do the right thing" most of the time.

So, who among us constitutes this trusting 18 percent? Generally it's the wealthy, who on average claim to trust for the obvious reason that the system has treated them and those they know quite kindly. The privileged sometimes use their wealth to escape from the inconvenience of other people, in some cases insulating themselves in a "mansion on the hill" or in gated communities. The wider the income gap, the starker that isolation becomes, and the more likely the wealthy are to "trust" and the less wealthy—the great majority of Americans—to lose faith in a system over which they feel they have little say and less control.

In sharp contrast, Finland has a low level of economic inequality and a high level of social trust; roughly 70 percent of Finns say they trust both government and their fellow citizens. Economic models suggest that this trust correlates with economic growth, and also with more smoothly running markets. Trust reduces the demand for costly legal and insurance services and increases the flow of information among businesses. Citizens who feel more connected to one another are more willing to invest in their communities through taxes, and more likely to develop habits of cooperation and reciprocity that make government more efficient. In Finland government is so transparent, I was told, that almost any citizen can arrange a telephone meeting with the president.

University of Maryland political scientist Eric Uslaner has written extensively on trust and its role in economic growth and, in particular, innovation. "There's a belief out there that people innovate only to get rich," he told me. "That's not true. In some societies, the desire to innovate is almost ground into the culture. In the US, innovation often is just a matter of applying automation to cut jobs. In Finland, innovation often means creating opportunities."

The term *solidaristic individualism* was coined by sociologists to describe a system in which people are willing to support one another even when they don't agree with one another. The bargain is this: my goals and values may differ from yours, but I believe you have a right to your beliefs, and I will support you on the condition that you support me in mine. Such a bargain—though tacit—motivates the Finns to tolerate differences and support one another while maintaining a healthy regard for individual effort and achievement. Their high levels of trust come not from impartiality—the idea that one comes to the table with few opinions and an open mind—but truth telling, being honest and open about their views.

Finns value frankness and disdain flattery and boosterism. The idea of emblazoning one's chest with company swag—say, in the form of a Google hoodie—is not entirely alien in Finland, home to Rovio, the entertainment and media juggernaut built on the phenomenal success of the video game Angry Birds. But the culture at Rovio is entirely different from that of similar companies in the United States. Rovio management expects employees to work hard, produce, and innovate. But the company does not expect them to merge their identity with the firm, which, executives admit, is not a great thing to do. Rovio chief of marketing Peter Vesterbacka once confessed that the company's working environment can be chaotic. "People will tell you it pretty much sucks," he said. "People will tell you brutally what is wrong." It's hard to imagine a Silicon Valley executive admitting as much, unless, of course, he or she is a *former* Silicon Valley executive.

Paul Romer, until January 2018 the chief economist at the World Bank, teaches at the Stern School of Business at New York University. Romer has argued that the future of work depends most critically on "meta-ideas" that support the production and transmission of other ideas. The nation that takes the lead in this effort, he contends, will be the one that most effectively supports productivity and growth in both the private and the public sectors. In a speech at the National Academy of Sciences he made the point that "even if technology has been improving rapidly enough to raise average income, somehow the benefits of that are being distributed in a way that favors those on the upper rungs of the economic ladder so that median income is not growing." Income inequality contributes heavily to our nation's work disorder, a disorder Romer predicts will be solved not by technology but by a "change in the rules." For example, modifications in the tax structure to incentivize employers to create not just more jobs but better jobs. Through long and painful experience, the Finns have come to understand the importance of changing the rules in response to progress. Americans—some of whom continue to pray for the reascendency of coal and the banishment of immigrants—not so much.

This chapter began with the acknowledgment that Finland is not the United States. I'll stand by that. But we can certainly take lessons from a nation that so quickly rose from a state of utter stagnation and despair to become among the happiest and most innovative on the planet. By opening their minds and putting their trust in one another, Finns found a way to address the problem of work head-on, with policies that lift up the less fortunate, sustain the middle class, and encourage true innovation. What the Finnish story tells us is that foretelling the future of work is no easier than foretelling the future of anything—"common wisdom" can lead us astray. Clearly, it is time to think—and act—anew.

ABOLISH HUMAN RENTALS

In our society, labor is one of the few productive
factors that cannot legally be bought outright.
Labor can only be rented.
—PAUL SAMUELSON

I have always been fully persuaded that, through
co-operation, labor could become its own employer.
—LELAND STANFORD

Robert Owen, father of the modern worker-cooperative movement, was born in Newtown, North Wales, on May 14, 1771, the sixth of seven children. His father was an ironmonger and his mother the daughter of farmers. Though the family was not poor, its fortunes were uncertain, and the children were encouraged to fend for themselves. A precocious and eager student, Robert left school at age nine and home at age ten for London, where he apprenticed with a manufacturer of ladies' clothing. His master, a benevolent Scotsman, offered the boy access to his extensive library. Young Robert took full advantage, immersing himself in the great works of history, philosophy, and religion. Gradually his reading turned him away from the idea of free will and toward the belief that human character is formed by circumstances over which individuals do not have total control. Society, he concluded, must take responsibility for all its members.

At age seventeen Owen left London for Manchester and with

a partner formed a company specializing in the manufacture of steam-driven cotton-spinning machines. He sold the business and invested his profits in the aptly named Chorlton Twist Company, a prosperous steam cotton mill. It was then, on a business trip to Glasgow, that he met Anne Caroline Dale.

Anne was daughter of David Dale, a wealthy banker and owner of the New Lanark Mills, the largest cotton-spinning conglomerate in Scotland. Owen befriended Dale, married his daughter, and with a few partners bought Dale's four booming textile factories, coaxing them into becoming an even more profitable enterprise. He grew rich but also was scandalized by the horrifying abuses he witnessed daily on the factory floor.

For, while manufacturing had once been largely a matter of widely dispersed home-based cottage industries, home was not the place for mass production. The British industrial class was galvanized by the new machines and the opportunity to grow capital through the centralization of labor. Through the concentration and magnification of human effort, factories made it possible for the few to gorge on the fruits of the labor of many. And in this, cotton was truly king.

The invention in 1779 of the steam-driven cotton-spinning mule upended a six-hundred-year-old English guild system, and forced tradesmen to abandon their workshops for factories. In just one generation England transformed from a nation of independent entrepreneurs to a nation of wage earners—or, as some carped, "human rentals."

Owen found himself a reluctant general on the front lines of this revolution. He likened the life of factory workers to that of American slaves, or even worse. He decried "the great attention given to the dead machinery, and the neglect and disregard of the living machinery." And he saw no business advantage in cruelty. To the contrary, he was sure that humane treatment of workers would lead to higher profits. At New Lanark he built schools, housing, a day nursery, and a kindergarten. He installed a dining hall, a library, and to the disdain of his Calvinist neighbors, a theater and dance hall. He whittled the workday down from fourteen hours to ten and banished young children from the factory floor. He organized a cooperative store for his workers and encouraged them to garden and take up handicrafts. His partners objected to these and other indulgences and eventually broke with him. Owen took on new partners. His business flourished. Trust prevailed.

Owen harbored great hopes that his enlightened thinking and practices would catch on, and why not? Just as contented cows produce better milk, he reasoned, contented workers produce better products. But his arguments, while persistent, did not change the minds of many of his peers. As long as there were more people in search of paid work than there was paid work available, factory owners saw no advantage to improving labor's lot. If anything, working conditions worsened in Britain. In the words of one historian, factories of the period were "perfect infernos: places in which those who entered did so without hope of emerging except blind or maimed or tubercular wreckages." A survey commissioned by the House of Commons warned of "factories, no means few in number, nor confined to the smaller mills, in which serious accidents are continually occurring," adding that the workers were "abandoned from the moment that an accident occurs; their wages are stopped, no medical attendance is provided, and whatever the extent of the injury, no compensation is afforded." A German visitor, observing the machine-mangled workers staggering through the streets of Manchester, compared the carnage to "living in the midst of the army just returned from a campaign."

Horrified by all this, Owen continued to lobby for reforms. In 1815 he proposed a bill that would prohibit the hiring of workers younger than age ten, and set a maximum ten-and-a-half-hour workday for those under eighteen. Parliament settled on a nine-year-old age limit and a twelve-hour working day for children sixteen years and younger. So Owen took another tack, reasoning that not only were factories killing children but that automation was idling hands. "Men being more expensive than mechanical or chemical inventions and discoveries . . . the men were discharged, and the machines were made to supersede them," he wrote in his autobiography.

Idle hands, Owen reminded his countrymen, were the devil's workshop. Among other reforms, he advocated setting up a series of villages where residents would engage in a mix of agricultural and industry and labor cooperatively. Parliament's enthusiasm for this proposal was, to put it kindly, muted. Owens reports the response thus: "Mr. Owen—this committee is not prepared to consider a report so extensive in its recommendations, so new in principle and practice, and involving great national changes."

Undaunted (and possibly deluded), Owen set sail for America, specifically, New Harmony, Indiana, a community carved out of a twenty-thousand-square-acre patch of wilderness by Lutheran immigrants who had separated from their home church in Germany. After the Lutherans pulled up stakes and moved to Pennsylvania, Owen purchased the town for $125,000, nearly his entire fortune. Owen's plan was to found a utopian community, where "labour exchanges" and "labour bazaars" eliminated middlemen, essentially putting workers in control. His intention was to build a "new moral world" where men and women would work cooperatively, owning both the means and the fruits of their efforts.

Owen's work at New Harmony was widely heralded. Social progressives flocked there, and a joint session of Congress convened to which Owen was invited to express his views. Outgoing president James Monroe and president-elect John Quincy Adams were terribly impressed, and a scale model of New Harmony was put on display in the White House. But approbation was not enough to sustain the cooperative. Ravaged by internal squabbles and poor management, New Harmony fell apart in three years. Owen returned to England, where, having lost most of his fortune, he was no longer a flourishing capitalist. Still, he enthused that scientific advances had pushed civilization beyond "a boundary never before reached in the history of man: . . . [beyond] the regions of poverty arising from necessity and . . . into those of permanent abundance." He died nearly penniless, with these last words on his lips: "I gave important truths to the world, and it was only for want of understanding that they were disregarded. I have been ahead of my time."

Medrick Addison had heard a lot about Robert Owen, and he couldn't help but admire him. While he was not sure Owen's dream would come true for everyone, he seemed fairly sure it would come true for him. A big man in his midforties, Addison had a soulful look that could easily pass for sadness. When we met it was a steamy day in early June, and his shirt clung damply to his back as we strolled through the Cleveland neighborhood where he grew up. The streets were peaceful and neat as a graveyard. Addison pointed toward his childhood home, a brick apartment complex with thick plywood sheets blinding the window holes. He said he hoped to see the day the plywood got switched out for glass. But, he added, he wasn't holding his breath.

Addison was born in Itta Bena, Mississippi, where he said his father once taught sociology at Mississippi Valley State University and his mother worked as a dietician. At eighteen months, he moved with his mother and siblings to Cleveland and his dad drifted out of the picture. "When I was sixteen I started taking care of myself," he said. "At eighteen, I enlisted in the army." Army life didn't quite suit him; he liked having things his own way. So when his wife got pregnant with their third child, he took a general discharge and returned home. He wasn't worried. He had military service, a high school degree, and every reason to expect he'd land a job. But Cleveland wasn't hiring, at least not him. Undaunted, he suited up to surf the zeitgeist—entrepreneurship! He'd read all about it, and he knew just what to do. He enrolled in community college and focused on business, marketing mostly. A year later, he dropped out. "I had no one to lean on but myself," he told me. "With three kids, I needed money, now. So I made a bad choice."

That choice was to deal cocaine, a job that was harder than it might seem. First, you have to negotiate with shady people you may fear. Second, you have to find a way to steer clear of the law. Addison had difficulty on both counts, but it was the second hurdle that changed his mind.

"Jail is no place you want to go back to," he told me.

But he did go back. And after the second time, he'd had enough. He cobbled together a loan and opened a restaurant. That work wasn't easy either. His plan was to do everything but cook. But when the cook quit Addison had to do that too. "It worked out for a while," he said. "Then the economy crashed and I had no clientele." He closed the restaurant, returned to college, and this time completed an associate's degree in business administration, management, and operations. Still, no offers, so he signed up for job-training programs. "I'd do the training, pay for transportation and fees, and then I'd be trained—but for what?" he said. "There were no jobs. Not even a hint of a job."

Addison felt branded, as though the word *unworthy* was tattooed on his forehead. Desperate, he signed on with Towards Employment, a nonprofit agency he'd heard helped people who'd run out of options. Given his previous disappointments, it was a leap of faith to fill out the forms, answer the questions. And it was a leap of faith to even consider the job interview the agency set up. "At first I said, no way I'm going to do that," he said. "But my wife thought I should go have a look. So I did."

The job on offer was manager of Evergreen Cooperative Laundry, a commercial laundry carved out of a former automotive machine shop. It wasn't the dark, dingy, and rundown place Addison thought it would be. It was dolled up with skylights, glass-block ribbon windows, bike racks out front, and a trio of murals hand-painted across the polished brick exterior. It looked good. But decor, the surface of things, was never Addison's priority. What mattered to him was work he could own. And Evergreen was a worker-owned cooperative, built on the utopian vision that Robert Owen imagined so long ago.

"They told me that after six months I could buy into the place, have an ownership share," he said. "That sold me." Thanks to his previous experience running his own business, Addison got the job and within a year rose from manager to official Evergreen spokesperson and evangelist. Ownership, he said, made all the difference. "I've seen a lot of lives transformed at Evergreen Cooperative," he told me. "And one of them is mine."

Launched to great fanfare in 2009, the laundry was the first venture undertaken by the Evergreen Cooperatives Corporation, a holding company that in 2010 launched Evergreen Energy Solutions, a cooperative specializing in solar panel and LED installations, and in 2013 Green City Growers, the nation's largest urban hydroponic greenhouse. Five years from launch, the energy company and the laundry were making a tidy profit, a feat that to locals seemed nothing short of a miracle. That's because in Glenville, the neighborhood where Addison grew up and where the laundry and energy cooperative reside, the median household income hovers around $23,205, the crime rate greatly exceeds the national average, and more than half of children grow up below the poverty line.

Glenville is the sort of place where much is promised and not much is delivered. But Evergreen tries not to make promises, especially promises it can't keep. The organization was built on Robert Owen's insight that "free will" doesn't really mean much when people don't have the opportunity and the means to apply it. No amount of training or education is going to create demand for work unless someone is willing to pay for that work to get done.

The Evergreen strategy is to create work that meets a real demand and then give workers the opportunity to buy into it. "When I hire, I'm not necessarily looking for any particular skills," Addison told me. "People can learn skills on the job. I'm looking for attitude, and heart."

Addison drove me to the laundry, where I introduced myself to a woman in a hairnet and a blue uniform top urging fitted sheets through a machine that folded them flat, neat as a magic trick. Thirty-one years old, a single mother of two, she told me that this was her first full-time job. She'd worked retail—mostly fast food and discount stores—but the erratic hours and paltry pay sustained neither her family nor her peace of mind. She needed something steady and sure, work she could count on and grow into. Until Evergreen, she didn't see that happening. For one thing, she didn't have a car, and since there were almost no jobs in Glenville, that made things pretty tough. For another, she did not possess the attitude most bosses seemed to favor. She admitted to being blunt and stubbornly independent, traits not many employers seek in an entry-level hire. "I'm not going to lie," she told me. "I wasn't sure I'd make it through the first six months here at the laundry. But I kept thinking, I'm going to own a piece of this one day, and that kept me going. I can see a future now."

"Seeing a future" was a phrase I heard more than once that day, as I watched as sheets, towels, and other linens trucked in by the ton from nearby hospitals, clinics, hotels, and nursing homes were laundered by careful hands. The entire cycle—from first wash through folding—took twenty-eight minutes. Every employee was expected to learn every piece of equipment and also to master basic skills in customer service and sales. In a worker-owned operation, the bottom line is not theoretical, it's very real and very personal. Every man and woman really counts.

Evergreen CEO John McMicken signed onto the effort in 2013, about a year after his young son, Charlie, had a heart transplant.

While he did not make a direct link between his personal and professional life, he made it clear that he saw his family's challenge and the challenges of Evergreen in a similar light. "They were both problems to be solved," he told me flatly. "A lot of companies tell their employees to 'take ownership,' but what does that mean? At Evergreen, we mean it literally. Our people invest, they own an equity share in the company, and they have a say in how it's run. They have a say in who gets hired, and they sit on the board and share in the profits. Being successful here means all of us working together, not as a 'team' in the sense the term is generally used, but as co-owners where everyone has skin in the game."

Evergreen Cooperatives had a bumpy start. In the early years not all voices were heard and mistakes were made, some of them grave. Clients disappeared and deals dried up. Money ran short, and some workers had trouble cashing their paychecks. McMicken said that he was once "a whisker away" from closing the laundry for good. But that was then. When we last spoke, in early 2018, the laundry was about to double its capacity and its payroll.

Evergreen is often described as an essential pivot point, "proof of concept" that in a networked world, good work for the average Joe and Jane can be driven and sustained through local needs and demands, with the profits retained by the community. Ohio native Ted Howard, a veteran social activist, was one of its principal architects. Howard is cofounder and president of the Democracy Collaborative, a modest think tank based at the University of Maryland. The collaborative pioneered the concept of creating worker-owned cooperatives to serve "anchor institutions": hospitals, universities, museums, schools, nursing homes, and other facilities that by definition are moored in a particular neighborhood. The idea was to nurture a give-and-take relationship between these organizations and the cooperatives that served them—that is, to reboot the virtuous cycle of work that once powered places like Cleveland.

Cleveland was once the fifth-largest city in the United States, and unimaginably vibrant. Glimmers of this grandeur can still be seen in its majestic institutions: the Cleveland Clinic, Case Western Reserve University, University Hospitals of Cleveland, the Cleveland Symphony, and the stunning Cleveland Museum of Art. These and many other humbler establishments—nursing homes, day-care centers, schools—generate a voracious demand for food, energy, transportation, business services, and, in some cases, clean laundry. Most of that demand is outsourced to large corporations with no particular attachment to the local community. These large businesses serve the needs of investors, and that's fine, for the investors. But the focus on shareholders often leaves employees, and good work, by the wayside.

The Democracy Collaborative leadership urged representatives of a number of Cleveland's most venerable institutions to rethink their obligations to the public, challenging them to carefully consider where and from whom they procured goods and services. Their argument was this: Would it not be fairer and wiser to turn closer to home and invest in the people and community that hosts you? As the primary example of how this all might work, they cited the Mondragon Cooperative Corporation (MCC), a federation of more than two hundred worker-owned cooperatives clustered in a lush mountain valley in the Basque region of northwest Spain.

Mondragon's creation story goes something like this: Long ago, in the turbulent wake of Spain's bloody civil war, Father José María Arizmendiarrieta, a charismatic young priest, was sent by his archbishop to a beleaguered manufacturing village deep in the Pyrenees Mountains. Aghast at the poverty he found there, Arizmendiarrieta gathered the community into a fund-raising effort to build a technical school. The funds were raised, the school was built, and more than a decade later, in 1956, five graduates, all engineers, formed a small company to hand-build paraffin heaters, a worker cooperative in which each would have a vote and a share in the profits. Spain's economy had by then to some degree recovered from the war, and the cooperative prospered and the model grew, with more and more businesses joining on, all financed by a bank that Arizmendiarrieta also helped found.

Today MCC is one of Spain's largest commercial conglomerates, encompassing more than 120 cooperatives in every sector—from the bicycle maker Orbea to the Eroski supermarket chain. Together these firms employ a reported eighty-three thousand workers directly and many thousands more through subsidiary companies in Portugal, France, Germany, Brazil, China, and other nations (though not all subsidiaries are cooperatives—and not all workers in these subsidiaries are owner-members). MCC operates on a policy of "network resource sharing," a buddy system that ensures that when one cooperative starts to slip, the others rush in to assist with loans or other supports. Each business contributes 10 percent of pretax profits to a central fund to finance new cooperatives, with a focus on stability. In the midst of the 2007–2010 global financial crises, when 3.7 million Spanish citizens were added to the nation's unemployment roster, Mondragon kept its payroll steady. To avoid layoffs, the members agreed to a 5 percent cut in salary, with managers going first.

Mondragon has for decades been a mecca for labor activists and other progressives, hordes of whom make pilgrimages to admire this living testament to "responsible capitalism." The cooperatives, which together boast roughly $15 billion in annual sales, played a seminal role in the rise of the Basque region from rural poverty to relative wealth. Mondragon maintains its own schools, university, technical institute, and research centers, as well as one of the largest banks in Spain. It operates on a decentralized strategy, whereby firms collaborate to form networks to respond quickly to volatile markets—when there's an unfilled niche, workers are free to jump in to fill it without the burden of a bulky management apparatus. The companies are lean, with relatively few managers, and are specifically directed at sustainable job creation. (This is also typical of cooperatives in Italy, where in the prosperous Emilia Romagna region 40 percent of GDP is generated by worker-owned cooperatives.)

To its many admirers, Mondragon is living proof that the modern corporate model—where the demands of investors trump the needs of workers—is ripe for disruption. Not a few Americans aspire to something similar. Whether that aspiration can be fulfilled on a significant scale remains an open question that experiments like Evergreen are poised to address.

In Cleveland, a five-mile drive from the laundry brings me to Green City Growers, a $17 million, 174,240-square-foot hydroponic greenhouse sprawled across a former brownfield site. The newest of Evergreen's three cooperatives, Green City Growers was also the most expensive to build and operate, and by far the most ambitious; with an annual yield of three million heads of lettuce and three hundred thousand pounds of cilantro, parsley, and basil, it's hard to overlook. The greenhouse is precisely calibrated to be both high-tech and labor intensive, a duet of human and machine. It's already the largest urban food-producing operation in America, and McMicken told me that a new, multiyear deal to grow basil for a major buyer makes future expansion all but inevitable.

Cleveland may seem like the wrong place to grow food, but in some ways it's perfect: it harbors thousands of vacant buildings surrounded by thousands of acres of vacant land. Agriculture, as it turns out, is a reasonable way to put all that empty space to good use. Cleveland ranks second in the nation in local food and agriculture; it's home to a few dozen for-profit farms and over two hundred community gardens. Most of the smaller farms peddle their wares in the city's lush farmers' markets or directly to restaurants— that is, to the elite. But Green City Growers can compete on a much larger scale; its customers include many of the city's anchor institutions and several large supermarket chains. To account for the relatively high wages and benefits of its workforce, the cooperative's prices are slightly higher, but the quality and freshness of its products result in less waste and reduce overall costs.

Green City Growers donates about 1 percent of its crop to Cleveland food banks, where its worker-owners are no longer likely to be clients. Mack Squire, one of the coop's twenty-five original employees, was pretty happy about that. Squire got his start at Green City dropping pelletized lettuce seeds—one by one—into squares of spongy growth medium. At fifty-three, he had a high school degree in business and commerce and a master technician certificate from Ohio Technical College. Before signing on with the greenhouse, neither of these distinctions brought him steady work. He mentioned that his previous employer, an industrial stamping plant, had let him go after losing a contract to a company in China. "But here," he said, "no one has to worry about competition from China. It's all about making things work here, in Cleveland."

The Cleveland experiment is just that, an experiment. It's not meant to employ hundreds of thousands, and it's not for everyone. But it may well be part of the solution, one way to bring good work back to local communities. Atlanta, New Orleans, Detroit, Baltimore, and New Haven, Connecticut, all have voiced interest in the model. Rochester, New York, has invested in its first cooperative—an energy company, and Richmond, Virginia, is planning to do the same.

When we first spoke, Evergreen architect Ted Howard had just returned from giving a speech in Amarillo, Texas, where about a quarter of the US beef supply is processed. A vegetarian, Howard had a tough time navigating the menus there (seventy-two-ounce steaks!), and he worried that he'd also have a tough time connecting with his audience. "It's such a politically conservative place that people remind you that in 1964 Lyndon Johnson lost to Goldwater in Amarillo," he recalled. In his speech, Howard envisioned Amarillo's anchor institutions—hospitals, colleges, even the large meatpackers—as customers for a slew of worker-owned cooperatives in transportation, cleaning, and food services. When he finished his talk, the city's Republican mayor shot up a hand with a question. Howard braced himself for harsh words, but the mayor surprised him. "This sharing thing, where everyone owns a piece," he said. "That really makes sense to me."

Indeed, "this sharing thing" makes sense to many Americans, and always has. Farmers have since colonial times formed cooperatives to pool resources, consolidate their market power, and insulate themselves from lean years. Robert Owen's New Harmony, though not itself a rousing success, inspired hundreds of manufacturing worker-owned cooperatives to emerge in response to industrial age struggles over wages and working conditions. Worker-owned cooperatives were also a key element in early labor unions: in the mid- to late 1800s there were more than five hundred worker cooperatives across the country, some of them quite large. The Knights of Labor, with seven hundred thousand members at its peak in 1886, mobilized factory labor into what it called the "co-operative commonwealth," an alternative economic system built on worker democracy and the abolition of "wage slavery."

In the twentieth century, public support for worker cooperatives rose with the Great Depression, when hundreds of worker cooperatives were revived or created with the explicit purpose of job creation. The post–World War II boom years and the rise of unions contributed to a decline of enthusiasm for the form until the 1960s and '70s, when worker cooperatives resurfaced as part of the larger social justice movement, only to get buried in the neoliberal policies of the Ronald Reagan administration.

Throughout this checkered history, the appeal of worker ownership remained undeniable, even to its detractors. In a 1987 speech Reagan shared his thoughts: "I can't help but believe that in the future we will see in the United States and throughout the western world an increasing trend toward the next logical step, employee ownership. It is a path that befits a free people."

As history shows, our national enthusiasm for worker ownership correlates with the ebb and flow of the economy: when times are bad, our interest peaks. Melissa Hoover, president of the US Federation of Worker Cooperatives, believes we live in one of those "bad" times. There are about 350 worker-owned cooperatives nationwide, and interest is growing rapidly. That is partly due to the resounding success of a handful of worker-owned cooperatives, notably the Cooperative Home Care Associates (CHCA). Based in the South Bronx neighborhood it also serves, the cooperative is the largest in the nation, with 2,200 staff members, many of them recent immigrants and single mothers. CHCA is of special interest because home health care and personal aides constitute not only the largest single occupation in the United States but the fastest-growing occupation, with a projected ten-year growth of more than 40 percent. Three million jobs strong and growing, home health care is very big business in the US.

Of the more than $3.4 trillion spent annually on health care, more than half is spent on labor, a truly astonishing figure that has not gone unnoticed by investors. Laurie Orlov is founder and principal analyst at Aging in Place Technology Watch, a consulting firm with a special focus on the technology market aimed at older adults. She told me that in 2017 there were seventeen thousand companies operating in the home health care sector alone and $200 million of venture capital investment in new endeavors. "There are two factors driving the demand for home health care," she said. "First, growing longevity of the population aged sixty-five and older. And second, that assisted living [arrangements for the elderly] are so costly as to be out of reach for all but the wealthiest. The demand for home health aides and services is only going to grow as the baby boomers move into their eighties and beyond. In many urban areas, demand has already outstripped supply."

Despite this unquestioned demand, home health care aides hover at the very bottom of the health care hierarchy, well below doctors and nurses. They earn an average annual wage of about $21,000, and that only if they are able to find stable, steady employment. This leads to a painful question: Given their soaring demand, why has the market not lifted the prospects of these vital caregivers? Obviously, the job cannot be outsourced, and robots, Orlov assured me, are not up to the task; the work is far too varied and unpredictable. Yet beyond a handful of broad-brush standards required for Medicaid approval, there are no federal regulations covering the nation's three million home-care workers, and—incredibly—only about half of all states require agencies to offer these specialists *any* training. Given this lack of training, low status, and low compensation, perhaps it is no surprise that roughly a third of all criminal convictions for Medicaid fraud involve a personal or home health care aide. Nor is it a surprise that, nationwide, there is only one health care aide available for every three sick or disabled people in need of their services.

CHCA, which is unionized, is rising to the challenge. The cooperative invests $2 million a year in training its members, more than half of whom have ownership in the company (for which they invest $1,000 payable over several years). Owners get an equity share and the opportunity to have a seat on a board composed mostly of worker-members. Ownership and equity are key: in an industry with almost constant turnover, the average tenure at CHCA is seventeen years, meaning that worker-owners tend to stay put, building experience and skills that they apply to benefit their community.

The rise of CHCA was one of several factors leading to New York City's Worker Cooperative Business Development Initiative, which has since 2016 led to the launch of thirty-six new worker-owned businesses. Hoover, of the US Federation of Worker Cooperatives, said that New York is one of a growing number of cities turning to cooperatives as a way to revitalize threatened neighborhoods. "Minneapolis, Austin, New York, Oakland, and Boston are deeply exploring and investing in employee ownership," she said. "Of course, you might expect cities like these to take an interest. But we've also had other, less likely partners—small cities and rural communities that want to preserve or revive their local businesses."

Cooperative ownership is one economic strategy that spans political divides—both conservatives and progressives have noted its advantages. On one end of the spectrum are reformers taking a stand for what they call "democratic ownership," and on the other are residents of struggling flyover America aiming to revitalize devastated local economies. With so many big box stores pulling up stakes and leaving—in early 2018, Walmart shuttered 63 outlets and closed 250 in 2016—these towns are often left with no grocery, no pharmacy, and fewer jobs. In these communities cooperatives are seen as a lifeline.

Co-ops are sometimes misunderstood, regarded not as a challenge to existing business models but as an escape from business altogether. But the financial crisis, Hoover said, changed public thinking. "I'd say there is less talk of democratic control these days than in an overwhelming interest in economic issues," she told me. The major concerns are income inequality, job stability, and the problem of low-wage and contingent work, where a few people skim off the profits and leave society with the liabilities. Suddenly people see worker ownership as a viable alternative to a system that is leaving middle-wage work behind."

Hoover sees a particularly strong opportunity for growth in the conversion to worker ownership of traditional, privately held small businesses. Baby boomers own roughly two-thirds of existing businesses, meaning that over the next couple of decades a "silver tsunami" of retirements will result in trillions of dollars in asset transfers. The question is, where will those assets land? It's estimated that 15 percent of family-owned businesses will stay in the family and that others will be scooped up by private equity firms.

But private equity is not always available, and even when it is, it is not always the first choice of business owners. Passing the business on to employees in a cooperative arrangement is a way to serve their employees, retain their customers, and preserve their legacy.

Meanwhile, the cooperative movement has widened and found common cause in some unlikely places, like union halls. At a national gathering of cooperative owners and advocates I met lawyers, video game designers, cabdrivers, a maker of photovoltaic cells, and Rob Witherell, a contract negotiator for United Steelworkers (USW), the nation's largest industrial labor union. Burly and soft-spoken, Witherell is every inch the union man, but he sees cooperatives as the next big thing. "At the most basic level, labor unions and cooperatives have a lot in common," he told me. "It's all about workers helping each other to make a better life. Unions have had these very public battles in Wisconsin, Michigan, Indiana, and Ohio, and we've lost most of them. There is a pretty well-organized and well-funded opposition to what we do. So if we go back to that primary concept of what it is we should be doing—workers helping each other to improve our standard of living—that opens the doors to trying something new, like a union-cooperative alliance. Rather than just try to convince workers at an existing employer that they would be better off joining the union, it probably makes sense for us to also think about how we can create our own jobs, cooperatively. And by that I mean sustainable jobs, where the rug does not get pulled out from under us because the company can make something five cents cheaper in China."

In the 1950s, unions represented more than one-third of the labor force, and for decades the very threat of unionization kept nonunion-shop practices and wage differentials in check. But with union membership at 6.4 percent of the private sector workforce, the power of unions to negotiate a middle-class life for the majority of American workers is greatly diminished. Economist Eileen Appelbaum of the Center for Economic and Policy Research focuses on the impact of public policy and industry practices on labor. She told me that without the "countervailing force" of unions, "wages are no longer necessarily a way to secure a decent living."

For millions of middle-class Americans, this is not exactly news. In the early 2000s many of us saw our net worth reflected less in our paychecks than in the inflated paper value of our homes and (to a far lesser degree) investments. This powerful "wealth effect" led to the glossing over of the dual problem of stagnating wages and precarious employment. As we've seen, since the 1980s temporary and contract work and self-employment have grown faster than have permanent, full-time jobs. Secure opportunities, especially those offering benefits and a possible career path, have certainly become scarcer, but that's only part of the problem. As one labor attorney told me, "Most people are blissfully unaware of just how vulnerable they are to job loss or downgrades."

America's at-will employment doctrine, the default private sector employment agreement, effectively treats workers as providers of labor with no legal stake in their workplace or, for that matter, their job. This is a terribly slender reed on which to hang a working life. As legal scholar Clyde W. Summers once observed: "The [employment at will] law, by giving total dominance to the employer, endows the employer with divine right to rule the working lives of its subject employees." In the legal sense, this "divine right" has reduced employment arrangements to the state of "human rentals" that Robert Owen and his followers so fervently decried.

Regarding ourselves as "human rentals" makes it more difficult for us to make meaning of our work, for the very reason that we are human and therefore subject to certain assumptions, including what social scientists call the "reciprocal obligation." In the employment context, the reciprocal obligation involves a psychological contract between employers and employees—the implication that each party will work together for mutual benefit. Employment at will essentially breaches this implicit contract: since it allows employees to be fired for almost any reason, or no reason at all, it puts all but a privileged few at a great disadvantage. For example, a Los Angeles accountant might accept a job offer from a firm in Charleston, South Carolina, quit her job, urge her husband to quit his job, sell their apartment, yank the kids out of school, move her family across the country to a new home, only to receive a text message that her services are not needed—with no explanation. "People believe they have a right to work, but in truth they don't have shit," Boston labor attorney Joe Sandulli told me. "Outside of unions, there is very little worker protection."

At-will employment lowers the barrier to hiring by giving employers the opportunity to grow or downsize their workforce and thereby gain competitive advantage. This, proponents argue, has led to more jobs being created more quickly in the United States than in other developed economies. All true. But while employment at will does offer employers more flexibility, it also greatly reduces the ability of workers to negotiate for better jobs, in particular since those jobs are not backed by a union.

In 2015, Harvard economist Richard Freeman and colleagues published "How Does Declining Unionism Affect the American Middle Class and Intergenerational Mobility?" Their conclusions were stunning. Not only did union workers have higher incomes compared to nonunion workers, but the adult children of union members had higher incomes than did adult children of otherwise comparable nonunion parents. Equally alarming, given the decline of unions, was that people living in communities with higher union density had higher average incomes relative to their parents than did people in communities with lower union density. That is, the very presence of unions in a community improved employment prospects for everyone. The authors conclude: "A strong union movement is not simply sufficient for high levels of intergenerational mobility and middle-class membership, but it could be necessary. If that is the case, it will be difficult to meaningfully increase intergenerational mobility and rebuild the middle class without also rebuilding unions or some comparable worker based organizations."

The decline of labor unions and the ascendance of at-will employment arrangements neatly coincided with the rise in the knowledge economy, in which workers are expected to negotiate for individual advantage rather than to bargain collectively toward common goals. The IT sector in particular seemed to consider unions a special threat. In the 1970s, Intel cofounder Robert Noyce declared, "Remaining non-union is an essential for survival for most of our companies" and "a very high priority for management." Twenty years later, Steve Jobs denounced unions as the "essential problem," and venture capitalist and Netscape cofounder Marc Andreessen observed that "there may have been a time and a place for unions, but not sure I see it anymore."

Nevertheless, efforts to unionize the digital workforce have succeeded in fits and starts, and, critically, public support for unions has been on the rise for nearly a decade: in 2017, a solid majority of Americans voiced their approval. Still, it's not likely that unions as we know them will ever return to their industrial-era glory days, as it's all but impossible to bargain collectively when the collective is scattered across the globe.

"The economy is moving away from the way work was organized in the twentieth century, when ten thousand workers gathered in a single workplace, and where a strike of five hundred thousand steel workers could all but paralyze the nation," labor historian Max Fraser told me. "Current attempts—the one-day strikes by fast-food employees and the online protests—are exciting and innovative, but they lack strategic focus. As a scholar of labor history, I know of no form of organizational power anything like the power of collective bargaining—unions were without a doubt the most effective way for workers to gain control over their work. But we're in a moment in history where this no longer works, and we're looking for new models."

Rob Witherell is part of a movement crafting what he hopes will become one of those new models—worker cooperatives that unite workers, owners, and consumers in a common cause that will benefit all stakeholders. "If we think of unions and worker ownership as complementary parts of the same broad labor movement, then we have a greater chance of success of building that movement and making change," he explained. One of the most attractive aspects of worker ownership is that it guarantees a relatively even distribution of profits and earnings, and narrows the gap between the highest and lowest earners. Cooperatives also hold the possibility of offering greater flexibility to respond to the erratic demands of a distributed economy. Consider energy. Fossil fuels like coal, natural gas, and oil rely on enormous, vertically organized operations where capital resides in very few hands and workers wield little power. But starting in 2013, wind, solar, and other renewables accounted for roughly two-thirds of the new capacity added to the nation's power grid, far outpacing the growth in fossil fuels. While in many states large, investor-owned utilities operate legal monopolies, making it difficult to transfer to renewables, the appeal of residential rooftop solar threatens those monopolies with a cooperative model of "community solar" or "shared solar" networks. So some argue that the future of energy may lie not in large corporations serving investor demands, but in networks of nimble cooperatives responding to the needs of worker-owners who also happen to be customers.

Equally promising, and perhaps even more unexpected, is the online "platform cooperative" designed to allow workers to exchange their labor without the interference—and cost—of a middleman. Platform cooperatives rose as an alternative to old-school online labor brokerages like Upwork and Amazon's Mechanical Turk (MTurk), currently the most popular online work "marketplace." MTurk is an online platform that employers (or "requesters") use to "distribute" what Amazon calls "Human Intelligence Tasks," snippets of work like filling out surveys, tagging photos, transcribing podcasts, or entering data into Excel spreadsheets. Generally, the tasks are broken down into bits that can be completed in a matter of seconds or minutes. For example, perhaps the job is to translate a memo from English to French. Rather than bid out the whole job, Amazon breaks it down into sentences, then bids the project out to hundreds of Turkers, each of whom grabs as many sentences as possible at a rate of maybe a penny or two a sentence. Amazon claims to engage five hundred thousand "Turkers" worldwide, the vast majority of them in the United States and India. In the United States, Turkers are thought to average about $1.50 to $3.50 an hour. Amazon facilitates the process and takes a cut. If the requester is unhappy with a worker's efforts, he can refuse to pay them, and the worker gets stiffed.

Mechanical Turk is wildly popular, for example, to verify and "clean up" data and to train AI algorithms for language-recognition and machine-learning applications. Yet, while demand is growing, satisfaction with the service is not. Requesters complain of workers doing a slipshod job, and workers accuse Amazon of "crowd-fleecing," preying on a desperate worldwide digital workforce to grab the lion's share of profits. (As filmmaker Alex Rivera put it in his cult hit *Sleep Dealer*, "all the work without the worker.") Amazon's own website all but confirms this charge, boasting that the company "significantly lowers costs" by "leveraging the skills of Mechanical Turk Workers from around the world."

MIT mathematician and philosopher Norbert Wiener once warned that under capitalism the very job of new technology was to intensify the exploitation of workers. "Crowd-sourced" work marketplaces have certainly contributed to this problem. Many labor advocates and scholars believe that online platforms like MTurk are ripe for disruption, and some have designed alternatives. One of the more ambitious is Daemo, a comprehensive worker-cooperative platform currently under development at Stanford University's Crowd Research Collective. On Daemo, described as a "self-governed crowd sourcing marketplace," "requesters" are instructed to pay a minimum of $10 an hour, well above the Mechanical Turk average. The site has set up a system to screen workers and to screen out requesters who are exploitative or inappropriate. At this writing, Daemo is still in test mode, and it's too soon to know whether it will scale. But there are a handful of other worker-owned marketplace platforms already in place, both in the United States and in Europe.

California-based Loconomics is a mobile work marketplace linking customers to freelancers in work ranging from math tutoring, accounting, and tax preparation to wedding photography and dog walking. Rather than pay a commission to a Silicon Valley overlord, Loconomics members keep their earnings and chip in a monthly ownership fee that grants them a vote, an equity share, and the opportunity to serve on the executive board. Since no commissions are paid, the revenue stays in the (virtual) community. Likewise, Fairmondo is a digital, cooperative version of eBay where sellers are also owners. Launched in Germany in 2013, the platform was supported by a series of crowdfunding campaigns in which it raised hundreds of thousands of euros in member equity. (The funders are also members.) Rather than offer direct work opportunities, Fairmondo enables the work of its members—both merchants and craftspeople. Relatively new, the site already sells roughly two million "ethically sourced" products.

Worker ownership is often overlooked by those in power, but in recent years a number of powerful people have publicly acknowledged its promise. Among these is the Harvard economist Larry Summers, former Harvard president and US secretary of the Treasury, who in 2015 published a report on "inclusive prosperity" that advocated worker ownership. He concludes: "As wage growth and productivity growth have diverged, an increasing share of the net income of business has gone to management pay and to shareholders. In addition to measures that support wage growth, there is a need to create institutional change that will allow more inclusive capitalism in which profit income is more broadly shared."

In March 2017, the Senate Banking Committee overwhelmingly approved the bipartisan Encouraging Employee Ownership Act proposed by Republican senator Pat Toomey and Democratic senator Mark Warner, thereby easing the way for private companies to award stock as part of an employee's compensation plan. In the press release announcing the bill, Senator Warner explained: "When employee ownership is spread across a growing business, it has a huge impact on workplace culture, employee productivity and wealth creation. The Encouraging Employee Ownership Act will encourage fast-growing companies and start-ups to give more employees an ownership stake by reducing the paperwork burden on privately held businesses. This will allow greater distribution of equity beyond just the C-suite."

Joseph Blasi, the J. Robert Beyster Distinguished Professor at Rutgers University School of Management and Labor Relations, is an expert on corporate governance. He reminded me that while true worker-owned cooperatives are relatively rare, worker-owners are not. "Although I believe this is a special moment in time for cooperatives, we have to avoid tricks to make co-ops seem bigger than they are," he told me. A more viable approach, he said, and the one to which Warner likely alluded, is Employee Stock Ownership Plans (ESOP), a tax-advantaged retirement plan that allows workers to buy out all or part of an owner's interest in an established company. To participate, workers do not have to use their savings or wages to buy stock. Rather, a trust is arranged to borrow the money that the company repays, leaving the employee with the asset but not the risk.

Louis Kelso, a San Francisco lawyer and investment banker, is credited with constructing the first ESOP in 1956 to help employees of a closely held newspaper chain buy out the retiring owners. To make the purchase, the company's value was used as collateral to obtain a loan, and the company's future earnings were earmarked to pay off the loan. This way, employees did not have to risk their own money to complete the deal.

A corporate attorney, Kelso was an unabashed supporter of business. But he noted an essential fact that many economists of the time (and some today) overlook: that in the modern free-market economy technological change does not make individuals more valuable so much as it makes tools, machines, structures, and processes more valuable. Yes, a worker's productivity is enhanced by machines, but if he does not own that machine he does not actually "own" that productivity; rather, his employer does. The result is that the primary distribution of income through the free-market economy—"Each according to his or her own productivity"—delivers progressively more to the owners of machines and other forms of capital (stocks, bonds, real estate) and progressively less to the rank and file who contribute through their labor. This fact, Kelso argued, explained why the free-market economy was so unstable, with exhilarating highs followed by terrifying lows, such as the financial collapse he experienced as a young man in the Great Depression. The concentration of capital in so few hands, Kelso argued, reduced consumer demand and job growth and threw many of those who relied on wage income into poverty. His solution was to offer workers an ownership stake, the opportunity to amass wealth not only through their labor but through their holdings—in other words, to allow the average worker to benefit just a bit more by his or her productivity. "In human terms," Kelso wrote in 1989, "[an ESOP] is a financing device that gradually transforms labor workers into capital workers."

Today, there are nearly ten thousand ESOPs and related plans representing about fifteen million Americans, or about 10 percent of the US workforce. Forty percent of these companies are entirely employee owned, and about half are majority employee owned. Employees with ESOP plans on average earn more and have more than two times the retirement savings than do workers in similar companies without ESOPs. In a report entitled *How Did Employee Ownership Firms Weather the Last Two Recessions?* economists Fidan Ana Kurtulus and Douglas Kruse show that even modest levels of employee ownership—less than 12 percent of company shares—are associated with higher productivity and less employee churn. In their analysis they also found that worker ownership greatly enhanced stability: for every 1 percent uptick in the national unemployment rate, companies without worker ownership cut jobs by 3 percent, while companies with employee stock ownership plans cut them by just 1.7 percent. And for companies in which all workers were included in the ownership plan, only 0.7 percent of jobs were cut. One notable example: Florida-based Publix Super Markets, with 190,000 employee members the largest majority-employee-owned company in the world, has never had a layoff.

ESOPs are not universally admired. Some worry that encouraging employees to invest in their own company (as some also do through their 401K programs) makes them doubly vulnerable: if the company collapses, workers lose both their job and their retirement fund. This is not a trivial concern. When UAL Corporation, the parent company of United Airlines, went bankrupt in 2001–2002, workers in the company's shared-ownership plan lost about $2 billion in stock value. This led critics to condemn employee ownership as "lemon socialism" that saddles workers with the cost of management failures under the guise of making them "owners." But United was not a typical ESOP. For one thing, many employees had no stake in the company. For another, the stock plan was not freely given to employees but offered in exchange for massive wage and benefit concessions—a tactic ESOP advocates deplore.

"If a worker-ownership arrangement is well structured, the risk is minimal and the benefits substantial," Blasi said. "Even the Founders knew this, and advocated for it. They agreed that every family would own their land, which in those days essentially meant owning their own work. This was broad-based ownership, which was considered essential in a democracy. Really, there is still nothing more democratic than citizens owning their work."

Thomas Jefferson, a pastoralist, idealized farming and saw industry as a hotbed of corruption that treated workers not as partners or even stakeholders but as a means to an end. "While we have land to labor then," he wrote, "let us never wish to see our citizens occupied at a work bench. . . . Let our workshops remain in Europe." Alexander Hamilton, the nation's first treasury secretary, declared Jefferson's views elitist and reactionary, which, of course, they were—the farms Jefferson idealized were mostly plantations and his much-vaunted "laborers" mostly slaves. In contrast to Jefferson's vision of an agrarian economy of virtuous farmers, Hamilton envisioned a vibrant and innovative manufacturing sector manned in part by immigrants like himself.

Yet while Hamilton and Jefferson were notorious rivals, they did share some views. When British warships destroyed vital New England fisheries in the Revolutionary War, for example, Hamilton and Jefferson agreed to help revitalize the industry by lifting taxes under the condition that the shipowners give their crews profit sharing or an ownership share. Enacted in 1792, this worker ownership requirement remained in place until after the Civil War. Hence, the prospect of worker ownership informed the thinking— and ideals—of both men, as it informs that of many voters today. In recent years, there's been a groundswell of support for the form: since 2015, Colorado, California, Missouri, New York, and Massachusetts have all passed legislation lowering barriers to incorporation of worker-owned cooperatives. These and similar efforts reflect a growing awareness that broad-based ownership of work holds the potential to deliver more wealth to more of us, stimulate demand, and create and sustain more jobs worth having.

Back in Cleveland, I was fortunate to meet Loretta Bey, office manager of Evergreen Energy Solutions, the alternative-energy cooperative. She'd suffered through a lot of jobs, but this one, she said, was different. "In this economy, it's such a blessing to have a place to come to every morning," she told me. "And it's a blessing to be part of something bigger than yourself. We are like a close-knit family here, everyone gets listened to with respect." Bey's small windowless office was cluttered with family photos and artwork created by her grandson, of whom she was very proud. She mentioned she'd moved her grandson and a rotating cast of assorted family members (and two dogs) into a 2,100-square-foot five-bedroom home she'd purchased with the help of the Evergreen Housing Program. She's working hard to fix it up, to turn it into a place done "just so." But even "as is," it was more than she had imagined—the first home she'd ever owned. "Before I came to Evergreen, I was investing my money, time, and effort into other people's business," she said. "Now I'm working with a team of people who depend on me, and we're investing in *our* business. I'm not saying I'm going to stay here forever, but this experience has changed everything, and that confidence—that belief in myself—is going to stick."

PUNK MAKERS

It's cool to make things again.
—ANDREW KIMBALL

Brooklyn, New York, was once a manufacturing juggernaut, a maker of glass, iron, paper, rope, and glue, a refiner of oil, a distiller of spirits. In the early 1900s, Brooklyn-based American Sugar Refining Company (brand name Domino) was the largest sugar refinery in the world, churning out 1,200 tons a day, supplying more than half the nation with its daily fix. Brooklyn had slaughterhouses, bookbinders, weavers and dyers, and crafters of clocks and cigars. It was home to the Chandler Piano Company, the Grand Union Tea Company, and the Robert Graves Company, a maker of bespoke wallpaper.

But even in brawny Brooklyn, the Navy Yard stood out.

The Brooklyn Navy Yard was in its heyday the world's largest shipyard, and its ships sailed a timeline of American history. The *Fulton*, the nation's first oceangoing steamship, was launched there, as was the USS *Maine*, whose explosion in a quiet Havana harbor in 1898 sparked the Spanish-American War. The Yard birthed the boats that bracketed World War II—the USS *Arizona*, sunk by the Japanese in Pearl Harbor, and the USS *Missouri*, on whose foredeck the Japanese surrendered in 1945. And tucked behind its turreted gates lay a city unto itself, a dense network of drydocks, piers, and warehouses, a well-equipped laboratory and a medical complex. The residential streets were lined with grand mansard-roofed officers' quarters flanked by barracks for the enlisted men. Civilians came from nearby neighborhoods, arriving by foot or trolley car to join in the work. At its height in the mid-twentieth century, the Yard had a payroll seventy thousand strong. In grainy photographs the workers mug like movie stars, arms draped over one another's shoulders.

Dick Larregui, a Brooklyn native who retired in San Juan, Puerto Rico, recalled those times like yesterday. He wrote:

> I started working at eighteen years of age in an adminis-
> trative capacity at the Electric Shop 51 in June 1948. . . .
> I was drafted into the army due to the Korean War and
> returned to work at the Navy Yard after completing mili-
> tary service in 1953. My supervisor was Joe Levy, who un-
> fortunately has since passed away. I owe a huge gratitude
> to Joe who helped me progress during my twelve years. . . .
> A social accomplishment I contributed to was to join with
> the electricians to start an annual softball league with
> players competing against players from most of the other
> trade shops. Shop 51 became the league's winningest team
> each year. . . . Shop 51 Softball Team players were (I have a
> photo) R. Jackson, R. Larregui, V. Nicoletti, M. Baldinger,
> J. Scarfone, L. Pimenta, M. Flanagan, N. Protto, D. Gittens,
> C. Bacon, C. Willams, F. Carlucci, N. Cappadona (Captain),
> J. Di Bernado, J. Uliano, A. Motti. S. Harvey, A. Lontos.

Larregui barely mentions his actual duties, but from his recollections (all those names!) it seems that his work orientation was kinship, a priority similar to that of the firefighters we met in a previous chapter. Another worker, Rubena Ross, recalls her time at the Yard quite differently. From 1939 until 1946, Ross was one of hundreds of women who stitched flags for the boats—American flags, mostly, and also signal flags. Her nickname, "Betsy," sounds like a joke written especially for her (Betsy Ross!), but in truth every "flag girl" was nicknamed Betsy. The military used a lot of flags; a ship on convoy duty might go through an entire set of signal flags in a single mission. To keep pace, the flag loft was a twenty-four-hour-a-day/seven-day-a-week operation. Working there, Ross, an expert seamstress, did quite well: by the war's end she had saved enough to purchase two brownstones in Prospect Heights. (Decades later one of her buildings was featured in the PBS series *This Old House*.)

Rubena Ross left the Yard after the war, and in the late 1950s Dick Larregui also left, to start a management career at IBM. By then the nation's standing as a commercial seapower had sharply declined, as had the call for shipbuilding and repair. In light of this, Columbia University economist Seymour Melmen proposed a detailed plan to convert the shipyard into a viable commercial operation. Though well thought out and detailed, the plan was scrapped, and the Yard went into a slow decline. In 1966 the Navy decommissioned the Yard, and a few years later sold it to New York City for $24 million. In 1981 the nonprofit Brooklyn Navy Yard Development Corporation took over. By then the Yard was best known as a repository for towed cars and stray dogs. Fewer than one hundred people worked there. To skeptics, the revival of the site to its previous glory seemed as unlikely as the Dodgers returning to Ebbets Field.

The skeptics were half right: Ebbets Field is today covered by an apartment complex dotted with faded green signs forbidding residents to, among other things, play baseball. But the skeptics got it dead wrong on the yard, which against all odds is today a manufacturing mecca. Sprawled across three hundred acres of prime East River waterfront nestled between the Williamsburg and Manhattan bridges, the Yard is home to scores of new businesses. Preference is given to small- to medium-sized manufacturers working in concert with Brooklyn-based commercial artists, craftspeople, and designers. To qualify for a lease, candidate companies must project a viable long-term future in the local economy. When I visited in 2017, nearly 90 percent of the four hundred companies at the Yard sold their goods to customers in New York City, in transactions making up more than 70 percent of their total sales. The on-site employment office recruited and trained local residents to fill as many posts as possible.

David Ehrenberg is president and CEO of the Brooklyn Navy Yard Redevelopment Corporation, the nonprofit overseeing the site's rehabilitation. "Job creation is a core part of our mission," he told me. "I believe our best days are in front of us. Over the next five years we expect to have fifteen thousand workers, and in ten years twenty thousand. These are quality jobs that pay a living wage. Local workers—and this community—are why we are here."

Most of those workers make things: from movie sets, computer-generated designs, software, jewelry, "kinetic" furniture, and robots to tortillas, lamps, plastic bags, lawn sprinklers, and food packaging. They also make brain implants and boats, kitchen counters and bike racks. And to do this, many if not most rely on the synergies of unexpected partnerships, of sharing ideas, space, vision, contacts, and—critically—materials, skills, and tools. I heard of a baker trading pizza to a carpenter in exchange for wood scraps for his wood-burning oven, and a metalworker swapping a lighting fixture for the services of a web designer. I got a look at New Lab, an eighty-four-thousand-square-foot "innovation hub," its thickets of potted greenery punctuating rows of multi-hued workstations and workshops of every variety: CNC milling machines, metal and wood shops, an electronics lab for making circuits, a spray booth, laser cutters, and a 3D printing operation. Looped around an exposed steel beam very high overhead, a rusted crane hung like a vestigial memory of what the shipyard once was—and is planning to become once again. "Our vision is that New Lab will be a supportive and collaborative working environment for designers, engineers, and entrepreneurs—people trying to accomplish really hard things—not in Silicon Valley or at MIT but right here in Brooklyn," Ehrenberg said. "Our tenants feel a level of commitment to us, and to each other, and to staying here. We're all about innovation, but the sort of innovation that involves making things here in Brooklyn."

David Belt, one of the developers behind this ambitious public-private partnership, said that the synergies that New Lab offers manufacturers of "hardware" are analogous to those that have launched many successful software start-ups. "Hardware is hard to do almost anywhere, but especially in New York," he told me. "It requires space, and lots of it." In New York, as in many cities, old warehouses and factories are often regarded as eyesores to be gutted and repurposed; after all, office, retail space, and housing stock generally command several times the rent of industrial facilities. Landlords sometimes keep factories and warehouses empty for years, awaiting approval to convert them into more lucrative real estate. The Navy Yard didn't exactly buck this gentrification trend—recent years have brought a smattering of fancy cafés and luxury condos. But the vast bulk of its four million square feet is reserved for industry.

Jonathan Bowles, executive director of the city's Center for an Urban Future, said that New York is awash in entrepreneurs, scores of thousands of whom incorporate new start-ups every year. But these start-ups tend to be small and short-lived operations of the one-(wo)man-and-a-laptop variety. Some will certainly succeed, and a few will grow. But not many are likely to be significant creators of work, especially for the 3.3 million New Yorkers whose educations ended in high school. Technology has brought a slew of new occupations—game designer, systems architect, biomedical engineer, roboticist, virtual reality developer, content provider, multimedia specialist—and some argue that we should "train up" more people to work in these and related disciplines. But not all of us are inclined toward this sort of work, and as we've seen, it's not clear that more of us should be. Our twenty-first-century dilemma is that ever more companies are creating ever less work of the sort that equips enough of us to pay the rent, let alone purchase a pair of brownstones in New York City. In its own way, the Navy Yard is taking steps toward righting that wrong. And the Navy Yard is far from unique—hubs for small manufacturing are sprouting around the country. And it's none too soon.

Traditional manufacturing jobs have declined by roughly one-third since 1989, while "real" production (adjusted for inflation) has soared by 71 percent. Outsourcing and automation are the obvious culprits, but Christine Owen, executive director of the National Employment Law Project, said there is another equally important factor: political will. "Germany has a specific commitment to maintaining an industrial sector, and is willing to invest in it," she told me. "In the US we've walked away from manufacturing, we've allowed our capacity in that sector to wither because we've bought into an elitist view that there are higher uses for our human capital."

To be fair, the United States is second only to China in the value of goods we produce: were our manufacturing sector a nation unto itself, it would boast the world's ninth-largest economy. For consumers this is easy to miss, as many of these goods are not of the sort that get sold at the mall, but rather things like chemicals, airplanes, iron, and steel. Still, we import more than we export, imports that go beyond T-shirts and toasters to include sophisticated goods like semiconductors, medical equipment, and pharmaceuticals. In 2017, the United States ran an $83.136 billion trade deficit in *advanced* technology products, the largest in our history. That's not good news for good work.

In the new economy, many large multinational corporations

capture most of the value of their products through invention, design, marketing, and distribution, rather than through manufacture. For example, an analysis of Apple's iconic iPad and iPhone concludes:

> While these products, including most of their components, are manufactured in China, the primary benefits go to the U.S. economy as Apple continues to keep most of its product design, software development, product management, marketing and other high-wage functions in the U.S. China's role is much smaller than most casual observers would think. . . . With its control over the supply chain, Apple has the power to make and break the fortunes of many of its suppliers. A key finding for policymakers is that there is little value in electronics assembly. Bringing high-volume electronics assembly back to the U.S. is not the path to "good jobs" or economic growth.

Apple's uncanny capacity to maximize profits while minimizing production costs has drawn kudos from investors and has created jobs for Apple engineers, marketers, and sales staff. And there's no doubt that the company's policy to "outsource almost every part of the production process to low-wage nations" has helped make it the world's most profitable brand. But this "winner take most" strategy also threatens innovation of the sort that creates and sustains stable middle-class jobs.

Manufacturing is the largest contributor to spending on research and development in the United States, and the largest employer of engineers. And the manufacturing process is critical to the successful commercialization of scientific discoveries and technological innovation. The production process is—in its own right—a driver of innovation, and production workers are—in their own right—knowledge workers. In other words, invention and production are complementary processes, and sending production abroad risks cramping innovation at home. As economist Paul Samuelson once wryly observed: "Invention abroad that gives to [other countries] some of the comparative advantage that had belonged to the United States can induce for the United States permanent lost per capita real income."

Innovation tends to bubble up from a synergy of research, development, and production, and an ongoing conversation among engineers, designers, factory managers, and the customers they serve. Psychologists have shown that individuals working at a distance from one another are at a considerable disadvantage and that face-to-face interaction is key. Knowing this, many American companies have quietly installed major research and development centers close to their factories and suppliers overseas, a long list of firms that includes Google, Microsoft, IBM, Dow Chemical, and Apple. And while corporate America has built up an enormous cache of cash, it shows no inclination to invest that cash in innovations that will sustain a lot of American jobs.

American manufacturers once relied on hordes of workers to operate costly equipment that factory owners could not risk growing idle in strikes or other worker disruptions. Technology has atomized many of these jobs—various tasks are peeled off and either automated or outsourced. This highly efficient unbundling of work brings great levels of productivity. And as workforce productivity soars, the workforce itself has contracted.

Consider aircraft, consistently among the nation's top three exports. Officially, the European aerospace giant Airbus "manufactures" its A320 family of aircraft in a facility in Mobile, Alabama. But this so-called manufacturing facility resembles not a factory but an overblown operating room—immaculate, silent, and focused on the "patient"—in this case an airplane, flayed and ready for its operation. The parts for the plane are made elsewhere— wings, fuselage, vertical stabilizer, and all the rest built in factories in other parts of the world, notably Germany and France. In Mobile, a handful of workers dressed in jeans, blue polo shirts, and protective eyewear assemble these pieces in a series of complex tasks. I was not surprised to learn that most of these employees have years—even decades—of specialized training and experience and that many have military records and some college degrees. But there were only about 350 of them, a small fraction of the number of workers one would expect in such a large facility.

Alabama dug deep to lure Airbus—with $158.5 million in state and local entitlements that included a twenty-five-thousand-square-foot facility to train Airbus employees at the taxpayer's expense. In March 2017, of the 915 workers who had been enrolled at the training center, Airbus had hired only 231—roughly two-thirds of their entire team at the time. This led some Alabamans to question the Airbus hiring process. For example, a listing for "Quality Control Inspector," at a starting pay rate of $20 an hour, prompted a number of responses. "The job posting for 'Quality Inspector' highlights the questionable net-return from state monies invested in buying companies for the state," wrote one commenter. "The monies spent in bringing these companies to Alabama would provide far greater return through investment in true education of our state's population." Wrote another: "Be honest, how many local, unemployed people will find work at Airbus? Very few. The local people who do work at Airbus will be ones with a strong work experience, most of whom will come from other employers after building a decent work resume."

In some EU nations, the unions allow multinational companies to outsource less skilled, lower-value jobs to low-wage nations, while insisting that high-wage work stay put. This applies to Airbus: the precision parts are made in Germany, often by small firms linked to the global production chain through union efforts. Before opening the Alabama assembly plant, Airbus outsourced final assembly of the A320 to Chinese factories. It seems that Alabama was competing not with Germany for the high-wage, high-value jobs, but with China for the relatively low-wage, low-value jobs.

In March 2010, manufacturing employment in the United States bottomed out at roughly 11.45 million jobs—down from a high of 19.6 million in 1979. Five years later, 900,000 new factory positions had been created, most of them in southern states. In addition to the aircraft assembly jobs, Alabama's burgeoning auto parts industry employed 26,000 workers in 2017. Georgia and Mississippi have seen similar job growth in the auto parts sector. These manufacturing jobs are avidly sought after, as they are assumed to be more stable and higher paying than service or retail jobs. But as we saw on the visit to Kentucky, that is not always the case. Today, US manufacturing jobs pay an average hourly rate of $20, roughly 7.7 percent below the overall average hourly wage. And that $20 hourly average is propped up by legacy union jobs, most of them in the northern United States. In southern states, wages can be half that amount, and working conditions in some plants—especially foreign-owned plants—can be treacherous. As columnist Harold Meyerson wrote, "The role of the South in the global production chain increasingly resembles that of the pre–Civil War era, when it provided the cheapest labor in a chain that created the millionaire clothing manufacturers of Manchester, England."

An anticipated spurt of "advanced-manufacturing" jobs has led to predictions of a shortage of skilled labor to fill them and a call for more training. Entire books have been written making this claim, as have many urgent white papers and reports and newspaper headlines. Many of the economists and other social scientists I interviewed for this book echoed that claim, as did many educators. Manufacturers and lobbyists insist on it, and politicians preach it. But as we've seen in earlier chapters, there is little if any actual evidence of this so-called skills shortage, at least on a national level. Roughly one-third of US factory workers already hold a college degree, and, like the mechanics, engineers, welders, and other Airbus employees in Mobile, many have gained skills in the military or in previous jobs. Given the rapid advances in factory automation, it's unclear just how many people should be trained up for jobs in mass manufacturing, no matter how "advanced."

In May 2017, Apple CEO Tim Cook announced a $1 billion advanced-manufacturing fund to bolster US manufacturers by offering skills training, such as teaching people to write code to create apps. But the announcement came with a caveat: the cost of this program would be paid with "US money which we have to borrow to get." Cook was intentionally reminding us that a substantial portion of Apple's cash holdings is registered overseas and cannot be used in the United States unless repatriated under the US tax code, triggering the collection of income tax. Apple has kept earnings abroad and has borrowed money from its own foreign subsidiaries to pay dividends and make new investments. Because the interest paid on loans is also deductible, Apple ends up reaping a second tax benefit. That's why, Cook said, "comprehensive tax reform is so important to this economy"—that is, the sort of "reforms" that would encourage foreign-based money to return to the United States. Part of that money, he implied, would go toward supporting manufacturing. "If we can create many manufacturing jobs—those manufacturing jobs create more jobs around them, because you have a service industry that builds up around them," he said.

In late 2017, Cook got what he asked for—comprehensive tax reform. As part of that reform, Apple, Google, and other companies sheltering profits overseas were given the opportunity to return those profits to the United States at a greatly reduced tax rate. But the $1 billion "advanced-manufacturing fund" that Cook had promised looked less like a job-preparation program than an investment. A $390 million "award" to Finnair, one of Apple's suppliers, went not for training but to build a plant to make vertical-cavity surface-emitting lasers for the new iPhoneX and other devices, and a $200 million award to supplier Corning Glass went to support a glass factory in Harrodsburg, Kentucky, that over a decade earlier had invented the scratch-resistant "gorilla glass" used by Apple and other manufacturers. In other words, there was no sign that the fund would do much if anything to enhance American job readiness, or grow manufacturing jobs in the United States.

Industrialization—in Adam Smith's words—reduced work to "a few simple operations, of which the effects are perhaps always the same, or very nearly the same." This led to better, more consistent products, greater affordability, and greater demand. Today, the demand for cheap goods can be met by manufacturers around the globe striving to automate—and obviate—as many jobs as possible. And while we can't be sure how many factory jobs will be automated out of existence, one thing is certain: thanks to the unbreakable law of supply and demand, the more workers we train for manufacture, "advanced" or otherwise, the less power individual workers will have to negotiate the terms of their employment.

The most compelling manufacturing problem, then, is not to train more humans to manufacture stuff even more cheaply—we've pretty much mastered that challenge. The most compelling challenge is to restart the "virtuous cycle" by which fairly paid workers produce quality goods at a price within reach of enough of us to stimulate the demand that creates more work worth doing.

The "Third Industrial Revolution," as some call it, attempts to respond to this challenge with a production strategy that harkens back to the cottage industries of our past. While large multinationals churn out commodities aimed at broad generic markets, this new approach involves smaller companies leveraging technology to manufacture higher-value products tailored to the needs and desires of local, regional, and niche markets.

"Over the last century there was so much negativity about manufacture, but recently there's been an enormous change," Jonathan Bowles told me. "There are many, many manufacturing companies starting up. We don't know how many of these new ventures can hang on, or whether they can grow into sizable companies that employ sizable numbers of people. But the potential is certainly there."

Adam Friedman is director of the Pratt Center for Community Development in Brooklyn, based just blocks from the Navy Yard. An expert on urban manufacture, he said that—paradoxically—it seems that digital technology has sparked our desire for locally made goods. "This trend represents a fundamental shift in values," he told me. "People want tactile, they want to touch what they buy, and they want to know where it comes from. In a world where almost everyone has access to so many things online, buying custom—or making custom—is a way to distinguish yourself as an individual. It's about being human."

Friedman alerted me to a landmark study by the Pratt Center in partnership with the Brookings Institution that singled out urban manufacturers as key players in the nation's economic recovery. And while web-based market platforms certainly play a role, the change goes beyond individuals buying and selling their crafted goods online. It's also about small manufacturers using new tools to both create and reach a wider audience.

Steven Hoffman and his brother, Dennis, own New York City–based Buttonwood Corporation, one of the last remaining button-manufacturing companies in the United States. "Young designers say they prefer to use American-made," Steven told me. "And every designer who discovers us tells us how glad they were to find us. So they buy from us. We plan on surviving, but not the way some people say we will. 'Cause no matter what [President] Trump claims, we can never go back—our trade links to China and other countries are just too profound. There's no way we are ever going to beat China on price. But that doesn't mean we can't compete in other ways. China is where most apparel is made, and no Chinese apparel maker would source buttons from the US. And when Chinese workers demand higher wages, the companies just move manufacturing to a lower-wage country, like North Korea. So we can't compete with plastic buttons. But we can compete with wooden buttons. Our wooden buttons are sustainable and cost maybe 15 percent more than wooden buttons made abroad. That cost has very little impact on the final price of a garment. So we've been able to sustain our business, and if circumstances improve, we could grow it. It's a matter of getting more public support, and of consumers thinking about the impact of what they buy. We've also got to level the playing field. The city needs to offer cheap power, cheap real estate, and tax breaks to small manufacturers. This is a matter of policy that, when you think about it, could create an awful lot of jobs, and not just manufacturing jobs. We use mechanics and electricians in our business, and they'd also benefit, and so would other trades and service providers."

Technology sent manufacturing jobs overseas, and technology, it is hoped, will return some of those jobs closer to home but in an entirely different form. For example, 3-D printers assemble objects of almost any shape through an "additive process" in which successive layers of material—ceramic, plastic, metal, biologics—are laid down by a machine taking its cues from a digitized computer model. The printers are one of a growing array of digital fabrication tools that offer tremendous flexibility to users, allowing them to quickly customize and modify products—whether a tennis racket, a brain implant, or a drone—without the need to retool an entire factory or even the machine itself. In theory, these technologies could do for objects what the Internet has done for information: make them *instantly* accessible and available to almost anyone.

Digital fabrication technology is sometimes likened to having a "Walmart in the palm of your hand." While that's a stretch, these tools do offer small producers significant advantages over traditional manufacturing—namely, exquisite control over the process of making the sorts of things that resist mass manufacture. Designs of clothing, shoes, furniture, engine parts, even human tissue can be calibrated precisely to individual requirements and then encoded on digital templates, to be accessed—and modified—as needed. Judiciously applied, these technologies could minimize transportation and overhead costs as well as waste—as they are not only more precise than traditional manufacturing methods but made to respond to actual, not predicted, demand. Basically, these new technologies make it possible for those with little capital to get a grip on a market that would otherwise be out of reach. It makes it possible for the little guy (or gal) to innovate in three dimensions.

Some years ago, designer Dan Provost used a 3-D printer to prototype two devices he designed in collaboration with his partner, Tom Gerhardt: the "Glif," a tripod mount for cell phones, and the "Cosmonant," a wide-grip stylus for touchscreens. Both gizmos were aimed at a niche market and were funded via a Kickstarter campaign. Useful and beautifully designed, they sold far beyond Provost's expectations and eventually became the foundation for a design company focused on the "small batch" production of a variety of carefully crafted objects.

Provost's company, Studio Neat, is based in Austin, Texas, and its products are manufactured at Premier Source, a small firm based in Brookings, South Dakota. "Just because Apple makes their stuff in Shenzhen doesn't mean we have to," Provost told me. Provost said two friends discouraged him from even considering a foreign manufacturer. The friends, both designers, also launched a product on Kickstarter, a stainless-steel writing implement called "Pen Type A." They then hired—and fired—two different Chinese manufacturers, neither of which met their quality standards. They moved on to a Vermont manufacturer who shared their vision. "Manufacturing is hard," they wrote in a note to Provost. "There are no shortcuts. No magic, no secrets, and always lots of surprises."

Products crafted in small batches and for a specific purpose tend to be more durable than mass-produced products and are often better suited for the job that needs to get done. For example, the most costly factors in the making of clothes are fabric and labor. Cutting corners on either of these results in a garment that may fit poorly and is more likely to wear out quickly. For these reasons, despite their higher initial price, better made garments often offer better value. Most of us understand this, and given the right incentives, many of us would be willing to pay a bit more for goods we know will serve us a lot better. Indeed, the popular notion that only elites desire quality merchandise is in itself a sort of elitism that is both narrow-minded and wrong. Americans are certainly willing to pay more for quality automobiles, and no one would accuse Ford at aiming at "elites" when it touts the durability of its cars and trucks.

Mass manufacture does a terrific job of getting huge quantities of stuff to huge numbers of consumers on a global scale, but it often does a poor job of distributing the wealth created by those objects. Small manufacture holds the potential to mitigate this problem. The New Lab, the Navy Yard manufacturing incubator, was explicitly created to help turn that potential into a reality. When we met at the lab a few years ago, industrial designer Edward Jacobs called the facility "a dream come true," and he seemed to mean that literally. At the time, Jacobs was working on two seemingly unrelated projects: a futuristic chassis design for Triumph Motorcycles and a solar collector for the Lowline, a much-anticipated underground park planned to be carved out of an abandoned trolley terminal deep beneath New York's Lower East Side. Jacobs, who trained both as an architect and as an industrial designer, told me he tries to approach most design and engineering problems fresh, with as few preconceived ideas as possible, an approach that does not always sit well with large, established manufacturers. "In most companies, everything is looked at as a 'retail opportunity,' which is fine to a degree—everyone needs to make money," he said. "But people who have ideas, who create, aren't really motivated by maximizing financial gain. They want to make things that matter. Being forced to focus so hard on retail opportunities shuts them down. It just kills innovation."

Jacobs started a company, Design Necessities Initiative (DNI), to create a line of what he called highly durable "utility products"—

basics like pocketknives, pens and pencils, and clothing. New Lab was built to accommodate this sort of niche design and manufacture, smoothing the path from concept to prototype to finished product and encouraging "cross-platform" collaborations. Jacobs's solar-collector design is just such a project. The collector is made of six hundred laser-cut hexagonal and triangular anodized aluminum panels. The panels are formed into a tessellated canopy designed to reflect light filtered from remote skylights down into the tunnel's subterranean space, where it was part of a system to bring light to plants underground.

A few years ago Jacobs teamed up with investor Francois-Xavier Terny to form Vanguard, a start-up where he actually built his dream: a twin-engine motorcycle that looks like no other motorcycle I've ever seen—sleek, minimalist, futuristic, more like an artist's fantasy than an actual motorcycle. A modular construction, the machine was designed for easy manufacture, and it comes together with only five bolts. "Working alone or in a company you can get overspecialized tunnel vision," Jacobs told me. "But we did not rely on heritage or nostalgia. We relied on design and engineering to create our own language. We don't design for the luxury market, and this bike is not elite. It's utilitarian, and every part, every component, is there for a reason."

I had been introduced to Jacobs's work by David Belt, a founding sponsor of New Lab. A self-made entrepreneur, Belt backed the lab (through his real estate firm, Macro Sea) in response to a gnawing realization that business as usual was no longer working for too many Americans. "Since the financial downturn in 2008, people have been continuously trying to figure out what to do," he told me. "First they thought making mittens was the answer, you know, selling crafted things on Etsy. Well, nice try, but not the solution. Then they started making apps, but apps will only take you so far, and they can be made and marketed anywhere around the globe, so there's no hometown advantage. What I realized is that Americans are good at design, good with ideas, and really good at marketing.

But it's the middle of the sandwich—actually making the stuff—where we fall short. So I figured we should focus there."

Belt sees no sign of a "skills gap" and no need to urge Americans to seek more education purely to train up for employment. He's seen legions of highly educated friends and colleagues fail to flourish while he soared without a college degree. "I was planning to go, like everyone else, but family finances got in the way," he said. "So I joined a rock band instead. Then I moved to California and worked in construction, just hard labor, nothing skilled. I learned the real estate business on my own and started out building condos, projects I wasn't really proud of. Without a degree I felt I had to prove myself constantly. I worked really hard, accumulated a billion dollars in billings, and then moved to New York. I thought I'd build skyscrapers, because I figured, well, bigger is better."

Belt made money in commercial real estate, but struggled to make meaning from his career. One day, cruising through his hometown in the Philadelphia suburbs, it occurred to him it was unlikely that meaning *could* be made from his career. "I just felt awful, realizing that at that minute our legacy as Americans was shitty strip malls," he said. "This was 2007, and a lot of them were empty, just vacant lots filled with junk. I got to thinking, maybe I could do something about that. I became obsessed with repurposing these spaces." Belt spent the next few months driving around the country in search of vacant malls to buy and repurpose. While scouting a project in Georgia, he and a couple of friends came across a backyard "dumpster pool" made by Curtis Crowe, most famous as the drummer for the eighties rock band Pylon. Belt and his pals were impressed with the concept of turning junk into something useful and decided to build their own dumpster pool. Back in Brooklyn, they scored some secondhand dumpsters from a construction company, sealed the seams, added a liner, filled the bottom with sand, installed a filter, pumped in thousands of gallons of water and threw an invitation-only block party. The pool was an instant hit. A few years later, the city opened three dumpster pools along Park Avenue for the month of August. Belt's plan was to install dumpster pools in strip malls like the one in his hometown, with the goal of provoking interest and investment to rejuvenate the sad, empty spaces. But that's not what happened.

"Through that stupid pool I met all these great people—artists, visionaries," he told me. "And after meeting them, my focus shifted."

Belt loved building things and he knew a lot of other people who did as well. But building things was not what most people he knew *did*; they didn't have the time. Most were tinkering at the margins, struggling to make meaning of their jobs. For example, his former assistant Alex Escamilla had taken a sure path to success—top schools, impressive internships, powerful contacts, tireless effort. But she wondered why she'd gone to all the trouble. I asked her about her first postgraduate school job, as a client solution manager at Google, the world's most sought-after employer. She laughed. "We called it 'JFE,' just funky enough, because Google knows how to treat its employees well, and it is fun to work there," she told me. "But basically it's a big corporation wrapped in pink bubble wrap. The company does some cool things, but in the end it's mostly just a bunch of people selling and tracking media advertising. Making meaning, are you serious? A lot of us didn't even understand the business model."

Belt, too, was puzzled by what he called "all this focus on software." His new artist friends were all about *hardware*: they manifested their visions in real time, in real, three-dimensional objects. And that is precisely what excites Belt about New Lab—turning ideas into useful and sometimes beautiful things. Nearly half of New Lab consists of workrooms tricked out with every conceivable tool, from table saws and drill presses to massive, industrial-size 3-D printers and laser cutters. The intent is to recapture the synergistic relationship of manufacturing and design that's so often sacrificed in mass manufacture.

The Navy Yard serves as an exemplar of how and in what form manufacturing jobs might return to the United States. Rather than attempt to compete on a global scale through economies of scale built on automation and low-wage labor, the "Third Industrial Revolution" leverages the diversity and talents of the individuals we are, not the "team players" we are told we should be. Duke neuroscientist Ted Hall described this as the "opposite" of the traditional industrial model that requires workers to bend to the demands of the machine. "In digital production, the power is inherently in the hand of the maker, not the machine," he told me. In the 1990s Hall invented and designed the ShopBot, a computerized cutting and shaping tool—or router—for making boats, furniture, cabinets, and other things. ShopBot and other high-tech tools of the "maker" movement are intended to amplify rather than obviate human talent and effort. In contrast to mass production tools churning out precisely the same item for millions of customers the world over, these technologies were created to bring customization within reach of the average consumer, and—ideally—to enable at least some workers to build things that comport with their values and vision.

Oakland, California, designer Jeffrey McGrew trained as an architect and dreamed of building things that—at the very least—had a reason for being. But his job at an international architectural firm wasn't about that—it was about fast and cheap and on to the next assignment. "You go to school for years, hoping to make things," he said. "Then you find a job and it's soul killing, and you work at it for years, hoping that some day you'll get to make things you want to make. But no matter how good you are, no matter how passionate you are, unless you somehow push your way to the top you don't get that chance. And I really wanted that chance." So, for reasons they can't quite articulate, McGrew and his wife, graphic designer and photographer Jillian Northrup, sank $7,000 into a ShopBot. They weren't sure what they were going to do with the device, but they sensed it would lead them somewhere more meaningful than the place they were at the time. They started making stuff for themselves, then for friends, and then for friends of friends. They made desks, light fixtures, bookcases, and coffee tables, and they designed spaces—offices, restaurants, schools, and homes. Word got out, and demand grew to the point where they felt able to quit their jobs and start their own company. They called it Because We Can.

"When you work for a big company, you are realizing *their* vision," Jillian Northrup told me. "We wanted to realize our own vision. But with traditional manufacturing that's a huge risk. A designer can create something, no problem. But to get it made you have to send out the job to a large factory, which, if a project is intricate or complicated, can add enormously to the costs. With the ShopBot we could take risks with design—rather than working around the limitations of the tool, we could use the tool to realize our vision. With these new tools, a person who has an idea can *make* that idea. It's huge."

McGrew described his venture as "a mash-up of architects, artists, builders, designers, and fabricators" who use robot-empowered fabrication to make precisely what they design. He likened this collaborative to the punk movement of the 1970s, where musicians, designers, artists, and writers strove for a new level of self-expression. "Before punk you had to be a big star signed with a big label making big productions," he said. "But punk changed that. With punk, anyone with a guitar and a lot of passion could make music. They wouldn't get rich necessarily, but some of them could make a living. So this is punk manufacturing. Suddenly, thanks to cheap hardware, cheap software, and the Internet, all of us can make stuff. If this movement launches a slew of small businesses like mine, I think it will have an impact every bit as great as the Internet."

The nineteeth-century philosopher and essayist Ralph Waldo Emerson once famously spoke out against the strictly utilitarian criteria of value, whereby one was judged not by one's character but by one's productivity, which he compared to gazing into the ocean and seeing only the price of fish. His insight was that the emerging corporation and its factory system had atomized work and robbed workers of their humanity. He wrote: "The state of society is one in which the members have suffered amputation from the trunk, and strut about so many walking monsters—a good finger, a neck, a stomach, an elbow, but never a man."

The maker movement represents a reversal in the process by which overspecialization reduces work to a series of disembodied tasks and workers to a pile of parts. Ideally, digital fabrication technologies allow individuals to bring their "whole selves" to work and to build on their talents and instincts, while acquiring knowledge and skills as they go along. The action of making informs the thinking, and the thinking informs the making.

The Institute for Defense Analysis predicts that by 2030 digital fabrication will be "so powerful" as to begin to challenge traditional manufacturing. To people like Belt, that's wonderful news. But the maker movement is not without critics, some of them notable. The American economist Michael Spence, a Nobel laureate, worries that a "powerful wave of digital technology is replacing labor in increasingly complex tasks. This revolution is spreading to the production of goods, where robots and 3-D printing are displacing labor." Spence makes the important point that traditional manufacture is by its nature labor intensive, and that labor outsourced from the United States still provides jobs for hundreds of millions of people. At least theoretically, digital manufacturing reduces the need for labor, low-wage or otherwise. Once the initial design is complete, the marginal cost of replicating the software drops to essentially zero, largely because there is no additional labor required to generate or maintain it. Transportation costs—including labor costs—are also reduced, as designs can be shipped electronically and fabricated directly on machines located anywhere. Essentially, digital fabrication allows workers to transform data into things, cutting out the middlemen and many other men and women in the process. Spence concludes: "Unlike the preceding wave of digital technology, which motivated firms to gain access to and deploy underutilized pools of valuable labor around the world, the driving force in this round is cost reduction via the *replacement* of labor."

Spence's point is that all countries—not just developing countries—will need to reorient their growth models around this change. And that is almost certainly a good thing. The Old Economy model is once again being challenged by technology, and with it our thinking on what constitutes meaningful work. When almost anyone can have the opportunity to own the means of production, the balance of power will almost certainly shift. The hope is that this shift will result in worker-owners profiting from their enhanced productivity rather than ceding that benefit to their employers.

"Once people recognize what we can accomplish here in terms of making products that really benefit consumers, the big bureaucracies of the world will have less of a hold on the great ideas," designer Ed Jacobs told me. "We won't need them to agree to our vision—we can build it ourselves. I think this is going to force big companies to change, to be more responsive to the public and more respectful of their workforce. This is going to change work, and not just for people like me. It's going to change work for everyone."

HOMO FABER

The free market sometimes needs referees.
—SENATOR BYRON DORGAN

Some years ago, Maine governor Paul LePage—by secret order—had a thirty-six-foot-long mural pried from the walls of the Maine Department of Labor and put into storage. The mural, commissioned by the US Department of Labor and painted by a Maine artist, depicted the lives of American workers in the early twentieth century. Its eleven linked panels portrayed textile workers pressing handkerchiefs to their mouths to filter noxious fumes, children lugging lunch buckets to their factory workbenches, and a bevy of female welders suited up for their jobs at the Bath Iron Works. To most, the murals were a stirring, patriotic tribute. But to LePage, they were an outrage and abomination, "too pro-labor" for public eyes.

Helen Rasmussen, a resident of Maine, had one word to say about all this, and that word was "dumb." A draperies and textiles designer, Rasmussen strongly identifies with the workers the murals portray. She, too, makes her living with her hands, shaping the look of films like *American Hustle*, *In the Company of Men*, and *The Last Samurai*, and of TV shows like *Mad Men*. She chooses and creates objects—couches, lampshades, rugs, curtains, pillows—that set the scene for these and other productions.

Unlike most of the workers pictured in the murals, Rasmussen does not work in a factory. She works from her home studio, in Portland. But that doesn't mean she works alone, far from it. She's a proud member of the International Alliance of Theatrical Stage Employees, Moving Picture Technicians, Artists and Allied Crafts of the United States, Its Territories and Canada (IATSE). It is IATSE, Rasmussen told me, that makes possible her working life. "Without IATSE," she said, "I'm not sure where I'd be."

As we've seen over the past half century, attempts to adopt federal legislation aimed at restoring the nation's private sector unions have largely failed. Underlying this failure is a fundamental and intractable problem: collective bargaining. Built for an era of standardized industrial production, collective bargaining is a negotiation process between employers and a group of their employees to set the terms and conditions of work at a particular facility, typically a factory. Unfortunately, this system offers far fewer advantages today, when far fewer of us are working in manufacturing. Indeed, the portion of American workers currently covered by collective bargaining agreements is so small it seems wrong to call it a "system."

As we've also seen, in the absence of unions, the terms and conditions of work are under the unilateral control of employers, with individuals having little to no power to engage in meaningful negotiations. Labor advocates agree that we need a new mechanism, one that can unite workers and sustain their bargaining power in a global economy where decentralized, dispersed work is increasingly the norm. Yet while these advocates readily acknowledge the dwindling power of industrial-age unions, they sometimes fail to give serious consideration to the many real alternatives already in place. Among the most promising of these alternatives are worker organizations that negotiate and set standards not company by company but across industry sectors. In that sense, IATSE, founded at the dawn of the film age in 1893, was well ahead of its time.

In contrast to most other private sector unions, IATSE has in recent years grown its membership through grassroots efforts that reflect the needs of workers in nearly every corner of show business—from lighting technicians and animators to makeup artists and theater ushers. Part of the reason for its success, Rasmussen said, is IATSE's openness and flexibility—its acceptance of the changing nature of work and the people who do it. "The film industry is full of misfits who fall into things by accident," she told me. "I'm one of them. I was an art school dropout, working as a waitress. I had skills, but I didn't learn them in school or a training program. My mother taught me and my sisters to sew, and it was sewing that opened doors. I love manual labor, and I'm proud I can create things and repair them. People want to feel able, they want to contribute, they want to be useful, and I feel that way. Thanks to the union I've been able to do that, and make a good living doing it."

When Governor LePage cried foul on the Maine "pro-labor" murals, he wasn't acting in a vacuum. It was 2011, a time when most Americans distrusted unions, sensing corruption in their well-paid bureaucrats and economic stagnation in their rules. Like LePage, many of us pinned our hopes on a "free-agent nation" of market-driven *employment relationships*, whereby each of us would be free to negotiate our own best terms based on our perceived value to employers and customers. The idea of a "sharing economy" in which some of us started "sharing" our homes, cars, or other assets for a fee had just taken hold, and some of us felt ourselves well liberated from the yoke of "old-fashioned" employment contracts. But recently that thinking has shifted.

In 2017, public support for unions was at a ten-year high, with roughly 60 percent taking a positive view. The number was even higher among workers aged eighteen to twenty-five, 75 percent of whom reported a "favorable view" of unions. Part of the reason for that shift has been the realization that despite a tightening labor market, labor's share of income has fallen steeply since the 1970s, when union membership was high. With no civic entity to represent them, few workers have the power to claim their fair share of rewards, no matter how robust the economy. Apparently, not all boats lift with the rising tide.

Not all Americans bemoan the decline of factory jobs, including many of those who actually worked in factories—a quarter of whom in 2013 earned less than $12 an hour. But they do miss what factory work once offered: the opportunity to engage with colleagues and come together to promote their common interests. Even those of us who choose to work independently—like Helen Rasmussen—do best when working in solidarity with others similarly inclined.

Going forward, the very technological advances that have allowed some of us to declare our work independence will ease the way for more of us to unite for a better working life. One perhaps surprising example of this is the residential real estate sector. In national ratings, real estate agents have by several metrics "the happiest job in America," or at least among the happiest. Why do real estate agents feel so satisfied with their work? The industry cites several theories, but to get beyond those, I thought it best to put that question to an actual real estate agent.

When I called to set our appointment, John Bigelow had just closed one of the biggest deals of his career: a five-bedroom colonial revival tucked behind a white picket fence in a toney neighborhood on the outskirts of Boston. He suggested we meet at the house later that week, and I arrived a few minutes early to encounter him stepping out of a Jaguar, wearing Paul Stewart boots, a Hermès tie, and a fabulous Rolex watch, circa 1977. Noting my quizzical look, he laughed. "I loathe paying retail," he told me. "I bought the Jag from a client for five hundred dollars. The car didn't run, so I spent maybe another twelve hundred to fix it up. I bought the boots on sale at Neiman Marcus, and I got the watch and the tie in a trade with an antiques dealer, traded him stuff I had found on the sidewalk left out for garbage collection. You wouldn't believe what people throw away."

Bigelow is compact and boyish, with a rakish flop of salt-and-pepper hair. On fine days, he navigates town by bicycle decked out in a sports jacket and a pocket square. He studied Asian culture and Mandarin in college and took his first job in Beijing, working as a sales representative for an American maker of spectrometers and optical systems. He returned to the States to raise a family and found a job at another company through the grandmother of a friend. Eventually the company was swallowed by a bigger company and started to shed employees. "They told me if I wanted to stay on I had to move my family to Switzerland," he said. "I was tired of living abroad. So I quit."

Bigelow was young then and cocky, certain that his college degree, language skills, and extensive experience would land him what he called "another fancy, China-ish" job. He was wrong. Months went by and then more months. The steady stream of bills kept flowing, and his confidence tanked. "I got my real estate license, almost out of self-defense," he told me. "I was reluctant. I felt proud of my previous job, it felt accomplished, fancy. With real estate, the pride just wasn't there. Anyway, that's what I thought at first."

Bigelow's second thought was that his previous job was not as fancy as he fancied it had been. Yes, it offered exotic travel and the opportunity to mix and mingle with top executives. But when he looked back, those "perks" seemed as trivial as gratis espresso in a sweatshop. The job itself was what mattered, and his old job was, well, blah. Since the technical aspects bored him, he'd focused almost entirely on the social aspects—settling clients into hotel rooms, running airport pickups, once even escorting a delegation of Pakistani businessmen to a strip club in Rhode Island. "I'd do anything to make clients happy," he said. But on reflection, he realized that efforts to make people happy in that way did not make him happy. Nor did the infighting, or the near-constant and unspoken threat of termination. He courageously disclosed a low point: getting a colleague fired in order to protect his own job. "When you're worried about just keeping your job, the survival instinct kicks in, and that brings out the weasel in you," he said.

"The cruelty of it—the harshness, the capriciousness—that was terrible. I decided I didn't want any more of that. And now I'm so glad I made the change. In real estate we're free agents, accountable only to our clients. I can't tell you how big that is, no one looking over your shoulder. We work sixty- to seventy-hour weeks—we don't get weekends off. But we value our independence and freedom. An enormous part of this job is just helping people out, gaining and winning their trust. That's rewarding, and I love it. And not working for the man, *that* is huge for me . . . just uncalculatingly gratifying."

Real estate sales, Bigelow said, allow him to make human connections while giving him a sense of autonomy and competence—all pillars of a happy life. While the risks are real, to him the job is less a crapshoot than a treasure hunt, where diligence brings reward. And while he's certainly a free *spirit*, he's not technically a free *agent*. Like most realtors, he connects daily with a dense network of colleagues, both nationally and locally. Text messages are his lifeline. Critically, he's also a member of the National Association of Realtors, a trade association with 1.2 million members and one of the nation's most powerful and influential political lobbies. Effectively, he is part of a very large online working *community* that supports and defends his efforts and strives to sustain the value of his work. The same or something similar holds true for workers in a number of other licensed professions—physicians have long had the support of the powerful American Medical Association, teachers of the National Education Association, and attorneys of the American Bar Association. Not all physicians, teachers, and attorneys are members of these politically active professional organizations, but enough are to ensure that their interests are represented. This does not necessarily mean they all are happy—young lawyers employed by large firms seem to be especially frustrated in their work, as are young physicians struggling to deal with outlandish caseloads. But these affiliations do enforce at least some protections not available to the vast majority of "contingent" workers in many other sectors.

As we've seen, an unfettered, fragmented labor pool—in which workers around the world battle one another for dwindling opportunities—is not a hopeful one. So it is hopeful indeed that as traditional unions fail to recruit younger workers, organizations better able to adapt to the challenges of the demands of the digital marketplace are rising to fill the gaps.

Sara Horowitz, executive director of the Freelancers Union, first confronted this challenge more than a quarter century ago. Shortly after arriving at a new job, she learned that she had been hired as an independent contractor, with no retirement plan, no health insurance, no vacation days, and no job security. In response she and two other young associates formed the Transient Workers Union, with the motto "The union makes us not so weak." Of course, this was a joke . . . there was no union, so Horowitz quit to start one.

Horowitz's grandfather was vice president of the International Ladies' Garment Workers' Union, and her father a union lawyer. But she harbored no nostalgia that unions as they once were would rebound. "You can't bargain collectively when people are all over the place," she told me. "The nature of work has changed; cultural norms have changed. People don't have leverage at the job level anymore, so we needed to find another way. The question was, what are the levers?" Certainly they weren't what they once were, when large numbers of workers in a single industry were prepared to walk off the job in solidarity. So rather than organize around a particular institution, or even a particular industry, Horowitz pulled together workers from across business sectors—consultants, accountants, nannies, writers, web designers, lawyers, and eBay entrepreneurs—into a motley collective she called the Freelancers Union.

The Freelancers Union is today the nation's fastest-growing labor organization, with several significant victories under its belt. Perhaps most notable, the union ushered in the so-called Freelance Isn't Free Act, a New York City law requiring employers to offer contingent employees written contracts for work valued at $800 or more and to honor those contracts in a timely manner. Still, there is much left to be done. "Making sure people have enough work is the biggest issue we have," Horowitz told me. "For that we need new structures, new strategies."

Estimates are that within decades nearly 50 percent of Americans will be working independently, at least some of the time, and the Freelancers Union does offer some protection. But Minneapolis entrepreneur Kyle Coolbroth agrees with Horowitz that demand is key, and he also agrees that new strategies to generate that demand are a must. Interestingly, his strategy relies not only on new technology but on literally bringing people together—in space. "The way work is done has radically changed in my lifetime," he told me. "People who before were defined by their workplace, by their job, by a particular career path, that's falling apart. Millennials don't expect to build a life around just one skill, and they don't expect to spend a life with one company. They live in a world where people can work anywhere and collaborate with anyone. I wanted to build on that."

Coolbroth once worked as an independent architect, and he felt stifled by the pressure of having to sell himself as "better than the rest." Other people—friends, colleagues—told him they felt the same way. So with a partner he designed a physical space where people who worked for a range of companies, ventures, and projects could gather under one roof. Since these people didn't all work for the same company or even in the same industry, the culture would not be that of "teamwork" but rather of people of different backgrounds, skill sets, and visions coming together in mutual support. This strategy brought camaraderie, of course, and also the opportunity to brainstorm new approaches and ventures that allowed the workers themselves to generate demand for their services.

It's been nearly a decade since Coolbroth opened his first co-working space in downtown St. Paul. When he made his start, there were only a handful of such operations outside the large coastal cities, and it was thought that without a huge population to draw from, these arrangements would almost certainly fall apart. But formal coworking establishments have since caught on across the country and around the globe. Today, Coolbroth co-owns five, the largest a high-tech wonderland sprawled across what was once the trading pit of the majestic Minneapolis Grain Exchange Building. On a short visit there, I met software designers, lawyers, analysts, artists, and marketing expert George McGowan III, an MBA with a résumé thick with consulting stints. "Co-working represents the rise of the freelance class—a more mature version where people want to pursue their craft, but not at their kitchen table," he told me. "It fills a void that companies no longer fill. Could this model replace IBM? Maybe."

IBM, notorious for its multiple and massive layoffs of highly skilled veteran staff, may well be a model worth replacing. By contrast, coworking holds great appeal for millions of workers, and that appeal is likely to grow. A few years ago, work scholars Gretchen Spreitzer, Peter Bacevice, and Lyndon Garrett published an analysis of coworking arrangements in the *Harvard Business Review*. They wrote, "There seems to be something special about co-working spaces. As researchers who have, for years, studied how employees thrive, we were surprised to discover that people who belong to them report levels of thriving that approach an average of 6 on a 7-point scale"—at least a full point higher than the average for traditional employees. The authors considered this finding so surprising that they checked their data twice. Spotting no mistakes, they set out to probe deeper through a survey of several hundred coworkers across the United States. Compared with traditional office workers, coworkers experience little pressure to compete with one another, but rather consult with one another, a process that apparently makes the work seem more distinctive and interesting *to them*. "A traditional company is a means to an end, but coworking is different—it's a beehive of energy, engaging and exciting," George McGowan told me. "Coworking has the power of community facilitated by like-minded people doing very different things. Ideas are always in the air."

Coolbroth's partner, Don Ball, described this as an "abundance mentality," the belief that there's enough to go around, and that what's good for you is actually good for me too. "The attitude of sell, sell, sell, that doesn't work here," he told me. "What works is authenticity, generosity, openness. People give back. It's like you find yourself in others."

Coworking arrangements, twenty-first-century unions, and other coalitions offer hope to the growing cadre of Americans laboring independently. But what of the majority of us who are—and will continue to be—employed by a single institution, nearly half of us by very large institutions with five thousand or more employees? Historically, our needs have taken a backseat to other stakeholders, for reasons that many economists once agreed were both legitimate and unavoidable. Milton Friedman, the leading monetary economist of the twentieth century, famously declared that companies that invested in their employees and communities beyond the absolute minimum were derelict in their duty to provide investors with income and customers with good deals. He and his contemporaries in the Chicago school of economics forged an indelible link in the public mind between free markets and freedom itself. But Friedman did not mistake the invisible hand for a perfect legal instrument. In his writings he outlined the nation's responsibility to "establish a framework of law" by which business would be held accountable, and he insisted that people harmed by the externalized costs of doing business be compensated, arguing that market forces, though powerful tools of progress, cannot ensure a *distribution of income* that guarantees all citizens a decent life. To compensate for this uneven distribution of income, Friedman proposed a negative income tax for low-wage earners.

Under Friedman's scheme, the government would award qualifying workers regular payments and would also play a pivotal role in regulating business and labor practices. Corporate leaders agreed. It wasn't that business elites relished taxes or government intrusions; rather, they feared the alternative—economic disruptions, social unrest, and lagging demand for their goods and services. One way to ward off these problems was to offer Americans sufficient wage income to justify any discomforts or indignities they experienced on the job—Henry Ford's famous "$5 a day" tactic. Another was for government to prime demand by putting money directly into workers' pockets through social welfare and job creation programs. Business applauded these and similar proposals and promoted tax hikes to support them: in the 1950s, the statutory corporate tax rate was more than 50 percent and accounted for more than 30 percent of federal revenues. Labor not only received a larger share of its growing productivity but also benefited by corporate contributions to the general welfare.

Today, corporations no longer play that role, and corporate profits are at all-time highs. But markets and financial stability hinge on trust, and as we've seen, public trust is at a low point. This has raised concern not only among labor advocates, but also among business experts. Harvard economist Rebecca Henderson keeps a keen eye on the ways in which large organizations respond to technological shifts, including the automation of jobs. "Business well run is an enormous instrument for human good, a major source of prosperity and freedom," she told me. "But business leached of any sense of value or purpose, well ... no one relishes the idea of coming home exhausted from the office, and explaining to one's spouse, 'I'm late because I had to spend more time maximizing shareholder value.' That's not a life that would make sense to many people."

To at least some degree, the mid-twentieth-century "Golden Age of Capitalism" was—as Adam Smith might put it—constrained by "common sense": government, business, and labor somehow managed to work together for mutual interests and, perhaps incidentally, the common good. Business needed workers to produce and distribute goods and services, and labor relied on business for a paycheck. Government needed to sustain both its legitimacy and its tax base. But in the twenty-first century, these commonsense constraints have been swept away in a tsunami of technological change. Automation and globalization have made it possible for business to produce more with much less American labor, and also—through its lobbies—to purchase the favor of government. In the absence of a national economic strategy to respond to this change, we have come to expect little of our political system and less still of our employers.

At the same time, a cult of personality in the business community has led to the rise of towering corporate leaders, some of whom have become public icons. Like the Wizard of Oz who hid behind his curtain, these "wizards" of business obscure the reality of the enterprises they represent. Many of these companies rely for their profits on financial machinations—mergers, stock buybacks, acquisitions, secondary offerings—rather than on their avowed function of delivering real value. And the collateral damage of corporate decision making—for example, pollution and underemployment—is borne by society. Workers go largely unheard, their concerns and needs overlooked or disregarded until election time brings politicians bearing promises of "more and better jobs." The hollowness of these promises has led millions of frustrated American voters to cast a vote to "blow up" the system, in a desperate attempt to clear the way for almost any alternative.

"People, ordinary people, have this uneasy feeling that something is not working," Henderson told me. "They see the decline in our political institutions and the way these institutions don't seem to reflect what we need as a healthy society. The reawakening of business's social mission, and the difference business can make—in terms of the jobs we need to create and the purpose and meaning people can get from valuable work—is enormous."

Henderson contends that corporations and their managers have a special duty to sustain the larger interests of capitalism, even at the expense of corporate and shareholder interests. The stakes, she told me, are staggeringly high: the plummet in public trust weakens the underpinnings of both our capitalist system and our democracy. Henderson is not alone in this belief. In January 2018, Larry Fink, CEO of BlackRock, the largest investment fund in the world with $6 trillion in assets, informed the chief executives of most of the world's largest public companies to take action in the social interest if they expected his firm to invest in their businesses. He wrote: "Society is demanding that companies, both public and private, serve a social purpose. To prosper over time, every company must not only deliver financial performance, but also show how it makes a positive contribution to society. Companies must benefit all of their stakeholders, including shareholders, employees, customers and the communities in which they operate. . . . Without a sense of purpose, no company, either public or private, can achieve its full potential."

Given his position—and enormous wealth—you have every right to be skeptical of Fink's manifesto. I certainly was—firms like his often claim credit for taking social responsibility merely to appease customers, investors, and regulators. But Fink's missive carried substantial weight, particularly since it put BlackRock at odds with some of its own business partners. Jeffrey Sonnenfeld, a senior associate dean of Yale School of Management, told the *New York Times* that Fink's action was a "lightning rod" to business and the entire investment industry.

Fink went futher, to address not only business but the public at large. He wrote, "Many governments [are] failing to prepare for the future, on issues ranging from retirement and infrastructure to automation and worker retraining. As a result, society increasingly is turning to the private sector and asking that companies respond to broader societal concerns." Companies that fail to respond, he continued, will "ultimately lose the license to operate from key stakeholders."

Fink's "license to operate" seems to correlate with what business scholars call the "triple bottom line," a phrase coined in the late 1990s to describe the "three P's" of purpose-driven business: profit, people, and planet. While clearly not all businesses have embraced all three of these priorities, Henderson believes more would if business leaders were freed to do so. "I work with managers who are keen to make a difference," she told me. "But they lack a business model that will allow them to move in that direction."

Jay Coen Gilbert believes he has unleashed just such a model— a new way, as he puts it, "to use the power of business to solve social problems." Coen Gilbert is the former CEO of AND 1, an athletic apparel company he and two partners founded straight out of business school. The company sold a made-in-China basketball shoe promoted the world over by NBA stars like Rafer Alston, Kevin Garnett, and Jamal Crawford. Thanks to these and other endorsements, the company grew to be the second-biggest basketball shoe brand in the United States, and in 2005 Coen Gilbert and his partners sold it for $240 million.

"The typical arc of the cashed-out entrepreneur is 'Let's do another one,'" he told me. "But I figured, the world's problems are not going to be solved by creating another company."

Coen Gilbert took a sabbatical to join his wife (whom he described as a "yogini") and their two kids on a lengthy sojourn to Australia and Costa Rica. Distance brought perspective, and it occurred to him that work in America was on a collision course. Companies like his that catered explicitly to shareholders pushed costs onto the backs of workers and taxpayers (in his case, largely Chinese workers and American taxpayers). At the same time, the nation's intense focus on wealth creation had undermined the essential human need to derive purpose and meaning from one's efforts. Having learned back in college that business generates the vast bulk of the nation's GDP—as much as 80 percent—he believed that business had an obligation to take the lead in cleaning up this mess. The first step, he decided, was to change the rules.

For nearly a century, corporate social responsibility was subjugated to—and some argued legally trumped by—a fiduciary duty to make shareholders as much money as possible. This duty—later articulated by Milton Friedman—was first made law through the case of *Dodge v. Ford Motor Company* in 1919, in which Henry Ford was overturned in his effort to employ as many men as possible so as to spread prosperity (and presumably demand for his cars). Oddly, the ruling also thwarted Ford's efforts to lower the price of his cars and to raise wages. The Michigan Supreme Court declared that Ford shareholders must take precedence over the needs of employees and even customers. Over time, through both law and custom, the concept of "shareholder primacy" became the default position for all publicly held companies.

Given the mandate to put shareholders' needs first and foremost, the injunction that business seek a "higher purpose" seems unrealistic, if not absurd. What possible "higher purpose" could be served in efforts to sate the hunger of investors for profits? Clearly a puzzlement, but not an intractable one. Coen Gilbert gathered a small team of like-minded colleagues, who together sketched out a blueprint for a new organizational form that "merges the power of business with the needs of a purpose-driven society." For lack of a more felicitous title, they called their creation the Certified B Corporation.

Certified B Corporations become certified through the auspices of B Lab, a nonprofit Coen Gilbert and his colleagues created to evaluate a firm on its "triple bottom line." Firms that pass muster are free to amend their corporate charters to honor a governance philosophy fundamentally different from that of traditional corporations—that is, they can legally put the needs of the workers and their communities ahead of the demands of their shareholders.

By early 2018, B-Corps legislation had been passed in thirty-two states, and six more states had taken it under consideration. Coen Gilbert told me that the victory in Delaware was especially sweet. Thanks to its generous tax policies, the state had wooed more than half of *all* US public firms, including two-thirds of all Fortune 500 companies. The legislation offered those firms the option to do right by all of their stakeholders, not just shareholders and executives.

Coen Gilbert likened social responsibility in the workplace to a "team sport" that Americans—especially young Americans—are aching to play, as long as the other teams play fair. "There's plenty of research showing that the millennial generation—when asked a battery of questions about life—want to make meaning at work," he said. "They're not talking about the work/life balance because for them it's not about balance, it's about integration. They bring their values into the workplace."

It's not only millennials, of course. In 2012, Patagonia, the iconic outdoor clothing retailer, was the first company to qualify for B-Corp status. Patagonia's much-publicized commitment to environmental responsibility and social justice made their certification unsurprising. But since then over 2,390 companies have also qualified, representing 130 industries—financial and investment, insurance, engineering, architectural and law, textile and apparel, furniture, food and medical, biomedical, and IT. These companies seek the legal benefits of incorporation, as well as the legal right to hold themselves accountable to a basic standard of fairness—that is, to distinguish themselves from companies whose pledge to be "disruptive" so often seems to translate as "generate as much revenue as quickly as possible, no matter the consequences."

Coen Gilbert is not alone in his belief that many of the major crises of our time—social, environmental, and political—have come as the result of bad business practices. But the modern corporation is a market creation, not a political one. The rise of new corporate forms like B Corps requires us to reimagine that business can—as Henderson suggests—become part of the solution. "We're at an inflection point," Coen Gilbert told me. "In the next generation,

this is just the way people will do business. Maybe it will be called
B Corps, or maybe it will be called something else, but what's defi-
nite is that there will be a shift away from shareholder capitalism
to stakeholder capitalism."

Yet management at many companies, especially publicly held
companies, still believe they have no choice but to minimize the
cost of labor to remain competitive in a brutally competitive
global economy. But is this really their only choice? MIT economist Zeynep Ton makes a compelling argument that it is not, and
that for most companies, leaving workers behind in a rush to profits is, from a strictly business perspective, not a good choice.

Turkish by birth, Ton was raised to imagine America as a land
of endless opportunity. And for her, it was. Tall and lanky, she ex-
celled in sports and arrived in the United States at age sixteen via
a basketball scholarship to Pennsylvania State University. (Speaking little English, she walked into team practice having memo-
rized the media team guide, and addressed teammates in this
fashion: "Hi [fill in the name] from [fill in the hometown].") Ton
grew fascinated by America's sprawling marketplace, and later focused her doctoral research at Harvard on the retail sector. It was
then that she made the (to her) surprising discovery that many
American companies treated their employees as interchangeable
commodities.

"Really, I was shocked," she told me. "I know that sounds naive,
but from what I'd been told about America I could not understand
it." What she could not understand, she said, was why citizens in
a free-market-driven economy would endure the indignities show-
ered upon them every day in the workplace. As an example, she
recalled visiting the electronics department of a large retail store,
where she met with a manager. The manager, who she figured was
about fifty years old, told her of the many years she'd spent clawing her way up and into the perch from which she now supervised
a staff of more than a dozen people. Ton was astonished to learn

that for these efforts the manager earned "poverty wages" and also that her work schedule varied erratically from week to week. The manager could neither plan her days nor contribute significantly to her granddaughter's future. Making matters worse, her hard-won "manager" status appeared to be no more than a technicality, a way to legally disqualify her for overtime pay while offering no real chance of *genuine* advancement in the company. "There are many millions of adults like this manager," Ton told me. "Hardworking people with bad jobs."

Over time, Ton gathered her thoughts on how this "bad jobs strategy" came to be. Many of America's largest companies, she theorized, suffer from an inferiority complex. They make or import and sell standardized goods—burgers, pencils, gasoline, books, underwear, mass-market electronics, small appliances, and other stuff consumers can find almost anywhere, increasingly, online. Convinced that they have nothing special to offer, these companies strive to distinguish themselves through a single metric: low price. The quickest and easiest way to lower prices is to cut labor costs up and down the supply chain—that is, to squeeze the company's workforce and insist that suppliers and other business partners do the same.

The repercussions of this "bad jobs strategy" can flatten entire communities, as one business after another rushes to cut labor costs to keep up with their low-price competitors. But what many companies fail to recognize, Ton said, is that over the long term this "Walmart" model won't necessarily work for them, or for their investors. Sometimes shooting low just means shooting yourself in the foot.

Home Depot offers a great example of this problem and also a natural experiment from which other companies can draw their own conclusions. In 1990, Home Depot was the nation's largest home improvement center, a darling of Wall Street, and certainly a darling of mine. The stores were everywhere and offered quality merchandise at decent prices. Most important, the staff knew things about stuff I didn't—paint, sandpaper, toilet plungers—basically, it seemed, almost anything involving home maintenance and improvement. I loved the joint, and so did many other people—Home Depot was the world's fastest-growing retailer, and the youngest retailer in history to hit $50 million in sales. By 1999, the company was doing so well that shareholders literally cried with joy at shareholder meetings. Cofounder Arthur Blank attributed the company's astonishing success to its happy, capable workforce. Checkout clerks were sent to "cashier college." Skilled craftspeople and tradespeople—plumbers, electricians, painters—roamed the sales floor, ready and able to serve. Dubbed the "Orange Apron Cult," these employees—most of them full time—were encouraged to make decisions for themselves and to help customers make their own decisions too. Store managers were empowered to do the same. To ensure loyalty, employees were issued shares in the company, and some became millionaires. The company was pronounced "the greatest retail organization today" by none other than David Glass, then the CEO of Walmart. (And yes, he included Walmart in that assessment.)

But not all went smoothly. The company lacked discipline and fell behind in basic efficiencies—like neglecting to set up a company-wide e-mail system or to automate its billing process. Customer service, though often excellent, grew inconsistent. Customers balked, and the stock price fell. In 2000, the company board brought in a new CEO, Robert Nardelli of General Electric, a company known for instilling tough operational discipline in its workforce.

Nardelli made the call to replace skilled and experienced full-time employees with less knowledgeable, cheaper, and more "flexible" staff members willing to put in unpredictable and in some cases part-time hours. Costs shrank and profits grew, as expected. Nardelli's total compensation soared to $38.1 million, and shareholders breathed a collective sigh of relief. But the customers . . . well, let's just say we were not impressed. Over time, Home Depot sank to the very bottom of the University of Michigan's American

Customer Satisfaction Index. Five years later, when the company's share price dropped 24 percent, the investors took notice. The board dumped Nardelli and hired Frank Blake, a Harvard-trained lawyer who had once clerked at the Supreme Court. The "Orange Apron Cult" was revived and service greatly improved, and with that improvement came record sales and revenues. A win-win.

Years later, Ton encountered the power of this "good jobs strategy" firsthand while on a business trip in Texas. Driving with some colleagues through the midsummer heat, she was scouting for a cold drink when she noticed two convenience stores situated not far from each other. The parking lot of one store was nearly empty, while the parking lot of the other was jammed. The busy store featured an enormous QT logo on its marquee. Ton had never heard of QT, but her Texas colleagues knew it well. "They told me Quik-Trip was an amazing company," she said.

Headquartered in Tulsa, Oklahoma, QuikTrip is one of the nation's largest privately held corporations. An $11 billion company with nearly twenty thousand employees and 750 stores, in 2018 it had plans to add another 100 stores over the next few years. Company CEO Chester Cadieux III may well be proud of this, but he's careful not to let it show. Cadieux is a low-key guy who dresses pretty much the way his store clerks do: in a polo shirt and neatly pressed Dockers. The outfit seems to suit him—his father founded the company, but that didn't let Cadieux off the hook. Just like most other employees, he started his QuikTrip career on the night shift.

When I asked him to describe his hiring strategy, Cadieux said nothing about teamwork or passion, and not one word about "disruption" or "callings." He did not mention giving applicants a test or requiring that they be trained in any particular fashion. Nor did he give any indication that he was looking for a cultural "fit." Rather, he said, he was looking for people who believed in themselves and believed that their efforts mattered.

"We center on finding people willing to work really hard to serve our customers, people who will stick by us," he told me. "And then we try to do right by them."

But how does he find these people? After all, many employers complain that hiring "good help" is nearly impossible, and blame the problem on drug use, bad parenting, bad schools, and a vaguely defined "dysfunctional system." This is especially true of sectors that hire "unskilled workers," like truck-driving operations, fast-food restaurants, and convenience stores like QT. But Cadieux seems to have no such difficulty. In fact, he claims to have his pick of applicants. How's that work? "We pay a lot and we trust," he said. "I believe that people come to work here, start with us, because of the pay. And they stay with us because they like the job. They come for the paycheck and stay for the people and the experience."

In an industry in which employee turnover averages nearly 100 percent, turnover of full-time QT store associates stands at a rock bottom 10 percent. Cadieux said that this is no accident—he simply can't afford to lose them, nor would he want to. "How could I be happy getting out of bed every morning knowing I'm going to have to tell people they will be laid off?" Cadiuex asked. "How is that even normal? That might work for some, but it doesn't work for me."

This stopped me for a minute—wasn't this precisely what I'd heard in Finland? That trust is essential and people are too valuable to squander? But this was Tulsa, not Helsinki, and Cadieux is a successful businessman, not a starry-eyed idealist. What does all this mean for his bottom line?

"We're growing," he said. "And when we transfer experienced employees to a new location, it's like sending marines on the beach in World War II—they don't know what to expect, and neither do we. When we set up in a new locality it takes us seven to ten years to break even, and it can take years more to turn a profit. So we have to be patient. We're building a culture, and it takes some time for the customers to learn about us, to figure out that we're different. But eventually, they do figure it out. And what they figure out is what's different about us is our people. Our customers deserve to be served by someone who cares about them."

I wanted to meet some of these caring employees, so Cadieux turned me over to his human resources head, who declined to screen them and told me to take my pick from a long list. I talked to a few. The youngest was Brian Larson. When we first spoke Larson was twenty-seven years old and the father of three young children, including a newborn. He was about to move his family from Kansas City to Charlotte, North Carolina, where he was to manage a new QT store—one of those "marines on the beach" situations Cadieux had described. It took five years for Brian to work his way up from night clerk to store manager, and he thought that was more than fair. The company cross-trains its employees to master almost every task from stocking shelves to sales, and there's a lot to learn. It takes time, he said, to get to know a business, time to win the trust of people. As a manager, his job is to anticipate customer needs. That takes insight, he said, the sort of insight that comes with experience. And he knew—always—that the company had his back.

When Larson moved his family to Charlotte, the company covered his expenses. His salary, he said, is ample and he gets generous benefits, including college tuition remission. Both Larson's parents attended college, and he, too, thought he would go someday. But now he sees no reason to do so. "I plan to spend forty years with this company," he told me. "Honestly, working here doesn't feel like just a job. It's a lot more than that."

QuikTrip is not the only successful company to invest in its employees. When I asked Ton if she could share other examples, she cited several, and the one that stood out in my mind was Market Basket supermarkets. In New England, where I live, Market Basket is a powerhouse, employing twenty-five thousand people in seventy-one stores in three states. The chain is known for the quality and the variety of its produce, its outstanding customer service, and its consistently low prices. But this comes not on the backs of its workforce. Market Basket employees, Ton told me, get a fair wage, benefits, and a profit-sharing plan. Perhaps that explains why every worker in its stores wears a badge proudly citing the number of years he or she has spent with the company. Cashiers, stockers, and managers all work together, and the chain has a fiercely loyal customer base. When in 2014 Market Basket board members proposed to change company policies that would benefit owners at the expense of the workers, customers united in seven weeks of protest and, ultimately, blocked the change. I was one of them. It wasn't out of sentiment: I simply knew of no other store where a clerk would sort through a huge pile of pineapples, methodically sniffing and squeezing each one to choose one just ripe enough for me to serve at dinner that evening.

Great stories, sure, but you have every right to ask, "What's your point?" It's one thing for a benevolent business owner to treat employees with respect, quite another for citizens across the nation to rise up to demand systematic reforms. I've offered thoughts on how individuals, labor advocates, and business may work toward solutions to our national work disorder, but what role should government play?

Widespread initiatives to empower workers and mend the unsightly holes in the social safety net are unlikely to gain broad support at a time when so many of us feel beleaguered. As mid-nineteenth-century German economist Adolph Wagner observed in what became known as "Wagner's Law," concerns for social welfare emerge naturally from prosperous free-market societies. Yet, while our free-market society is certainly prosperous, not all that many Americans feel that way. On the contrary, one might easily imagine we are operating under a "Wagner's Alt-Law," by which the growing income gap prompts a retreat from public generosity and support. Unchecked by sensible policies to protect us, the inexorable march of technology has left many of us feeling like collateral damage in a war we voted against.

We Americans are suspicious of centralized "solutions" and

reluctant to cede individual prerogative to collective control. But from all available evidence, American workers have already ceded control. Corporations spend nearly $3 billion annually on lobbying, roughly thirty-five times more than do lobbies that represent the interest of workers. Rather than demanding that government "stay out" of their businesses, corporations are increasingly partnering with government to achieve their ends—whether to "train up" more workers to do their bidding or to reduce and veto worker protections. That's not good for workers, and it's not good for democracy.

As we've seen, no free nation can flourish without capturing the full value of its human capital. This is not a matter of largesse; it's a matter of building a civil society. One step that government might take is to find new ways to incentivize good work of all sorts. Consider what follows a starting point, some thoughts on which we together might begin to build.

The late senator Daniel Patrick Moynihan denounced payroll tax as "a tax on work." Imposed on the first dollar earned by all workers regardless of income level, many consider it regressive because the largest portion of the tax, the part that covers Social Security, does not apply to earnings over a given income threshold—$127,200 in 2017. As a consequence, in 2017 most American workers, especially those with incomes under $100,000, paid more in payroll tax than they did in income tax. To thinkers like Moynihan, this was very bad policy. As we all know, taxes work best when imposed on things we want less of, like tobacco and booze and fossil-fuel consumption, rather than things we want more of, like earned income. In an age when good work is under threat, the payroll tax might be ripe for reform. Naturally, the things the tax pays for—Social Security, Medicare, unemployment benefits—are essential and cannot be put at risk. But since payroll tax is paid almost entirely by workers—

directly through deductions from their paychecks and indirectly through reduced wages—some experts believe it constrains earning power, and therefore our ability to generate demand. While there is not yet agreement on how to go about it, many economists contend that taking a step back from the payroll tax to look at new ways to pay for entitlements is worth serious consideration. Why not experiment?

Another way for government to boost good work involves offering tax credits to employers who offer stable, living-wage employment. This strategy is not new: in 1994 a Federal Reserve gathering of prominent US economists came to a near consensus that such a subsidy *should* be part of any economic policy aimed at reducing unemployment. Some social scientists worry that the subsidies will be sucked up by employers who would have hired the same number of workers without a subsidy. That's certainly a possibility. But experiments outside the United States suggest that hiring subsidies can be of great benefit. After the 2008 financial meltdown, tax subsidies for hiring workers contributed to recovery efforts in Austria, South Korea, Portugal, and Sweden. And while the American experience of hiring subsidies is limited, there is evidence that—properly managed—they can work here to stimulate hiring as well. For example, the New Jobs Tax Credit of 1977–1978 and the Hiring Incentives to Restore Employment Act of 2010 both correlated with new job creation. Studies of job subsidy programs in Michigan and Georgia showed similar results. None of these experiments offer proof that tax subsidies per se create good jobs: it's impossible to know whether job growth came as a result of the tax credits or simply correlated with them. But it makes sense that reducing the cost of hiring would encourage employers to take the leap. While no tax incentive is likely to induce employers to hire in the absence of need, tax incentives may encourage them to hire in anticipation of need and to offer their employees a better deal. Indeed, in order to receive tax concessions and other public supports, firms should be required to file a "worker impact statement," laying out precise, evidence-based projections of the quantity, quality, and duration of the jobs they pledge to create. Failure to follow through might result in substantial fines that would be applied to creating public-sector employment opportunities, perhaps related to alternative energy, infrastructure improvements, or other public needs.

Another much-debated solution to dealing with a stalled demand for living-wage labor is to reduce the average workweek to as few as twenty-one hours. Advocates of this strategy argue that capitalism works best when labor is in short supply. Some quote Karl Marx, who once warned of "a disposable industrial reserve army, that belongs to capital quite as absolutely as if the latter had bred it at its own cost." Some believe that the large segment of the population not currently working or looking for work represents our own "industrial reserve army," poised to jump in when conditions improve while at the same time making it all the more unlikely that conditions will improve.

As we've seen in earlier chapters, on some levels that argument holds. Clearly, when workers are scarce they are in a stronger position to leverage a better deal. Shortening the workweek should—at least in theory—contribute to that scarcity and therefore to more demand for workers. But there are quibbles, and questions. Which workers, specifically, should have this option? Can society afford to train up doctors, lawyers, teachers, social workers, engineers, plumbers, dentists, and others knowing their skills will be doled out so sparingly? And while white-collar Americans may feel overworked, many working-class Americans desire to be paid for more—not fewer—hours.

Still, in the 1950s, labor boss George Meany declared the "progress toward a shorter work-day and shorter work week [as a] history of the labor movement itself." And it's not only history: analysts estimate that the United States might expect a significant uptick in employment, and better employment, for every hour cut from the workweek. An added bonus is that fewer hours on the job would free working Americans to devote a larger portion of their time to family and community. And there is real-world evidence that such arrangements can be economically beneficial. In Germany, for example, reduced work hours have since the late 1990s helped save many well-paid jobs from cutbacks, thanks to government-business partnerships that addressed the needs of all stakeholders. And in Sweden, the city of Gothenburg implemented a six-hour workday for public workers to great success, with hospitals and even private firms following suit. They found that fewer hours made workers less stressed and more productive and in some cases led to the hiring of more employees who boosted profits and productivity still further. In both the German and Swedish experiments, the key was government subsidies that made up most or all of the income gap between full- and part-time employment, thereby eliminating the problem of part-time work for low-income workers. Would this work in America? Perhaps we should muster the political will to find out.

Meanwhile, a growing number of advocates have taken up the call for government support, not of shorter work hours, but of no work hours. The Basic Income Guarantee (BIG) has become central to almost any public consideration of the future of work, in particular by Silicon Valley elites who worry about the shrinking capacity of humans to compete with their ever-more-clever creations. BIG has been proposed in a variety of incarnations, the most common one being payments to all citizens for—well—being alive. Though a modest sum, BIG alone might constitute enough income for some hardy souls willing to live on less, and for others it would be a wage subsidy. Those with higher incomes would have the stipend clawed back through taxes. The goal is to grant Americans an allowance, albeit a humble one, and the free time in which to spend it—thereby stimulating growth and creating more and better jobs. All BIG recipients—meaning all US citizens—would have the opportunity to earn funds through a job or entrepreneurship or investments, but no one would be obliged to do so. In theory, this scheme would reduce competition for jobs, thereby giving those who chose to work more leverage to negotiate better wages, benefits, and working conditions, and perhaps even to decline the boring, demeaning, and underpaid gigs so many endure today. BIG would also presumably reduce public anxieties over automation, in the sense that low-paid or demeaning jobs better done by machines would be done by machines, for the benefit of all.

BIG has fans in every corner. Left-leaning sociologist Erik Olin Wright writes in *Envisioning Real Utopias* that the plan would "generate an incentive structure for employers to seek technical and organizational innovations that eliminate unpleasant work" and would result in "not just a labor-saving bias, but a labor-humanizing bias." Libertarian Charles Murray agrees, though for different reasons—he believes BIG would eliminate the need for "unearned" entitlements, like Social Security, Medicare, and unemployment benefits. And as I've mentioned, Silicon Valley, too, enthusiastically supports the idea. "Universal basic income might be the most meaningful way we could subsidize the earliest stages of innovation," venture capitalist Roy Bahat, the head of venture fund Bloomberg Beta, once enthused. "It could multiply, by many factors, the amount of time people can spend creating." Other besotted enthusiasts have gone so far as to call BIG the "social vaccine of the 21st century."

BIG's many detractors see it not as a vaccine but as a dangerous drug, an addictive public handout that would undermine human motivation to seek paid labor. Naturally, this prospect should be addressed: Without the incentive of avoiding poverty, would we all simply lose our will to labor? Certainly, there is reason to fear such a threat. But don't. For there is little evidence that it is real. If anything, it appears that BIG stimulates the will to work.

In 1974, roughly one thousand residents of the small farming town of Dauphin, Manitoba, got news of their good fortune: through the joint largesse of their federal and provincial governments, they would receive monthly payments. It was an experiment, the purpose of which was to assess the social impact of a guaranteed, unconditional annual income on people who had never had quite enough. First among the questions to be answered was the one paramount in many of our minds today: Does paying people just to be alive make them lazy? The stipend was set at 60 percent of the poverty threshold, not enough for a family to live on, but enough to make a difference. The stipend was directed specifically at elevating the poor, so for every dollar an individual earned from other sources, half a dollar was withdrawn from the monthly payout.

The payments were made from 1976 to 1979, when a federal push toward austerity and a change in regional politics stanched the flow of funds. The shutdown was so abrupt that researchers had no time to analyze their data. So they stuffed the mountain of paperwork into 1,800 cardboard boxes, put the boxes in storage, and walked away, leaving the good people of Dauphin in a daze.

Decades later, Evelyn Forget, an economist at the University of Manitoba, learned of the experiment. She unearthed the boxes, blew off the dust, and dug in. "I wanted to know what impact the program had on people's lives," she told me. "And what I found is that people prefer to work." In fact, while every citizen in Dauphin was eligible for the payments, only two subgroups decreased their work hours in response—new mothers, who thanks to the subsidy were able to extend their maternity leave beyond the then-mandated six to eight weeks, and teenage boys, who were able to stay in high school beyond the "normal leaving" in tenth grade. Forget observed that far from discouraging work, the monthly payments were a source of stability, shielding residents from financial ruin in the case of sudden illness, disability, or other unpredictable events and disasters. Thanks to the solace and opportunities made possible by the payments, hospitalizations declined significantly, as did injuries. And mental health greatly improved.

"The basic income was not generous," Forget reminded me. "It was not enough to allow people to escape poverty. But it allowed people room for creativity. It allowed them the opportunity to do the sort of work that needs to get done, or the work they wanted to do that did not generate wages." When I asked Forget if she had spoken with many residents who had received the subsidy, she said yes, and that one in particular stood out in her mind: Eric Richardson.

When I called him, Richardson told me he had been only twelve years old when the program got under way. He was the youngest of six children; his mother was a hairdresser and his father did odd jobs. They were poor, he said, but they didn't feel poor, because everyone around them was in a similar situation. "We never went hungry because we had a garden, and we fished," he said. "Most people at that time were self-reliant, they helped their neighbors and each other, and there was a strong volunteer ethic. But the payments helped us afford 'extras'—education, health care, improved food. It doesn't take a lot of money to improve people's situation. I went to the dentist for the first time, and had ten cavities filled. A friend of mine, his family was able to use the money to put a down payment on a truck, and they used it to haul their animals to market. It saved their farm." Today, Richardson is a carpenter and a teacher of carpenters.

In recent years, a sprinkling of governments—in Finland, Canada, the Netherlands, and Kenya—have engaged in tentative BIG experiments. So far results are mixed. Forget, a strong advocate of the program, said it all comes down to priorities. In Dauphin, the bit of extra cash helped mothers stay home with their infants and helped young men to complete high school. It allowed artists and craftspeople to pursue what they loved and to share what they loved with their communities. Maybe some people took advantage, but far more used the funds wisely, and to great benefit. "If you give people a little bit of money, and a little bit of trust, they'll surprise you with what they can do," Forget said. "And believe me, everyone wants—everyone needs—to work."

The first step toward curing National Work Disorder is to recognize a need to work as a fact of human nature. The drive to innovate is all but coded into our DNA, and generally that's a good thing: in an age of self-driving trucks, robotic surgery, and machines that teach themselves, who could deny the power of technology to change the world, let alone change work? But the overselling of innovation of a particular kind has led us to mistake every sort of mischief as "progress" and to act as though amassing great wealth—in and of itself—absolves corporations and individuals of their responsibility to repay the privilege that society has bestowed upon them, a privilege that we as workers have made possible.

Our National Work Disorder is not really about scarce opportunities: there will always be more than enough good work to go around. Nor is it about technology, which applied correctly should only enhance our lives. Our work disorder is about a deficit of political will to frame the challenges clearly and honestly. As citizens of a free-market democracy with a global reach, it's up to us to agree upon a set of shared principles and priorities. We might curb or remove health care costs from business ledgers through a health care system that uncouples good work from good health. Many—if not most—economists have for years argued that we should. Is it time to put their idea to the test? Thinking even more fundamentally, do we agree that every American is entitled to a shot at a liberal education, income security, and a purpose-driven life? If these are the basics, let's find a way to make them happen, whether in or out of the traditional employment context. Do we value caregiving, teaching, the arts? If so, do we need a new way to reward—and value—the workers who do it?

Finding better ways to support and sustain good work might become a centerpiece of public policy in which business and government play complementary roles. Political and economic innovations that incentivize those who contribute to that effort could—and I believe would—become the most important innovations of the future. Careless free-market ideology would give way to the politics of common sense, as we rid ourselves of the supply-side fantasy that the market gives each of us the work and income that we "deserve." The nation's history belies this myth, as does our personal experience—we know the wealthiest don't always "deserve" the lion's share they take.

In this global, digitalized economy we can't rely on the private sector to guarantee long-term employment. Nor can we expect—let alone demand—that the private sector employ people to do jobs that machines can do as well and more cheaply. In recent decades, technology's greatest impact has been not on the number of jobs but on their quality: secure, full-time employment with benefits and a future have given way to precarious arrangements that expose workers to the fits and starts of an uncertain world. Technology made these changes possible, but politics is what makes them happen. It's politics, too, that has widened inequalities through the fissuring of the workplace, whereby bits and pieces of work are peeled away and auctioned off to the lowest bidder. And it is politics that has torn a yawning chasm between the many and the few, and fueled a disturbing backlash against shared values and vital social institutions.

America was built on an economic platform by which citizens earn their income—and their sense of worth—through employment. That strategy has served us well. But in an age when so many able-bodied adults lack full-time, stable employment, it is not enough. Our challenge is not finding more ways to fit people into "meaningful" jobs. Our challenge is helping people find and sustain work that offers them an opportunity to make a contribution, to make them feel worthwhile, and to make meaning for themselves.

Growing efficiencies was a fixation of the industrial age. It's a fixation we can no longer afford. We must quell the GDP fetish, a metric that overvalues work of the sort that brings outsized profit to the few and underrates and even fails to measure what matters most—work of intrinsic value to those who do it and to those who need it done. This largely unrecognized work contributes mightily to the wealth of the nation, in some cases beyond measure. Finding ways to "count" these efforts in our calculations of national prosperity—and in some cases to compensate these efforts through tax relief or rebates—would bring immediate societal benefits and would encourage a more equitable distribution of income of the sort that powers the virtuous cycle of supply and demand.

The future of work depends less on our digital creations than on our collective imagination. New computational, statistical, and data-gathering techniques have made it possible for us to better assess what efforts contribute most to our sense of well-being. Thus the very technology disrupting so many forms of work today could be used to enable a new model by which compensation is based at least in part on an individual's "social contribution." By using these tools, rather than valuing only what we can measure, we can measure what we actually value. By finding new ways to take work's measure, the very work we so desperately want and need to get done—caring work, creative work, building work, healing work, artistic work—would be acknowledged and rewarded according to its real value.

The election in 2016 of real estate tycoon Donald Trump reflected the economic uncertainty of millions of Americans, the vast majority of whom lacked a bachelor's degree. This majority see their and their children's opportunities shrinking. In postelection polls, 63 percent of Trump supporters cited a lack of "job opportunities for working-class Americans" as a "very big" problem. At the same time, rising income inequality and racial and ethnic tensions drove away younger voters, many of them recent college graduates who had reason to believe that the existing system had failed them. They had come to doubt that work, no matter how demanding, consuming, or vital, would bring them a middle-class life. The good news is that the legitimate grievances of so many, and the political forces that fed on these grievances, have ignited a renewed public faith in collective action. What we've come to recognize is that bad jobs are not a law of nature to be obeyed but a societal construct to be remedied.

What I also hope we've come to recognize is that work is not a zero-sum game of winners and losers. On the contrary, work in a free-market democracy is meant to shrink, not grow, inequality. While education and expertise are always good things, we should pull back from our too-tight focus on "skills above all." It's not enough to train people to try to stay one step ahead of the machines. A better approach is to reverse-engineer our thinking—that is, to find new ways to use technology to leverage the power of people to create real value from work. And rather than credit employers with giving us the "gift" of "meaningful" work, let's agree that the meaning we gain from our work is no gift, but very much a product of our own efforts.

British economist John Maynard Keynes once wrote that nobody "can look forward to the age of leisure and of abundance without a dread." We more or less live in that age, at least when it comes to abundance. Let's shake off the dread and recalibrate our priorities. The Enlightenment ideal of human advance lifting us from a life of toil into a life of purpose and meaning is at our doorstep. We need only muster the political will—and the trust—to answer the bell. I hope you, like me, are eager to open the door. For in the end, ensuring good work for all is not only the highest purpose of any civil society. It is by any measure the most disruptive innovation of all.

Acknowledgments

The Job has its roots in conversations I've had over the years—and decades—with friends, colleagues, and students, all of whom played a role in informing the narrative. Thank you so much for having the courage to share your concerns and insights.

For encouraging me to stay the course I am eternally grateful to my agent, Michael Carlisle. Michael is the sort of person one rarely encounters outside the pages of Victorian novels: courtly, cultured, kind, intuitive, unwaveringly loyal and generous beyond measure. (Also, a tough negotiator.) Michael brought me to Crown and to Roger Scholl, a master editor whose patience, fortitude, and wise counsel have meant everything. Thanks to Roger and to his band of consummate pros at Crown: especially Megan Schumann, Nicole McArdle, Erin Little, and Campbell Wharton, for doing everything they do with such diligence, grace, and integrity.

Work is a subject on which almost everyone—including me—has opinions, but not everyone has the facts. My deep thanks to the hundreds of experts who guided me in an effort to push beyond received wisdom toward a more enlightened—and realistic—view. Among the many scores of experts I spoke with, I'd like to give special thanks to Amy Wrzesniewski of Yale University, for graciously allowing me entry into the May Meaning Meeting, as well as for sharing time made so very precious by the recent birth of her second child. Same goes for Zeynep Ton of MIT, who was pregnant with twins when we first met, and Michael Pratt of Boston College, a very busy and devoted father of three. For their advice, suggestions, and clarifications, a special shout-out also to Offer Sharone of the University of Massachusetts; Michel Anteby of Boston University; Claudia Goldin and Richard Murnane, both of Harvard; Kathyrn Edin of Johns Hopkins University; Alexandra Michel of the University of Pennsylvania; Ron Hira of Howard University; Andrew McAfee of MIT; Robert Anthony Bruno of the University of Illinois; Robert Pollin of the University of Massachusetts; and the peerless—and fearless—Bill Lazonick of the University of Massachusetts at Lowell.

At the Brooklyn Navy Yard, David Belt and his team were a tremendous help, and David Ehrenberg an energetic guide. It was through the Yard that I met designer Edward Jacobs, who reframed my take on the creative process, and also neuroscientist Ted Hall, who disavowed me of any hope that humans will forever trump machines.

In Finland, Veera Voutilainen, Maarit Kiviso, and Anu Lehtinen eased the way, and Sannakaisa Essang, Kimmo Paavola, Pekka Ylä-Anttila, Leo Pahkin, Pekka Pohjakallio, and Tommi Laitio led the way. Thanks also to the students at Kallahti Comprehensive School for allowing me access to their thoughts and, in a few cases, to their dreams.

In Dayton, thanks especially to Adam Murka, and to Steven Johnson, Daryl Curnutte, and others of the devoted and forward-thinking faculty and staff of Sinclair Community College. Thanks also to Richard Stock and Jane Dockery, whose frank observations of the vagaries of job-training programs were sobering.

In Cleveland, thanks in particular to Ted Howard and the entire team at Evergreen Cooperatives, some of whom literally walked me through their busy days. In Minnesota, thanks to Kyle Coolbroth and his team at CoCo, who shared their collective wisdom, not to mention strong coffee and exceptional pizza. In Detroit, visionary filmmaker Philip Laurie, director of *After the Factory*, served as both guide and truth teller, as did the legendary Maurice Cox. Also in Detroit, Morgan Willis, Ellie Schneider, Nina Bianchi, and Olga Stella pulled me into a fascinating ongoing conversation about the "redesign" of work for the digital age.

In Kentucky, the faculty and staff of Berea College threw their doors—and arms—open, encouraging me to sit in on classes, interview students, and spend hours wandering the bucolic campus, including its working farm and lush forest land. I'm especially indebted to Berea president Lyle Roelofs and dean of labor David Tipton, business scholar Peter Hackbert, and artist Daniel Feinberg, and also to Tim Jordon for organizing my visit. Also in Kentucky, I am grateful to Robert Renner, and especially to his parents for sharing their views over coffee in their kitchen late into the night when they had such tough jobs to attend to the next day.

In Portland, Maine, I'm grateful to draper-to-the-stars Helen Rasmussen, and in Lawrence, Massachusetts, to Brenna Nan Schneider, whose efforts make clear that technology—aptly applied—can create broadly based prosperity. David Rolf of Service Employees International spent hours with me explaining in detail ways that organized labor might be "disrupted" to accommodate twenty-first-century economic realities.

In Somerville, Massachusetts, fire chief Pat Sullivan not only schooled me in the psychology of his chosen profession, but insisted I take the view from the driver's seat of a fire engine, not my best moment. In Cambridge, John Bigelow offered living proof that making meaning from one's work is very much a do-it-yourself proposition and a challenge that he has mastered with verve, integrity, and style.

To Abe Gorlick and Amy Cotterman: making public your own stories in the hope of helping others with their struggles was an act of genuine courage. Thank you both.

To the many friends and colleagues who cheered on this effort and forgave my obsessions . . . priceless. Particular gratitude to Susan Blau and Ellie McCarthy, meticulous editors who not only volunteered to read early drafts, but strove to set right every comma splice and split infinitive (an impossible task). Thanks as always to Doug Starr, my dear partner in the teaching life, and to Charles Mann, Andrew Sullivan, Pagan Kennedy, Robin Marantz Henig, and Kate Childs, whose good counsel helped steady the sometimes turbulent writing life. I'd also like to thank the many editors whose support and guidance on earlier projects laid the foundation for this one: Judy Brown, Steve Petranek, Paul Trachtman, Corby Kummer, Andrew Miller, Bill Phillips, and in particular, William Whitworth, editor emeritus of *The Atlantic,* whose unerring guidance and support in years past made almost anything seem possible.

As for those who suffered most in the course of completing this project, I have this to say: Alison, your determination, honesty, intelligence, and poise in the face of almost any challenge is astonishing. You are a wonder. Joanna, your humor, insight, and resilience are an inspiration. You are a ray of hope, and a joy. And Marty—for your guidance, wisdom, good sense, even temper, and eternal forbearance . . . you've made every dream that matters come true.

Notes

EPIGRAPH

vii **"In the highest sense"** Edmond Bordeaux Székely, *Creative Work: Karma Yoga: A Western Interpretation* (San Diego, CA: Academy Books, 1973).

INTRODUCTION

1 **"A man's work does not satisfy"** Elliott Jaques, *Equitable Payment: A General Theory of Work, Differential Payment, and Individual Progress* (New York: Wiley, 1961), 25.

1 **even** *freedom* **takes a backseat to** *work* In all but the first of President Obama's State of the Union addresses, two of the three most used words were *jobs* and *work*. In her presidential campaign speeches, Hillary Clinton's number one word was *jobs*.

1 **"You watch, it'll happen"** Nick Gass, "Trump Promises to Create 25 Million Jobs with Economic Plan," *Politico*, September 15, 2016, http://www.politico.com/story/2016/09/donald-trump-jobs -economic-plan-228218.

2 **Americans spend more time on the job** US Department of Labor, Bureau of Labor Statistics, "American Time Use Survey—Charts," last modified June 27, 2017, https://www.bls.gov/tus/charts.htm.

2 **In the twenty-first century, job growth** Marianne Page, "Are Jobs the Solution to Poverty?," *Pathways* magazine (Stanford University), summer 2014, https://web.stanford.edu/group/scspi/_media/pdf/pathways/summer_2014/Pathways_Summer_2014_Page.pdf.

4 **"And what's true for books is true for so many other industries"** Thanks to Max Nussenbaum, CEO and cofounder of the Detroit-based property management firm Castle, which unfortunately closed its doors in early 2018.

4 **The mantra of our time** Thomas Friedman, "Average Is Over," *New York Times*, op-ed, January 24, 2012.

5 **Memorably, one of my own students** Of the 1,895,000 bachelor's degrees conferred in 2014–15, the greatest number were conferred in the fields of business (364,000) along with health professions and related programs (216,000). The largest percentage increases between 2003–4 and 2013–14 occurred in homeland security, law enforcement, and firefighting (122 percent, from 28,200 to 62,400) and parks, recreation, leisure, and fitness studies (108 percent, from 22,200 to 46,000).

7 **since 1973 our productivity has grown almost six times** "The Productivity-Pay Gap," Economic Policy Institute, updated October 2017, http://www.epi.org/productivity-pay-gap/.

7 **in 1971, 61 percent of Americans qualified as middle class** "The American Middle Class Is Losing Ground," Pew Research Center Social and Demographic Trends Project, December 9, 2015, http://www.pewsocialtrends.org/2015/12/09/the-american-middle-class-is-losing-ground/.

8 **yet it's not at all clear that the same can be said** The Canadian government took a stab at evaluating the value of just one form of free labor—uncompensated care—and estimated the value at one-third to one-half of the country's annual GDP, Canadian Centre for Policy Alternatives, B.C. Solutions Budget, 2006, p. 12. In the United States this would amount to something like $6 trillion. This is an unavoidably speculative figure, of course, but one that gives some idea of the vital importance of uncompensated labor.

9 **half of all American workers earn less than $30,000** US Social Security Administration, "Wage Statistics for 2015," accessed February 2, 2018, https://www.ssa.gov/cgi-bin/netcomp.cgi?year=2015.

9 **with a whopping $8,000 deductible** eHealth, "Ten Years of Health

Insurance Costs," https://resources.ehealthinsurance.com/affordable
-care-act/much-obamacare-cost-2017.

11 **"Rapid advancements in the field of robotics"** UNICRI Centre
for Artificial Intelligence and Robotics (The Hague, The Netherlands), homepage, http://www.unicri.it/in_focus/on/UNICRI_Centre
_Artificial_Robotics.

13 **Nor can it be dismissed as a mere happy side effect** For thinking
along this line I am indebted to many economists, historians, and
philosophers, and to the persuasive reasoning of Harvard philosopher Michael J. Sandel in his thought-provoking book *What Money
Can't Buy: The Moral Limits of Markets* (New York: Farrar, Straus and
Giroux, 2012).

PROLOGUE

15 **"The industrious races find it extremely difficult"** Friedrich
Nietzsche, *Beyond Good and Evil: Prelude to a Philosophy of the Future*
5.189, ed. Rolf-Peter Horstmann and Judith Norman (Cambridge:
Cambridge University Press, 2001).

16 **Todesco was a self-made man** Jill Lloyd, *The Undiscovered Expression-
ist: A Life of Marie-Louise von Motesiczky* (New Haven, CT: Yale University Press, 2007), 4.

16 **cyclists dazzle in white shirts and black trousers** You can see the bicycle dance club in action at the Archiv für die Geschichte der Sozi-
ologie in Österreich, "Die Arbeitslosen der Marienthal—Bilder," June
2010, http://agso.uni-graz.at/marienthal/bilder/097.jpg.

16 **The Great Depression smothered the Austrian economy** There is
no question that Austria suffered mightily in the Great Depression,
perhaps more than any other developed nation. From 1929 to 1933,
Austria lost more than 22 percent of its GDP, an astonishing drop
when compared to the Netherlands, Switzerland, Belgium, Norway,
Sweden, or the United Kingdom, which had real output losses ranging from 5.8 to 9.46 percent. Germany suffered a loss of just over
16 percent.

17 **Unemployment was rampant, he fumed** This accounting benefited
from a reading of Paul Neurath, "Sixty Years Since Marienthal,"
Canadian Journal of Sociology/Cahiers canadiens de sociologie 20, no. 1
(1995): 91, http://dx.doi.org/doi:10.2307/3340988.

18 **Deprived of their livelihood** Marie Jahoda, Paul Lazarsfeld, and

Hans Zeisel, *Die Arbeitslosen von Marienthal: Ein soziographischer Versuch über die Wirkungen langdauernder Arbeitslosigkeit* (Leipzig: Hirzel, 1933). First published in the United States as *Marienthal: The Sociography of an Unemployed Community* (Chicago: Aldine, Atherton, 1971).

18 **"When Men Eat Dogs"** Robert N. McMurry, "When Men Eat Dogs," *Nation*, January 4, 1933, 15–17, https://www.unz.com/print/Nation -1933jan04-00015/.

18 **"When a dog or cat disappears"** Jahoda, Lazarsfeld, and Zeisel, *Marienthal*, 22.

18 **the weirdest thing in Marienthal was not dog on dinner plates** Dog meat had been eaten in every major German crisis at least since the time of Frederick the Great and was commonly referred to as "blockade mutton." In the early twentieth century, high meat prices led to widespread consumption of horse and dog meat in Germany. "Germany: Dachshunds Are Tenderer," *Time*, November 25, 1940, http://content.time.com/time/magazine/article/0,9171,884181,00 .html.

19 **the community was atomized** One particularly harrowing example was a man being reported for playing the harmonica in public and accepting money for his efforts. Since the unemployed were not allowed to work for pay, the report resulted in the man being deprived of his unemployment benefits—at an enormous cost to his family.

19 **"Leisure proves to be a tragic gift"** Jahoda et al., *Marienthal*, 66.

19 **The Marienthal investigation was the first systematic effort** The Marienthal study was first published in 1933, just a few weeks before Hitler seized power in Germany. Given that the authors were Jewish, the German publisher, Hirzel, determined that it was safest to leave their names off the title page. Although widely acclaimed immediately after its publication, the monograph all but disappeared from scholarly notice for three decades, thanks to the more pressing concerns of World War II and to the relative postwar prosperity.

19 **linking the idleness and malaise in Marienthal** Neurath, "Sixty Years Since Marienthal."

19 **the factory was reopened and "Aryanized"** American sociologist David Sills described the "major finding" of the Marienthal study as "prolonged unemployment leads to apathy rather than revolution" and stated that this "foreshadowed the widespread lack of resistance to Hitler." David L. Sills, "Paul F. Lazarsfeld, February 13, 1901–August 30, 1976," in National Academy of Sciences, *Biographical*

Memoirs, vol. 56 (Washington, DC: National Academies Press, 1987), 287, https://www.nap.edu/read/897/chapter/11. In 1933, unemployment in Germany reached a high point of six million, a number that in two years was reduced drastically—to less than a million—thanks to a policy whereby municipalities received federal funds to support public works projects—like road building—using as little machinery as possible to maximize jobs. One condition of receiving these funds was that women were not allowed to take the jobs but would devote themselves to "motherhood."

20 **"Although I now have much less to do than before"** Jahoda et al., *Marienthal*, 75.

20 **"for the women are merely unpaid, not really unemployed"** Ibid., 74.

PART 1

21 **"We are going to fight"** President Trump promised to work to keep manufacturing companies in the United States and to lower taxes for businesses in a speech at the unveiling of the Boeing 787 Dreamliner on February 17, 2017, in North Charleston, SC.

CHAPTER 1

26 **economies with low labor union participation rates** Union membership in Israel was in the past as high as 80 to 85 percent of all workers, but it declined sharply in the 1980s and 1990s. In 2017, it stood at roughly 24 percent.

27 **"Standing out from the equally-qualified pack"** Kristin F. Kranias, "The #1 Thing Hiring Managers Are Looking For," The Muse, last modified August 27, 2012, https://www.themuse.com/advice/the-1-thing-hiring-managers-are-looking-for.

31 **pronouncing applicants over the age of thirty-five** Jon Swartz, "Ageism Is Forcing Many to Look Outside Silicon Valley, but Tech Hubs Offer Little Respite," *USA Today*, August 4, 2017, https://www.usatoday.com/story/tech/columnist/2017/08/04/ageism-forcing-many-look-outside-silicon-valley-but-tech-hubs-offer-little-respite/479468001/.

31 **a difficult time imagining most women as a "good fit" for the job** "In these occupations, there's been a persistent idea that women aren't a good fit, that by nature they're not good at the work—which

isn't true," University of Indiana sociologist Cate Taylor told the *Washington Post*. It's perhaps for that reason that only about 2 percent of members of the Iron Workers Union are women, and only about 10 percent of trucking and automotive technicians. Danielle Paquette, "America's Manliest Industries Are All Competing for Women," *Washington Post*, April 21, 2017, https://www.washingtonpost.com/news/wonk/wp/2017/04/21/americas-manliest-industries-are-all-competing-for-women/?utm_term=.195dd21eb161.

31 **"more closely resembling the choice of friends or romantic partners"** Lauren A. Rivera, "Hiring as Cultural Matching: The Case of Elite Professional Service Firms," *American Sociological Review* 77, no. 6 (2012): 999–1022, http://dx.doi.org/doi:10.1177/0003122412463213.

32 **since they "didn't need the money" they were more likely to quit** Lauren A. Rivera and András Tilcsik, "Class Advantage, Commitment Penalty: The Gendered Effect of Social Class Signals in an Elite Labor Market," *American Sociological Review* 81, no. 6 (2016): 1097–131, http://dx.doi.org/doi:10.1177/0003122416668154.

32 **judged less by the quality of their work** Sharon Koppman, "Different Like Me: Why Cultural Omnivores Get Creative Jobs," *Administrative Science Quarterly* 61, no. 2 (2015): 291–331, http://dx.doi.org/doi:10.1177/0001839215616840.

33 **"Thus, evaluators shifted the job criteria"** Julie E. Phelan, Corinne A. Moss-Racusin, and Laurie A. Rudman, "Competent Yet Out in the Cold: Shifting Criteria for Hiring Reflect Backlash Toward Agentic Women," *Psychology of Women Quarterly* 32, no. 4 (2008): 406–13, http://dx.doi.org/doi:10.1111/j.1471-6402.2008.00454.x.

33 **In the hiring of construction managers and police officers** Ibid.; Michael I. Norton, Joseph A. Vandello, and John M. Darley, "Casuistry and Social Category Bias," *Journal of Personality and Social Psychology* 87, no. 6 (2004): 817–31, http://dx.doi.org/doi:10.1037/0022-3514.87.6.817.

34 **some employers are turning to a new approach, "recrutainment"** Subhadra Mitra Channa, "Conclusion: Redefining the Feminine," in *Gender in South Asia: Social Imagination and Constructed Realities* (Cambridge: Cambridge University Press, 2013), 184–209, http://dx.doi.org/doi:10.1017/cbo9781107338807.008.

35 **such attributes as emotional intelligence** Dr. Halfteck is not alone in this observation. See Oliver Korn et al., "Defining Recrutainment: A Model and a Survey on the Gamification of Recruiting and

Human Resources," in *Advances in the Human Side of Service Engineering*, ed. Louis E. Freund and Wojciech Cellary, Advances in Intelligent Systems and Computing 601 (Cham, Switzerland: Springer, 2018), 37–49, http://dx.doi.org/doi:10.1007/978-3-319-60486-2.

35 **there's scant evidence that games** Rachel Martin, "Could Video Games Be the Next Job Interview?," WBUR, December 1, 2013, http://wbur.org/npr/246999632/playing-the-game-to-get-the-job.

35 **the average job announcement brought more than 250 résumés** "50 HR and Recruiting Stats That Make You Think," Glassdoor .com, last modified 2017, http://b2b-assets.glassdoor.com/50-hr-and -recruiting-stats.pdf.

36 **This loss of wealth was particularly dire for people of color** Fabian T. Pfeffer, Sheldon Danziger, and Robert F. Schoeni, "Wealth Disparities Before and After the Great Recession," *Annals of the American Academy of Political and Social Science* 650, no. 1 (2013): 98–123, http://dx.doi.org /doi:10.1177/0002716213497452; Rakesh Kochhar and Richard Fry, "Wealth Inequality Has Widened Along Racial, Ethnic Lines Since End of Great Recession," Pew Research Center, December 12, 2014, http://www.pewresearch.org/fact-tank/2014/12/12/racial-wealth -gaps-great-recession/.

36 **And college graduates are not immune** Jaison R. Abel, Richard Deitz, and Yaqin Su, "Are Recent College Graduates Finding Good Jobs?" *Current Issues in Economics and Finance* (Federal Reserve Bank of New York) 20, no. 1 (2014), https://www.newyorkfed.org/media library/media/research/current_issues/ci20-1.pdf.

37 **the United States had the lowest** Maximiliano Dvorkin and Hannah Shell, "A Cross-Country Comparison of Labor Force Participation," *Economic Synopses* (St. Louis Fed), no. 17 (2015), https://research .stlouisfed.org/publications/economic-synopses/2015/07/31/a -cross-country-comparison-of-labor-force-participation.

37 **the United States lagged behind Poland** "Employment Rate by Age Group," OECD Data, Organisation for Economic Co-operation and Development, last modified 2016, https://data.oecd.org/emp/ employment-rate-by-age-group.htm#indicator-chart. According to this data, the United States had a prime-age (ages twenty-five to fifty-four) labor participation rate of 78.2 percent in 2016; however, this figure represents not only employed workers but workers looking for work and workers who labored as little as one hour the previous week, or in some cases no hours thanks to an illness or temporary layoff.

38 **the dashing of this hope, rather than unemployment itself** Anne
Case and Angus Deaton, "Mortality and Morbidity in the 21st Century," *Brookings Papers on Economic Activity*, no. 1 (Spring 2017): 397–
476, http://dx.doi.org/doi:10.1353/eca.2017.0005.

38 **the United States is among the most anxious nations on the planet**
"Health Statistics and Information Systems—Disease Burden and
Mortality Estimates—Disease Burden 2000–2015," World Health
Organization, last modified 2015, http://www.who.int/healthinfo
/global_burden_disease/estimates/en/index2.html.

38 **excessive work stress costs the US economy** Zak Stambor, "Employees: A Company's Best Asset," *Monitor on Psychology* (American
Psychological Association), March 2006, http://www.apa.org/monitor
/mar06/employees.aspx. Interestingly, prior to 2016, the top stressors
for the US population remained steady, with Americans being most
likely to report money, work, and the economy as very or somewhat
significant sources of stress in their lives. During the spring of 2016,
however, American Psychological Association member psychologists
began reporting that their patients were increasingly concerned
and anxious about the 2016 US presidential election—a problem
that persisted into 2017, with well over half of Americans reporting
they felt stressed by the political climate and two-thirds reporting
stress over the prospects for the future. See American Psychological Association, *Stress in America: Coping with Change*, 10th ed., 2017,
https://www.apa.org/news/press/releases/stress/2016/coping-with
-change.pdf.

38 **demanding jobs that give us no agency** Erik Gonzalez-Mulé and
Bethany Cockburn, "Worked to Death: The Relationships of Job
Demands and Job Control with Mortality," *Personnel Psychology* 70,
no. 1 (2017): 73–112, http://dx.doi.org/doi:10.1111/peps.12206.

41 **"their superiors approved highly"** William Hollingsworth Whyte,
"How Hard Do Executives Work?," *Fortune*, January 1954.

41 **"Conspicuous abstention from labor"** Thorstein Veblen, *The Theory
of the Leisure Class* (New Brunswick, NJ: Transaction, 1992), 43.

41 **"he cannot distinguish between work and the rest of his life"** William Hollingsworth Whyte, *The Organization Man* (Philadelphia:
University of Pennsylvania Press, 2002).

41 **in the case of white-collar workers** David R. Francis, "Why High
Earners Work Longer Hours," *NBER Digest* (National Bureau of
Economic Research), July 2006, http://www.nber.org/digest/jul06
/w11895.html.

42 **the "workaholic in chief"** In February 2017, in an interview broadcast on Fox News, President Trump boasted of working "long hours, long hours, and right up to 12 a.m. or 1 a.m." He claimed that he slept no more than four or five hours a night and that he continued to work while he ate. David Caplin, "President Trump: I Get 4 to 5 Hours of Sleep," ABC News, February 8, 2017, http://abcnews .go.com/Politics/president-trump-hours-sleep/story?id=45339855.

42 **"the perceptions that a busy person"** Silvia Bellezza, Neeru Paharia, and Anat Keinan, "Conspicuous Consumption of Time: When Busyness and Lack of Leisure Time Become a Status Symbol," *Journal of Consumer Research* 44, no. 1 (June 2017): 118–38, http://dx.doi .org/doi:10.1093/jcr/ucw076.

44 **Even the seemingly innocuous open office** Survey by CoreNet Global, a professional association for corporate real estate managers. See, for example, Joshua Rivera, "Death to the Open Office Floor Plan!," *Fast Company,* January 10, 2014, www.fastcompany .com/3024697/death-to-the-open-offices-floorplan.

44 **"a web of control that did not exist"** Thanks to Charles Mauro, an expert in human factors engineering who helped me understand the link between office design and productivity (or the lack thereof). Mauro told me that while it has become received wisdom that an open office plan leads to greater collegiality and productivity, "there is not a single scrap of evidence" to support that claim. In fact, psychologists have linked open office plans to high levels of anxiety, anger, and aggression, and also to health threats including high blood pressure and the spread of airborne infections.

44 **garnered enthusiastic praise** Claire Suddath, "Why There Are No Bosses at Valve," Bloomberg.com, April 27, 2017, https://www .bloomberg.com/news/articles/2012-04-27/why-there-are-no -bosses-at-valve.

45 **"don't map really well"** Andrea Peterson, "Gabe Newell on What Makes Valve Tick," The Switch, *Washington Post,* January 3, 2014, www.washingtonpost.com/blogs/the-switch/wp/2014/01/03/gabe -newell-on-what-makes-valve-tick.

46 **consultants have advised American businesses** Raghuram G. Rajan and Julie Wulf, "The Flattening Firm: Evidence from Panel Data on the Changing Nature of Corporate Hierarchies" (NBER Working Paper No. 9633, National Bureau of Economic Research, 2003), http://dx.doi.org/doi:10.3386/w9633.

46 **companies have eliminated** David Jackson, *Dynamic Organisations: The Challenge of Change* (Houndmills: Macmillan Business, 1997), 106–7; Danielle Douglas, "Companies Embrace Structure with Fewer Managers," *Washington Post*, February 24, 2012, https://www.washingtonpost.com/business/capitalbusiness/companies-embrace-structure-with-fewer-managers/2012/02/23/gIQAZn6YYR_story.html?utm_term=.3886c92bb11a.

46 **This adjustment clearly correlates** Adam Goldstein, "Revenge of the Managers: Labor Cost-Cutting and the Paradoxical Resurgence of Managerialism in the Shareholder Value Era, 1984 to 2001," *American Sociological Review* 77, no. 2 (2012): 268–94, http://dx.doi.org/doi:10.1177/0003122412440093.

46 **The concept of "disruptive innovation"** See, for example, the cartoon strip *Dilbert*, in which the dog Dogbert, working as a consultant, advises a client, "To survive, you must create disruptive innovations to redefine the market." Scott Adams, *Dilbert*, February 16, 2004, http://dilbert.com/strip/2004-02-16.

46 **"an accusation rather than an irreplaceable"** Rosalind H. Williams, *The Triumph of Human Empire: Verne, Morris, and Stevenson at the End of the World* (Chicago: University of Chicago Press, 2013), 193–94.

47 **"a new iron cage whose bars are almost invisible"** James R. Barker, "Tightening the Iron Cage: Concertive Control in Self-Managing Teams," *Administrative Science Quarterly* 38, no. 3 (1993): 408, http://dx.doi.org/doi:10.2307/2393374.

48 **Ten percent of staff were dismissed every year** Stack ranking is an old strategy reinvigorated in the 1980s by GE CEO Jack Welch, who required managers across a company to assign their employees numeric ratings along a bell curve. This approach is controversial for several reasons, the most notable being that it requires that benefits offered to high performers be offset by the punishment of low performers.

48 **this certainly seemed to be the case at Megatech** H. Takahashi et al., "When Your Gain Is My Pain and Your Pain Is My Gain: Neural Correlates of Envy and Schadenfreude," *Science* 323, no. 5916 (2009): 937–39, http://dx.doi.org/doi:10.1126/science.1165604.

48 **"It's this treadmill"** Ofer Sharone, "Engineering Consent: Overwork and Anxiety at a High-Tech Firm" (Working Paper No. 36, Berkeley Center for Working Families, Berkeley, CA, May 2002), http://hdl.handle.net/2345/4123.

CHAPTER 2

51 **most of us fail to take them** Japan guarantees only ten paid vacation days and requires no paid holidays, and is the only wealthy nation where employers offer fewer vacation days than they do the United States. That said, almost one in four American workers has no paid vacation leave whatever, and the lowest earners are most likely to be in that category. See Tanzina Vega, "In Ads, the Workers Rise Up . . . and Go to Lunch," *New York Times*, July 7, 2012, https://mobile.ny times.com/images/100000001650931/2012/07/08/business/media /ads-for-mcdonalds-and-las-vegas-aimed-at-harried-workers.html. This article points to advertisements underwritten by fast-food companies and makers of other minor luxuries to encourage Americans to take the vacation time they've earned as well as to take a break for lunch. On a more recent survey of worker willingness to take vacation time, see Hugo Martin, "Vacation Time Goes Unused for Many Americans, Survey Says," *Los Angeles Times*, March 30, 2012, http:// articles.latimes.com/2012/mar/30/business/la-fi-mo-vacation -times-20120330.

51 **"Because the job *is* my life"** Sarah W. Gavin, "2013 Vacation Deprivation Study," Expedia Viewfinder, November 18, 2013, http:// viewfinder.expedia.com/features/2013-vacation-deprivation-study.

52 **"a tragedy of modern times"** Marshall David Sahlins, *Stone Age Economics* (Chicago: Aldine-Atherton, 1972), 30.

53 **hard labor was the one sure cure** Frank Parkin, *Max Weber* (London: Routledge, 2014).

53 **"The man is now a man"** Thomas Carlyle, *Past and Present* (1843; repr., London: Chapman and Hale, 1870), 244.

53 **"truest emblem of God"** Ibid., 170–71.

53 **"The inhabitant of Bridewell hates beating hemp"** Carlyle never held down what today would be described as a "job"; he supported himself through his writings and—sporadically—by serving as a tutor and lecturer, activities he deplored. This letter to his friend Matthew Allen, dated May 19, 1820, is in the Carlyle Letters Online, http://carlyleletters.dukeupress.edu/content/vol1/#lt-18200519-TC -MAL-01.

53 **break down the fibers in preparation for making rope** Bridewell was a prison for committed prostitutes, card sharks, and other transgressors. The beating of hemp with mallets to separate bark from stem was a grueling process, done mostly by women. This

custom was immortalized by the eighteenth-century English master William Hogarth in his painting *The Harlot Beating Hemp at Bridewell*.

54 **he had little tolerance for the older man's hypocrisy** Morris considered Carlyle one of the leading intellectual figures of the nineteenth century, but he was affectionately critical of the man. He once wrote that Carlyle was "on the right side in spite of all his faults." John Morrow, *Thomas Carlyle* (London: Hambledon Continuum, 2006), 219–20.

54 **"know but the horrors of idleness"** William Morris, "Useful Work Versus Useless Toil," in *The Collected Works*, vol. 23, *Signs of Change: Lectures on Socialism* (New York: Russell and Russell, 1996).

54 **a snobbish disdain for the laboring class** According to Noam Chomsky, the great linguist, political theorist, and humanitarian, scholars generally agree that "the Constitution was intrinsically an aristocratic document designed to check the democratic tendencies of the period," delivering power to a "better sort" of people and excluding "those who were not rich, well born, or prominent from exercising political power." Noam Chomsky, *What Kind of Creatures Are We?* (New York: Columbia University Press, 2016), 78.

55 **from destitution to prosperity** Alger was a self-confessed pedophile, who after being found guilty of abusing two boys in 1866 quit his post at the First Unitarian Church and Society of Brewster, Massachusetts, to write full time. Not a few critics have pointed out that while Alger's young heroes worked hard, many were also given a leg up thanks to a close relationship with a wealthy male patron.

55 **"they are apt to imagine"** Alexis de Tocqueville, *Democracy in America*, with commentary by John Stuart Mill, trans. Henry Reeve (New York: Schocken, 1967), 120.

57 **they also must know how best to apply** An annual survey by *Institutional Investor's Alpha* magazine reported that the twenty-five best-paid hedge fund honchos earned $13 billion in 2015, a sum that approached the gross domestic product of Iceland that year. "Alpha's Rich List," *Institutional Investor's Alpha*, last modified 2016, http://www.institutionalinvestorsalpha.com/HedgeFundRichList.html.

57 **people born into relative wealth** Economist Sendhil Mullainathan and psychologist Eldar Shafir have studied how scarcity of all sorts can constrain the brain to focus on easing pressing physical needs and thus reduce the mental bandwidth of individuals to plan ahead, exert self-control, and solve problems. They argue that scarcity can

lower mental performance as much as going a night without sleep
and can leave individuals unable to deal with complexity. Children
growing up in a household where food, clothing, or the roof over
their heads is in constant doubt are far less likely to engage in intel-
lectually challenging activities that prepare them for a future as analytic thinkers. See Sendhil Mullainathan and Eldar Shafir, *Scarcity:
Why Having Too Little Means So Much* (New York: Time Books, Henry
Holt, 2014).

58 **the American economy had since 1979** John Schmitt and Janelle
Jones, *Making Jobs Good* (Washington, DC: Center for Economic and
Policy Research, 2013), http://www.cepr.net/documents/publications
/good-jobs-policy-2013-04.pdf.

59 **linked to a general *decline* in job creation** In a 2014 poll of leading
academic economists conducted by the Chicago Initiative on Global
Markets on the impact of technology on employment and earnings,
43 percent agreed that "information technology and automation are
a central reason why median wages have been stagnant in the US
over the past decade, despite rising productivity," while only 28 percent disagreed or strongly disagreed. "Robots," IGM Forum, February 25, 2014, http://www.igmchicago.org/surveys/robots.

59 **its marginal benefit in terms of labor creation approaches zero**
Robert Gordon, "Is U.S. Economic Growth Over? Faltering In-
novation Confronts the Six Headwinds" (NBER Working Paper
No. 18315, National Bureau of Economic Research, Cambridge, MA,
August 2012), http://www.nber.org/papers/w18315.

60 **"beating out less-educated workers for barista and clerical jobs"**
Paul Beaudry, David Green, and Benjamin Sand, "The Great Reversal
in the Demand for Skill and Cognitive Tasks" (NBER Working Paper
No. 18901, National Bureau of Economic Research, Cambridge, MA,
March 2013), http://dx.doi.org/doi:10.3386/w18901.

62 **the demand for college instructors will grow** The US Department
of Labor's Bureau of Labor Statistics states that "the employment
of postsecondary teachers is projected to grow 13 percent from
2014 to 2024, faster than the average for all occupations." See Occupational Outlook Handbook, "Postsecondary Teachers," US
Bureau of Labor Statistics, last modified January 30, 2018, http://
www.bls.gov/ooh/education-training-and-library/postsecondary
-teachers.htm.

63 **The median pay in 2016 was $10.83 per hour** Occupational Out-
look Handbook, "Agricultural Workers," US Bureau of Labor Sta-

tistics, last modified January 30, 2018, https://www.bls.gov/ooh
/farming-fishing-and-forestry/agricultural-workers.htm.

64 **an increased demand for agricultural *workers* is unlikely** Ibid.

65 **"The flexibility so beloved of large corporations"** Lauren Weber,
"The Second-Class Office Workers," *Wall Street Journal*, September 14,
2017, https://www.wsj.com/articles/the-contractors-life-overlooked
-ground-down-and-stuck-1505400087.

65 **job stability remained a top priority** "Under Pressure to Remain
Relevant, Employers Look to Modernize the Employee Value Proposition: Global Findings Report: 2016 Global Talent Management
and Rewards, and Global Workforce Studies," Willis Towers Watson, September 9, 2016, https://www.willistowerswatson.com/en
/insights/2016/09/employers-look-to-modernize-the-employee
-value-proposition.

CHAPTER 3

68 **"as soon as man invented a machine"** Oscar Wilde and Linda C.
Dowling, *The Soul of Man Under Socialism and Selected Critical Prose*
(London: Penguin Books, 2001).

68 **roughly one of every nine American workers** In 1994 there were
3.5 million more Americans working in manufacturing than in retail. By 2016, those numbers had almost reversed. Over 80 percent
of private jobs are now in the service sector. See "FRED Graph: All
Employees: Manufacturing," FRED Graph, Federal Reserve Bank of
St. Louis, Economic Data, accessed February 3, 2018, https://fred
.stlouisfed.org/graph/?g=3OV6.

68 **more workers than in health care and construction *combined*** Derek
Thompson, "Death of the Salesmen: Technology's Threat to Retail
Jobs," *Atlantic*, June 2013, https://www.theatlantic.com/magazine/
archive/2013/06/death-of-the-salesmen/309309/.

69 **especially—hawking those things** "Retail Trade: NAICS 44–45,"
Industries at a Glance, US Bureau of Labor Statistics, last modified October 29, 2015, https://www.bls.gov/iag/tgs/iag44-45.htm
#workforce.

69 **sales per employee have in recent years doubled** David Neumark,
Junfu Zhang, and Stephen Ciccarella, "The Effects of Wal-Mart on
Local Labor Markets," *Journal of Urban Economics* 63, no. 2 (2008):
405–30, http://dx.doi.org/doi:10.1016/j.jue.2007.07.004.

69 **fastest-growing retail sector** More than eight million people—fully 6 percent of the workforce—earn their way as retail salespeople, stock clerks, and cashiers. See US Census Bureau, "Quarterly Retail E-Commerce Sales 4th Quarter 2017," news release, February 16, 2018, https://www.census.gov/retail/mrts/www/data/pdf/ec_current.pdf.

69 **the world's largest player in this rough-and-tumble sphere** In 2014, Alibaba broke records as the largest IPO in history, with proceeds of more than $25 billion. See Neil Gough, "Alibaba I.P.O. Underwriters Increase Deal Size to Record-Setting $25 Billion," *New York Times*, September 22, 2014. Still, thanks in part to concerns about China's weak track record on controlling counterfeiters, at this writing the company has not yet gained a large market share in either the United States or the European Union.

70 **Amazon is on the glide path** Eugene Kim, "This Chart Shows How Amazon Could Become the First $1 Trillion Company," *Business Insider*, December 7, 2016, http://www.businessinsider.com/how -amazon-could-become-the-first-1-trillion-business-2016-12.

70 **the nation's most efficient big-box retailer** In early 2018 each Walmart employee generated $225,000, each McDonald's employee $56,000. See CSIMarket, "Wal Mart Stores Inc.—Sales per Employee," CSIMarket, last modified January 2018, https://csimarket .com/stocks/WMT-Revenue-per-Employee.html.

70 **to also sell online, or to die trying** Best Buy is today the last standing big-box electronics retailer. The chain struggled for years and was sometimes derided as an "Amazon showroom," as so many customers scoped out merchandise in its stores before going online to make an actual purchase. But starting in 2015 the chain's outlook improved significantly, in part thanks to a lack of brick-and-mortar competitors, and in part due to a dramatic surge in online sales.

71 **But as the 1970s bled into the 1980s** After declining in the 1990s, the number of extremely poor neighborhoods in Chattanooga and the region—those with poverty rates above 40 percent—more than doubled from 2000 to 2009. See "The Re-emergence of Concentrated Poverty," in Elizabeth Kneebone, Carey Nadeau, and Alan Berube, *The Re-emergence of Concentrated Poverty: Metropolitan Trends in the 2000s* (Washington, DC: Metropolitan Policy Program at Brookings, 2011), https://www.brookings.edu/wp-content/uploads/2016/06/1103 _poverty_kneebone_nadeau_berube.pdf.

71 **A handful of naysayers objected to the president's choice of words** Perhaps the most vociferous objection came from the American

Booksellers Association. In a letter to the president, they called the choice of venue "greatly misguided" and explained that Amazon's business practices have cost the country far more jobs than they have created. "All told," the letter continued, "according to the Institute for Local Self-Reliance, every $10 million in spending that shifts from Main Street retailers to Amazon results in a net loss of 33 retail jobs." See David Grogan, "ABA Criticizes President's Choice of Venue for Jobs Speech," American Booksellers Association, news release, July 29, 2013, http://www.bookweb.org/news/aba-criticizes -president%E2%80%99s-choice-venue-jobs-speech.

72 **an inordinate number of Texans** Louise Story, "Texas Business Incentives Highest in Nation," *New York Times*, December 2, 2012, http://www.nytimes.com/2012/12/03/us/winners-and-losers-in -texas.html?pagewanted=all.

72 **independent contractors tied to labor platforms** See Lawrence Katz and Alan Krueger, "The Rise and Nature of Alternative Work Arrangements in the United States, 1995–2015" (NBER Working Paper No. 22667, National Bureau of Economic Research, Cambridge, MA, September 2016), http://dx.doi.org/doi:10.3386/w22667.

72 **like Chattanooga, Tennessee** Ana Campoy, "Amazon's Exit Spurs Tax Fight in Texas," *Wall Street Journal*, last modified February 17, 2011, https://www.wsj.com/articles/SB1000142405274870396110457 6148634038574352.

73 **Chattanooga worked hard to woo Amazon** When cities and states compete against one another for jobs, taxpayers shoulder the risk. Take Kansas City, for example, which straddles Kansas and Missouri, with State Line Road as a rough dividing line. In recent decades, thousands of businesses have held Kansas City hostage, threatening to move their jobs from one side of the line to the other. Each state bids against the other with tax breaks and other incentives to get companies to move to its side of the line. Nearly ten thousand companies have made the move, at an estimated cost to taxpayers of nearly half a billion dollars. One of these companies is Applebee's Bar and Grill, the casual dining restaurant chain. In 1993 Kansas lured Applebee's international headquarters to its side of the border. In 2007, Missouri enticed Applebee's back to its side. In 2011, Kansas upped the ante with a $12.9 million package funded in large part by the Missouri Quality Jobs Program. In 2015, the company announced it was moving its headquarters again—this time to California.

73 **Amazon promised 1,476 full-time jobs** In 2015, when Amazon announced it was hiring more workers in Chattanooga, the hourly wage on offer was $11.25, below the poverty line for a family of four. That meant that at least some of these workers would actually incur costs in the form of housing and other subsidies. See Jessica Bruder, "With 6,000 New Warehouse Jobs, What Is Amazon Really Delivering?," Reuters, June 17, 2015, http://blogs.reuters.com /great-debate/2015/06/17/with-6000-new-warehouse-jobs-what-is -amazon-really-delivering/.

73 **To ward off theft, employees were checked twice daily** In December 2014, the Supreme Court ruled unanimously that a contract agency was not required to pay workers at Amazon warehouses for the time they spent undergoing a twice-daily security screening, a process workers claimed can take as long as twenty-five minutes. See Supreme Court of the United States, Syllabus to *Integrity Staffing Solutions, Inc. v. Jesse Busk et al.*, No. 13-433, October term, 2014, https://www.supremecourt.gov/opinions/14pdf/13-433_5h26.pdf; "Supreme Court of the United States—9/12/2014—*Integrity Staffing Solutions, Inc. v. Jesse Busk et al.*, No. 13–433," *International Labor Rights Case Law* 1, no. 2 (2015): 239–43. Apparently, Amazon has no sympathy for employees who pilfer. In 2016, Bloomberg news reported that the company had installed big-screen monitors to broadcast streams of images of workers fired for stealing. The employees are seen in silhouettes, stamped with the words "Terminated" or "Arrested."

73 **"announcing a fitness initiative"** Helaine Olen, "President Obama's Amazon Jobs Pitch Is Hard to Buy with One Click," *Guardian*, August 6, 2013, https://www.theguardian.com/money/us-money-blog /2013/aug/06/obama-amazon-jobs-hard-to-buy.

73 **Jeff Bezos regularly offers workers** While Amazon CEO Jeff Bezos claimed the "pay to quit" option was instituted to rid the company of less-engaged employees, this explanation lacks credibility. The offer was extended only to low-wage warehouse employees, who could easily be replaced by even lower-wage temporary workers hired by a staffing agency. It was not extended to high-wage earners, such as Seattle-based engineers and technicians, who while in theory may be equally disengaged are far more difficult and costly to replace.

73 **While Bezos insists that none of these innovations** Bezos has a history of claiming that Amazon would enhance rather than destroy jobs—early on he insisted that the company was no threat to

the owners of independent bookstores but simply provided a different service from them. See, for example, Steve Wasserman, "The Amazon Effect," *Nation*, May 29, 2012, https://www.thenation.com/article/amazon-effect/.

73 **every human on the Amazon payroll** See, for example, Olivia LaVecchia and Stacy Mitchell, "Report: How Amazon's Tightening Grip on the Economy Is Stifling Competition, Eroding Jobs, and Threatening Communities," Institute for Local Self-Reliance, November 29, 2016, https://ilsr.org/amazon-stranglehold/.

73 **"Labor is the highest-cost factor"** Tim Linder, "New Patent Report," *Connected World Magazine*, January 28, 2014, https://connectedworld.com/new-patent-report-january-28-2014/.

75 **Sawyer (and his older brother, the two-armed Baxter robot)** Dr. Brooks gave $4 per hour as the approximate cost of employing Baxter in response to a question at the Technonomy 2012 Conference in Tucson. See John Markoff, Andrew McAfee, and Rodney Brooks, "Where's My Robot?," *Techonomy*, November 2012, http://techonomy.com/conf/12-tucson/future-of-work/wheres-my-robot/.

78 **the Weather Channel broadcasts 18 million forecasts** John Koetsier, "Data Deluge: What People Do on the Internet, Every Minute of Every Day," Inc.com, July 25, 2017, https://www.inc.com/john-koetsier/every-minute-on-the-internet-2017-new-numbers-to-b.html.

79 **continuously improving its performance** Many thanks to the very kind and patient data scientists who helped clarify this for me, and also see Christof Koch, "How the Computer Beat the Go Master," *Scientific American*, March 19, 2016, https://www.scientificamerican.com/article/how-the-computer-beat-the-go-master/.

81 **the third leading cause of death in America** Martin A. Makary and Michael Daniel, "Medical Error: The Third Leading Cause of Death in the US," *British Medical Journal*, May 3, 2016, i2139, http://dx.doi.org/doi:10.1136/bmj.i2139.

CHAPTER 4

80 **"over the next five years, machine learning"** "IBM Reveals Five Innovations That Will Change Our Lives Within Five Years," IBM news release, December 17, 2013, https://www-03.ibm.com/press/us/en/pressrelease/42674.wss.

84 **"starting and growing a business takes tremendous grit"** Donald
Trump, "President Donald J. Trump Proclaims November 2017 as
National Entrepreneurship Month," October 31, 2017, https://www
.whitehouse.gov/presidential-actions/president-donald-j-trump
-proclaims-november-2017-national-entrepreneurship-month/.

84 **Google, it seems, is the dream job** "Google Is Ranked as an Attractive Employer," Universum Global, last modified 2017, http://
universumglobal.com/rankings/company/google/.

84 **Google is also, after Apple, the world's most valuable brand** "Forbes
Releases Seventh Annual World's Most Valuable Brands List," *Forbes*,
May 23, 2017, https://www.forbes.com/sites/forbespr/2017/05/23
/forbes-releases-seventh-annual-worlds-most-valuable-brands-list
/#611e6a475b55.

85 **the odds of an applicant getting into Harvard** Max Nisen, "Here's
Why You Only Have a 0.2% Chance of Getting Hired at Google,"
Quartz, October 22, 2014, https://qz.com/285001/heres-why-you-only
-have-a-0-2-chance-of-getting-hired-at-google.

85 **a popular restaurant** Google brags that its Boston office is a mere
"529 Smoots (plus or minus a couple of ears)" from MIT's main
entrance. If you are among the majority who do not know what a
Smoot is, you might want to Google it.

85 **In the summer of 2016** Noam Scheiber and Nick Wingfield, "Amazon's Jobs Fair Sends Clear Message: Now Hiring Thousands," *New
York Times*, August 2, 2017, https://www.nytimes.com/2017/08/02
/technology/amazons-jobs-fair-sends-clear-message-now-hiring
-thousands.html.

86 **not one of these tech dynamos** Jerry Davis, "Re-imagining the Corporation," paper presented at the annual meeting of the American
Sociological Association, Denver, CO, August 2012.

87 **what one observer called the "yawning disparity"** Thanks for this
insight to sociologist Paul Starr, as expressed in his review of *The
Second Machine Age*, by Andrew McAfee and Erik Brynjolfsson. See
Paul Starr, "New Technology Doesn't Make Us All Richer," *New Republic*, July 6, 2014, https://newrepublic.com/article/118327/second
-machine-age-reviewed-paul-starr.

88 **At the Global Entrepreneurial Summit at Stanford University** See
"Remarks by the President at Global Entrepreneurship Summit,"
White House press release, June 25, 2016, https://obamawhitehouse
.archives.gov/the-press-office/2016/06/25/remarks-president-global
-entrepreneurship-summit-and-conversation-mark.

89 **six of ten jobs were generated by firms** David G. W. Birch, *The Job Generation Process* (Cambridge, MA: MIT Program on Neighborhood and Regional Change 1979), https://ssrn.com/abstract=1510007.

89 **new small businesses created fully eight of every ten new jobs** David G. W. Birch, *Job Creation in America: How Our Smallest Companies Put the Most People to Work* (New York: Free Press, 1987), https://ssrn.com/abstract=1496185.

90 **anachronisms but veritable job generation machines** For an eye-opening look at the rise of the small business myth, see Jonathan J. Bean, *Big Government and Affirmative Action: The Scandalous History of the Small Business Administration* (Lexington: University Press of Kentucky, 2001).

90 **Start-ups, by his reckoning** Tim J. Kane, "The Importance of Start-ups in Job Creation and Job Destruction," Kauffman Foundation Research Series: Firm Formation and Economic Growth, 2010, http://dx.doi.org/doi:10.2139/ssrn.1646934.

91 **Uganda had a per capita income of less than $700** "Uganda GDP per Capita," Trading Economics, last modified February 3, 2018, http://www.tradingeconomics.com/uganda/gdp-per-capita.

92 **David Birch came to question the power** In 1994 Birch told the *New York Times* he found his findings neither "interesting" nor "meaningful," and he bemoaned that the eight-out-of-every-ten number "won't go away." See Sylvia Nasar, "Myth: Small Business as Job Engine," *New York Times*, March 25, 1994, http://www.nytimes.com/1994/03/25/business/myth-small-business-as-job-engine.html?pagewanted=all.

93 **"Most entrepreneurial activity just generates churn"** See, for example, Kimberly Weisul, "Steve Case's Reddit AMA Reveals Striking Apology from Former Teen Hacker," Inc.com, April 23, 2014, http://www.inc.com/kimberly-weisul/steve-cases-best-advice-for-entrepreneurs-and-recent-graduates.html. As the *Wall Street Journal* reported in 2013, "[Start-ups] are reinventing the way companies work: Firing people before the ink is dry on their employment contracts." Stephanie Gleason and Rachel Feintzeig, "Startups Are Quick to Fire: New Hires Who Don't Measure Up Can Be Gone in Days or Weeks," *Wall Street Journal*, December 12, 2013, https://www.wsj.com/articles/no-headline-available-1386894031.

93 **"the spectacular yield you might think we'd get"** Scott Shane, "Why Encouraging More People to Become Entrepreneurs Is Bad

Public Policy," *Small Business Economics* 33, no. 2 (2009): 141–49, http://dx.doi.org/doi:10.1007/s11187-009-9215-5.

93 **to meet the immediate demands** Moshe Y. Vardi, "The Rise and Fall of Industrial Research Labs," *Communications of the ACM* 58, no. 1 (2014): 5, http://dx.doi.org/doi:10.1145/2687353. Also, economists Ashish Arora, Sharon Belenzon, and Andrea Patacconi report that the share of publicly traded corporations whose scientists publish in academic journals was just 6 percent in 2007, down nearly two-thirds from 1980. See Ashish Arora, Sharon Belenzon, and Andrea Patacconi, "Killing the Golden Goose? The Decline of Science in Corporate R&D" (NBER Working Paper No. 20902, National Bureau of Economic Research, Cambridge, MA, January 2015), http://dx.doi.org/doi:10.3386/w20902.

93 **as a share of the total federal budget** "R&D as a Percent of the Federal Budget," American Association for the Advancement of Science, last modified December 5, 2017, http://www.aaas.org/sites/default/files/Budget_1.jpg.

94 **the Trump administration, whose 2018 budget** Jeffery Mervis, "Little Holiday Cheer for U.S. Science Agencies as Congress Extends Spending Freeze," *Science*, December 22, 2017, http://www.sciencemag.org/news/2017/12/little-holiday-cheer-us-science-agencies-congress-extends-spending-freeze.

PART 2

95 **"Only if a man works can he live"** Langdon Gilkey, *Shantung Compound: The Story of Men and Women Under Pressure* (New York: Harper and Row, 1966).

CHAPTER 5

97 **"In every vocation, the meaning of the work"** Edward Howard Griggs, *Self-Culture Through the Vocation* (New York: B. W. Huebsch, 1914), 30.

99 **"so many mirrors in which we saw reflected our essential nature"** Karl Marx, "Comment on James Mill," in his *Economic and Philosophic Manuscripts of 1844.*

99 **"the tailor objected to the sewing machines"** George Howell, "American Competition #11," *American Gas and Light Journal* 71 (1899): 612.

102 **"burdens to be escaped as promptly as possible"** Mihaly Csikszentmihalyi, *Flow: The Psychology of Optimal Experience* (New York: Harper
Perennial Modern Classics, 2008), 149.

104 **"In the glorification of 'work'"** Friedrich Nietzsche, *A Nietzsche
Reader* (London: Penguin UK, 2003), p. 213.

105 **the term *follow your passion*** Google Ngram Viewer, Google Books,
accessed February 3, 2018, https://books.google.com/ngrams/graph
?content=follow+your+passion&year_start=1980&year_end=2018&
corpus=0&smoothing=3&share=&direct_url=t1%3B%2Cfollow%20
your%20passion%3B%2Cc0. Jobs's speech available at news.stanford
.edu/2005/06/14/jobs-061505.

105 **"You've got to find what you love"** " 'You've Got to Find What You
Love,' Jobs Says," *Stanford News,* June 14, 2005, https://news.stanford
.edu/2005/06/14/jobs-061505.

106 **It's not that fires aren't dangerous—of course they are** Workers in fishing and fishing-related occupations die on the job at a
higher rate than any other workers, and drivers/sales workers and
truck drivers (followed by structural metalworkers) have the highest injury rates, far outpacing those of firefighting. That said, when
compared to many other occupations, firefighting is dangerous.
Firefighters are twice as likely to die on the job as painters and automobile mechanics, six times more likely to die than janitors and
cashiers, and fourteen times more likely to die than those working
in food preparation and serving occupations. It does appear that
firefighter deaths are on the decline—in recent years the number of
deaths per year averaged fewer than seventy, with the vast majority of
those deaths occurring to part-time or volunteer firefighters rather
than full-time professional firefighters, and attributed primarily
to cardiac arrests. See "Firefighter Fatalities in the United States,"
National Fire Protection Association, June 2017, http://www.nfpa
.org/News-and-Research/Fire-statistics-and-reports/Fire-statistics
/The-fire-service/Fatalities-and-injuries/Firefighter-fatalities-in
-the-United-States.

109 **autonomy, complexity, and actions** Gladwell writes: "Those three
things—autonomy, complexity, and a connection between effort and
reward—are, most people agree, the three qualities that work has to
have if it is to be satisfying. Whether or not our work is fulfilling
is what ultimately makes us happy. Being a teacher is meaningful.
Being a physician is meaningful. . . . Hard work is a prison sentence
only if it does not have meaning. Once it does, it becomes the kind of

thing that makes you grab your wife around the waist and dance a jig." Malcolm Gladwell, *Outliers: The Story of Success* (2008; repr., New York: Back Bay Books, 2011).

109 **"often as intimate as our family relationships"** Charles McGrath, "The Prime-Time Novel: The Triumph of the Prime-Time Novel," *New York Times*, October 22, 1995, http://www.nytimes.com/1995/10/22 /magazine/the-prime-time-novel-the-triumph-of-the-prime-time -novel.html?pagewanted=all.

110 **he loathed his abusive parents** Maslow's father, Samuel, a heavy drinker, evidently kept his distance from the family home in order to avoid his wife, Ruth, a religious zealot whom Maslow diagnosed as "schizophrenogenic." Apparently, when Ruth caught her son feeding two stray kittens milk using her good china, she dashed the animals' brains out against the basement walls. When she died, Maslow did not attend her funeral. Algis Valiunas, "Abraham Maslow and the All-American Self," *New Atlantis*, Fall 2011.

111 **pundits publicly bemoaned the sad fate of the working stiff** D. Katz and B. S. Georgopoulos, "Organizations in a Changing World," *Journal of Applied Behavioral Sciences* 7 (1971): 342–70.

111 **"Overspecialization, petty rules, humiliation, and fatigue"** John Slocum Jr., "Dimensions of Participation in Managerial Decision Making," in *Contemporary Readings in Organizational Behaviour*, ed. Fred Luthans and Kenneth R. Thompson (New York: McGraw Hill, 1977), 129.

111 **"revulsion by young workers to working in mass production"** T. T. Herbert, *Dimensions of Organizational Behavior* (New York: Macmillan, 1977), 464.

112 **worker satisfaction in his heyday** Annamarie Mann and Jim Harter, "The Worldwide Employee Engagement Crisis," *Gallup Business Journal*, January 7, 2016, http://www.gallup.com/businessjournal /188033/worldwide-employee-engagement-crisis.aspx.

112 **as many as 92 percent of US workers** Robert P. Quinn, Graham L. Staines, and Margaret R. McCullough, "Job Satisfaction: Is There a Trend?," Manpower Research Monograph No. 30, US Department of Labor, 1974, https://www.psc.isr.umich.edu/dis/infoserv/isrpub/ pdf/Jobsatisfaction_3674_.PDF.

113 **fewer than half of all Americans** "2016 Employee Job Satisfaction and Engagement: Executive Summary," Society for Human Resource Management, 2016, https://www.shrm.org/hr-today/trends-and

-forecasting/research-and-surveys/Documents/2016-Employee-Job
-Satisfaction-and-Engagement-Report-Executive-Summary.pdf.

113 **The vast majority** Amy Adkins, "Employee Engagement in U.S. Stagnant in 2015," Gallup.com, January 13, 2016, http://www.gallup .com/poll/188144/employee-engagement-stagnant-2015.aspx.

114 **"His identity is thus at the mercy of another human being"** This comment and others that follow were in response to Ellen R. Shell, "Is Work Still Meaningful?," *Atlantic*, December 14, 2011, https:// www.theatlantic.com/business/archive/2011/12/is-work-still -meaningful/250131/.

CHAPTER 6

117 **Wrzesniewski was naturally drawn to this positive approach** C. R. Snyder et al., "The Future of Positive Psychology: A Declaration of Independence," in *Handbook of Positive Psychology*, ed. C. R. Snyder and S. J. Lopez (New York: Oxford University Press), 751–67.

118 **the nudge came from** *Habits of the Heart* Robert Bellah, *Habits of the Heart: Individualism and Commitment in American Life* (Berkeley: University of California Press, 1985).

118 **any activity that made life "perceptibly significant to a person"** John Dewey, *Democracy and Education: An Introduction to the Philosophy of Education* (New York: Macmillan, 1922), 358–59.

118 **a calling was not always socially relevant** Many thanks to Hamilton College political scientist Joel Winkelman for introducing me to Dewey's thinking and writing on work. I'm particular indebted to him for his (now published) manuscript: Joel Winkelman, "John Dewey's Theory of Vocation," *American Political Thought* 5, no. 2 (April 2016), http://www.journals.uchicago.edu/doi/abs/10.1086/685761? journalCode=apt.

119 **she and her team at Yale surveyed two hundred workers** A. Wrzesniewski et al., "Jobs, Careers, and Callings: People's Relations to Their Work," *Journal of Research in Personality* 31, no. 1 (1997): 21–33.

119 **one-third as a calling** Ibid. The Wrzesniewski et al. study included a separate survey of administrative assistants only, as well as a larger study (196 participants) that included a broad array of occupations.

121 **a poignant illustration** J. S. Bunderson and Jeffery A. Thompson, "The Call of the Wild: Zookeepers, Callings, and the Double-Edged Sword of Deeply Meaningful Work," *Administrative Science Quar-*

terly 54, no. 1 (2009): 32–57, http://dx.doi.org/doi:10.2189/asqu.2009
.54.1.32.

121 **in 2017 the average pay was reported as $11.95 per hour** "Zookeeper
Salary," PayScale, accessed February 4, 2018, https://www.payscale
.com/research/US/Job=Zookeeper/Hourly_Rate.

124 **His every move was followed and videoed** Apparently, video surveillance is not a terribly powerful tool of law enforcement. In 2012,
several TSA agents were indicted for drug trafficking after waving
through suitcases packed with cocaine and methamphetamine at
Los Angeles International Airport. The same year, according to the
Hartford Courant, "three Transportation Security Administration
officers, two police officers and more than a dozen drug dealers in
Florida, New York and Connecticut were charged in a smuggling
conspiracy that delivered illegal oxycodone pills from Florida to
the Waterbury [Connecticut] area. Authorities said that the TSA
officers—two in Florida and one in New York—were paid to help drug
couriers move pills and the stacks of cash they generated through
airport screening systems." See Edmund H. Mahony, "TSA Officer
Admits Working for Drug Smugglers," *Hartford Courant*, April 17,
2012, http://articles.courant.com/2012-04-17/news/hc-tsa-drugs
-0418-20120417_1_drug-couriers-move-pills-tsa-officers-oxycodone
-pills.

125 **Electronic surveillance of employees** The market for employee-
monitoring software is large and varied. One company welcomes
customers "to the age of smart network monitoring with Net
Spy Pro. Discover for yourself what network users are up to and how
they are behaving. Have control over their systems to run things
smoothly within the network. Watch them LIVE with viewing system activity in real time!" "Network users" means employees.

125 **nearly half keep tabs of their employees' keystrokes** "The Latest on
Workplace Monitoring and Surveillance," American Management
Association, last modified March 13, 2008, http://www.amanet.org
/training/articles/The-Latest-on-Workplace-Monitoring-and
-Surveillance.aspx.

125 **employer-provided cell phones that track them** David Kravets,
"Worker Fired for Disabling GPS App That Tracked Her 24 Hours
a Day," *Ars Technica*, last modified May 11, 2015, http://arstechnica
.com/tech-policy/2015/05/worker-fired-for-disabling-gps-app-that
-tracked-her-24-hours-a-day.

126 **gathering around the coffee machine results in higher overall productivity** Benjamin N. Waber et al., "Sensing Informal Networks in Organizations," Humanyze, November 21, 2017, https://www.humanyze.com/sensing-informal-networks-in-organizations/.

126 **"there are implicit pressures to share the information"** Thanks to Matt Beane for speaking with me so freely on this delicate matter.

126 **MIT business professor Andrew McAfee** Andrew McAfee, "In Praise of Electronically Monitoring Employees," *Harvard Business Review*, October 24, 2013, https://hbr.org/2013/10/in-praise-of-electronically-monitoring-employees.

126 **a study of surveillance he had completed** Lamar Pierce, Daniel Snow, and Andrew McAfee, "Cleaning House: The Impact of Information Technology Monitoring on Employee Theft and Productivity," *Management Science*, May 13, 2015, https://pubsonline.informs.org/doi/abs/10.1287/mnsc.2014.2103.

128 **surveillance vastly increases workplace stress** Since the 1980s, a number of empirical studies have produced strong evidence linking electronic monitoring in the workplace with increased levels of stress. In one survey of monitored workers, fully 81 percent of respondents complained that electronic observation made their jobs more stressful. Another study compared the attitudes of electronically monitored insurance workers with nonmonitored workers who performed comparable jobs and found that monitored workers reported feeling far more stressed. On stress, decreased job satisfaction, increased feelings of social isolation, and increased perceptions of the importance of quantity over quality, see John R. Aiello and Kathryn J. Kolb, "Electronic Performance Monitoring and Social Context: Impact on Productivity and Stress," *Journal of Applied Psychology* 80, no. 3 (1995): 339–53, https://www.ncbi.nlm.nih.gov/pubmed/7797458.

128 **a recent analysis aptly entitled "Watching Me Watching You"** Sally A. Aplin and Michael D. Fischer, "Watching Me Watching You (Process Surveillance and Agency in the Workplace)," International Symposium on Technology and Society, in *2013 IEEE International Symposium on Technology and Society (ISTAS): Social Implications of Wearable Computing and Augmediated Reality in Everyday Life: 27–29 June 2013, University of Toronto, Toronto, Canada* (Piscataway, NJ: IEEE, 2013), http://ieeexplore.ieee.org/document/6613129/?reload=true&tp=&arnumber=6613129&url=http:%2F%2Fieeexplore.ieee.org%2Fxpls%2Fabs_all.jsp%3Farnumber%3D661312.

128 **workers who sense they are not trusted are less productive** Barry A. Friedman and Lisa J. Reed, "Workplace Privacy: Employee Relations and Legal Implications of Monitoring Employee E-Mail Use," *Employee Responsibilities and Rights Journal* 19, no. 2 (2007): 75–83, http://dx.doi.org/doi:10.1007/s10672-007-9035-1.

131 **inflation-adjusted CEO compensation** For statistics on executive compensation, see Alyssa Davis and Lawrence Mishel, "CEO Pay Continues to Rise as Typical Workers Are Paid Less," Economic Policy Institute, Issue No. 380, June 2014, http://www.epi.org/publication/ceo-pay-continues-to-rise/.

131 **"roughly proportional to their market value"** Elizabeth Anderson, *Private Government: How Employers Rule Our Lives (and Why We Don't Talk About It)* (Princeton, NJ: Princeton University Press, 2017).

PART 3, CHAPTER 7

137 **"work in the school as in the factory will become drudgery"** Margaret A. Haley, "Why Teachers Should Organize," *Journal of Education* 60, no. 13 (1904): 215–16, 222.

138 **"Our nation is at risk"** US Department of Education, Commission on Excellence in Education, "A Nation at Risk," April 1983, http://www.ed.gov/pubs/NatAtRisk/risk.html.

138 **Japan, then an economic and technological juggernaut** *Japan as Number One: Lessons for America* (Cambridge, MA: Harvard University Press, 1979), by Harvard sociologist Ezra F. Vogel, is at this writing still the all-time best-selling book in Japan by an American author and has been highly influential in the United States as well. It was "a matter of urgent national interest for Americans to confront Japanese successes," Vogel warned, before Japan took control of the global economy.

139 **"In science and mathematics, Japanese test scores lead the world"** Committee for Economic Development, *Investing in Our Children: Business and the Public Schools: A Statement* (Washington, DC: CED, 1985), 2.

139 **IBM chief executive Louis Gerstner** For general background on Gerstner, I consulted, among other sources, Doug Garr, *IBM Redux: Lou Gerstner and the Business Turnaround of the Decade* (New York: HarperCollins, 1999). Prior to joining IBM, Gerstner headed RJR Nabisco, the multinational conglomerate that under his leadership

reaped roughly 57 percent of its revenues from the sale of cigarettes, notably Camels. In tests, nine out of ten six-year-olds were able to link the child-friendly icon "Joe Camel" to the cigarette brand. After the introduction of the Joe Camel mascot, the brand's share of the under-eighteen-year-old cigarette market jumped from 0.5 percent to 32.8 percent, representing a $470 million increase in annual sales. Some argued that this fact alone should disqualify Gerstner as an advocate for children. See, for example, this commentary on Gerstner's appointment as "education Pope": Derrick Z. Jackson, "Ex-Tobacco Chief Now Singing a Different Tune," *Boston Globe*, April 15, 1996.

139 **"spent a lot of time" on it and had "the scars to prove it"** Gerstner was not a fan of consensus governance but very clearly a fan of top-down leadership. He declared at that congressional hearing that turning around the nation's educational system was not a job that could be delegated: it had to be tackled by a fearless "CEO" willing to "expel the people and the organizations that are throwing up roadblocks to the changes you consider critical." 141 Cong. Rec. 1660 (August 5, 1995), https://www.gpo.gov/fdsys/pkg/CREC-1995 -08-05/html/CREC-1995-08-05-pt1-PgE1660-3.htm.

139 **almost all of them white and male** J. J. Lagowski, "The Education Summit: A Different Signal," *Journal of Chemical Education* 73, no. 5 (1996): 383, http://dx.doi.org/doi:10.1021/ed073p383.

140 **a "'Field of Dreams' optimism"** Alyson Klein, "Historic Summit Fueled Push for K-12 Standards," *Education Week*, September 23, 2014, https://www.edweek.org/ew/articles/2014/09/24/05summit.h34 .html.

141 **"incomplete and unlikely to work"** Thomas L. Good, "Educational Researchers Comment on the Education Summit and Other Policy Proclamations from 1983–1996," *Educational Researcher* 25, no. 8 (1996): 4, http://dx.doi.org/doi:10.2307/1176481.

141 **"the finest pillar of republican government"** "The Eagle, No. 4," *Columbia Phoenix and Boston Review*, February 1800, 109.

141 **little of this "useful knowledge" was passed down** Literacy rates are difficult to trace, as people tend not to leave much of a mark. While some keep wills, letters, or other documents, many do not, and without physical evidence it's difficult to know whether individuals could read or write. University of Montana scholar Kenneth Lockridge's groundbreaking book *Literacy in Colonial New England* (New York: Norton, 1974) garnered evidence from legal records and

offered provisional conclusions that among white New England men about 60 percent of the population was literate between 1650 and 1670, a figure that rose to 85 percent between 1758 and 1762 and to 90 percent between 1787 and 1795. In cities such as Boston, the rate had come close to 100 percent by century's end. The figures for other parts of the country—and for women—are not as conclusive, but it is thought that the vast majority of white men and about half of all white women could read and write by the early 1800s.

142 **"he was looked upon as a wizard"** Francis G. Blair, *The One Hundredth Anniversary of the Birth of Abraham Lincoln* (Springfield: Illinois State Journal Co., 1908), 22–23.

142 **"a pool of intellectual stagnation"** Dana Goldstein, *The Teacher Wars* (New York: Doubleday, 2014).

142 **high school attendance soared** US Census Bureau, *Statistical Abstract of the United States, 2003* (Washington, DC: US Census Bureau, 2003), No. HS-20, Education Summary—Enrollment, 1900 to 2000, and Projections, n.d., https://www.census.gov/library/publications /2003/compendia/statab/123ed.html.

142 **students in rural regions graduated** In 1924, high school graduation rates exceeded 35 percent in Idaho, while in urban New Jersey they stood at 20 percent. By 1928 fully 45 percent of Idaho students were graduating, while in New Jersey only 25 percent managed to earn their high school diploma. See "How America Graduated from High School: 1910 to 1960" (NBER Working Paper No. 4762, National Bureau of Economic Research, Cambridge, MA, June 1, 1994), http://www.nber.org/papers/w4762.

142 **old enough to snare a work permit** Wages of immigrants often fell well below those of their colleagues, making it necessary for their children to quit school and help support the family.

143 **"factories in which the raw products"** Alfie Kohn, *What Does It Mean to Be Well Educated?* (Boston: Beacon Press, 2004), p. 20.

143 **"skilled hands and trained minds"** Theodore Search, "Resolutions Regarding Technical Education [President's Annual Report]," in *Proceedings of the Second Annual Convention of the National Association of Manufacturers* (Philadelphia: National Association of Manufacturers, 1897).

143 **"the people yield themselves with perfect docility"** Frederick T. Gates, *The Country School of Tomorrow* (New York: General Education Board, 1913).

143 **guiding them across a threshold of independent thought** In the late 1800s, educational reformer Johann Heinrich Pestalozzi, a strong advocate of universal education, insisted that teachers use the environment and experience of the child as the most valuable means and material of his or her instruction. His curriculum favored observation and investigation over memorization. Pestalozzi's disciple Johann Friedrich Herbart argued that appealing to individual interest was the most important element in good teaching, and he designed a five-step approach to teaching that emphasized the adaptation of instruction to the past experiences of the pupil. The publication in 1892 of a primer by Illinois Normal School professor Charles McMurray entitled *The General Method* popularized Herbart's principles, which were applied in schools across the country. Though this was the height of the industrial age, the focus was not on "training" a docile workforce but on encouraging independent thought.

144 **"Our K–12 system largely still adheres"** "The New Normal: Doing More with Less: Secretary Arne Duncan's Remarks at the American Enterprise Institute," US Dept. of Education, Nov. 17, 2010.

144 **"We must open up the education industry"** Betsy DeVos, "Competition, Creativity and Choice in the Classroom," speech presented at SXSW EDU Conference, March 2015, http://www.federationfor children.org/wp-content/uploads/2015/03/Betsy-SXSWedu-speech -final-remarks.pdf.

146 **the relative decline in the market value of education** Claudia Dale Goldin and Lawrence F. Katz, *The Race Between Education and Technology* (Cambridge, MA: Belknap Press of Harvard University Press, 2009); also my own interview with Dr. Goldin.

146 **"being squeezed out of white collar work"** Paul Douglas, "What Ever Happened to the White-Collar Job Market," *System: The Magazine of Business* 49 (December 1926): 719.

146 **inequality declined** Thomas Piketty and Arthur Goldhammer, *Capital in the Twenty-First Century* (Cambridge, MA: Belknap Press of Harvard University Press, 2014).

146 **an "educational slowdown"** Goldin and Katz, *Race*, 7.

147 **the nation's "poorly educated" workforce** See, for example, David C. Berliner and Bruce J. Biddle, *The Manufactured Crisis: Myths, Fraud, and the Attack on America's Public Schools* (New York: Perseus, 1995), 133.

147 **In 2007 high school graduation rates started to rise** "Public High School Graduation Rates," National Center for Education Statistics,

last modified April 2017, http://nces.ed.gov/programs/coe/indicator_coi.asp.

147 **in 2015 they topped out at 91 percent** Camille L. Ryan and Kurt Bauman, "Educational Attainment in the United States: 2015," US Census Bureau, *Current Education Reports*, March 2016, https://www.census.gov/content/dam/Census/library/publications/2016/demo/p20-578.pdf.

147 **an "economic imperative"** Mary Bruce, "Snob? Obama Renews Higher Education Push," ABC News, February 27, 2012, http://abcnews.go.com/m/blogEntry?id=15802130&cid=77.

147 **33.4 percent of Americans hold at least a bachelor's degree** "Highest Educational Levels Reached by Adults in the U.S. Since 1940," US Census Bureau, news release, March 30, 2017, https://www.census.gov/newsroom/press-releases/2017/cb17-51.html.

147 **we pay heavily for the privilege** Peter Cappelli, *Will College Pay Off? A Guide to the Most Important Financial Decision You'll Ever Make* (New York: Public Affairs, 2015).

148 **the selectivity of the college from which they graduated** Stacy Dale and Alan Krueger, "Estimating the Return to College Selectivity over the Career Using Administrative Earnings Data" (NBER Working Paper No. 17159, National Bureau of Economic Research, Cambridge, MA, June 2011), http://dx.doi.org/doi:10.3386/w17159.

148 **children from families in the top quintile** Sean F. Reardon, Rachel Baker, and Daniel Klasik, "Race, Income, and Enrollment Patterns in Highly Selective Colleges, 1982–2004," Stanford Center for Education Policy Analysis, August 3, 2012, https://cepa.stanford.edu/content/race-income-and-enrollment-patterns-highly-selective-colleges-1982-2004.

149 **states have slashed education funding** Michael Leachman, Kathlee Masterson, and Michael Mitchell, "Funding Down, Tuition Up: State Cuts to Higher Education Threaten Quality and Affordability at Public Colleges," report, Center on Budget and Policy Priorities, last modified August 15, 2016, http://www.cbpp.org/sites/default/files/atoms/files/5-19-16sfp.pdf.

149 **where a majority of students** Nick Anderson and Danielle Douglas-Gabriel, "Nation's Prominent Public Universities Are Shifting to Out-of-State Students," *Washington Post*, January 30, 2016, https://www.washingtonpost.com/local/education/nations-prominent-public-universities-are-shifting-to-out-of-state-students/2016/01/30/07575790-beaf-11e5-bcda-62a36b394160_story.html?utm

_term=.71089c3d19a5. For the most recent specifics on the University of Alabama enrollments, see "Quick Facts," University of Alabama, n.d., https://www.ua.edu/about/quickfacts.

149 **getting closed out of classes** Rachel Baker, "The Effects of Structured Transfer Pathways in Community Colleges," *Educational Evaluation and Policy Analysis* 38, no. 4 (June 2016): 626–46, http://dx.doi.org/doi:10.3102/0162373716651491.

149 **Some of the poorest have been lured to for-profit colleges** "Figure A: Annual Median Family Income of Students by Type of College in 2008," Government Accountability Office, 2011, http://www.epi.org/files/2012/med_fam_income_college_students.png.

149 **the fastest-growing sector in higher education** The 2015–16 National Postsecondary Student Aid Study (https://nces.ed.gov/pubs2016466.pdf) found that 96 percent of students attending four-year for-profit schools borrowed money to finance their education, compared with an average of 62 percent at private institutions and less than 50 percent at public four-year institutions. The difference in borrowing for students at nonprofit public and for-profit two-year schools was ever starker: 17 percent versus 64 percent, respectively. Students at for-profits acquired larger loans, were far less likely to graduate, and were far more likely to default on their loans.

149 **households with less than $30,000 in annual income** Jennifer Ma and Sandy Baum, "Trends in Community Colleges: Enrollment, Prices, Student Debt, and Completion (April 2016)," College Board, 2016, https://trends.collegeboard.org/content/trends-community-colleges-enrollment-prices-student-debt-and-completion-april-2016.

149 **only about one in four entering students** See the table "Undergraduate Retention and Graduation Rates," in J. McFarland et al., *The Condition of Education 2017,* NCES 2017-144 (Washington, DC: US Department of Education, National Center for Education Statistics, 2017), https://nces.ed.gov/pubs2017/2017144.pdf.

150 **for-profits consumed one in four** Michael Stratford, "Study Finds For-Profit Colleges Drove Spike in Student Loan Defaults," *Inside Higher Ed*, September 11, 2015, https://www.insidehighered.com/news/2015/09/11/study-finds-profit-colleges-drove-spike-student-loan-defaults.

150 **the *average* incomes of those who don't** See the table "Unemployment Rates and Earnings by Educational Attainment," in "Employment Projections," US Department of Labor, Bureau of Labor

Statistics, last modified October 24, 2017, http://www.bls.gov/emp /ep_chart_001.htm.

151 **graduates of institutions ranked just a step or two below** For a truly insightful articulation of this, see Philip Brown, Hugh Lauder, and David Ashton, *The Global Auction: The Broken Promises of Education, Jobs, and Incomes* (New York: Oxford University Press, 2012), 116.

151 **borrowers are having great difficulty repaying it** See Federal Reserve Bank of New York Center for Microeconomic Data, *Quarterly Report on Household Debt and Credit, August 2016* (New York: Federal Reserve Bank of New York, 2017), http://admin.issuelab.org /permalink/resource/25718.pdf. While this data seems to indicate that only 11.2 percent of student loan debt is delinquent, the fine print reveals that delinquency rates for student loans are likely to understate effective delinquency rates because about half of these loans are currently in deferment, in grace periods, or in forbearance and therefore temporarily not in the repayment cycle. This implies that among loans in the repayment cycle delinquency rates are roughly twice as high.

152 **college graduates who started life poor** Brad Hershbein, "A College Degree Is Worth Less If You Are Raised Poor," Brookings Institute, February 19, 2016, https://www.brookings.edu/blog/social-mobility -memos/2016/02/19/a-college-degree-is-worth-less-if-you-are-raised -poor/.

152 **"a glass ceiling that even a bachelor's degree does not break"** Timothy J. Bartik and Brad Hershbein, "Degrees of Poverty: Family Income Background and the College Earnings Premium," *Employment Research* 23, no. 3 (2016): 1–3, https://doi.org/10.17848/1075 -8445.23(3)-1.

152 **South Korea is the world's largest producer** Karin Fischer, "When Everyone Goes to College: A Lesson from South Korea," *Chronicle of Higher Education*, May 1, 2016, https://www.chronicle.com/article /When-Everyone-Goes-to-College-/236313.

153 **37 percent of young adults hold a bachelor's degree** See Ryan and Bauman, "Educational Attainment." Note that only 26.7 percent of Americans of traditional retirement age, sixty-five and older, had bachelor's degrees.

153 **compared with 25 percent of jobs** See the table "Employment, Wages, and Projected Change in Employment by Typical Entry-Level Education," in "Employment Projections," US Department of Labor,

Bureau of Labor Statistics, last modified January 30, 2018, https://www.bls.gov/emp/ep_table_education_summary.htm.

153 **nearly half of all recent college graduates are underemployed** Jaison R. Abel and Richard Dietz, "Are the Job Prospects of Recent College Graduates Improving?," *Liberty Street Economics* (blog, New York Federal Reserve), September 4, 2014, http://libertystreeteconomics.newyorkfed.org/2014/09/are-the-job-prospects-of-recent-college-graduates-improving.html.

153 **a college degree has become a vetting mechanism** Mike Swift, "Blacks, Latinos and Women Lose Ground at Silicon Valley Tech Companies," *San Jose Mercury News*, last modified August 13, 2016, https://www.mercurynews.com/2010/02/11/blacks-latinos-and-women-lose-ground-at-silicon-valley-tech-companies/.

154 **a credential held by only 19 percent** "Moving the Goalposts: How Demand for a Bachelor's Degree Is Reshaping the Workforce," Burning Glass Technologies, September 2014, http://burning-glass.com/research/credentials-gap/.

154 **do not technically require a high school diploma** "Occupations with the Most Job Growth," under "Employment Projections," US Department of Labor, Bureau of Labor Statistics, last modified January 30, 2018, https://www.bls.gov/emp/ep_table_104.htm.

154 **the vast majority of colleges** Gary Saul Morson and Morton Schapiro, *Cents and Sensibility: What Economics Can Learn from the Humanities* (Princeton, NJ: Princeton University Press, 2017), 66. The authors state that only roughly 350 colleges and universities—out of several thousand—are even modestly selective and that the vast majority accept "virtually everyone who applies."

154 **68 percent of those who attend** "Fast Facts: Graduation Rates," from US Department of Education, National Center for Education Statistics, 2017, https://nces.ed.gov/fastfacts/display.asp?id=40.

155 **this sorting process almost inevitably discriminates** *Indicators of Higher Education Equity in the United States: 2017 Historical Trend Report* (Washington, DC: Pellington Institute, 2017), http://pellinstitute.org/downloads/publications-Indicators_of_Higher_Education_Equity_in_the_US_2017_Historical_Trend_Report.pdf.

156 **"a fraudulent offer to the majority"** Paul E. Willis, *Learning to Labor: How Working Class Kids Get Working Class Jobs* (New York: Columbia University Press, 1977), 38–39.

156 **a proxy for inherited privilege** John Ermisch, Markus Jäntti, and Timothy M. Smeeding, "What Have We Learned," in *From Parents*

to Children: The Intergenerational Transmission of Advantage (New York: Russell Sage Foundation, 2012), 463–81. The authors write, "The evidence indicates that . . . [the] net effect [of educational systems] is not to reduce the relationship between parental SES [socioeconomic status] and child achievement, but to maintain or strengthen patterns of differences in outcomes already evident at younger ages."

157 **"the educational factor"** Thomas Piketty and Arthur Goldhammer, *Capital in the Twenty-First Century*, 315.

CHAPTER 8

158 **"there is little to be gained from increasing potential supply"** Lawrence Summers, "The Jobs Crisis," Reuters, June 13, 2011, https:// www.reuters.com/article/column-usjobs-summers/rpt-column-the -jobs-crisis-lawrence-summers-idUSN1227995720110613.

158 **after they were married, Leroy and Susan** Kathryn Edin kindly shared the true story of Leroy and Susan with me but stipulated that their real names not be used. I've honored that agreement.

159 **a couple of questions on a Target job application** As research for this book, I attempted to apply online for an entry-level position at both Target and Walmart. The experience was not only confusing and frustrating but intrusive. I was asked for personal details—for example, whether I considered myself cocky and whether I was satisfied with my life. No explanation was offered as to why these questions were relevant to the job.

159 **like Ellen, she was raised with religion** Ellen DeGeneres makes no secret that she was raised as a strict Christian Scientist.

162 **go into deep debt while waiting for the check to arrive** Sarah S. Greene, "The Broken Safety Net: A Study of Earned Income Tax Credit Recipients and a Proposal for Repair," *New York University Law Review* 88, no. 2 (2013): 515–88, https://scholarship.law.duke .edu/faculty_scholarship/3107.

162 **" 'Skills' is a smokescreen for other things"** Economist Andrew Michael Spence is known for his job-market signaling model, whereby employees signal their respective skills to employers by acquiring a certain degree of education that is costly. Employers will pay higher wages to more educated employees because they know that the proportion of employees with high abilities is higher among the educated ones, as it is less costly for them to acquire education than it is

for employees with low abilities. For the model to work, it is not even necessary for education to have any intrinsic value if it can convey information about the sender (employee) to the recipient (employer) and if the signal (education) is costly. A. M. Spence, "Job Market Signalling," *Quarterly Journal of Economics* 87, no. 3 (1973): 355–74.

163 **"he more nearly resembles"** Frederick Winslow Taylor, *The Principles of Scientific Management* (New York: Harper, 1911), 59.

163 **"began to stop having as many vocational kinds of skills"** Shawn Langlois, "Tim Cook Says This Is the Real Reason Apple Products Are Made in China," MarketWatch, December 21, 2015, http://www .marketwatch.com/story/tim-cook-apple-doesnt-make-its-products -in-china-because-its-cheaper-2015-12-20.

163 **a significant "negative impact" factor on their bottom line** "The Boiling Point? The Skills Gap in the United States," Deloitte and Manufacturing Institute, 2011, http://www.themanufacturinginsti tute.org/~/media/A07730B2A798437D98501E798C2E13AA.ashx. Many journalists and policy makers have echoed these complaints. See Rahm Emanuel, "Chicago's Plan to Match Education with Jobs," *Wall Street Journal*, December 18, 2011, https://www.wsj.com/articles /SB10001424052970203893404577100772663276902; Thomas A. Hemphill and Mark J. Perry, "U.S. Manufacturing and the Skills Crisis," *Wall Street Journal*, February 26, 2012, https://www.wsj.com /articles/SB10001424052970204880404577230870671588412; Thomas L. Friedman, "If You've Got the Skills, She's Got the Job," op-ed, *New York Times*, November 17, 2012, http://www.nytimes.com /2012/11/18/opinion/sunday/Friedman-You-Got-the-Skills.html.

166 **tests were routine at more than 80 percent of all US companies** According to a survey conducted at the time by the American Management Association. See Lydia De Pillis, "Companies Dry Test a Lot Less Than They Used to Because It Doesn't Work," *Washington Post*, March 10, 2015.

166 **When illicit drug use started to decline through the early 2000s** https://drug-abuse-statistics/#drug-abuse-statistics-and-addiction -research.

166 **require candidates to pass a drug test** William C. Becker et al., "Racial/Ethnic Differences in Report of Drug Testing Practices at the Workplace Level in the U.S.," *American Journal on Addictions* 23, no. 4 (2013): 357–62, http://dx.doi.org/doi:10.1111/j.1521-0391.2013 .12109.x.

166 **a serious obstacle to filling job vacancies** Lauren Weber, "Greater Share of U.S. Workers Testing Positive for Illicit Drugs," *Wall Street Journal*, September 15, 2016, https://www.wsj.com/articles/greater -share-of-u-s-workers-testing-positive-for-illicit-drugs-1473901202. More recently, in testimony on the impact of opioid abuse before the Senate Banking Committee in July 2017, then Federal Reserve chair Janet Yellen opined, "I do think it is related to declining labor force participation among prime-age workers. I don't know if it's causal or if it's a symptom of long-running economic maladies that have affected these communities and particularly affected workers who have seen their job opportunities decline." Jeanna Smialek, "Yellen Says Opioid Use Is Tied to Declining Labor Participation," Bloomberg.com, July 13, 2017, https://www.bloomberg .com/news/articles/2017-07-13/yellen-says-opioid-use-is-tied-to -declining-labor-participation.

167 **"decreasing the need for skill"** The thinking is not entirely new. For example, see: David Card and John DiNardo, "Skill Biased Technological Change and Rising Wage Inequality: Some Problems and Puzzles," *Journal of Labor Economics* 20, no. 4 (October 2002), http:// dx.doi.org/doi:10.3386/w8769.

167 **a good head for numbers and strong customer service skills** See, for example, J. W. Carpenter, "Bank Teller: Career Path and Qualifications," Investopedia, last modified December 16, 2015, http:// www.investopedia.com/articles/professionals/121615/bank-teller -career-path-qualifications.asp.

167 **new, higher-skilled jobs that pay better** See, for example, Thomas L. Friedman, *Thank You for Being Late: An Optimist's Guide to Thriving in the Age of Accelerations* (New York: Farrar, Straus and Giroux, 2016). Friedman, a columnist for the *New York Times*, has used the example of cash machines repeatedly to make the point that automation can create jobs. But while it is true that in the 1990s ATMs led to an increase in the number of bank branches, and therefore opportunities for people to work in those new branches, additional new technologies have since led to a radical decline in both bank branches and their associated jobs.

167 **higher-skilled employees, like loan managers** "Digital Disruption: How FinTech Is Forcing Banking to a Tipping Point," Citi GPS: Global Perspectives and Solutions, March 1, 2016, https://ir.citi .com/D%2F5GCKN6uoSvhbvCmUDS05SYsRaDvAykPjb5subGr7f1 JMe8w2oX1bqpFm6RdjSRSpGzSaXhyXY%3D.

When I visited the Cambridge site, there was only one customer service rep, who told me he had a bachelor's degree in communications and said his core duties involved "promoting the brand" and directing customers to the "right person, regardless of their banking needs."

167 **demand for skilled bank employees will continue to decline** Nathaniel Popper, "'Fintech? Start-Up Boom Said to Threaten Bank Jobs," *New York Times*, March 30, 2016, https://www.nytimes .com/2016/03/31/business/dealbook/fintech-start-up-boom-said -to-threaten-bank-jobs.html. Popper reports projections of up to a 30 percent reduction of then-current bank employees due to new technologies.

168 **self-interested parties to overproduce graduates** Of eight hundred engineers age fifty or older responding to a 2011 survey, 16 percent were unemployed, and 48 percent had been out of engineering entirely for at least two years. See Brian Fuller, "Help for Unemployed Engineers," *EE Times*, May 20, 2011, http://www.eetimes.com/author .asp?section_id=28&doc_id=1285160. Four years later, in 2015, high-tech firms in the United States cut nearly eighty thousand employees, including forty-seven thousand announced layoffs from Hewlett-Packard, Intel, Unisys, and Microsoft. See "Tech Sector Shed Over 79K in 2015, 13 Percent of All Cuts," Challenger, Gray & Christmas, Inc., news release, January 20, 2016, https://www .challengergray.com/press/press-releases/tech-sector-shed-over-79k -2015-13-percent-all-cuts. While there is no question that recent graduates in engineering tend to have excellent job prospects, experienced engineers often find themselves underunemployed.

168 **down from about 385,000 in 2002** Patrick Thibodeau, "What STEM Shortage? Electrical Engineering Lost 35,000 Jobs Last Year," *Computerworld*, January 16, 2014, http://www.computerworld .com/article/2487847/it-careers/what-stem-shortage—electrical -engineering-lost-35-000-jobs-last-year.html.

168 **The supply of STEM graduates** For every two students graduating with a STEM degree, only one is employed in STEM. See Ibid.

168 **"We're not seeing indicators of a talent shortage"** According to the industry website Indeed.com, the average annual wage of all workers in the software services sector was roughly $100,000 in January 2017, about $1,000 less than five years earlier, as reported by TechAmerica Foundation in its annual Cyberstates report. While this wage may

appear high when compared with other industries, the fact that it has not grown significantly in five years is an indication that demand for these services is at best uncertain. As well, this number is heavily skewed by a relative handful of companies like Apple, LinkedIn, PayPal, and Google, where significant numbers of engineers earn salaries averaging as much as $144,000 annually, while software engineers at less glamorous companies earn less than $80,000.

169 **"The training pipeline produces more scientists"** B. Alberts et al., "Rescuing US Biomedical Research from Its Systemic Flaws," *Proceedings of the National Academy of Sciences* 111, no. 16 (2014): 5773–77, http://dx.doi.org/doi:10.1073/pnas.1404402111.

169 **Krugman once coined the term** *zombie idea* Paul Krugman, "Life, Death and Deficits," op-ed, *New York Times*, November 15, 2012, http://www.nytimes.com/2012/11/16/opinion/life-death-and-deficits.html.

170 **Unemployment for bachelor's-degreed computer scientists** Daniel Costa, "STEM Labor Shortages? Microsoft Report Distorts Reality About Computing Occupations," Policy Memorandum No. 195, Economic Policy Institute, November 19, 2012, http://www.epi.org/publication/pm195-stem-labor-shortages-microsoft-report-distorts/.

170 **"We teach our people to squeeze the orange harder"** For an excellent and comprehensive analysis of this issue, see David Rosnick and Dean Baker, "Missing the Story: The OECD's Analysis of Inequality," report, Center for Economic Policy Research, July 2012, http://cepr.net/publications/reports/missing-the-story-the-oecds-analysis-of-inequality. Also, there is a fairly consistent correlation between massive layoffs of employees and soaring stock prices, especially in the high-tech sector. In July 2014, when Microsoft reported that it was laying off 14 percent of its staff, the company's stock price in premarket trade soared 3.68 percent on top of the previous day's huge gains. Following Hewlett-Packard's second-quarter earnings report, where it announced up to sixteen thousand additional layoffs, its stock price rocketed nearly 7 percent in early trading. The HP workforce reduction came on top of the company's previously announced thirty-four thousand job cuts.

171 **the number of jobs listed as available** Bart Hobijn and Patryk Perkowski, "The Industry-Occupation Mix of U.S. Job Openings and Hires" (Working Paper No. 2012-09, Federal Reserve Bank of San Francisco, July 2012), https://www.frbsf.org/economic-research/files/wp12-09bk.pdf.

172 **"it rejects almost any applicant for no clear reason"** "MathWorks—Good for 1–2 Years, Move Out if You Don't Want to Work with Incompetent People," anonymous comment, Glassdoor, May 6, 2012, http://www.glassdoor.com/Reviews/Employee-Review-MathWorks -RVW1492717.htm.

173 **the yawning income disparity that is a hallmark of our age** Greg J. Duncan and Richard J. Murnane, *Whither Opportunity? Rising Inequality, Schools, and Children's Life Chances* (New York: Russell Sage Foundation, 2011).

173 **many workers have little *political* power** A. B. Atkinson, *Inequality: What Can Be Done?* (Cambridge, MA: Harvard University Press, 2015).

CHAPTER 9

176 **"Through the whole of his life"** Adam Smith, *The Theory of Moral Sentiments* 7.8, 10, ed. Knud Haakonssen (Cambridge: Cambridge University Press, 2002).

178 **who the hell even knew?** *The Last Truck: The Closing of a GM Plant*, directed by Steve Bognar and Julie Reichert (Home Box Office Films, 2009).

180 **"a great white whale washed ashore"** Mary Anne Hunting, *Edward Durell Stone: Modernism's Populist Architect* (New York: Norton, 2013).

180 **the highest-paid government employee in the county** Lynn Hulsey, "RTA Drivers' Pay Among Highest," *Dayton Daily News*, August 2, 2009, http://www.daytondailynews.com/news/news/local/rta-drivers -pay-among-highest/nM3Mt.

183 **well above the median wage of $29,930.13** See "Occupational Employment and Wages, May 2016: 51-4111. Tool and Die Makers," US Bureau of Labor Statistics, Division of Occupational Employment Statistics, September 9, 2016, https://www.bls.gov/oes/current /oes514111.htm#nat.

183 **I checked out recruitment notices** "Position for Tool and Die Maker," HNI Careers, last modified February 28, 2013, http://hni careers.com/JobDetails.aspx?ID=14293. Judging the nation's prosperity by average incomes can be misleading, as the average is skewed by very high salaries at the top. The median is the midpoint: half of all workers earn more and half of all workers earn less than this amount.

183 **a company in Georgia** Widely advertised recruitment announcement for a tool and die maker position in Cedartown, Georgia; TRC Professional Solutions, "Tool & Die Maker," ZipRecruiter, last modified March 1, 2012, http://www.ziprecruiter.com/job/Tool-Die -Maker/37918f8d/?source=cpc-simplyhired.

185 **but not all of them looked ready for it** From this job description, it seems that tool and die makers might have a higher-than-average risk of occupation-related injuries. Of the nearly sixty-one million Americans getting Social Security benefits in 2016, roughly 17.5 percent were disabled workers or their dependents—almost six times the number who received benefits in 1970.

185 **Dave Brat told the House Small Business Committee in 2017** see insidesources.com.skillgap-hurting-small-businesses/.

185 **for lack of skills** see still4hill.com/2016/07/29/Clintonkaine-2016 -at-knex-toy-factory-in-hatfield-pa/.

186 **"In China, you would have to have multiple football fields"** This quote comes from an interview with Cook that Charlie Rose conducted for the news series *60 Minutes*: "Inside Apple, Part Two," *60 Minutes*, CBS News, December 15, 2015, https://www.cbsnews .com/video/inside-apple-part-two, but Cook has said pretty much the same thing in far more recent interviews with a number of media outlets in both the United States and China.

186 **nearly half a million tool and die makers in the United States** Occupational Outlook Handbook, "Machinists and Tool and Die Makers," US Department of Labor, Bureau of Labor Statistics, January 30, 2018, https://www.bls.gov/ooh/production/machinists-and -tool-and-die-makers.htm.

186 **companies like Apple** Bill Canis, "The Tool and Die Industry: Contribution to U.S. Manufacturing and Federal Policy," Congressional Research Service Report for Congress, March 16, 2012, http://www .ntma.org/uploads/general/Tool-and-Die-Industry.pdf.

186 **"Our tooling department"** "Tool Making," Inventix Manufacturing, last modified 2013, http://www.inventix.com/toolmaking /index.php.

187 **one in four drop out after just one semester** Meredith Kolonder, "Why Are Graduation Rates at Community Colleges So Low?," *Hechinger Report*, May 5, 2015, http://hechingerreport.org/new-book -addresses-low-community-college-graduation-rates.

187 **firefighters earn an average wage of $46,870** Brian A. Reaves, *Local Police Departments, 2013: Personnel, Policies, and Practices* (Washing-

ton, DC: Bureau of Justice Statistics, Department of Justice, 2015), https://www.bjs.gov/index.cfm?ty=pbdetail&iid=5279.

188 **the Association of Unmanned Aerial Vehicle Systems** Darryl Jenkins and Bijan Vasgh, "The Economic Impact of Unmanned Aircraft Systems Integration in the United States," report, Association for Unmanned Aerial Vehicle Systems International, June 16, 2017, http://www.auvsi.org/our-impact/economic-report.

188 **more than 13,700 people flooded in to take the commercial drone licensing test** "Will There Be Too Many Drones?," KALB News, September 16, 2016, http://www.kalb.com/content/news/Will-there-be-too-many-drones-393790761.html.

188 **industry claims that their services were in booming demand** Conversations with industry experts provided this insight.

189 **"there are a lot of people who know how to fly drones"** "Why Most Drone Pilot Salaries Are So Low (and How to Increase Yours)," *Drone U* (blog), May 21, 2017, https://www.thedroneu.com/blog/why-most-drone-pilot-salaries-are-so-low/.

189 **who graduated from the JTPA program** James Bovard, "What Job 'Training' Teaches? Bad Work Habits," *Wall Street Journal*, September 12, 2011, https://www.wsj.com/articles/SB100014240531119043 32804576538361788872004.

189 **similar employment histories but with somewhat lower earnings** Ronald D'Amico and Peter Z. Schochet, "The Evaluation of the Trade Adjustment Assistance Program: A Synthesis of Major Findings," Mathematica Policy Research, December 30, 2012, https://www.mathematica-mpr.com/our-publications-and-findings/publications/the-evaluation-of-the-trade-adjustment-assistance-program-a-synthesis-of-major-findings.

192 **an Oklahoma-based consulting firm** Thomas Gnau, "Fuyao Spent Nearly $800K with Consultant in Union Battle," *My Dayton Daily News*, December 26, 2017, http://www.mydaytondailynews.com/business/fuyao-spent-nearly-800k-with-consultant-union-battle/zBIqg0Wtb KGhVmJbtNOjjI/.

192 **a "little bit like a 'hostage situation'"** Noam Scheiber and Keith Bradsher, "Culture Clash at a Chinese-Owned Plant in Ohio," *New York Times*, June 10, 2017, https://www.nytimes.com/2017/06/10/business/economy/ohio-factory-jobs-china.html.

CHAPTER 10

196 **the nation's "top liberal arts college" for the third year in a row** "2017 College Guide and Rankings," *Washington Monthly*, last modified 2017, https://washingtonmonthly.com/2017college-guide.

196 **The total estimated annual cost of attending Colgate** "Estimated Cost of Attendance," Colgate University, accessed February 13, 2018, http://www.colgate.edu/admission-financial-aid/financial-aid /prospective-first-year-students/estimated-cost-of-attendance.

198 **"a kind of Rosetta Stone for blue America"** Sarah Jones, "J. D. Vance, the False Prophet of Blue America," *New Republic*, November 17, 2016, https://newrepublic.com/article/138717/jd-vance-false-prophet -blue-america.

200 **arts and crafts play a major role in the economy** Paul Kern, "Arts and Culture Grows at Faster Pace in 2013," Bureau of Economic Analysis, news release, February 16, 2016, https://www.bea.gov /newsreleases/general/acpsa/acpsa0216.pdf.

203 **nearly half of all rural jobs lost to displacement** John Cromartie, Christine Von Reichiert, and Ryan Arthun, "Factors Affecting Former Residents' Returning to Rural Communities," Economic Research Report No. ERR-185, Economic Research Service, US Department of Agriculture, May 21, 2015, https://www.ers.usda.gov /publications/pub-details/?pubid=45364.

207 **"in the heart of a thousand-square-mile area"**: Judy Jones, "Rural Kentucky Addresses Doctor Shortage," *Rural Health Update*, Spring 2002, 1–3.

209 **what the average service worker earned in four or five months** Amy K. Glasmeier, "Living Wage Calculation for Kentucky," Living Wage Calculator, Massachusetts Institute of Technology, last modified 2018, http://livingwage.mit.edu/states/21.

PART 4, CHAPTER 11

214 **substantial Swedish-speaking minority** In 2005, Finnish-language author Arto Paasilinna said that he believed the issue of Swedish-speaking Finns "will be resolved naturally. The Swedish speakers will die off, taking their language with them." www.trelocal .se/20071204/9292.

214 **some bitterly resent it** Katariina Mäkinen, "Struggles of Citizenship and Class: Anti-immigration Activism in Finland," *Sociological Review* 65, no. 2 (2017): 218–34.

214 **alcohol abuse and domestic violence** Kris Clarke, "The Paradoxical Approach to Intimate Partner Violence in Finland," *International Perspectives in Victimology* 6, no. 1 (2011): 9–19; Edward Dutton, "Finland's the Best Place to Be," *Telegraph*, January 26, 2010, http://www .telegraph.co.uk/expat/expatlife/7073648/Finlands-the-best-place -to-be.html.

214 **the country did not have much to offer in trade** Kari Rutio, "The Growing Years of Finland's Industrial Production," Statistics Finland, last modified May 15, 2007, http://www.stat.fi/tup/suomi90 /toukokuu_en.html.

215 **the deepest recession endured by any industrialized country** Yuriy Gorodnichenko, Enrique Mendoza, and Linda Tesar, "The Finnish Great Depression: From Russia with Love" (NBER Working Paper No. 14874, National Bureau of Economic Research, Cambridge, MA, 2009), http://dx.doi.org/doi:10.3386/w14874.

215 **Unemployment peaked at 18.5 percent** Ibid.

215 **the "world leader" in teen suicides** Anniina Lahti et al., "Youth Suicide Trends in Finland, 1969–2008," *Journal of Child Psychology and Psychiatry* 52, no. 9 (2011): 984–91, http://dx.doi.org/doi:10.1111 /j.1469-7610.2011.02369.x.

216 *Newsweek*'s **list of the world's best countries** "Interactive Infographic of the World's Best Countries," *Newsweek*, August 15, 2010, https://web.archive.org/web/20101030031732/www.newsweek .com//2010//08//15//interactive-infographic-of-the-worlds-best -countries.html. Note: the interactivity no longer works but the site is imaged by the Wayback Machine.

216 **named second-happiest nation** Francesca Levy, "In Depth: The World's Happiest Countries," *Forbes*, July 14, 2010, https://www .forbes.com/2010/07/14/world-happiest-countries-lifestyle-real estate-gallup_slide_3.html#541c96406dbe.

216 **world's "happiest country":** http://worldhappiness.report/.

216 **no working person need fear losing a home** Iipo Airio, "In-Work Poverty and Unemployment in Finland: Dual Labour Market or Reserve Workers?," paper presented at the Sixth International Policy

and Research Conference on Social Security, Luxembourg, January 10, 2010.

218 **The nation's "youth guarantee"** "Youth," Ministry of Education and Culture, accessed March 18, 2013, http://www.minedu.fi/OPM /Nuoriso/?lang=en.

218 **world-class symphony conductors** Kari Uustkyla and Jane Piirto, "The Development of Orchestra Conductors in Finland," in *Musikaalisuuden ytimessä: Juhlakirja Kai Karmalle / In the Heart of Musicality: Essays in Honour of Kai Karma*, ed. Marjut Laitinen and Marja-Liisa Kainulainen (Helsinki: Sibelius-Akatemia, Musiikkikasvatuksen Osasto, 2007).

225 **CEO of Helsinki-based 925 Design** The firm has since been acquired by the consulting firm HINTSA Performance.

227 **it does little to help employees make meaning of their work** Thanks to human factors expert Charles Mauro, founding director of MauroNewMedia, for sharing his view on what he described as "Facebook culture" with me in a telephone conversation.

228 **brainstorming rarely leads to novel solutions** Michael Diehl and Wolfgang Stroebe, "Productivity Loss in Brainstorming Groups: Toward the Solution of a Riddle," *Journal of Personality and Social Psychology* 53, no. 3 (September 1987): 497–509, http://dx.doi.org /doi:10.1037//0022-3514.53.3.497.

232 **The CEO of Snellman** Harvard Business School Economist Rebecca Henderson has found evidence that trust and a shared sense of purpose are hallmarks of high-performing companies. See, for example, Robert Gibbons and Rebecca Henderson, "Relational Contracts and Organizational Capabilities," *Organization Science* 23, no. 5 (September–October 2012): 1350–64, http://dx.doi.org/doi:10.1287 /orsc.1110.0715.

233 **"freeing him to do work he finds meaningful"** Aditya Chakrabortty, "A Basic Income for Everyone? Yes, Finland Shows It Really Can Work," *Guardian*, October 31, 2017, https://www.theguardian.com /commentisfree/2017/oct/31/finland-universal-basic-income.

234 **less engaged in educational, religious, and political organizations** Robert D. Putnam, "Bowling Alone: America's Declining Social Capital," *Journal of Democracy* 6, no. 1 (1995): 65–78, http://dx.doi.org/ doi:10.1353/jod.1995.0002.

234 **a mere 18 percent of Americans** "Public Trust in Government: 1958–2017," Pew Research Center, May 3, 2017, http://www.people -press.org/2017/05/03/public-trust-in-government-1958-2017/.

234 **Finland has a low level of economic inequality** "Income Inequality," OECD Data, Organisation for Economic Co-operation and Development, last modified 2015, https://data.oecd.org/inequality /income-inequality.htm.

235 **"People will tell you brutally what is wrong"** Vesterbacka was speaking at the annual Mobile Summit sponsored by the Massachusetts Technology Leadership Council. Linda Tucci, "Mobile Business Advice from Peter Vesterbacka of Angry Birds," https://searchcio .techtarget.c.myopinion/Mobile-business-advice-from-PeterVester backa-of-Angry-Birds.

236 **"even if technology has been improving"** Brandon Fuller, "Paul Romer's National Academy of Sciences Lecture," presented at New York University Marron Institute, February 1, 2013, http:// urbanizationproject.org/blog/paul-romers-national-academy-of -sciences-lecture/#.U9qq2qhPLmU.

CHAPTER 12

237 **"Labor can only be rented"** Paul Anthony Samuelson and William D. Nordhaus, *Economics*, 10th ed. (New York: McGraw-Hill, 1976), 569.

237 **"through co-operation, labor could become its own employer"** Leland Stanford, "Stanford on Cooperation," in *Biennial Report of the Bureau of Labor Statistics of California for the Years 1887–1888*, vol. 3 (Sacramento, CA: State Office, 1888), 320.

238 **the largest cotton-spinning conglomerate in Scotland** J. F. C. Harrison, *Quest for the New Moral World: Robert Owen and the Owenites in Britain and America* (New York: Scribner, 1969), 5–6.

238 **"the neglect and disregard of the living machinery"** B. L. Hutchins, *Robert Owen, Social Reformer* (London: Fabian Society, 1912), 8.

239 **banished young children from the factory floor** Erik Reece and James Patrick Cronin, in their inspiring book *Utopia Drive*, note that prior to Owen's taking over, 500 of 1,800 workers at New Lanark were children. The reason for this was that to keep the cotton supple, the factories were kept so hot that many adults refused to work in

them, leaving the door wide open to children as young as five, whose small fingers were considered an advantage, until—as happened in many cases—they were mangled in the machines. Erik Reece and James Patrick Cronin, *Utopia Drive: A Road Trip Through America's Most Radical Idea* (Old Saybrook, CT: Tantor Media, 2016).

239 **factory owners saw no advantage to improving labor's lot** Contemporary notions of "unemployment" do not really apply to the mid-nineteenth-century labor market, when patterns of work varied with individuals and region. There are no statistics. It is known, however, that Britain experienced an economic depression and increase in unemployment in the late 1850s, brought about in part by a severe downturn in the American economy.

239 **"maimed or tubercular wreckages"** Richard E. Banta, *The Ohio* (Lexington: University of Kentucky Press, 1949), 373.

239 **"living in the midst of the army just returned from a campaign"** See John Simkin, "Child Factory Accidents," Spartacus Educational, last modified February 2015, http://spartacus-educational.com/IR accidents.htm.

240 **"Men being more expensive"** Robert Owen, *The Life of Robert Owen*, vol. 1–1A (London: E. Wilson, 1857), 124.

240 **"involving great national changes"** Ibid.

240 **New Harmony fell apart in three years** See, for example, "Robert Owen and New Harmony," American Studies at the University of Virginia, accessed February 13, 2018, http://xroads.virginia.edu /~hyper/hns/cities/newharmony.html.

241 **"a boundary never before reached in the history of man"** Robert Owen, "Address to the Agriculturalists, Mechanics, and Manufacturers of Great Britain and Ireland, Both Masters and Operatives," *Cooperative Magazine*, 1827, 438.

241 **"ahead of my time"** Max Beer, *A History of British Socialism*, Vol. 2 (New York: Harcourt, Brace and Howe, 1921), p. 174.

243 **median household income hovers around $23,205** "Glenville Demographics and Statistics," Point2 Homes, accessed February 13, 2018, https://www.point2homes.com/US/Neighborhood/OH /Cleveland/Glenville-Demographics.html.

247 **3.7 million Spanish citizens** Economic Research, Federal Reserve Bank of St. Louis, accessed June 20, 2018, at research.stlouisfed.org /dashboard/770.

248 **40 percent of GDP is generated by worker-owned cooperatives** Christopher D. Merrett and Norman Walzer, *Cooperatives and Local Development* (New York: Routledge, 2004).

248 **thousands of acres of vacant land** Kathy A. Carr, "Urban Farmers, Advocates Cite Challenges in Cultivating Business," Craine's Cleveland Business, August 30, 2010, www.crainsclevelandbusiness.com /article/20100830/FREE/308309951/1016/smallbusiness&template =printart.

252 **roughly a third of all criminal convictions for Medicaid fraud** Office of Inspector General, *Medicaid Fraud Control Units Fiscal Year 2015 Annual Report,* OEI-07-16-00050 (Washington, DC: Department of Health and Human Services, 2016), https://oig.hhs.gov/oei/reports /oei-07-16-00050.asp.

254 **preserve their legacy** There's a tax advantage as well: a provision in the tax code—Section 1042—allows business owners to defer capital gains taxes when they sell their company to an eligible worker cooperative.

254 **the power of unions to negotiate a middle-class life** For a detailed discussion of the impact of labor unions on wage inequality, see Bruce Western and Jake Rosenfeld, "Unions, Norms, and the Rise in U.S. Wage Inequality," *American Sociological Review* 76, no. 4 (August 1, 2011): 513–37, https://doi.org/10.1177/0003122411414817.

255 **the inflated paper value of our homes** In 2007 nearly three-quarters of Americans with incomes of $30,000 to $79,000 held stocks, as did nearly two of three Americans. See Justin McCarthy, "Little Change in Percentage of Americans Who Own Stocks," Gallup.com, April 22, 2015, http://www.gallup.com/poll/182816/little-change-percentage -americans-invested-market.aspx. Since then, stock ownership has plummeted to roughly 52 percent of adults in 2016.

255 **This powerful "wealth effect"** The wealth effect is a psychological phenomenon that causes people to spend more as the value of their assets rises. The premise is that when consumers' homes or investment portfolios increase in value, they feel more financially secure, so they increase their spending. See, for example, Karl E. Case, John M. Quigley, and Robert J. Shiller, "Comparing Wealth Effects: The Stock Market Versus the Housing Market," *Advances in Macroeconomics* 5, no. 1 (2005), http://dx.doi.org/doi:10.2202/1534-6013.1235.

255 **America's at-will employment doctrine** Employees can be fired for any or no reason as long as the decision to fire them is not unlaw-

ful according to a specific law, such as the National Labor Relations Act or federal, state, or local antidiscrimination statutes and ordinances. That said, proving discrimination is extremely difficult.

255 **"divine right to rule the working lives of its subject employees"** Clyde W. Summers, "Employment at Will in the United States: The Divine Right of Employers," *University of Pennsylvania Journal of Business Law* 3, no. 1 (2000), http://scholarship.law.upenn.edu/jbl/vol3/iss1/2/.

255 **reciprocal obligation involves a psychological contract** Wendy R. Boswell, Julie B. Olson-Buchanan, and T. Brad Harris, "I Cannot Afford to Have a Life: Employee Adaptation to Feelings of Job Insecurity," *Personnel Psychology* 67, no. 4 (December 1, 2014): 887–915, https://doi.org/10.1111/peps.12061.

257 **"rebuilding unions"** Richard Freeman et al., "How Does Declining Unionism Affect the American Middle Class and Intergenerational Mobility?" (NBER Working Paper No. 21638, National Bureau of Economic Research, Cambridge, MA, 2015), http://www.nber.org/papers/w21638.

257 **to bargain collectively toward common goals** See, for example, Charles E. Sporck, *Spinoff: A Personal History of the Industry That Changed the World* (Saranac, MI: Saranac Lake, 2001), 271: "It would have been impossible to move ahead with the rapidly developing technology of semiconductors in an organization hampered by union formalities.... No semiconductor facility in Silicon Valley was ever unionized."

257 **"there may have been a time and a place for unions"** Kevin Rose, "Silicon Valley's Anti-Unionism, Now with a Side of Class Warfare," *New York Magazine*, July 2013. Still, it's worth pointing out that not a few of these new economy employers recognize the value of collective action in pursuit of their own goals. Consider, for example, the sudden involvement of industrial leadership in immigration reform. In April 2013, Facebook founder and CEO Mark Zuckerberg collaborated on the launch of Fwd.us, a proimmigration collective whose members included Bill Gates, Google's Eric Schmidt, Yahoo CEO Marissa Mayer, and Silicon Valley venture capitalist and billionaire John Doerr.

258 **narrows the gap between the highest and lowest earners** Derek C. Jones, "The Ombudsman: Employee Ownership as a Mechanism to Enhance Corporate Governance and Moderate Executive Pay Levels," *Interfaces* 43, no. 6 (December 1, 2013): 599–601, https://

doi.org/10.1287/inte.2013.0709. Also, in Europe at least, employee-owned firms in every industry have been shown to be at least as efficient as investor-owned firms. See, for example, Fathi Fakhfakh, Virginie Pérotin, and Mónica Gago, "Productivity, Capital, and Labor in Labor-Managed and Conventional Firms: An Investigation on French Data," *ILR Review* 65, no. 4 (October 1, 2012): 847–79, https://doi.org/10.1177/001979391206500404.

258 **far outpacing the growth in fossil fuels** "Renewable Generation Capacity Expected to Account for Most 2016 Capacity Additions," "Today in Energy," US Energy Information Administration, January 10, 2017, https://www.eia.gov/todayinenergy/detail.php?id=29492.

258 **the interference—and cost—of a middleman** Trebor Scholz, "Platform Cooperativism vs. the Sharing Economy," *Medium*, December 5, 2014, https://medium.com/@trebors/platform-cooperativism-vs-the-sharing-economy-2ea737f1b5ad.

261 **"capitalism in which profit"** Lawrence H. Summers and Ed Balls, "Report of the Commission on Inclusive Prosperity," Center for American Progress, January 15, 2015, https://www.americanprogress.org/issues/economy/reports/2015/01/15/104266/report-of-the-commission-on-inclusive-prosperity/.

262 **"In human terms"** Louis O. Kelso and Patricia Hetter Kelso, "Why Owner-Workers Are Winners," *New York Times*, January 27, 1989.

263 **workers lose both their job and their retirement fund** See, for example, Sean M. Anderson, "Risky Retirement Business: How ESOPs Harm the Workers They Are Supposed to Help," *Loyola University Chicago Law Journal* 41, no. 1 (2009), https://ssrn.com/abstract=1363879.

263 **many employees had no stake in the company** Benjamin B. Dunford, Deidra J. Schleicher, and Liang Zhu, "The Relative Importance of Psychological Versus Pecuniary Approaches to Establishing an Ownership Culture," *Advances in Industrial and Labor Relations* 16 (2009): 1–21, https://doi.org/10.1108/S0742-6186(2009)0000016004.

264 **reactionary, which, of course, they were** Hamilton made this clear in, among other things, his "Report on the Subject of Manufacturers," in which he wrote: "It has been maintained that agriculture is not only the most productive, but the only productive species of industry. The reality of this suggestion, in either respect, has, however, not been verified by any accurate detail of facts and calculations; and the general arguments, which are adduced to prove it, are rather

subtil [*sic*] and paradoxical, than solid or convincing." Alexander Hamilton, "Report on the Subject of Manufacturers," in *The Works of Alexander Hamilton*, ed. John C. Hamilton, vol. 3 (New York: John F. Trow, 1850), 195.

264 **shipowners give their crews profit sharing or an ownership share** Findan Ana Kunetulus and Douglas A. Kruse, "How Did Employees Ownership Firms Weather the Last Two Recessions?," W. E. Upjohn Institute for Employee Research, 2017. See research.upjohn.org/up _press/241/.

264 **the potential to deliver more wealth to more of us** For example, ESOP participants earn 5 to 12 percent more in wages and have almost three times the retirement assets of workers in comparable non-ESOP companies.

CHAPTER 13

266 **"It's cool to make things again"** Joe Nocera, "How to Build a Spoon," *New York Times*, April 26, 2013, http://www.nytimes.com/2013/04/27 /opinion/nocera-the-navy-yards-revival.html.

266 **the USS *Missouri*** Writers' Program of the Work Projects Administration in the State of New York and Barbera La Rocco, *A Maritime History of New York* (Brooklyn, NY: Going Coastal, 2004), 264–65.

267 **recalled those times like yesterday** Tom Vigliotta, "Inside the Brooklyn Navy Yard," *Thirteen*, January 26, 2009, http://archive.is/5m8uP.

268 **featured in the PBS series *This Old House*** Ibid. Ms. Ross was ninety years old when she was interviewed about her experience at the Yard in 2009 in one of her homes. She concludes, "It was a good experience. It helped make my life. That's it!"

268 **the call for shipbuilding and repair** In 2010 the United States ranked twentieth in number of oceangoing vessels, having fallen from a top-ten ranking in just a few years. See Transportation Institute, "Know Our Industry—Present Industry Status," accessed February 13, 2018, http://www.trans-inst.org/present-status.html.

268 **the Yard went into a slow decline** Will Lissner, "Plan to Convert Navy Yard Urged," *New York Times*, December 11, 1964, http://www .nytimes.com/1964/12/11/plan-to-convert-navy-yard-urged.html.

271 **less work of the sort that equips enough of us to pay the rent**
Middle-wage jobs made up about 37 percent of the jobs lost in the
meltdown but only about 26 percent of the jobs gained in the recovery. See "Tracking the Low-Wage Recovery: Industry Employment and Wages," Data Brief, National Employment Law Project,
April 27, 2014, http://www.nelp.org/publication/tracking-the-low
-wage-recovery-industry-employment-wages/.

271 **the world's ninth-largest economy** See "Top 20 Facts About Manufacturing," National Association of Manufacturers, 2014, http://
www.nam.org/Newsroom/Top-20-Facts-About-Manufacturing/.

271 **semiconductors, medical equipment, and pharmaceuticals** William B. Bonvillian, "Reinventing American Manufacturing: The
Role of Innovation," *Innovations: Technology, Governance, Globalization*
7, no. 3 (2012): 97–125.

272 **"Bringing high-volume electronics"** Kenneth Kraemer, Greg Lin-
den, and Jason Dedrick, "Capturing Value in Global Networks:
Apple's iPad and iPhone," Personal Computing Industry Center,
University of California, Irvine, and Syracuse University School of
Information Studies, July 2011, http://pcic.merage.uci.edu/papers
/2011/Value_iPad_iPhone.pdf.

272 **jobs for Apple engineers, marketers, and sales staff** Apple CEO
Tim Cook claims that the company has created "two million" American jobs (https://apple.com/newsroom/2018/01/apple-accelerates-us
-investment-job-creation), but only eighty thousand of the holders of
these jobs are actual Apple employees. Almost 1.5 million are members of what he describes as the "developer community" who write
the apps he says have "changed the world." Unfortunately, changing the world doesn't always bring them much revenue—those lucky
enough to peddle their apps on Apple hardware average about $4,000
per app, with a total yearly revenue stream of roughly $21,000. And
these, it bears repeating, are the lucky ones.

273 **"permanent lost per capita real income"** Paul A. Samuelson, "Where
Ricardo and Mill Rebut and Confirm Arguments of Mainstream
Economists Supporting Globalization," *Journal of Economic Perspec-
tives* 18, no. 3 (2004): 137, https://doi.org/10.1257/0895330042162403.

273 **face-to-face interaction is key** See J. R. Hackman, "Six Common
Misperceptions About Teamwork," *Harvard Business Review*, June 7,
2011, https://hbr.org/2011/06/six-common-misperceptions-abou.

Hackman, a Harvard psychologist who studied teams of workers as varied as airplane pilots and undercover agents, points out that while digital technology allows us to work independently, organizations that rely entirely on "virtual" interactions among departments tend to have lower productivity.

275 **US manufacturing jobs pay an average hourly rate of $20** Table B-8, "Average Hourly and Weekly Earnings of Production and Non-supervisory Employees on Private Nonfarm Payrolls by Industry Sector, Seasonally Adjusted," Economic News Release, US Bureau of Labor Statistics, Division of Labor Force Statistics, n.d., accessed February 13, 2018, https://www.bls.gov/news.release/empsit.t24.htm.

275 **some plants—especially foreign-owned plants** Peter Waldmen, "Inside Alabama's Auto Jobs Boom: Cheap Wages, Little Training, Crushed Limbs," Bloomberg.com, March 23, 2017, https://www.bloomberg.com/news/features/2017-03-23/inside-alabama-s-auto-jobs-boom-cheap-wages-little-training-crushed-limbs.

275 **"The role of the South in the global production chain"** Harold Meyerson, "Germany Shows the Way on Labor," *Washington Post*, April 29, 2015, https://www.washingtonpost.com/opinions/germany-shows-the-way-on-labor/2015/04/29/b9bc811c-ee9e-11e4-8666-a1d756d0218e_story.html?utm_term=.52f1077d3efc.

276 **"US money which we have to borrow to get"** Katie Benner and Nelson D. Schwartz, "Apple Announces $1 Billion Fund to Create U.S. Jobs in Manufacturing," *New York Times*, May 3, 2017, https://www.nytimes.com/2017/05/03/technology/apple-jobs.html.

278 **urban manufacturers as key players** See "The Federal Role in Supporting Urban Manufacturing," report, Pratt Center for Community Development, April 6, 2011, http://prattcenter.net/report/federal-role-supporting-urban-manufacturing.

278 **the companies just move manufacturing** As wages creep up in China, China and other nations are outsourcing apparel manufacture to factories in North Korea, where wages are extremely low. See, for example, Jane Perlez, Yufab Huang, and Paul Mozur, "How North Korea Managed to Defy Years of Sanctions," *New York Times*, May 12, 2017, https://www.nytimes.com/2017/05/12/world/asia/north-korea-sanctions-loopholes-china-united-states-garment-industry.html.

284 **Google, the world's most sought-after employer** Katie Little and Denise Garcia, "The 40 Most Attractive Employers in America, Ac-

cording to LinkedIn," CNBC, June 20, 2016, http://www.cnbc
.com/2016/06/19/the-40-most-attractive-employers-in-america
-according-to-linkedin.html.

286 **seeing only the price of fish** Ralph Waldo Emerson, *The Complete
Works of Ralph Waldo Emerson* (New York: Sully and Kleinteich), 9:9.

287 **"strut about so many walking monsters"** This from Emerson's lecture "The American Scholar," delivered to a class at Harvard College
in 1837; Ralph Waldo Emerson, *Essays and English Traits* (New York:
P. F. Collier, 1909).

287 **digital fabrication will be "so powerful"** Stephanie Shipp et al.,
Emerging Global Trends in Advanced Manufacturing, IDA Paper P-4603
(Alexandria, VA: Institute for Defense Analysis, 2012).

288 **"cost reduction via the *replacement* of labor"** Michael Spence, "Labor's Digital Displacement," Project Syndicate, May 22, 2014, https://
www.project-syndicate.org/commentary/michael-spence-describes
-an-era-in-which-developing-countries-can-no-longer-rely-on-vast
-numbers-of-cheap-workers?barrier=accessreg.

CHAPTER 14

289 **"The free market sometimes needs referees"** Sam Stein, "Glass-
Steagall Act: The Senators And Economists Who Got It Right," *Huff-
ington Post*, June 11, 2009, https://www.huffingtonpost.com/2009/05
/11/glass-steagall-act-the-se_n_201557.html.

291 **a "favorable view" of unions** Shiva Maniam, "Most Americans See
Labor Unions, Corporations Favorably," Pew Research Center, Fact
Tank, January 30, 2017, http://www.pewresearch.org/fact-tank/2017
/01/30/most-americans-see-labor-unions-corporations-favorably.

291 **labor's share of income has fallen steeply since the 1970s** Jay Sham-
baugh et al., "Thirteen Facts About Wage Growth," The Hamilton
Project, hamiltonproject.org/thirteen-facts-about-wage-growth.

292 **less than $12 an hour** Ken Jacobs et al., "Producing Poverty: The
Public Cost of Low-Wage Production Jobs in Manufacturing," report, Center for Labor Research and Education, May 10, 2016, http://
laborcenter.berkeley.edu/producing-poverty-the-public-cost-of-low
-wage-production-jobs-in-manufacturing.

292 **at least among the happiest** The online jobs site CareerBliss com-
piles an annual list of the "10 happiest jobs," based on analysis from

more than sixty-five thousand employee-generated reviews. Employees around the United States are asked to evaluate ten factors that affect workplace happiness, including relationships with bosses and coworkers, work environment, job resources, compensation, growth opportunities, company culture, company reputation, daily tasks, and control over the work one does on a daily basis. In 2013 real estate agents came out on top, with associate-level attorneys claiming the lowest spot. https://careerbliss.com/facts-and-figures/careerbliss /happiest-and-unhappiest-jobs-in-america-2013.

294 **he's not technically a free** *agent* Bigelow is a member of the National Association of Realtors (NAR)—with more than 1.2 million members, America's largest trade organization and an extraordinarily powerful lobbying group.

297 **formal coworking establishments have since caught on** At this writing, a single coworking franchise, WeWork, has 212 locations and 200,000 members.

298 **very large institutions** See Justin Fox, "Big Companies Still Employ Lots of People," Bloomberg.com, April 20, 2016, https://www .bloomberg.com/view/articles/2016-04-20/big-companies-still -employ-lots-of-people.

298 **derelict in their duty to provide investors with income** See Milton Friedman, "The Social Responsibility of Business Is to Increase Profits," *New York Times Magazine*, September 13, 1970.

298 **link in the public mind between free markets and freedom itself** Milton Friedman once wrote: "Underlying most arguments against the free market is a lack of belief in freedom itself." Milton Friedman, *Capitalism and Freedom* (Chicago: University of Chicago Press, 1962), 15.

299 **lagging demand for their goods and services** Concern over supply exceeding demand seems to be nearly as old as the nation. James Madison, writing in 1829, worried that within the following century people would be "necessarily reduced by a competition for employment to wages which afford them the bare necessities of life." See James Madison, *The Mind of the Founder: Sources of the Political Thought of James Madison*, ed. Marvin Meyers (Hanover, NH: University Press of New England, 1981).

299 **social welfare and job creation programs** This was partly out of fear—the Depression had left the nation cautious and humbled. In 1933 the value of stock on the New York Stock Exchange was less than

a fifth of what it had been at its peak in 1929. Historian Arthur M. Schlesinger cited management neglect of workers as an important underlying cause of the crash, writing: "Management's disposition to maintain prices and inflate profits while holding down wages and raw material prices meant that workers and farmers were denied the benefits of increases in their own productivity. The consequence was the relative decline of mass purchasing power. As goods flowed out of the expanding capital plant in ever greater quantities, there was proportionately less and less cash in the hands of buyers to carry the goods off the market. The pattern of income distribution, in short, was incapable of long maintaining prosperity." Arthur M. Schlesinger, *The Crisis of the Old Order, 1919–1933*, vol. 1 of *The Age of Roosevelt* (1957; repr. New York: Houghton Mifflin, 2002), 159–60.

299 **promoted tax hikes to support them** Ganesh Sitaraman, *The Crisis of the Middle-Class Constitution: Why Income Inequality Threatens Our Republic* (New York: Knopf, 2017), 202.

301 **"Society is demanding that companies"** "A Sense of Purpose," Larry Fink's Annual Letter to CEOs, BlackRock (2017), https://www.blackrock.com/corporate/investor-relations/larry-fink-ceo-letter.

302 **the "triple bottom line"** See, for example, John Elkington, *Cannibals with Forks: The Triple Bottom Line of 21st Century Business* (Oxford: Capstone, 1997).

303 **the concept of "shareholder primacy"** The primacy of shareholders above other stakeholders was more recently reaffirmed by the case of *EBay Domestic Holdings Inc. v. Newmark*, H2O Classroom Tools, last modified February 24, 2014, https://h2o.law.harvard.edu/cases/3472, in which the Delaware Chancery Court stated that a nonfinancial mission that "seeks not to maximize the economic value of a for-profit Delaware corporation for the benefit of its stockholders" is inconsistent with directors' fiduciary duties.

304 **two-thirds of all Fortune 500 companies** It takes less than an hour to incorporate a company in Delaware, and the state regularly tops lists of domestic and foreign tax havens because it allows companies to lower their taxes in another state—for instance, the state in which they actually do business or have their headquarters—by shifting royalties and similar revenues to holding companies in Delaware, where they are not taxed. Between 2002 and 2012 the "Delaware loophole" had reduced taxes paid by corporations to other states by an estimated $9.5 billion. See, for example, Leslie Wayne,

"How Delaware Thrives as a Corporate Tax Haven," *New York Times*, June 30, 2012, http://www.nytimes.com/2012/07/01/business/how -delaware-thrives-as-a-corporate-tax-haven.html. For the latest statistics on how many businesses Delaware hosts, see the state's official website at State of Delaware, Division of Corporations, "About Agency," last modified 2018, https://corp.delaware.gov/aboutagency .shtml.

304 **Patagonia's much-publicized commitment** For example, the company prides itself in its reliance on "Fair Trade"–certified factories, and in December 2017 it joined a coalition of like-minded institutions to sue the Trump administration in an effort to strike down the president's "extreme overreach of authority" in revoking the national monument status of Bear's Ears in Utah.

307 **its happy, capable workforce** Bernie Marcus, Arthur Blank, and Bob Andelman, *Built from Scratch: How a Couple of Regular Guys Grew the Home Depot from Nothing to $30 Billion* (New York: Crown Business, 2000), 104.

307 **known for instilling tough operational discipline** Dr. Ton was kind enough to explain Home Depot and other cases to me over a series of meetings and conversations; and for some details I also referred to her excellent book, *The Good Jobs Strategy: How the Smartest Companies Invest in Employees to Lower Costs and Boost Profits* (Boston: Houghton Mifflin Harcourt, 2014).

307 **shareholders breathed a collective sigh of relief** Brian Grow, "Home Depot's CEO Cleans Up," Bloomberg.com, May 22, 2006, https:// www.bloomberg.com/news/articles/2006-05-22/home-depots-ceo -cleans-upbusinessweek-business-news-stock-market-and-financial -advice.

308 **the company's share price dropped 24 percent** Paula Rosenblum, "Home Depot's Resurrection: How One Retailer Made Its Own Home Improvements," *Forbes*, August 21, 2013, https://www .forbes.com/sites/paularosenblum/2013/08/21/home-depots -resurrection/#1a8583bf58c3.

310 **told me to take my pick** The QuikTrip "open book" policy presented a sharp contrast to an incident years ago, when a Target manager chased me from his store for attempting to interview an employee.

313 **tax credits to employers who offer stable, living-wage employment** Targeted versions of this, though quite different in their goals, have

been shown to be effective in the United States. The Work Opportunity Tax Credit (WOTC) program, made law in 1996, is a federal tax credit available to employers who hire and retain veterans and individuals from other target groups with significant barriers to employment, for example, ex-felons and food stamp recipients. Employers claim about $1 billion in tax credits each year under this program, which has led to more hiring of these target groups. However, this sort of program is meant to increase hiring of a certain kind, not employment overall.

313 **a subsidy *should* be part of any economic policy** L. F. Katz, "Active Labor Market Policies to Expand Employment and Opportunity," in *Reducing Unemployment: Current Issues and Policy Options* (Kansas City, MO: Federal Reserve Bank of Kansas City, 1994). See also Sagiri Kitao, Aysegul Sahin, and Joseph Song, "Subsidizing Job Creation in the Great Recession," FRB of New York Staff Report No. 451, Federal Reserve Bank of New York, May 1, 2010, http://dx.doi.org/10.2139/ssrn.1619507.

313 **job subsidy programs in Michigan and Georgia** Thanks once again to Peter Cappelli, professor of management at the Wharton School of the University of Pennsylvania, for helping me make sense of the research on hiring subsidies.

314 **the "progress toward a shorter work-day"** In Europe, work-sharing policies by which individuals were encouraged to share jobs led not to more job creation but to more leisure in the form of longer vacations. While longer vacations hold great appeal, this finding does not support a jobs growth policy predicated on shorter work hours. See "Work and Leisure in the United States and Europe: Why So Different? Discussion," *NBER Macroeconomics Annual* 20 (2005): 97–99, http://www.jstor.org/stable/3585414.

315 **devote a larger portion of their time to family and community** Thanks to Boston College economist Juliet Schor for a detailed discussion of the twenty-one-hour workweek. Professor Schor's ideal scenario is one in which productivity growth is channeled into shorter hours on the job rather than into increased income for the top 1 percent.

315 **In Germany, for example, reduced work hours** See, for example, Hartmut Seifert and Rainer Trinczek, *New Approaches to Working Time Policy in Germany: The 28.8 Hour Working Week at Volkswagen Company* (Dusseldorf: WSI, 2000).

316 **the "social vaccine of the 21st century"** Critics point to a conflict of

interest: rather than promote technology that contributes to general human flourishing, Silicon Valley elites favor UBI as a publicly supported solution that does not impede their profit-making activities. See, for example, Jathan Sadowski, "Why Silicon Valley Is Embracing Universal Basic Income," *Guardian*, July 14, 2017, https://www .theguardian.com/technology/2016/jun/22/silicon-valley-universal -basic-income-y-combinator.

316 **an addictive public handout** Predictions that a BIG (basic income guarantee) would result in many people laying around lazily are not supported by the evidence. In particular, Brazil's subsistence-level BIG program has resulted in very little change in workforce participation. Given a choice, most people choose to work, and the World Bank has determined that such supports even increase individual efforts to find work, as they allow people to take risks. In addition, people on these supports are mostly parents with children who actually do critically important work—as care providers. That said, it remains unclear whether income guarantees that go beyond providing the basics—of food, shelter, education, and health care—would deter people from seeking employment.

320 **the fits and starts of an uncertain world** Economists Lawrence Katz and Alan Krueger have shown that since 2005, 94 percent of net employment growth in the United States has come in the form of low-wage, short-term, part-time, on-call, and temporary jobs. See Lawrence F. Katz and Alan B. Krueger, "The Rise and Nature of Alternative Work Arrangements in the United States, 1995–2015" (NBER Working Paper No. 22667, National Bureau of Economic Research, Cambridge, MA, September 2016), http://www.nber.org /papers/w22667.

320 **to make a contribution, to make them feel worthwhile** Many thanks to David Nordfors, PhD, founder of the International Institute of Innovation Journalism and Communication (IIIJ) and organizer of a series of top-level conferences focused on innovation and the future of work. David, who was kind enough to invite me to the meeting in Lund, Sweden, was also kind enough to share his thoughts on the future of work in a private conversation.

322 **nobody "can look forward to the age of leisure"** John Maynard Keynes, "Economic Possibilities for Our Grandchildren" [1930], in *Revisiting Keynes: Economic Possibilities for Our Grandchildren*, ed. Lorenzo Pecchi and Gustavo Piga (Cambridge, MA: MIT Press, 2008), 23.

Index

Adams, John Quincy, 240
Addison, Medrick, 241–244
advanced manufacturing, 182
age and fitting corporate culture, 31
Airbus, 273–274
Alabama, 274–275
Alger, Horatio, 55, 338n55
Alibaba Group, 69, 341n69
Alphabet, 84–85. *See also* Google
AlphaGo, 79–80
Amazon
   automation and, 73, 74
   Chattanooga facility, 71, 73,
     343n73
   data collected by, 69–70
   government incentives given to,
     71–72, 73
   jobs with, 70, 72, 73, 343n73
   MTurk online platform, 258–259
   as one of Four Horsemen, 85–86
   share of US online market, 69
American Association for the
   Advancement of Science, 93–94

American Booksellers Association,
   341n71
American Institute for Stress,
   334n38
American Sugar Refining Company,
   266
analytic thinking skills, 56–57
AND 1, 302
Anderson, Elizabeth, 131
Andreessen, Marc, 255
Anteby, Michel, 123–124
anxiety
   office design and, 335n44
   stress and, 38–39
Appalachia, 194–200, 201–205,
   206–210
apparel industry, 278–280, 379n278
Appelbaum, Eileen, 254–255
Apple (technology company)
   cash holdings overseas, 276
   jobs created by, 378n272
   number of employees, 59
   as one of Four Horsemen, 85–86

Apple (technology company) (*cont.*)
  reason for overseas
    manufacturing, 186
  value to US economy, 272
Applebee's Bar and Grill, 342n73
aristocracy
  US founding fathers as, 54–55,
    338n54
  Victorian Era, 52
Arizmendiarrieta, José María,
  246
artificial intelligence
  AlphaGo, 79–80
  as job destroyer, 3, 82–83
  jobs not able to do, 3
  medical uses, 80–81
  replacement of human
    intellectual capital by, 11
arts and crafts
  economic role of, 200–201,
    202–203
  worker cooperatives and, 258
Atlantic (online magazine), 113–114
at-will employment, 255, 256, 257,
  374–375n255
Aukland, Shawn, 85
Austria
  Great Depression, 16–20, 329n16
  industrialization, 15–16
  noneconomic cost of joblessness,
    330n19
  tax subsidies for hiring workers,
    313
automation
  advantages of, 73–74, 75, 77–78,
    82, 344n75
  in coal mining, 206
  early, 238–240, 269n239
  manufacturing jobs, 271
  productivity and, 6, 262, 273
  self-driving cars, 75
  training former factory workers
    unemployed by, 183–186
  in warehouses/distribution
    centers, 73–75
autonomy
  defining, 107
  importance of, 65, 106, 348n109
Autor, David, 60

Bacevice, Peter, 297
"bad jobs strategy," 305–308
Ball, Don, 298
banking industry, 167
Barker, James, 47
Bartik, Tim, 151–152
Basic Income Guarantee (BIG),
  315–318, 385n316
Bauer, Otto, 17
Beane, Matt, 126
Beaudry, Paul, 60, 167
Because We Can, 286
Bellah, Robert N., 118
Belt, David, 270, 282–284
Berea College, 194–197, 198–200,
  204, 205, 209
Best Buy, 70, 341n70
Bey, Loretta, 264–265
Bezos, Jeff, 70, 73, 343n73
Bigelow, John, 292–294
"A Bill for the More General
  Diffusion of Knowledge"
  (Jefferson), 141
"Bill Gates effect," 150, 187
Birch, David L., 89–90, 92, 346n92
birth circumstances
  ability to acquire analytic
    thinking skills and, 57, 338n57
  ability to rise in class and, 55,
    338n55
  income and, 56, 151–152
  type of work and, 55

Blake, Frank, 308
Blank, Arthur, 307
Blasi, Joseph, 261, 263–264
Bowles, Jonathan, 270–271, 277–278
Bradski, Gary, 74
brainstorming, value of, 228
Brat, David, 185
Brazil, 385n316
Breckinridge, Mary, 207
Brooklyn, New York, 266–270, 271, 278, 281, 282, 284–285
Brooklyn Navy Yard, 266–270, 271
Brooks, Rodney, 74–75, 344n75
broom making, 204–206
Brown, Chris, 2
Bunderson, J. Stuart, 121–122
Bureau of Labor Statistics (BLS), 153, 154, 155
Burning Glass, 154
Burton, Justin, 203, 204–206, 209
Bush, George H. W., 140
Buttonwood Corporation, 278–279

Cadieux, Chester, III, 308–310
"the called," 109–110
calling(s)
   algorithms to discover job candidates with, 122
   careers and jobs versus, 118
   described, 118–119
   jobs as, 12
   sushi chef as, 120–121
   zookeeper as, 121–122
"The Call of the Wild: Zookeepers, Callings, and the Double-Edged Sword of Meaningful Work" (Thompson and Bunderson), 121–122

Canada
   GDP components in, 328n8
   government guaranteed basic monthly income, 316–318
   prime-age labor participation, 37
Capital in the Twenty-First Century (Piketty), 157
Capitalism, Socialism, and Democracy (Schumpeter), 88–89
Cappelli, Peter, 170
"career self-help industry," 27
careers versus callings and jobs, 118
Carlyle, Thomas, 53–54, 337n53, 338n54
Case, Anne, 37–38
Certified B Corporations, 303–305
Chattanooga, Tennessee, 70–71, 73, 341n71, 343n73
"chemistry game," 27–28
child labor, 269n239
child labor laws, 142
China, 271, 272, 274, 278, 379n278
Chinchilla, Najahyia, 43
Chomsky, Noam, 65
Chorlton Twist Company, 238
Christensen, Clayton, 46
Christopher Ranch, 63–64
"city workers," 109–110
Clark, Dave, 72
class system
   belief in ability of those of low or moderate birth to rise, 55, 338n55
   middle class, 7, 53, 58, 256–257
Cleveland, Ohio, 242–246, 248–249
Clinton, Hillary, 88, 185, 327n1
coal industry, 199–200, 206, 207
"Code wins arguments" ethic, 227
Coen Gilbert, Jay, 302–305
"coffinizing," 50

college graduates
  BLS predictions about percent of
    jobs requiring degree, 153, 154
  credential creep and, 153–154
  degree as economic imperative,
    147
  from for-profit institutions,
    149–150, 358n149
  income of, and family
    socioeconomic status, 151–152,
    361n156
  market value of degrees, 148–150
  most popular majors of, 170
  as percent of freshman class, 154
  as percent of US workforce, 153
  underemployment among, 36
Collins, Randall, 162–163
Colombia, 37
commerce
  brick-and-mortar retail, 68–69,
    340n68
  online, 69–73, 341nn69–70
community colleges, 179–183,
  186–189, 191–193
"comparative advantage"
  principle, 75
compensation. See wages
"competitive self-management,"
  47–48
Conn, Randall, 202–203
Conn, Regina, 202, 203
connectedness, 109–110, 348n109
Connelly, Steven, 201–202
contract work
  coworking and, 297
  evaluation of product/
    performance, 61–62
  flexibility, 64, 65
  increase in, 64–65
  lack of benefits, 64
  Loconomics and, 260

"pay to quit" option and, 343n73
  as portable, 61
  unions and, 289–290, 295–296
  wages, 72–73, 100, 343n73
Cook, Tim, 163, 186, 276
Coolbroth, Kyle, 296–297
Cooperative Home Care Associates
  (CHCA), 251, 252
cooperative ownership. See worker
  cooperatives
Corning Glass, 276–277
Cornyn, John, 168
"corporate culture"
  gender and criteria for fitting, 33
  Hamilton's Rule and, 30–31
  need to fit, 28, 29–30
  reflecting in job interviews, 28
cost of living versus wages, 9
Cotterman, Amy, 49–51, 66–67
coworking arrangements, 296–298
creative destruction, 88–89
creative economy, 201
"credential creep," 153–154
Cronin, James Patrick, 269n239
"crowdfleecing," 259
Crowe, Curtis, 283
Csikszentmihalyi, Mihaly, 100–104
Cubberley, Ellwood, 143
"cultural industry," 200–201
cultural résumés, 31, 32
Curnutte, Daryl, 182–183
Curry, Trace, 188

Daemo, 259–260
Dale, Anne Caroline, 238
Dale, David, 238
Darden Restaurants, Inc., 127
Darwin, Charles, 215
Dashi Dash, 35
Dayton, Ohio, 49, 178–179
Deaton, Angus, 37–38

Delaware, incorporation in, 304, 382n304

Democracy Collaborative, 245, 246

Design Necessities Initiative (DNI), 281–282

destiny, individual control of, 55

Detroit, Michigan, 201

"developer community," 378n272

DeVos, Betsy, 144

Dewey, John, 118–119

digital economy
  arts and crafts sales, 203
  broadband access, 206–207
  characteristics needed to thrive in, 57
  culture of, 227
  decline in job creation, 59
  "developer community," 378n272
  e-commerce, 69–73, 341nn69–70
  inequality and, 2, 3–4
  jobs in, 2, 170
  online work "marketplaces," 258–259
  replacement of human intellectual capital with technology, 11
  "skill gap" in, 163, 164–165
  skills required in, 56–57, 59–60
  tools, structures, and processes as more valuable than people, 262
  unionization of technology workforces, 257, 375n257
  wage stagnation and, 339n59

"disruptive innovation," 46

Dockery, Jane, 191, 192, 193

Dodge v. Ford Motor Company (1919), 303

Doerr, John, 375n257

Douglas, Paul, 146

drone pilots, 180, 188–189

Drug-Free Workplace Act (1986), 166

drug use, 166–167, 363n166

dumpster pools, 283–284

Duncan, Arne, 144

Earned Income Tax Credit (EITC), 161–162

Eastman, George, 86, 87

Eastman Kodak, 86–87

e-commerce, 69–73, 341nn69–70

Edin, Kathryn, 159–161, 162

education. *See also* college graduates
  Berea College, 194–197, 198–200, 204, 205
  community colleges, 179–183, 186–189, 191–193
  compulsory, 142, 355n142
  at elite institutions, 148–149, 150–151
  Finnish, 218, 219–224, 225
  Frontier Graduate School of Midwifery, 207, 208
  future employment as purpose of, 2–3, 5, 142–143, 188, 328n5
  importance, in late eighteenth and nineteenth centuries, 141–142, 354n141
  income and, 146, 147, 151–152, 361n156
  income of college dropouts compared to high school graduates, 155
  industrialization and, 142, 355n142
  job-market signaling model and, 358n162
  liberal arts, as best preparation for future, 199
  market value of higher and, 145–146, 147–148

education (*cont.*)
  overselling, as prerequisite of
    employment, 156
  quality of public, 147
  STEM disciplines, 168–169,
    364n168
  student loans, 151, 358n149,
    359n151
efficiency, 6–7. *See also* productivity
Ehrenberg, David, 269, 270
Ellsworth, Jeri, 45–46
Emerson, Ralph Waldo, 286–287
employee-employer relationship
  at-will employment and, 255,
    374–375n255
  Great Depression and,
    381–382n299
  market driven, 291
  Maslow and, 111–112
  mid-twentieth century, 111,
    299–300
  reciprocal obligation, 255–256
Employee Stock Ownership Plans
  (ESOPs), 261–264
Encouraging Employee Ownership
  Act (proposed 2017), 261
entrepreneurs and entrepreneurship.
  See also worker cooperatives;
  specific individuals
  age of company and productivity,
    92–93, 346n93
  "developer community," 378n272
  as engine of growth, 88, 346n93
  family-owned businesses,
    253–254, 374n254
  industry deregulation and, 89–90
  jobs created by start-ups, 89–90
  jobs destroyed by start-ups, 90–91
  manufacturing start-ups, 277–278
  nations with most, 91
  in New York City, 270–271
  percent of total jobs from start-
    ups, 94
  replicative *vs.* innovative, 91–92
  start-ups defined, 91
  worker ownership of stock,
    261–264
ephemeralization, 59
equality of opportunity, false nature
  of, 56
Escamilla, Alex, 284
Essang, Sannakaisa, 222–223
Evergreen Cooperative Corporation,
  242–245, 248–250, 264–265
Evergreen Cooperative Laundry,
  242–243, 244
Evergreen Energy Solutions, 243
Ewing Marion Kauffman
  Foundation, 90

Facebook, 85–86, 87
Fairlie, Paul, 229
Fairmondo, 260
family-owned businesses, 253–254,
  374n254
Fink, Larry, 301–302
Finland
  economy, 215, 216, 219, 232
  education, 218, 219–224, 225
  immigration, 213, 220–221,
    223–224
  monthly income to unemployed,
    232–233
  national character trait,
    216–217
  population, 213, 214, 369n214
  public services, 215–216
  similarities to US, 214
  trust in government, 233
  wealth inequality, 234
  work malaise, 225, 226
Finnair, 276

firefighters, 106–109, 348n106

flat corporate organizational structures, 44–48

"flight from work," 37

"flow," 101–104, 227

food services, 217–218

Forget, Evelyn, 317–318

"Four Horsemen," 85–86

France, 37

Franklin, Ben, 142

Fraser, Max, 255

freelancers
  coworking and, 297
  evaluation of product/ performance, 61–62
  flexibility of, 64, 65
  increase in, 64–65
  lack of benefits, 64
  Loconomics and, 260
  "pay to quit" option and, 343n73
  as portable, 61
  unions and, 289–290, 295–296
  wages, 72, 100

Freelancers Union, 295–296

Freeman, Richard, 256–257

free-market democracy, digital economy as threatening, 2, 3–4

Freud, Sigmund, 51

Friedman, Adam, 278

Friedman, Milton, 298–299

Friedman, Thomas, 363n167

Frontier Graduate School of Midwifery, 207, 208

Frontier Nursing Service (FNS), 207–208

"full-body rebellion," 43

Fuller, Buckminster, 59

Fuyao Glass Industry Group, 190–192

Garrett, Lyndon, 297

Gates, Bill, 375n257. *See also* "Bill Gates effect"

Gates, Frederick T., 143

gender
  effects of joblessness and, 19–20
  fitting corporate culture and, 31, 331–332n31
  increase in number of unemployed who are not looking for work and, 36–37
  shifting job criteria and, 32–33

General Motors, 176–178

Georgia (US state), 275, 313

Gerhardt, Tom, 280

Germany
  Great Depression, 329n16, 330n19
  manufacturing jobs, 271
  prime-age labor participation, 37
  reduced work hours, 315

Gerstner, Louis, 139–140, 353–354n139

"ghost jobs," 171–172

"gig" economy, 5, 11. *See also* contract work

Girls (television program), 28–29

Gladwell, Malcolm, 348n109

Glass, David, 307

Glassdoor, 35

The Global Achievement Gap (Wagner), 224

globalization, 7–8

Goldin, Claudia, 145, 146

Good, Thomas, 140–141

Google (aka Alphabet)
  artificial intelligence and, 79
  daily searches on, 78
  as employer of choice, 84
  as one of Four Horsemen, 85–86
  products, 84
  revenue sources, 85

Gordon, Robert, 59

Gorelick, Abe, 23–25, 31, 48

government

American trust levels in, 233–234, 299

corporations as partners of, 312

failure of, to prepare for future, 301–302

Finnish, monthly income to unemployed workers, 232–233

Finnish trust levels in, 233

incentives to lure jobs, 71, 72, 73, 274, 342n73

mid-twentieth century employee-employer relationship and, 299–300

negative income tax proposed by Friedman, 298–299

political will to cure National Work Disorder, 319–320

social welfare and job creation programs, 299, 312–314, 316, 381–382n299

subsidies for reduced work hours, 315, 384n314

wealth and, 234

will needed to cure National Work Disorder, 319–320

"grand career narrative," 2

Great Depression, 16–20, 329n16, 381n299

Great Recession (2007–2011), 36, 61

Green City Grocers, 243, 248–249

Gross Domestic Product (GDP) components, 8, 328n8

Grubb, Norton, 141

Grund, Francis, 54

Grusky, David, 56–57, 58

Habits of the Heart (Bellah), 118

Hackbert, Peter, 200, 201, 207, 208

"hacker" mentality, 227

Hackman, J. R., 379n273

Halfteck, Guy, 34–35

Hall, Ted, 285

Hamilton, Alexander, 264, 376n264

"Hamilton's Rule," 30–31

handicraft revival movement, 202

Harrington, Jason Edward, 124–125, 129

health

absence of work-life balance and, 43

flat corporate organizational structure and, 47

home health care industry, 251–252

increase in midlife mortality, 37–38

office design and, 335n44

stack ranking and, 48

24/7 work and, 50

wages and job prospects and, 37–38

Hegel, Georg Wilhelm Friedrich, 52

Henderson, Rebecca, 299, 300–301, 302, 371n232

Herbart, Johann Friedrich, 356n143

Herlin, Antti, 216

Hershbein, Brad, 151–152

Highhouse, Scott, 34

high school graduates

income of college dropouts versus, 151

percent decline in compensation for, 36

wages of community college graduates versus, 186

Hillbilly Elegy (Vance), 197–198

Hira, Ron, 168–169

"hire yourself" phenomenon, 31–32

Hiring Incentives to Restore
   Employment Act (2010), 313
Hoffman, Dennis, 278–279
Hoffman, Steven, 278–279
holidays and vacation, average
   annual not taken, 51, 337n51
Home Depot, 306–308
home health care, 251–252
Hoover, Melissa, 251, 252–253
Horowitz, Sara, 295, 296
Howard, Ted, 245, 249–250
*How Did Employee Ownership Firms
   Weather the Last Two Recessions?*
   (Kurtulus and Kruse), 263
"How Does Declining Unionism
   Affect the American Middle
   Class and Intergenerational
   Mobility?" (Freeman), 256–257
"Human Intelligence Tasks,"
   258–259
"human rentals," 238, 255
Humanyze, 125–126
Hunnicutt, Benjamin, 52–53
Hyden, Kentucky, 207, 208–210

IBM, 80
identity, job as individual's, 25, 27,
   28, 51, 132–133, 235
immigration
   collective action in technology
      sector, 375n257
   in Finland, 213, 220–221, 223–224
"inclusive prosperity," 260–261
income. *See also* wages
   Basic Income Guarantee, 315–318,
      385n316
   birth circumstances and, 56,
      151–152, 256–257, 361n156
   of children of members of unions,
      256
   of college dropouts, 155

   of college dropouts versus high
      school graduates, 151
   college education at elite
      institutions and, 148–149,
      150–151
   distribution and prosperity,
      381–382n299
   distribution of, 236
   distribution to rentiers, 61
   education and, 146, 147, 151–152,
      361n156
   Finnish monthly, to unemployed,
      232–233
   median household, 36
   worker cooperatives and, 258,
      376n258
independent contractors. *See*
   contract work
indispensability, 42
industrial economy
   efficiency in, 6, 320
   textiles and factories, 238–239
industrialization, 99–100, 142, 227,
   355n142
Industrial Revolution, 15–26
innovation
   as complementary to production
      process, 272–273
   as creative destruction, 88–89
   as creator of abundance, 86, 88
   "cross-platform" collaborations,
      281–282, 283–285
   cultural meanings of, 235
   "disruptive," 46
   as driver of productivity, 6
   face-to-face interaction and, 273
   hubs, 269–270
   investment in, by US firms, 273
   job satisfaction and, 113
   loss of jobs and, 58–59
   negative effects of, 11

innovation (*cont.*)
real economic impact of, 87–88
reflection needed for, 228
research and, 93
"small batch" production, 286
sustaining good work as goal of, 13–14
360 degree feedback and, 45
working in teams to encourage "disruptive," 228
The Innovator's Dilemma (Christensen), 46
"In Praise of Electronically Monitoring Employees" (McAfee), 126–127
Instagram, 86, 87
intergenerational mobility, 56, 151–152, 256–257, 361n156
International Alliance of Theatrical Stage Employees, Moving Picture Technicians, Artists and Allied Crafts of the United States, Its Territories and Canada (IATSE), 290–291
"interpersonal chemistry," 27–28
"Investing in Our Children" (Committee for Economic Development, 1985), 138–139
Irving, Texas, 71–72
Israel, 26, 331n26

Jacobs, Edward, 281–282, 288
Jahoda, Marie, 17, 19
Japan
average annual vacation and holidays, 337n51
fear of, as economic and technological threat, 138–139, 353n138
prime-age labor participation, 37
Jefferson, Thomas, 54, 55, 141, 264

Jiro Ono, 120–121
"job crafting," 129
job creation
age of company and, 92–93, 346n93
by Apple, 375n272
at-will employment and, 256
digital economy and decline in, 59
by entrepreneurs and entrepreneurship, 89–90
government incentives to companies to lure, 71, 72, 73, 274, 342n73
government social welfare and job creation programs, 299, 312–314, 316, 381–382n299, 383–384n313
retail industry as most important, 68, 340n68
by start-ups, 89–90
types and wages of, since 2005, 385n320
The Job Generation Process (Birch), 89–90
job interviews
desire to discover candidates with callings, 122
percent of applicants receiving, 35
"recrutainment" as replacement for, 34–35
reflecting "corporate culture" during, 28
similarity of candidate to interviewer, 30–32
simulation of job task as, 34
value of, 34
joblessness. *See also* skills scam/ smokescreen
blaming self for, in US, 25, 27, 28
blaming system for, in Israel, 26
effects on society, 19–20, 330n19

Finnish government monthly
income and, 232–233
identity and, 25, 27, 28, 132–133
increase in number of
unemployed who are not
looking for jobs, 36–37
Social Security disability
payments and, 37
job-market signaling model,
361n162
job openings. *See also* skills scam/
smokescreen
algorithms to discover job
candidates with callings, 122
average number of résumés per, 35
drug tests and, 166–167, 363n166
"ghost jobs," 171–172
in low-wage, low-skilled, 164–165
online applications, 159, 361n159
"plug and play" strategy, 170
ratio of applicants to, 35
job performance. *See* productivity
jobs
at-will employment and creation
of, 256
"bad jobs strategy," 305–308
BLS predictions about percent
requiring college degree, 153,
154
as callings, 12, 118–121
careers and callings versus, 118
in coal compared to renewable
energy, 199–200
decrease in, with middle level
wages, 378n271
decrease in "good," 58–59
decrease in living-wage, 7
defining, 9
defining "good," 58
demand for college instructors,
61–63, 339n62

demand for farm labor, 52–53
destroyed by start-ups, 90–91
Eastman Kodak, 87
e-commerce and, 71–72, 341n71
EITC and, 162
fastest growing, 60
gender and shifting criteria for,
32–33
"good job strategy," 308–311
as identity, 25, 27, 28, 51, 132–133,
235
increase in number of
unemployed, who are not
looking for, 36–37
layoffs and stock prices, 365n170
most desired benefits, 65
most threatened, 81–82
nontradable defined, 218
as not defining relationship to
work, 132–133
percent of total, from start-ups, 94
prime-age labor participation, 37,
333n37
"psychological ownership" of, 39
readiness for, as focus of
education, 142–145, 356n143
in science and tech sector,
168–170
"specs game" versus "chemistry
game" in obtaining, 27–28
stress and agency over, 38–39
surveillance of employees,
123–128, 227, 351n124, 351n125
technology and skill level of, 167
true meaning of "freedom" and
"flexibility" in, 61–62, 64–65
work versus, 100–101
Jobs, Steve, 105, 255
job satisfaction. *See also* calling(s)
company loyalty to and trust in
staff and, 230–232

job satisfaction (*cont.*)
  decline in, 113, 229
  "following your passion,"
    105–106, 110
  "happiest jobs in America," 292,
    380–381n292
  self-actualization and,
    112–113
  surveillance of employees, 128,
    352n128
JobsOhio, 191–192
Joe the Welder, 101–103
Johnson, Steven, 180–181, 187,
  191
Jones, Janell, 58
Joseph, Carol Graham Lewis,
  208–209
Jumpstart Our Business Startups
  (JOBS) Act (2012), 90

Kallahti Comprehensive School
  (Finland), 219–224
Kane, Tim J., 90
Kansas City (Kansas and Missouri),
  342n73
Katz, Lawrence, 145, 146, 385n320
Kauffman Foundation, 90
Kelso, Louis, 261–262
Kentucky, 275, 276–277
Keynes, John Maynard, 322
Knack, 34–35
knowledge economy. *See* digital
  economy
Kodak, 86–87
Koppman, Sharon, 32
Krieger, Mike, 86
Kroger (grocery chain), 59
Krueger, Alan, 385n320
Krugman, Paul, 169
Kruse, Douglas, 263
Kurtulus, Fidan Ana, 263

Laitio, Tommi, 232, 233
Larregui, Dick, 267, 268
Larson, Brian, 310
Latvia, 37
Lawrence, Massachusetts,
  173–175
Lazarsfeld, Paul, 17
*Learning to Labor: How Working
  Class Kids Get Working Class Jobs*
  (Willis), 155–156
leisure
  as natural human condition in
    absence of hunger, 52
  as sign of progress, 52–53
"lemon socialism," 263
LePage, Paul, 289, 291
"license to operate," 301–302
Lindner, Tim, 73–74
Lipson, Hod, 81, 82–83
Lockridge, Kenneth, 354n141
Loconomics, 260
Lyft, 72

Ma, Jack, 69
Madison, James, 55
Maitlis, Sally, 132–133
"maker" movement, 285, 287
Manpower Development and
  Training Act (1962), 112
manufacturing industry and jobs.
  See also entrepreneurs and
  entrepreneurship
  "cross-platform" collaborations,
    283–285
  goods produced in US, 271
  Hamilton on, 376n264
  as innovation contributor,
    272–273
  loss of, 68, 271, 340n68
  outsourcing of, 271, 272, 274,
    379n278

recent growth since bottoming
  out, 275
skills shortage and, 275–276
"small batch" production, 280,
  281, 285, 286
start-ups in, 277–278
urban, 278–279
Marienthal, Austria
  Great Depression, 16–19
  industrialization, 15–16
Market Basket, 310–311
Marx, Karl, 99, 314
Maslow, Abraham, 110–112, 130,
  349n110
"Maslow needs," 111
Massive Open Online Courses
  (MOOCs), 62
MathWorks, 171–172
Mauro, Charles, 335n44
May, Warren A., 202
Mayer, Marissa, 375n257
McAfee, Andrew, 85–86, 88,
  126–127
McGowan, George, III, 297–298
McGrath, Charles, 109
McGrew, Jeffrey, 285–286
McKinley, William, 64
McMicken, John, 244–245
McMurray, Charles, 356n143
Meaning Meetings, 122–124,
  132–133
Meany, George, 314
Mechanical Turk (MTurk), 258–259,
  260
Medoff, James, 92
Mehta, Jal, 140
Melmen, Seymour, 268
"mere exposure effect," 30–31
Meyerson, Harold, 275
Michel, Alexandra, 39–40, 42–44
Michigan, 313

middle class
  decline of, 58
  dignity of work and, 53
  smaller percent of Americans
    in, 7
  unions and, 256–257
Miller, Bob, 140
Mississippi, 275
Mondragon Cooperative
  Corporation (MCC, in Spain),
  246–248
"moneyball for business," 125–126
Monroe, James, 240
Moraine, Ohio, 176–178, 190–193
Morris, William, 54, 58, 338n54
Moynihan, Daniel Patrick, 312
Mullainathan, Sendhil, 338n54
Murka, Adam, 176–178, 179
Murray, Charles, 316
Music Makers, 202–203

Nardelli, Robert, 307–308
National Association of
  Manufacturers (NAM), 163
National Commission on Excellence
  in Education report (1985),
  138–139
National Education Summits (1989
  and 1996), 139–140
national policy of winner-take-all, 4
National Work Disorder, political
  will needed to cure, 319–320
Net Spy Pro, 351n125
Newell, Gabe, 45
New Harmony, Indiana, 240
New Jobs Tax Credit (1977–1978),
  313
New Lab, 269–270, 281, 282
Newsweek, 216
New York City, 266–271, 278, 281,
  282, 284–285

New York Times, 109, 168, 301, 346n92

Nietzsche, Friedrich, 104

Nightingale, Paul, 92–93

99 Degrees Custom, 173–175

Nixon, Richard, 112

Nokia, 216, 226, 232

Norris, Deb, 181–182

North Korea, 379n278

Northrup, Jillian, 285–286

Noyce, Robert, 257

Obama, Barack
  e-commerce as future and, 70–71, 73, 341n71
  on entrepreneurship as engine of growth, 88
  on importance of college degree, 147
  use of word "work" or "jobs" in State of the Union addresses, 327n1
office design and 24/7 work and, 43, 44, 335n44
offshoring of jobs. *See* outsourcing
online commerce, 69–73, 341nn69–70
The Organization Man (Whyte), 40
Orlov, Laurie, 251, 252
Osterman, Paul, 164–165
outsourcing
  effects of, 5
  government incentives and, 274
  manufacturing jobs, 271, 272, 274, 379n278
Owen, Christine, 271
Owen, Robert, 237–241

Paasilinna, Arto, 369n214
Paavola, Kimmo, 220–222, 224
Pahkin, Leo, 224

Panel Study of Income Dynamics (PSID), 151–152

Patagonia, 304, 382n304

payroll taxes, 312–313

Perry, Rick, 72

Pestalozzi, Johann Heinrich, 356n143

Piketty, Thomas, 157

platform cooperatives, 258–260

Pohjakallio, Pekka, 225–230, 231–232

Poland, 37

Pollin, Robert, 200

Portugal, 37, 313

Pratt, Michael, 97–98, 106, 107, 109–110

"precariat" and "precarity," 61–63, 64

Premier Source, 280

prime-age labor participation in developed world, 37, 333n37

productivity
  age of company and, 92–93, 346n93
  automation and, 6, 262, 273
  CEO-to-worker compensation ratio and, 131
  of ESOPs, 263
  face-to-face interaction and, 379n273
  increase in worker, and "shareholder primacy," 131, 260
  in industrial economy, 6
  making meaning of work and, 129
  surveillance of employees and, 126–127, 128–129
  wages and, 7, 260
  working in teams to maximize, 228

Program of International Student Assessment (PISA), 225

progress, assumptions about, 6
Protestant work ethic, 53
Provost, Dan, 280
public trust
  Certified B Corporations and,
    303–305
  economic growth and, 235
  at end of twentieth century,
    233–234, 300
  in Finland, 233
  in mid-twentieth century,
    299–300, 381–382n299
  need of long-term prosperity and,
    300–301
  "shareholder primacy" and, 301
  solidaristic individualism and,
    235
  wealth inequality and, 234
Public Welfare Amendment to the
  Social Security Act (1962), 112
Publix Super Markets, 263
Putnam, Robert, 233–234

Quicken Loans, 201
QuikTrip, 308–310

The Race Between Education and
  Technology (Goldin and Katz),
  145, 146
Rasmussen, Helen, 289–290, 291
Reagan, Ronald, 166
recession of 2007–2011, 36, 61
"recrutainment," 34–35
Reece, Erik, 269n239
renewable energy, 199–200, 258
Renner, Bobby, 194, 198
Renner, Robert, 194–195
"rentiers," 61
research, 93–94
residential real estate sector jobs,
  292–294, 380–381n292

retail industry
  as most important job creator, 68,
    340n68
  wages, 68–69
retirement
  assets and ESOPs, 263, 377n264
  delaying of, 37
Richardson, Eric, 318
Rivera, Lauren, 31–32
"Robo Madness" conference (2015,
  Cambridge, Massachusetts),
  75–77
robots, 74–76, 344n75. See also
  automation
Roelofs, Lyle, 196–197, 199–200
Romer, Paul, 236
Roosevelt, Franklin Delano, 142
Ross, Rubena, 267–268, 377n268
Rovio, 235
Royal Worcester Corset Company, 68
Rus, Daniela, 76

Sahlins, Marshall, 52
salaries. See wages
Samuelson, Paul, 273
Sandulli, Joe, 256
Sawyer (industrial robot), 74–75,
  344n75
scarcity, 42, 338n54
Schlesinger, Arthur M., 382n299
Schmidt, Eric, 375n257
Schmitt, John, 58
Schumer, Chuck, 168
Schneider, Brenna Nan, 173–175
Schor, Juliet, 384n315
Schumpeter, Joseph, 88–89
Search, Theodore, 143
The Second Machine Age (McAfee), 85
security, 104, 112
self-actualization, 111–113
self-driving cars, 75

self-employment, 61–62, 64–65

self-esteem
"chemistry game" and, 28
joblessness and, 25, 27, 28, 132–133
money as measure of, 42–43

"self-made man," 55

Selman, Bart, 80–81

service workers, 60, 340n68

Shafir, Eldar, 338n54

Shane, Scott, 93

"shareholder primacy"
Dodge v. Ford Motor Company (1919), 303
increase in productivity and, 131, 260
public trust and, 301

Sharone, Ofer, 25–28, 35, 38–39, 47

shipbuilding, 266–268, 266–270, 271, 377n268

ShopBot, 285, 286

"simulation" as part of job interview, 34

Sinclair Community College, 179–183, 187, 188–189, 191–193

"Skill Demands and Mismatch in U.S. Manufacturing" (Osterman and Weaver), 164–165

skills scam/smokescreen
business's desire for oversupply, 171
employers claim of lack of trained workers is more than century old, 163, 164
is favorite argument of politicians and business leaders, 163
job-market signaling model and, 361n162
lack of workers with vocational skills, 185–186

low-wage, low-skilled were unfilled, 164–165, 361n162
in manufacturing jobs, 275–276
obsolescence and, 188
training former factory workers unemployed by automation and, 185–186
wages in science and technology sector, 161n168, 168–169, 364n168
as zombie idea, 169

Snellman, 230–232

Snyder, Gary, 46

Social Security disability payments, percent of prime-working-age unemployed men receiving, 37

solidaristic individualism, 235

Sonnenfeld, Jeffrey, 301

South Korea, 152, 313

Spain, 37, 246–248

"sparks," 110

"specs game," 27

Spence, Andrew Michael, 287–288, 361n162

Sprecher, Leo, 76–78

Spreitzer, Gretchen, 297

Squire, Mack, 249

stack ranking, 48, 336n48

Standing, Guy, 61–62

Stanton, Elizabeth Cady, 142

Startup Acts 2.0 and 3.0, 90

start-ups
defined, 91
jobs created by, 89–90
jobs destroyed by, 90–91
in manufacturing, 277–278
percent of total jobs from, 94

Stock, Richard, 188–189

Stone, Edward Durell, 179–180

"Store Teller Machines" (STMs), 167

Strahorn, Fred, 192
stress
    cost to US economy, 38
    increase in, 334n38
    major cause of, 334n38
    stack ranking and, 48
    surveillance of employees and,
        128, 227, 352n128
Studio Neat, 280
success
    costs of, 67
    defining, 66
Sullivan, Patrick, III, 107–109, 110
Summers, Clyde W., 255
Summers, Larry, 260–261
sushi chef as calling, 120–121
Sweden, 37, 313, 315
Systrom, Kevin, 86

tax credits, 313–314, 383–384n313
taxes, 276–277, 298–299, 312–313,
    382n304
Taylor, Cate, 331–332n31
Taylor, Frederick, 163
Taylor, Mary, 190
teamwork, 228
technology. *See also* digital economy
    digital fabrication, 279–281,
        287–288
    distribution of benefits of, 236
    Finnish economy and, 216, 218,
        219
    replacement of human
        intellectual capital and, 11
    skill level of jobs and, 167
    worker cooperatives, 258–260
Terny, Francois-Xavier, 282
Texas, 71–72
textile industry, 238
The Theory of the Leisure Class
    (Veblen), 41

"There's a Lot of Month Left at
    the End of the Money" (Edin),
    160–161
"Third Industrial Revolution"
    "cross-platform" collaborations,
        281–282, 283–285
    digital fabrication technology,
        279–281, 287–288
    manufacturing start-ups, 277–278
    "small batch" production, 280,
        281, 285, 286
    urban manufacturers, 278–279
Thompson, Jeffery, 121–122
"360 degree feedback," 45
Tipton, David, 209–211
Tocqueville, Alexis de, 55
Todesco, Hermann, 15–16
Ton, Zeynep, 305–306, 308, 310–311
Toomey, Pat, 261
Training Within Industry program,
    169
"triple bottom line," 302, 303
Trump, Donald
    election of, 321
    entrepreneurship and, 88
    use of words "work" or "jobs" in
        campaign, 1
    as "workaholic in chief," 42,
        335n42
TSA employees, 124–125, 351n124
"Turkers," 258–259
24/7 work
    flat corporate organizational
        structure and, 47
    health and, 43, 50
    office design and, 43, 44, 335n44
    pride in, 50

UAL Corporation, 263
Uber, 72
Uganda, 91

unemployed workers. *See also* skills
    scam/smokescreen
  Finnish government monthly
    income to, 232–233
  increase in number of, who are
    not looking for jobs, 36–37
  percent of prime-working-age
    males receiving Social Security
    disability payments, 37
unions
  collective bargaining, 290
  decline in membership in Israel,
    331n26
  decline in membership in US, 254
  incomes of children of members,
    256
  for independent contractors,
    289–290, 295–296
  middle class and, 256–257
  outsourcing in EU nations and,
    274
  support for, 291
  technology workforce and, 257,
    375n257
  wages and, 255
  worker cooperatives as similar to,
    254
  worker protections and, 256
United Kingdom, 37
Up in the Air (film), 50–51
Upward Bound, 194–195
Uslaner, Eric, 235
Utopia Drive (Reece and Cronin),
    372n239

vacation and holidays, average
    annual not taken, 51, 337n51
Valve Corporation, "Flatland,"
    44–46
Vance, J. D., 197
Vanguard, 282

Vardi, Moshe, 79
Veblen, Thorstein, 41
Vesterbacka, Peter, 235
Victorian Era aristocrats, 52
Vogel, Ezra F., 353n138
Volkswagen, 71

wages
  automation and, 73–74, 82
  "bad jobs strategy," 307–308
  CEO-to-worker compensation
    ratio, 131
  community college graduates
    versus high school graduates,
    186
  of contract employees, 72–73, 100,
    343n73
  cost of living versus, 9
  cost of robots versus workers', 75,
    77–78, 344n75
  current manufacturing jobs, 275
  decrease in jobs with middle level,
    378n271
  decrease in living-wage jobs, 7
  e-commerce jobs, 72–73, 343n73
  ESOPs and, 262
  of European outsourced jobs, 274
  of fastest growing jobs, 60–61
  in Finland, 217
  globalization and, 7, 379n278
  of "good" job, 58
  "good jobs strategy," 308–310
  of home health care aides, 252
  labor shortage and, 63–64
  lagging demand for goods and,
    299
  low-wage, low-skilled as unfilled,
    164–165
  percent decline in, for high school
    graduates, 36
  productivity and, 7, 260

purchasing power and, 381–382n299

retail jobs, 68–69

stagnation in digital economy, 339n59

in STEM sector, 168–169, 364n168

tool and die makers, 183–185

unions and, 255

worker cooperatives and, 260, 377n264

Wagner, Adolph, 311

Wagner, Tony, 224–225

Wall Street bankers

as "coin operated," 42

flat corporate organizational structure, 44

office design, 43, 44, 335n44

24/7 work, 43

Walmart, 70, 341n70

Warner, Mark, 75–76, 261

Washington, George, 55

Waste Pro USA, 123–124

wealth

average household losses during 2007–2011 recession, 36

trust in government and, 234

of US founding fathers, 54–55, 338n54

during Victorian Era, 52

"wealth effect," 255, 374n255

wealth inequality

birth circumstances and, 55, 56, 151–152, 361n156

consumer demand and, 262

currently in US, 4

income distribution rules, 236

prosperity and, 381–382n299

"small batch" manufacturing and, 281

technology and, 236

trust in government and, 234

Weaver, Andrew, 164–165

Weber, Max, 53

Weiss, Howard, 114–115

Welch, Jack, 336n48

welfare, 161, 299, 381–382n299

Why Good People Can't Get Jobs (Cappelli), 170

Whyte, William H., Jr., 40–41

Wicks-Lim, Jeanette, 156

Wiener, Norbert, 259

Williams, Rosalind, 46

Williams-Steiger Occupational Safety and Health Act (1970), 112

Willis, Paul, 155–156

Willis Towers Watson, 65

Witherell, Rob, 254, 257–258

work. *See also* 24/7 work

in absence of need, is not natural human inclination, 52

average hours in 1950s of executives, 41

average hours in 2000s of executives, 41–42

centralization of, 99–100

as "cornerstone of humanness," 51

craft and industrialization of, 99

defining, 8–9

dignity of, and middle class, 53

"Do now, think later" strategy, 227–228

feeling passionate about, 104–105

glorification of, 104

inventing, for humans, 75–76

jobs versus, 100–101

"malaise" described, 226–227

myth of control over, 25

as outside employment context, 10

passion for, but not for job, 132–133

work (*cont.*)
reducing hours of, 314–315, 384n314, 384n315
as "requirement" of citizenship, 161
sanctity of, 1
as source of happiness, 54
sustaining good, must be goal, 13–14
unpaid, 20
use of word by politicians, 1, 327n1
"youth guarantee" of employment, 218
work, meaningful
elements of, 106, 348n109
making, 12, 129–130, 227
for millennial generation, 304
as product of own efforts, 322
quest for meaning through, 97, 98
reciprocal obligation between employers and employees, 255–256
seeing selves as "human rentals," 255
"workaholics," 41–42, 335n42. *See also* 24/7 work
Work Colleges Consortium, 195–196
Worker Cooperative Business Development Initiative (New York City), 252
worker cooperatives
arts and crafts movement and, 258
current laws, 264
Democracy Collaborative, 245, 246
Evergreen Cooperatives, 242–245
Founding Fathers and, 264
growth of, 252–254, 374n254

"inclusive prosperity" and, 260–261
incomes in, 258, 376n258
IT platform, 258–260
Mondragon Cooperative Corporation, 246–248
number in US, 251
Owen and, 239, 240, 251
ownership and equity as key, 252
wages and, 377n264
as way to revitalize threatened neighborhoods, 252–253
work-life balance. *See* 24/7 work
Work Opportunity Tax Credit (WOTC) program (1996), 384n313
workweek, reducing hours of, 314–315, 384n314, 384n315
World Health Organization, 334n38
Wright, Erik Olin, 316
Wrzesniewski, Amy
background, 116–119
jobs as answering a calling, 12
on making meaning of work, 129–130
Meaning Meetings, 122–124, 132–133
on productivity and surveillance of employees, 128–129

Yellen, Janet, 363n166
Ylä-Anttila, Pekka, 218–219

Zeisel, Hans, 17
"zero-drag employees," 51
"zombie ideas," 169
zookeeper as calling, 121–122
Zuckerberg, Mark, 232, 375n257

DATE DUE

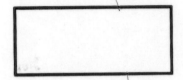

**This item is Due on
or before Date shown.**

OCT - - 2018